朱派龙 主编
陈天宏 唐电波 副主编

Diagrammatic Professional English of Mechanical Manufacturing

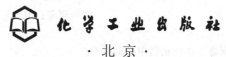

·北京·

图书在版编目（CIP）数据

图解机械制造专业英语（增强版）/朱派龙主编．—北京：化学工业出版社，2014.1（2025.1重印）
ISBN 978-7-122-18838-0

Ⅰ.①图… Ⅱ.①朱… Ⅲ.①机械制造-英语 Ⅳ.①H31

中国版本图书馆CIP数据核字（2013）第257139号

责任编辑：贾　娜	文字编辑：张燕文
责任校对：边　涛	装帧设计：王晓宇

出版发行：化学工业出版社（北京市东城区青年湖南街13号　邮政编码100011）
印　　装：大厂回族自治县聚鑫印刷有限责任公司
787mm×1092mm　1/16　印张25　字数568千字　2025年1月北京第1版第15次印刷

购书咨询：010-64518888　　　　　　　　　　售后服务：010-64518899
网　　址：http://www.cip.com.cn
凡购买本书，如有缺损质量问题，本社销售中心负责调换。

定　价：69.00元　　　　　　　　　　　　　　　　　　　　版权所有　违者必究

前　言

专业英语是专业知识与英语知识的结合。许多词汇在公共英语和专业英语两个领域有着截然不同的含义，以致纯外语专业的人士往往难以胜任专业技术翻译工作，而具有工科专业背景且外语优秀的人才越来越受到欢迎。随着技术全球化程度的提高及我国进出口贸易的发展，掌握一定的机械制造专业英语成为了机械领域从业人员的必备技能。

考虑到机械专业的专业特点，辅以图形会使专业内容更加直观、具体、形象、生动，基本可以达到"望图知意"的程度，更易于读者理解，所以本书以"看图识字"的方式编写专业英语，内容紧扣机械制造领域，形式上采用图文、英汉同步跟随的编写形式，对机械图做了新形式的表达。这种方式可使读者在学会某个名词、动词的英语表达时，进一步巩固、加深对机械本身专业术语的理解。

本书是《图解机械制造专业英语》的增强版，前一版在2009年出版后，因特色鲜明、形式新颖、内容实用，而得到了读者的认可与好评，至今已5年，考虑到部分内容比较陈旧，不适应技术发展的要求。我们根据读者反馈的意见和建议，结合行业发展情况，在保留前版基本框架风格以及使用丰富的图形、英汉同步等形式进行表达的基础上，在内容方面做了进一步更新和完善。同时，为了使本书更加贴近生产实际，特邀请了日立电梯（中国）有限公司高级工程师唐电波、广汽吉奥汽车有限公司生产和质量管理部部长何健斌、四川省机械研究设计院雷宇航参与编写，使本书内容得到进一步增强。

本书由朱派龙担任主编，陈天宏、唐电波担任副主编，何健斌、雷宇航、余岩、郭剑、余尚行参与了编写。具体分工为：陈天宏编写 Unit1~Unit3；余岩编写 Unit4.1 中（1）~(19)；朱派龙编写 Unit4.2~Unit4.5；何健斌编写 Unit5.1、Unit5.2、Unit9.1~Unit9.3；郭剑编写 Unit6.1~Unit6.3 和附录；雷宇航编写 Unit5.3、Unit5.4、Unit7；唐电波编写 Unit8.1~Unit8.5，余尚行编写 Unit4.1 中（20）~(23)、Unit6.4、Unit6.5、Unit8.6、Unit9.4。

由于编者水平所限，书中不妥之处在所难免，敬请广大专家和读者批评指正。

编　者

目 录

Unit 1　Safety and Its Measures at Work　劳动安全与防护 …… 1
　1.1　Human need　人类需求 …… 1
　1.2　Test and measuring gauge　测试仪器 …… 2
　1.3　Shielding setups　隔离屏蔽装置 …… 3
　1.4　Fire extinguisher　灭火设备 …… 6
　1.5　Crane signals　起重设备指挥信号 …… 7
　1.6　Short passage for reading　阅读短文 …… 8

Unit 2　Engineering Drawing　工程制图 …… 10
　2.1　Various types of views　视图类别 …… 10
　2.2　Drawing instruments　绘图仪器 …… 11
　2.3　Types of lines and notation　线型和标注 …… 12
　2.4　Types of geometry shapes　各种几何图形 …… 17
　2.5　Basic knowledge on mechanical engineering drawing　机械制图基本知识 …… 19
　2.6　CAD representation　CAD 绘图 …… 22
　2.7　Short passage for reading　阅读短文 …… 23

Unit 3　Engineering Metrology and Tolerance/Fits　技术测量与公差配合 …… 25
　3.1　Measuring parameters and instruments　测量参数和测量仪器 …… 25
　3.2　Tolerance and fits　公差与配合 …… 37
　3.3　Short passage for reading　阅读短文 …… 39

Unit 4　Mechanical Transmission and Equipments　机械传动与设备装置 …… 41
　4.1　Parts，components and mechanism　传动零（部）件及机构 …… 41
　4.2　Various types of machining equipment　各种机械加工设备 …… 89
　4.3　Cutting tools　切削刀具 …… 122
　4.4　Collection of commonly used machinery parts and tools　机械零部件和工具列表 …… 146
　4.5　Short passage for reading　阅读短文 …… 160

Unit 5　Hydraulic and Pneumatic Drives　液压与气动传动 …… 162
　5.1　Hydraulic and pneumatic elements　液压气动元件 …… 162
　5.2　Hydraulic and pneumatic auxilary component　液压气动附件 …… 171
　5.3　Hydraulic and pneumatic system　液压气动系统 …… 176
　5.4　Short passage for reading　阅读短文 …… 180

Unit 6　Mechanical Manufacturing Technologies　机械制造技术与方法 …… 182
　6.1　Outline of manufacturing processes　各种制造工艺技术简图要览 …… 182
　6.2　Cutting principle　切削原理 …… 188
　6.3　Heat process for metals　金属的热加工工艺 …… 195
　6.4　Non-traditional processes　非传统加工（特种加工）工艺方法 …… 219
　6.5　Short passage for reading　阅读短文 …… 242

Unit 7　NC Machining and NC Machine Tools　数控加工与数控机床 …… 245
　7.1　Basic knowledge on numerical control　数控基本知识 …… 246

7.2　CNC machining tools　数控加工机床 …… 252
7.3　CNC functional components and appendix　数控机床功能部件及附件 …… 262
7.4　CNC programming　数控加工编程 …… 268
7.5　Short passage for reading　阅读短文 …… 275

Unit 8　Manufacturing Processes and Procedures　机械加工工艺过程 …… 278
8.1　Various commonly used processes　多种常用的工艺方法和过程 …… 278
8.2　Machining procedures　工艺过程 …… 302
8.3　Convey setups　物料运送装置 …… 304
8.4　Jig and fixture, tooling　工装夹具 …… 315
8.5　CAD/ CAM/ CAPP/ FMS/ CIMS　与计算机相关的先进系统 …… 320
8.6　Short passage for reading　阅读短文 …… 327

Unit 9　Engineering Materials and Mould　工程材料和模具 …… 330
9.1　Engineering materials　工程材料 …… 330
9.2　Mould and die for metals　金属模具 …… 337
9.3　Die and mould for plastics　塑料模具 …… 347
9.4　Short passage for reading　阅读短文 …… 353

Vocabulary with Figure Index　词汇及图形索引（英中对照） …… 355
Vocabulary with Figure Index　词汇及图形索引（中英对照） …… 374
Dactylology: One-hand Alphabet　附录　单手势字母表 …… 393
参考文献 …… 394

Unit 1　Safety and Its Measures at Work
劳动安全与防护

1.1　Human need　人类需求

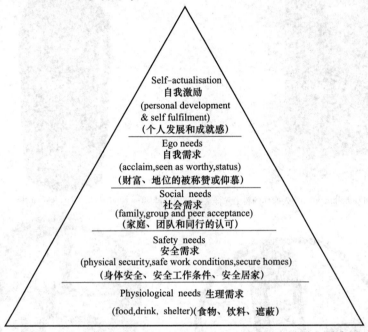

Fig 1.1　Maslow's hierarchy of human need　马斯洛人类分级需求图

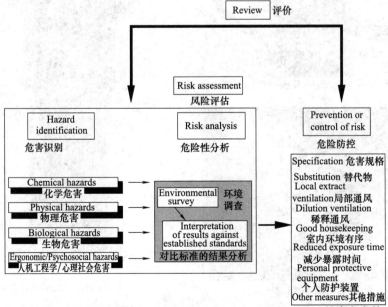

Fig 1.2　Diagram of strategy for protection against health risks　防止健康危害策略图解

1.2　Test and measuring gauge　测试仪器

(a) Personal dust sampling pump 个人操作的粉尘采样泵

(b) Industrial hand-held sound level meter 工业手持声压计

(c) Portable oxygen analyser 便携式氧气分析仪

(d) Smoke tube 风烟试验管

(e) Vane anemometer 叶片式风速计

Fig 1.3　Test and measuring gauge　测试仪器

1.3 Shielding setups 隔离屏蔽装置

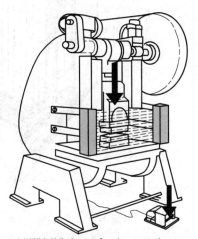
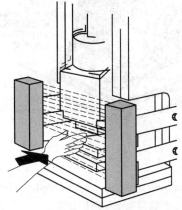

(a) With light beams forming a curtain across the zone of operation
光束在操作区形成幕帘

(b) Breaking the curtain of light beams by operator's hands sets brake on machine and disconnects clutch
操作者的手进入光束幕帘将启动机器制动器并断开离合器

Fig 1.4   Presence-sensing device   存在（"有无"）感应装置

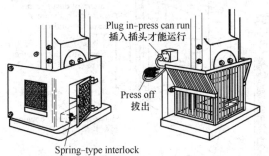

(a) Spring-type interlock shuts off power to machine when guard door is opened
防护罩门打开时，弹簧式互锁开关将切断机器电源

(b) Guard can only be removed by removing the plug, which then shuts off power to machine
只有拔出插头防护罩才能移走，从而切断机器电源

(a) Single lamp indication 单灯显示

(b) Dual light indication 双灯显示

Fig 1.5   Barrier guards   障碍防护罩

Fig 1.6   Interlocking switch condition indication lights   互锁开关状态指示灯

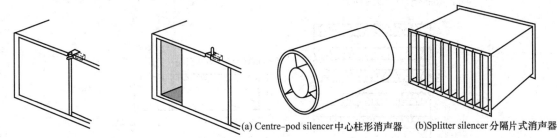

(a) Centre-pod silencer 中心柱形消声器   (b) Splitter silencer 分隔片式消声器

Fig 1.7   Direct manual switch interlock
手动互锁开关

Fig 1.8   Silencer   消声器

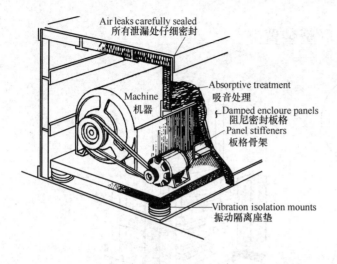

Fig 1.9　Cross section of a simple complete enclosure
简易完全围蔽断面图

Fig 1.10　A typical baghouse
典型布袋式除尘室

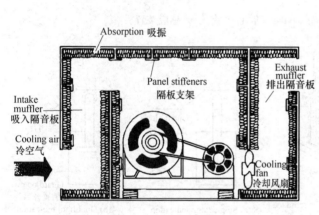

Fig 1.11　Schematic sectional view of a partial enclosure with mufflers
隔音板部分封闭的剖面图

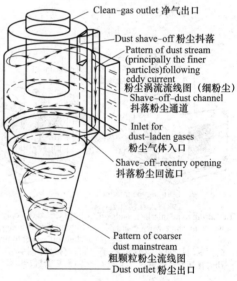

Fig 1.12　Flow pattern through a typical cyclone separator
典型旋风式粉尘分离器流线图

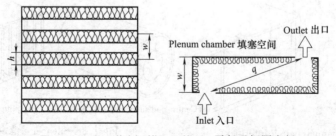

Fig 1.13　Parallel baffle muffler　平行吸振隔音板

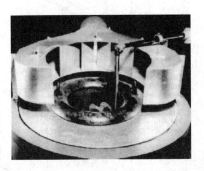

Fig 1.14　Captor-type claw hood for a furnace
加热炉捕捉型爪式围蔽罩

Fig 1.15　Bag filters　袋式过滤器

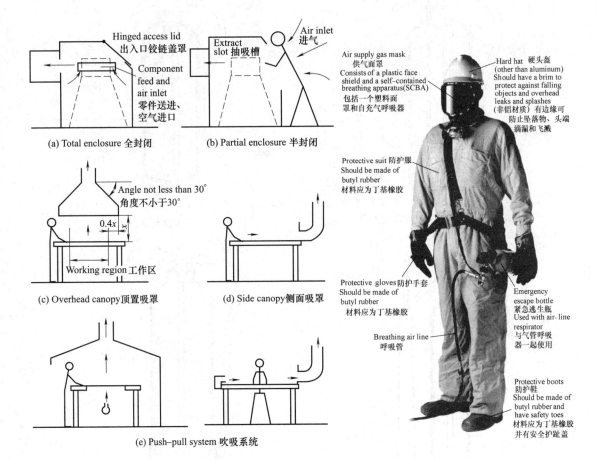

Fig 1.16　Typical local extract hoods and enclosures
典型局部抽吸罩和围蔽设施

Fig 1.17　Protective clothing and equipment
防护服及其装备

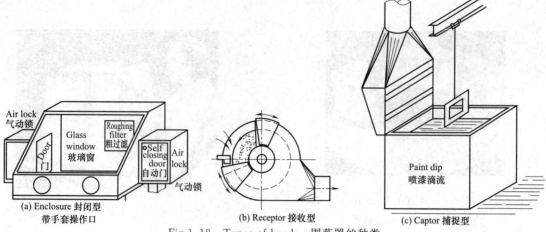

Fig 1.18　Types of hoods　围蔽罩的种类

1.4　Fire extinguisher　灭火设备

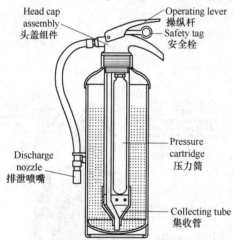

Fig 1.19　Section through a dry powder extinguisher　干粉灭火器剖面图

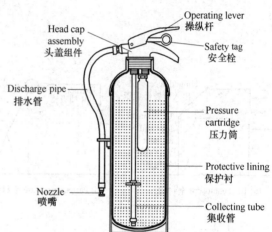

Fig 1.20　Section through a water extinguisher　水灭火器剖面图

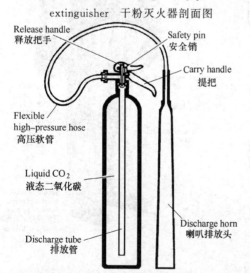

Fig 1.21　Section through a carbon dioxide extinguisher　二氧化碳灭火器剖面图

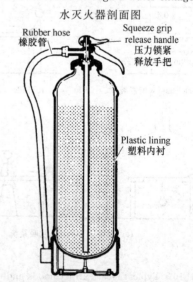

Fig 1.22　Section through a stored pressure type of water extinguisher　储存压力水灭火器剖面图

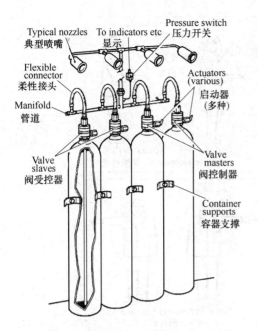
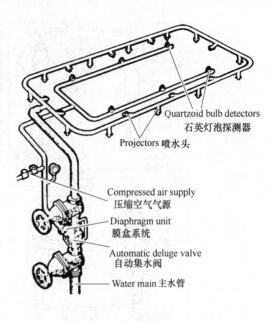

Fig 1.23 Diagram of battery of CO_2 cylinders supplying a small gas installation
二氧化碳缸筒组供给少量气体装置图

Fig 1.24 Diagram of a typical drencher (deluge) system
典型喷淋（集水）系统图解

1.5 Crane signals 起重设备指挥信号

Fig 1.25

Fig 1.25 Crane signals 起重设备的指挥信号

1.6 Short passage for reading 阅读短文

Risks to health at work

The main hazards are of three kinds, physical, chemical and biological, although occupational psychological factors may also cause illness.

1. Physical hazards

Noise, vibration, light, heat, cold, ultraviolet and infrared rays, ionising radiations.

2. Chemical hazards

These are liable to occur as a result of exposure to any of a wide range of chemicals. Ill-effects may arise at once or a considerable period of time may elapse before signs and symptoms of disease are noticed. By this time the effects are often permanent.

3. Biological hazards

These may occur in workers using bacteria, viruses or plants or in animal handlers and workers dealing with meat and other foods. Diseases produced range from infective hepatitis in hospital workers (virus infection) to ringworm in farm labourers (fungus infection).

4. Stress

This may be caused by work or may present problems in the time spent at work. Work related stresses may be due to difficulties in coping with the amount of work (quantitative stress) or the nature of the job (qualitative stress).

工作场所面临的健康危害

（工作场所面临的健康）危害主要分为三类，即物理危害、化学危害和生物危害，当然职场心理因素也可能导致疾病。

1. 物理危害：噪声、振动、光、热、受冻、紫外线、红外线和粒子辐射。

2. 化学危害：暴露在各种化学品中易于引起这些危害。病况可能会立即出现，也可能经历相当长时间而消失。但在疾病的预兆和征兆发现之后，此时的影响将会是长期的。

3. 生物危害：可能发生在那些接触细菌、病毒或动、植物处理以及肉类或其他食品的相关从业人员中。产生的疾病遍及医院从业人员感染的传染性肝炎（病毒感染）到田间地头农夫感染的金钱癣（真菌感染）。

4. 压力：工作本身或工作期间呈现的问题可能引起压力。工作相关的压力起因一方面是工作量太大难于处理（定量压力），另一方面是工作性质（定性压力）。

Unit 2　Engineering Drawing　工程制图

2.1　Various types of views　视图类别

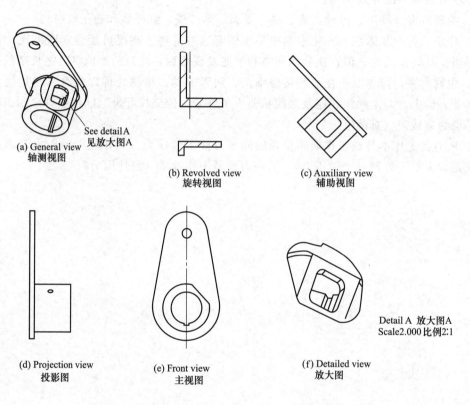

Fig 2.1　The five main types of views　五种主要的视图

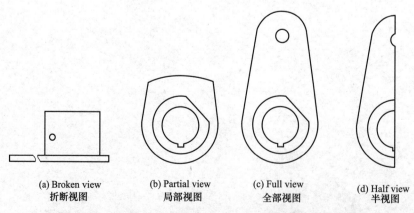

Fig 2.2　Some other commonly used views　其他常用视图

2.2 Drawing instruments 绘图仪器

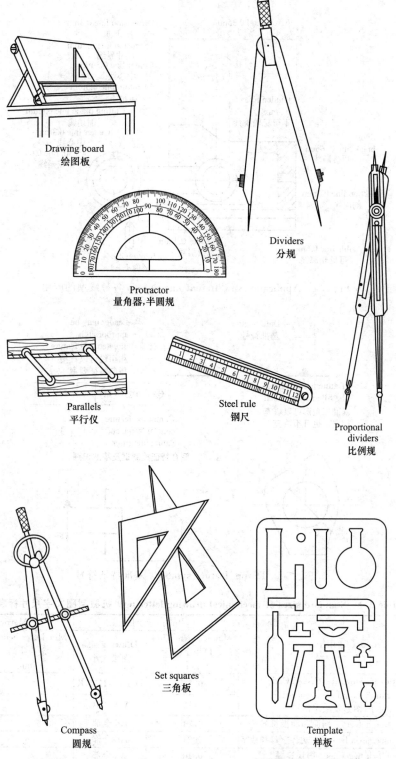

Fig 2.3 Drawing instruments 绘图仪器

2.3 Types of lines and notation 线型和标注

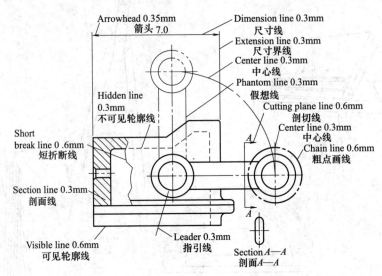

Fig 2.4 Application of different line types 各种线型的应用

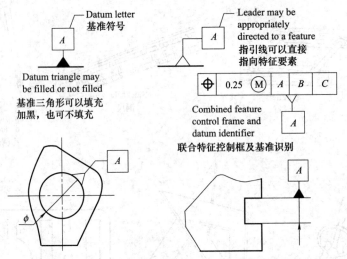

Fig 2.5 Datum feature symbol 基准特征符号

Table 2.1 Standard sizes of mechanical drawing lettering 机械制图文字尺寸标准值

Use for 适用于	Inch 英制		Metric 公制	
	Min. letter heights 最小字高 /in	Drawing size 图纸大小	Min. letter heights 最小字高 /mm	Drawing size 图纸大小
Drawing title, drawing size, CAGE Code, draw-ing number, and revision letter 图名、大小、图号及版本字样	0.24	D,E,F,H,J,K	6	A0,A1
	0.12	A,B,C,G	3	A2,A3,A4
Section and view letters 剖面和剖视符号	0.24	All 全部	6	All 全部
Zone letters and numerals in borders 边界字母和数字	0.24	All 全部	6	All 全部
Drawing block headings 图块标题	0.10	All 全部	2.5	All 全部
All other characters 其他	0.12	All 全部	3	All 全部

Table 2.2 American national standard for engineering drawings 工程制图美国标准

Line type	Appearance	Weight
Visible line 可见轮廓线	————————————	Thick 粗
Hidden line 不可见轮廓线	– – – – – – – – – –	Thin 细
Section line 剖面线	————————————	Thin 细
Center line 中心线	— - — - — - — - — -	Thin 细
Symmetry line 对称线	‖— - — - — - — -‖	Thin 细
Dimension line Extension line and leader 尺寸线、尺寸界线和指引线	Leader 指引线 / Extension line 尺寸界线 / Dimension line 尺寸线 3.50	Thin 细
Cutting plane line or viewing plane line 剖切线或投影线	⬆— — — — —⬆ ⬆━━━━━━⬆	Thick 粗
Break line 折断线	∼∼∼∼∼∼∼∼∼ —⋀—⋁—	Thick 粗 Short breaks 短折断 / Thin 细 Long breaks 长折断
Phantom line 假想线	— - - — - - — - -	Thin 细
Stitch line 缝合线(虚线)	- - - - - - - - - - · · · · · · · · · ·	Thin 细 / Thin 细
Chain line 粗点画线	— · — · — · — · —	Thick 粗

Table 2.3 American national standard symbols for section lining 剖面阴影填充线美国国家标准

Symbol	Material	Symbol	Material
▨	Cast and malleable iron(also for general use of all materials) 铸铁、可锻铸铁(及各种材料通用)	▨	Titanium and refractory material 钛合金、难熔材料
▨	Steel 钢	▦	Electric windings, electro magnets, resistance, etc 电绕组、电磁铁、电阻等
▨	Bronze, brass, copper, and compositions 青铜、黄铜、紫铜和复合材料	▨	Concrete 混凝土
▩	White metal, zinc, lead, babbitt, and alloys 白色金属、锌、铅、巴氏合金及合金	▨	Marble, slate, glass, porcelain, etc 大理石、石板、玻璃、陶瓷等

续表

▨	Magnesium, aluminum, and aluminum alloys 镁、铝和铝合金	▨	Earth 泥土
▨	Rubber, plastic electrical insulation 橡胶、塑料电绝缘材料	▨	Rock 岩石
▨	Cork, felt, fabric, leather, fiber 软木、毛毡、编织物、皮革、纤维	▨	Sand 砂子
▨	Sound insulation 隔音材料	▨	Water and other liquids 水和其他液体
▨	Thermal insulation 绝热材料	▨	Wood-across grain 横纹木材 Wood-with grain 纵纹木材

Table 2.4 Comparison of ANSI and ISO geometric symbols ANSI 美国国家标准和 ISO 国际标准的比较

Symbol for 符号	ANSI Y14.5M	ISO	Symbol for 符号	ANSI Y14.5M	ISO
Straightness 直线度	—	—	Circular runout 圆跳动	↗	↗
Flatness 平面度	▱	▱	Total runout 全跳动	↗↗	↗↗
Circularity/Roundness 圆度	○	○	At maximum material condition 最大实体条件	Ⓜ	Ⓜ
Cylindricity 圆柱度	⌭	⌭	At least material condition 最小实体条件	Ⓛ	Ⓛ
Profile of a line 线轮廓度	⌒	⌒	Regardless of feature size 不计特征尺寸	None 无	None 无
Profile of a surface 面轮廓度	⌓	⌓	Projected tolerance zone 延伸公差带	Ⓟ	Ⓟ
Angularity 倾斜度	∠	∠	Diameter 直径	ϕ	ϕ
Perpendicularity 垂直度	⊥	⊥	Basic dimension 基本尺寸	50	50
Parallelism 平行度	∥	∥	Reference dimension 参考尺寸	(50)	(50)
Position 位置度	⌖	⌖	Datum target 基准目标	$\phi6$/A1	$\phi6$/A1
Concentricity/Coaxiality 同心度/同轴度	◎	◎	Target point 目标点	×	×
Symmetry 对称度	⩵	⩵	Dimension origin 尺寸起点	⌭	⌭
Radius 半径	R	R	Spherical radius 球半径	SR	SR
Between 两者之间	↔	None 无	Controlled radius 受控半径	CR	None 无

续表

Symbol for 符号	ANSI Y14.5M	ISO
Feature control frame 特征控制框	⊕ φ0.5 Ⓜ A B C	⊕ φ0.5 Ⓜ A B C
Datum feature 基准特征	A	OR A
All around profile 周围轮廓	⟲	⟲ (Proposed) 建议
Conical taper 锥度	▷	▷
Slope 斜度	◁	◁
Counterbore/Spotface 沉孔/点锪	⊔	⊔ (Proposed) 建议
Countersink 锪锥形沉孔	∨	∨ (Proposed) 建议
Depth/Deep 深度	↧	↧ (Proposed) 建议
Square(shape) 正方形	□	□
Dimension not to scale 尺寸不成比例	15	15
Number of times/places 次数/位置数	8X	8X
Arc length 弧长	⌒105	⌒105
Spherical diameter 球直径	Sφ	Sφ
Statical tolerance 静公差	⟨ST⟩	None 无

Table 2.5 Application of geometric control symbols 几何控制符号的应用

Type 类别	Geometric characteristics 几何特征		Pertains to 相关要素	Basic dimensions 基本尺寸	Feature modifier 特征修正	Datum modifier 基准修正
Form 形状	─	Straightness 直线度	Only individual feature 只需自身特征		Modifier not applicable 不需修正	No datum 无基准
	○	Circularity 圆度				
	▱	Flatness 平面度				
	⌭	Cylindricity 圆柱度				
Profile 轮廓	⌒	Profile(line) 轮廓(线)	Individual or related 独立或相关	Yes if related 相关则有		RFS implied unless MMC or LMC is stated 不管特征尺寸 除非注明 MMC 或 LMC
	⌓	Profile(surface) 轮廓(面)				
Orientation 定向	∠	Angularity 倾斜度	Always related feature(s) 总需相关特征	Yes 有	RFS implied unless MMC or LMC is stated 不管特征尺寸 注明 MMC 或 LMC	
	⊥	Perpendicularity 垂直度				
	∥	Parallelism 平行度				
Location 位置	⊕	Position 位置度		Yes 有		
	◎	Concentricity 同轴度				
	═	Symmetry 对称度				
Runout 跳动	╱	Circular runout 圆跳动			Only RFS 不管特征尺寸	Only RFS 不管特征尺寸
	╱╱	Total runout 全跳动				

注：RFS——regardless of feature size 不管特征尺寸。

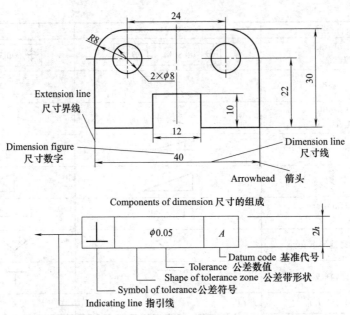

Fig 2.6 Code for shape and location tolerance 形位公差代号

Table 2.6 Commonly used symbols and abbreviation in dimensioning
常用尺寸标注符号和缩写

Description 描述	Symbols and abbreviation 符号缩写	Description 描述	Symbols and abbreviation 符号缩写
Diameter 直径	ϕ	Equally spaced 等距、均布	EQS
Radius 半径	R	Square 正方形	□
Spherical diameter 球直径	$S\phi$	Depth 深度	↓
Spherical radius 球半径	SR	Counterbore 沉孔	⊔
Thickness 厚度	t	Countersink 沉坑	∨
45°Chamfer 45°倒角	C	Taper 锥度	▷

Table 2.7 Morse tapers 莫氏锥度

Morse taper 莫氏锥度号	Taper per foot 每英尺的锥度值	Morse taper 莫氏锥度号	Taper per foot 每英尺的锥度值	Morse taper 莫氏锥度号	Taper per foot 每英尺的锥度值
0	0.62460	2	0.59941	4	0.62326
1	0.59858	3	0.60235	5	0.63151

Table 2.8 Tolerance modifiers 公差修正符号

Ⓕ	Ⓜ	Ⓛ	Ⓣ	Ⓟ	⟨ST⟩
Free state 自由状态	MMC 最大实体状态	LMC 最小实体状态	Tangent plane 相切平面	Projected tolerance zone 延伸公差带	Statical tolerance 静公差

2.4 Types of geometry shapes 各种几何图形

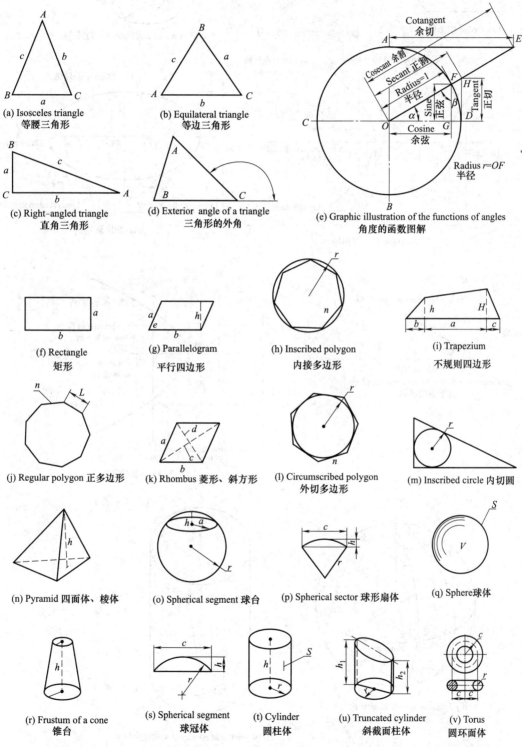

Fig 2.7

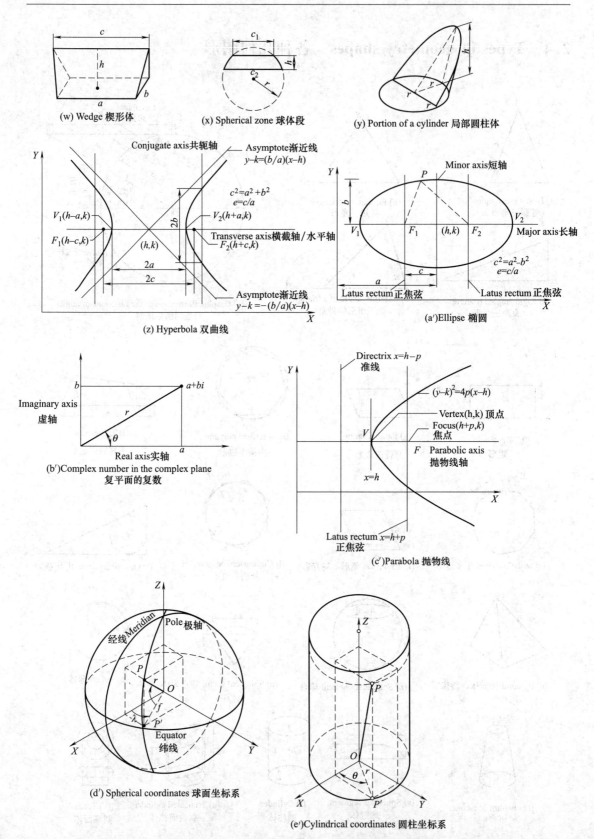

Fig 2.7　Types of geometry shapes　各种几何图形

2.5 Basic knowledge on mechanical engineering drawing 机械制图基本知识

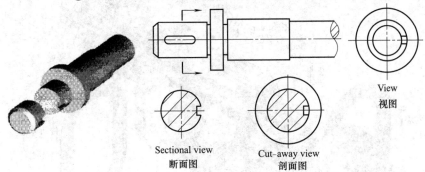

Fig 2.8 Comparison between sectional view with cut-away view 断面图与剖面图的比较

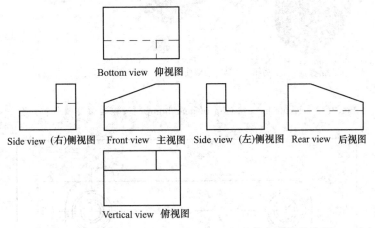

Fig 2.9 Location of the six views 六个基本视图的位置

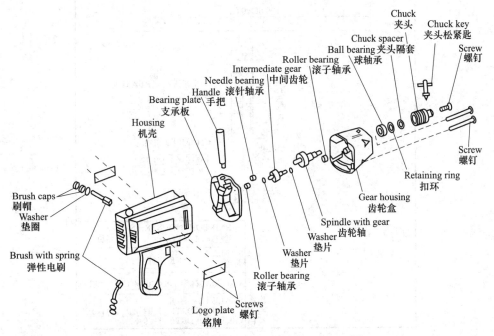

Fig 2.10 Exploded drawing 爆炸（分解）图

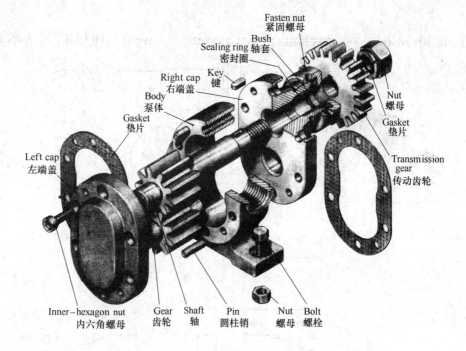

Fig 2.11　Exploded drawing of gear bump　齿轮泵爆炸（分解）图

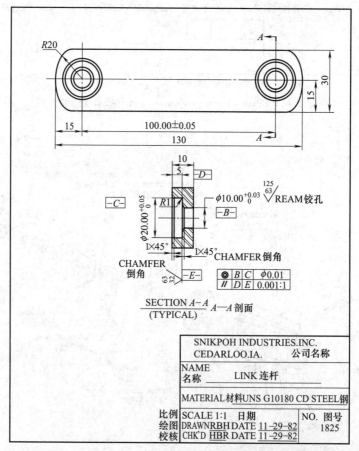

Fig 2.12　An example of a detail drawing　零件图例

Unit 2 Engineering Drawing 工程制图

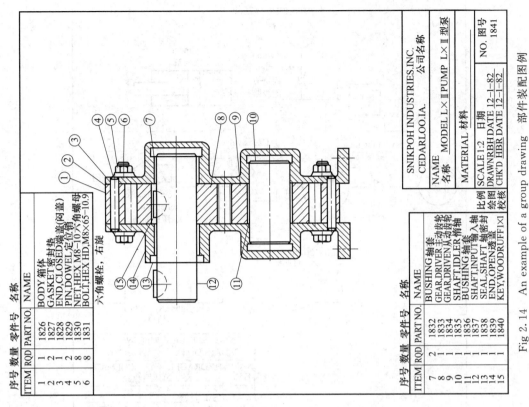

Fig 2.14 An example of a group drawing 部件装配图例

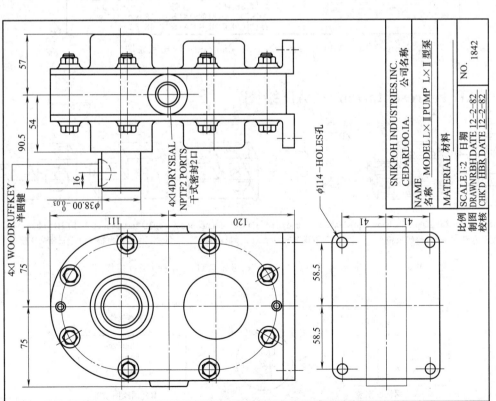

Fig 2.13 An example of an installation drawing 安装图例

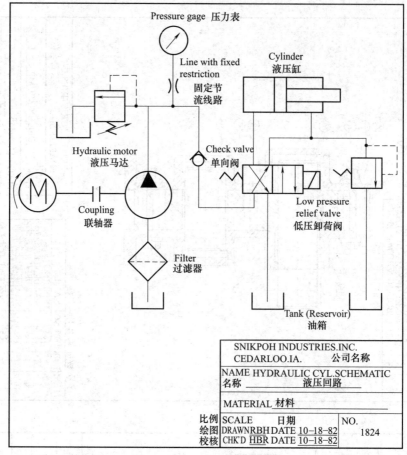

Fig 2.15　A hydraulic schematic diagram　液压示意图

2.6　CAD representation　CAD 绘图

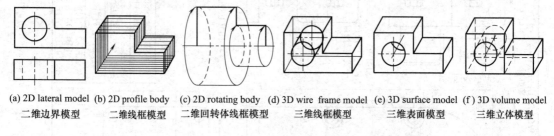

(a) 2D lateral model　(b) 2D profile body　(c) 2D rotating body　(d) 3D wire frame model　(e) 3D surface model　(f) 3D volume model
二维边界模型　　　二维线框模型　　　二维回转体线框模型　　三维线框模型　　　三维表面模型　　　三维立体模型

Fig 2.16　Various types of modeling for CAD　几种 CAD 建模

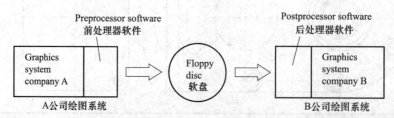

Fig 2.17　IGES (Initial Graphics Exchange Specification)　原始图形转换规格

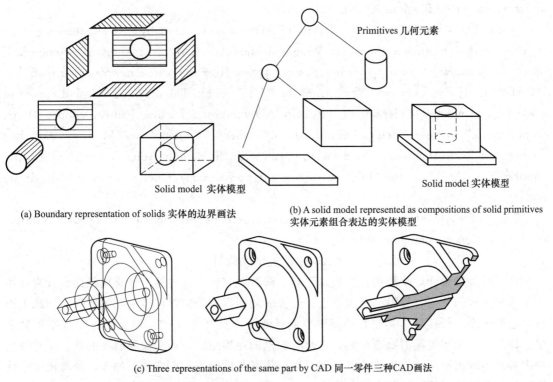

(a) Boundary representation of solids 实体的边界画法

(b) A solid model represented as compositions of solid primitives 实体元素组合表达的实体模型

(c) Three representations of the same part by CAD 同一零件三种CAD画法

Fig 2.18　CAD representations　　CAD 画法

2.7　Short passage for reading　阅读短文

AutoCAD

CAD (computer-aided design) is a technique of using a computer to create, modify, and refine a design. It, normally used in engineering departments, has greatly changed these departments. Drawings used to be made on paper with pencil or pen and drawing instruments. The drawings were very time-intensive to produce. They were then copied, and the copies were sent to the floor for production. The originals were stored in large drawers. Even a small job shop could have thousands of large blueprints on file. If changes were necessary, the engineer would get the original out of the file drawer, make the changes, copy it, and send the new print to the floor. Nowadays the computer can eliminate the need for all of the physical storage of prints. The computer also allows for rapid and easy modifications.

The engineer or designer first draws the part on the screen of computer. This part drawing is the actual part geometry. The sizes and locations are all correct so that the information can be used later to create a program to machine the part. Actually, you can also draw the geometry of a workpiece with CAD software on a computer. You may create the design model by applying graphics commands stored in the computer. You have complete freedom to zoom and view the model at different orientations and then represent the design as a set of points, lines, arcs, and so on by using basic CAD software. Actually, graphics editing commands allow for easy modifications as required.

AutoCAD is a computer-aided design (CAD) program used by just about every engineering and design office in the world. When you start AutoCAD, the AutoCAD window will open. The window is actually your design work space. How to create a new drawing with AutoCAD? Firstly, you choose "New" from the "File" menu. The dialogue box will appear in the command window underside of the AutoCAD window. Secondly, you can choose "Start from Scratch". Under "Select Default Setting" select "English" or "Metric", and then choose "OK". In this way, the drawing opens with the default AutoCAD settings. Finally choose "Save As" from the "File" menu and enter a file name, then you can save the drawing.

The AutoCAD interface has several different components, each of which provides different information of command options for the user.

CAD 计算机辅助设计

计算机辅助设计就是利用计算机来创建、修改并完善设计内容。计算机辅助设计常常用于工程相关部门并使它们得到巨大改变。过去的制图靠使用铅笔或钢笔及绘图仪在图纸上进行，绘制图纸十分耗时。绘制好的图纸复制件送到车间用于生产而原始图纸保存在资料柜里。即使是一个小规模的修造车间，它都有大量的存档图纸。如果需要改变的话，工程师就得去资料柜取出原图，作出修改并复制，最后将复制件送到生产车间。如今，计算机可以使得图纸的所有物理层面的储存工作没有必要，图纸的修改工作也变得方便快捷。

工程师或设计师首先在计算机屏幕上绘出零件图，其几何尺寸为零件实际值。零件图的尺寸和位置必须是正确值，这样就可以在以后的加工时创建其加工信息的程序。实际上，使用计算机里的 CAD 软件还可绘制零件的几何构形。使用计算机储存的图形命令可以创建设计模型。设计模型可以自由放大和在不同位置视图，然后通过采用基础的 CAD 软件输出一整套的由点、线条、弧线等构成的设计图。使用图形编辑指令会让修改变得十分便捷。

AutoCAD 是在全世界几乎每一个工程或设计部门所采用的计算机辅助设计程序软件。启动 AutoCAD，其窗口就会打开，实际上这个窗口就是人们的设计空间。AutoCAD 如何创建新图？第一步，"File" 文件菜单选定 "New" 更新，AutoCAD 视窗下侧边的命令窗口里出现对话框。第二步，选定 "Start from Scratch" 新建（从零开始）。在 "Select Default Setting" 默认选项下选取 "English" 英制或 "Metric" 公制，再点击 "OK" 确认。这样绘图窗口以默认项设置打开。最后，在 "File" 文件菜单选取 "Save As" 另存为，输入文件名，接着存储绘制图样。

AutoCAD 界面有多种不同的组件，每个组件为用户提供不同的命令选项信息。

Unit 3　Engineering Metrology and Tolerance/Fits　技术测量与公差配合

3.1　Measuring parameters and instruments　测量参数和测量仪器

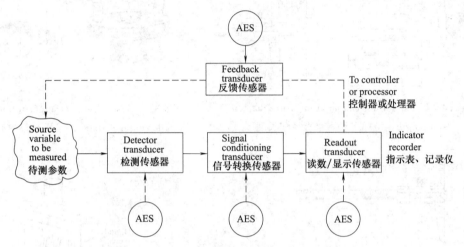

Fig 3.1　The generalized measurement system　通用的测量系统

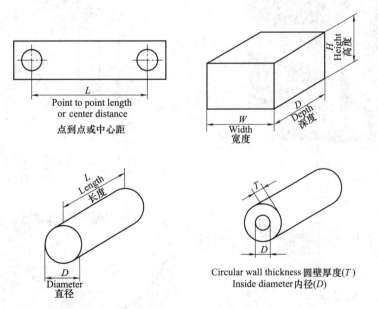

Fig 3.2　The measurement length may appear under several names
长度的测量可有不同的名义出现

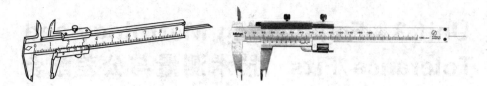

Fig 3.3　Vernier caliper　游标卡尺

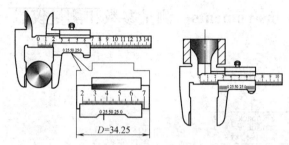

Fig 3.4　Use a vernier caliper to measure diameter and length　游标卡尺测量直径和长度

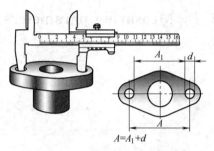

Fig 3.5　Use a vernier caliper to measure the center distance　卡尺测量中心距

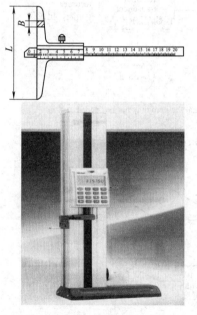

Fig 3.6　Vernier depth gauge 游标深（高）度尺

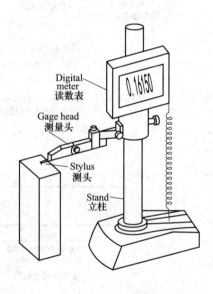

Fig 3.7　Digital vernier height gauge 数字高度尺

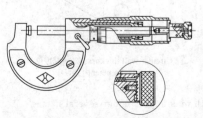

Fig 3.8　Micrometer for external diameter　外径千分尺

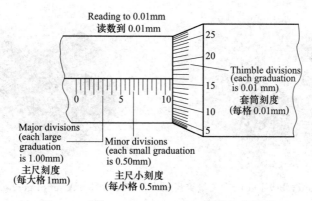

Fig 3.9 Micrometer principle 刻度细分原理

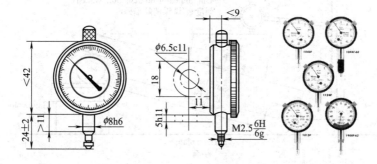

Fig 3.10 Centesimal dial indicator 百分表

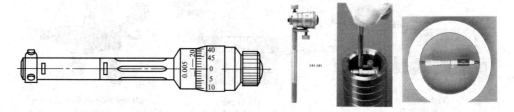

Fig 3.11 Three-jaw micrometer for internal (inner/inside) diameter 三爪内径千分尺

Fig 3.12 Optical projector
光学投影仪

Fig 3.13 Measuring of gear
齿轮公法线长度测量

Fig 3.14　Measuring miter/bevel gears　测量锥齿轮

Fig 3.15　A set of gear gauges　成套齿轮规

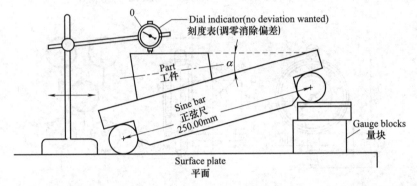
Fig 3.16　Angular measurement with a sine bar and dial indicator　正弦尺和刻度表测量角度

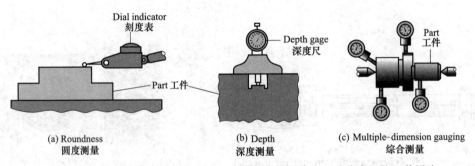
(a) Roundness 圆度测量　　(b) Depth 深度测量　　(c) Multiple-dimension gauging 综合测量

Fig 3.17　Three uses of dial indicator　刻度表（百分表、千分表）的三种用法

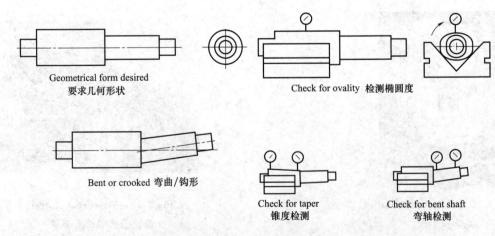

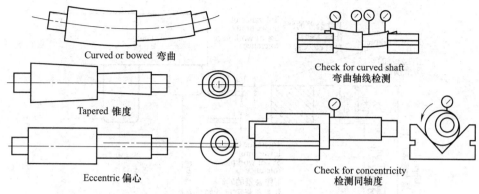

Fig 3.18　Checking for various shaft conditions　轴的多项检测

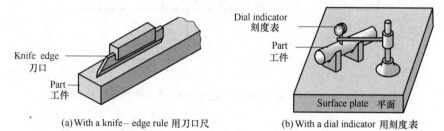

Fig 3.19　Measuring straightness manually　手工测量直线度

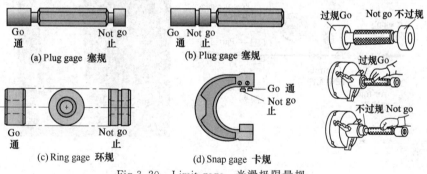

Fig 3.20　Limit gage　光滑极限量规

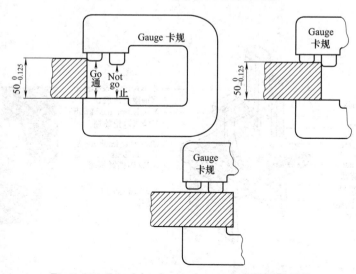

Fig 3.21　Principle of a snap gauge　卡规测量原理

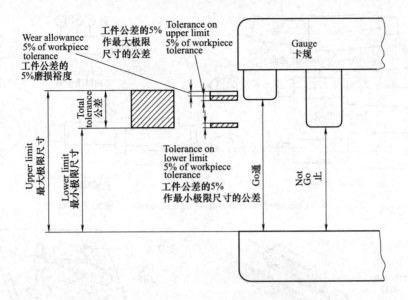

Fig 3.22 Disposition of wear in a snap gauge 卡规的磨损构成分解

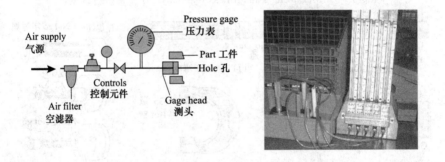

Fig 3.23 Air-gage system 气动测量仪

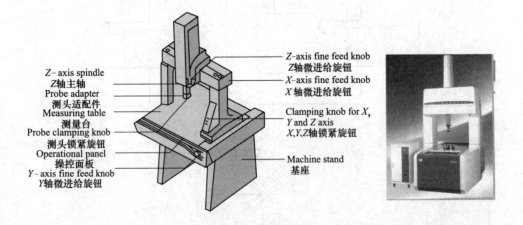

Fig 3.24 Coordinate-measuring machine (CMM) 坐标测量机

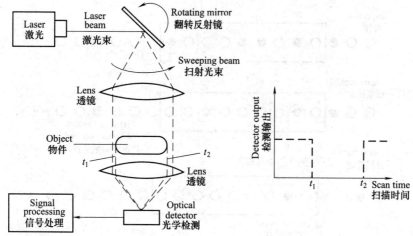

Fig 3.25 Schematic diagram showing operation of scanning laser beam system 激光束扫描工作图解

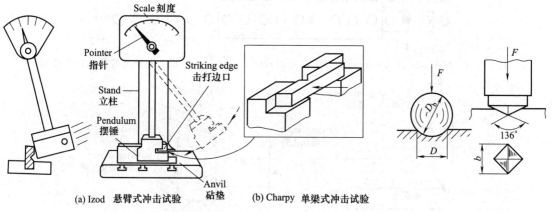

(a) Izod 悬臂式冲击试验   (b) Charpy 单梁式冲击试验

Fig 3.26 Impact-toughness tests
冲击强度试验

Fig 3.27 Hardness testing
硬度测量

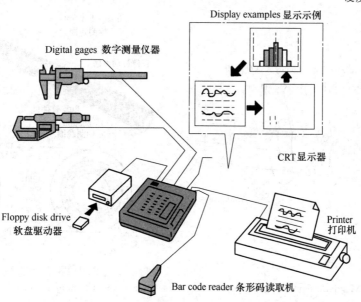

Fig 3.28 Integration of digital gages with microprocessor for real-time data acquisition and SPC/SPQ capabilities
数字测量仪器与微计算机集成用于实时数据查询和设备监控

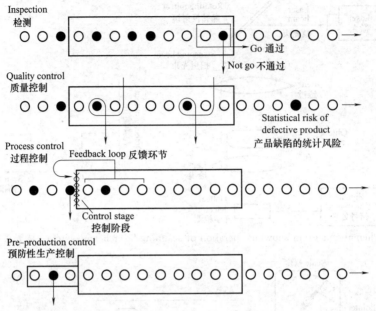

Fig 3.29 Methods of incorporating NDT into a production line 引入非破坏性检测的生产线

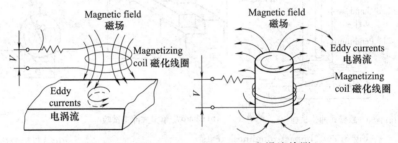

Fig 3.30 Eddy-current testing 电涡流检测

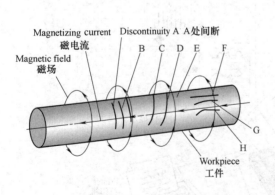

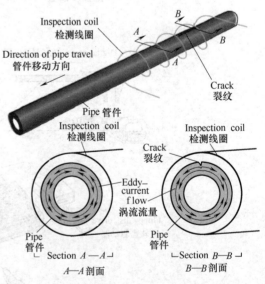

Fig 3.31 Magnetic-particle inspection of a part with a defect in it
工件内部缺陷的磁粒探伤检测

Fig 3.32 Changes in eddy-current flow caused by a defect in a workpiece
工件内部缺陷引起涡流流量改变

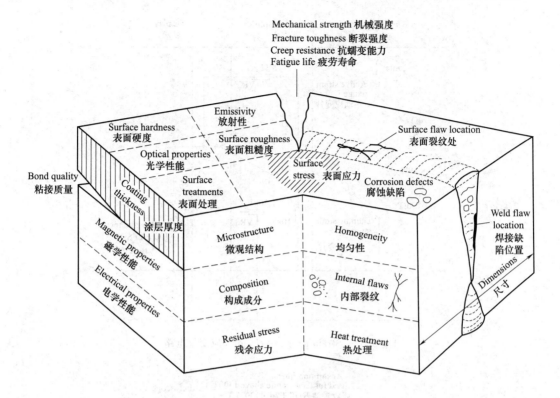

Fig 3.33　The scope of non-destructive testing　无损检测应用范围

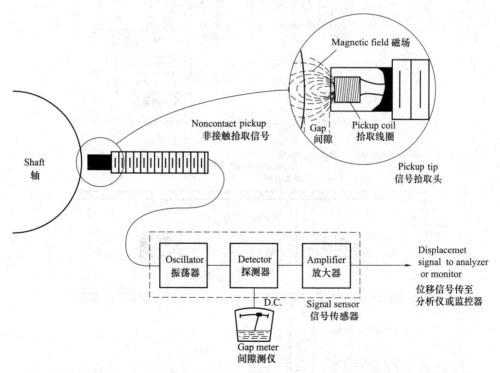

Fig 3.34　Displacement probe and signal conditioning system　位移探测和信号匹配系统

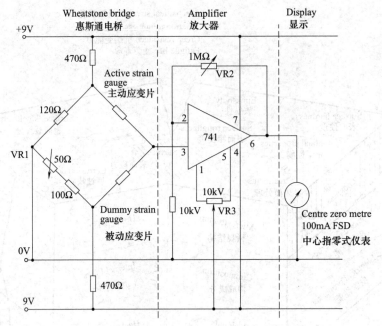

Fig 3.35 Strain gauge in circuit 应变仪电路

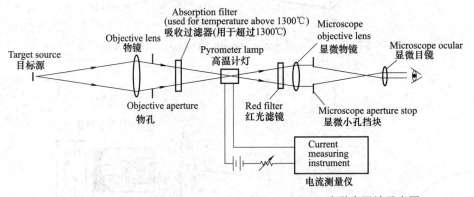

Fig 3.36 Schematic diagram of an optical pyrometer 光学高温计示意图

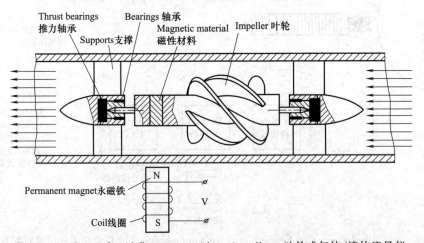

Fig 3.37 Gas or liquid flowmeter with an impeller 叶轮式气体/液体流量仪

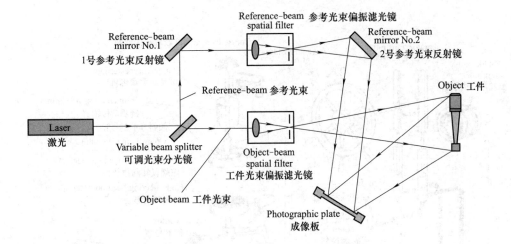

Fig 3.38 Basic optical system used in holography elements in radiography, for detecting flaws in workpieces

用于 X 射线全息摄影检测工件内部缺陷的基本光学系统

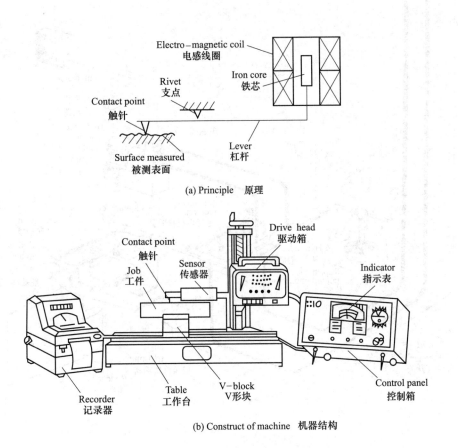

(a) Principle 原理

(b) Construct of machine 机器结构

Fig 3.39 Measuring principle of electrodynamic contourogragh

电动轮廓仪测量原理

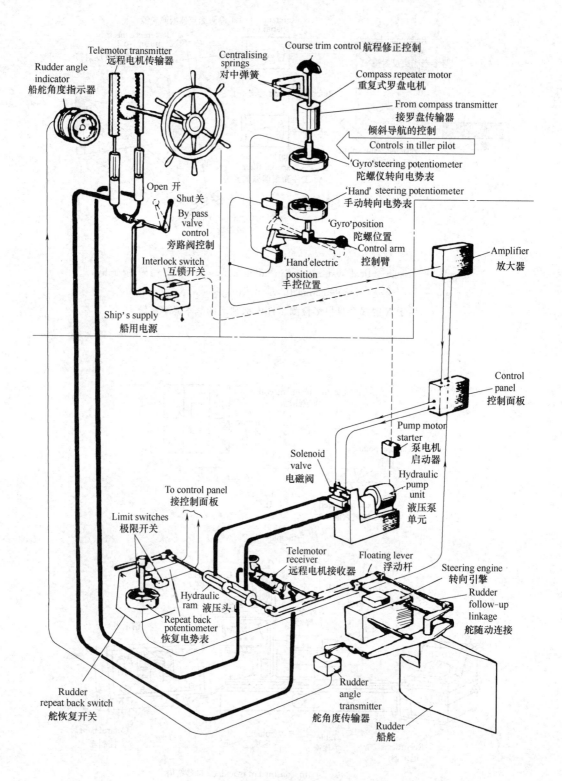

Fig 3.40 An early electro-mechanical autopilot system using telemotors
早期的采用远程电机机电式自动导航系统

3.2 Tolerance and fits 公差与配合

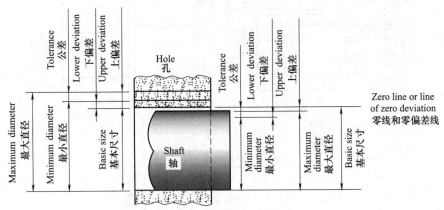

Fig 3.41　Basic size, deviation, and tolerance on a shaft, according to the ISO system
依据国际标准化组织的轴的尺寸、偏差和公差

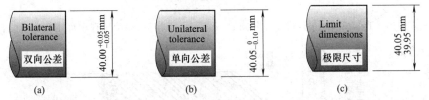

Fig 3.42　Various methods of assigning tolerance on a shaft　轴的公差标注方法

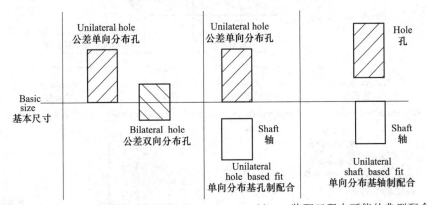

Fig 3.43　Typical fits possible in engineering assemblies　装配工程中可能的典型配合

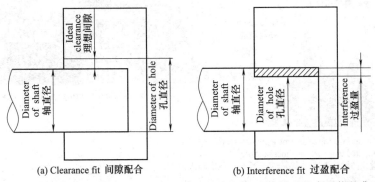

Fig 3.44　Typical fits possible in engineering assemblies　装配工程中可能的典型配合

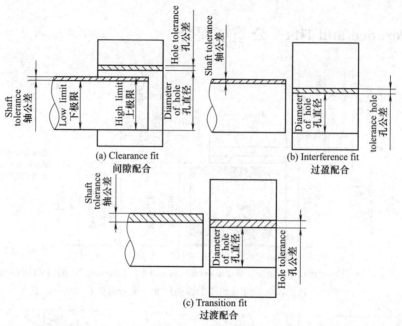

Fig 3.45　Typical fits possible in engineering assemblies　装配工程中可能的典型配合

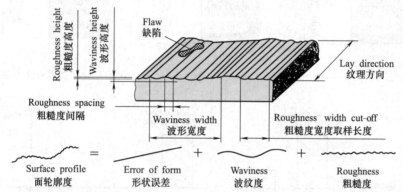

Fig 3.46　Standard terminology and symbols to describe surface finish　描述表面形貌的标准术语

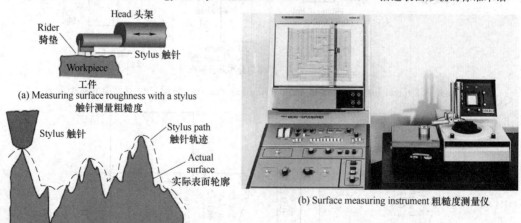

Fig 3.47　Measuring surface roughness with a stylus　触针测量粗糙度

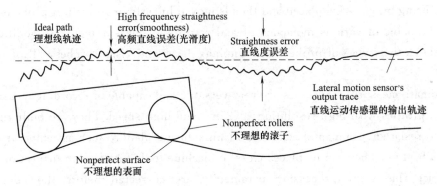

Fig 3.48 Straightness errors caused by surface form and finish errors
表面形状和粗糙度误差引起的直线度误差

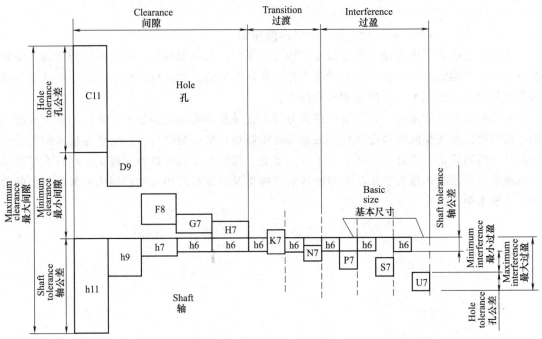

Fig 3.49 The recommended fits of shaft-basis system   基轴制推荐配合

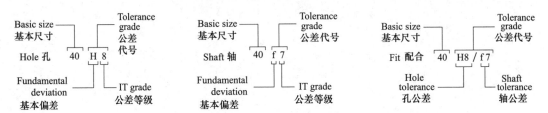

Fig 3.50 Nomenclature of tolerance and fit and symbols   公差配合符号及含义

3.3 Short passage for reading   阅读短文

Coordinate measuring machines

A coordinate measuring machine (CMM) basically consists of a platform on which the workpiece being measured is placed and then is moved linearly or rotated. A probe is attached to a head (capable of various movements) and records all measurements. In addition to the tactile probe, other types of probes are scanning, laser and vision probes, all of which are nontactile.

Coordinate measuring machines are very versatile and capable of recording measurements of complex profiles with high resolution (0.25m) and high speed. They are built rigidly and ruggedly to resist environmental effects in manufacturing plants, such as temperature variations and vibration. They can be placed close to machine tools for efficient inspection and rapid feedback; this way, processing parameters are corrected before the next part is made. Although large CMMs can be expensive, most machines with a touch probe and computer controlled three-dimensional movements are suitable for use in small shops and generally cost under $20,000.

坐标测量机

坐标测量机主要由测量工件放置平台构成,平台可以直线移动,也可以回转运动。安装在(可有多个运动的)测量头架上的探头记录各种测量值。除接触式探头外,还有其他类型的非接触探头,如扫描式、激光和影像探头。

坐标测量机功能多样,它能够快速高分辨率记录复杂轮廓的测量值。坐标测量机构造坚固,能够抵抗加工车间的温度变化、振动等环境影响。坐标测量机可以安装在机床附近及时检测并反馈测量值,由此,在下一个工件加工前,其加工参数可以得到修正。尽管大型的坐标测量机价格昂贵,适合于小型车间的接触式探头及计算机三维运动控制的大多数机型的价格通常低于两万美金。

Unit 4 Mechanical Transmission and Equipments
机械传动与设备装置

4.1 Parts, components and mechanism 传动零(部)件及机构

(1) Four-bar mechanism 四杆机构

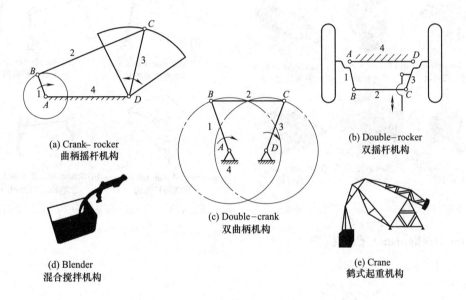

Fig. 4.1 Types of four-bar mechanism 四杆机构的类型

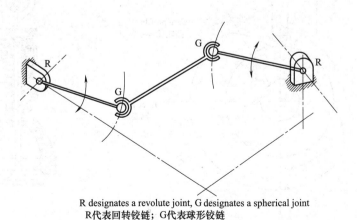

R designates a revolute joint, G designates a spherical joint
R代表回转铰链；G代表球形铰链

Fig. 4.2 An RGGR spatial linkage RGGR 空间连杆

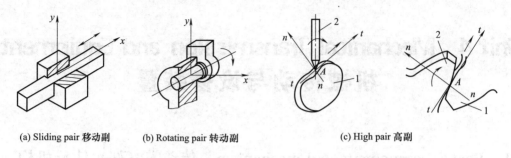

Fig 4.3　Common pairs in mechanical transmission　常见机械传动副

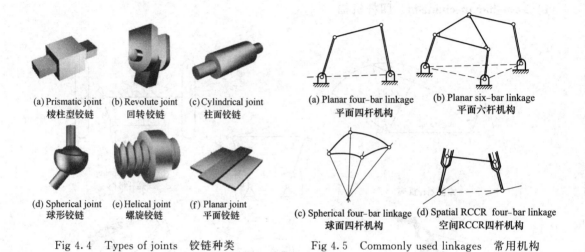

Fig 4.4　Types of joints　铰链种类

Fig 4.5　Commonly used linkages　常用机构

(2) Cam Mechanism　凸轮机构

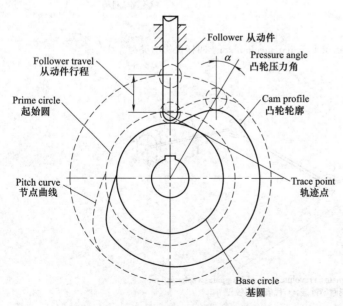

Fig 4.6　Basic components of cam mechanism
凸轮机构的基本构件

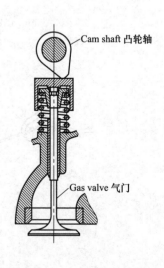

Fig 4.7　Valve mechanism
配气机构

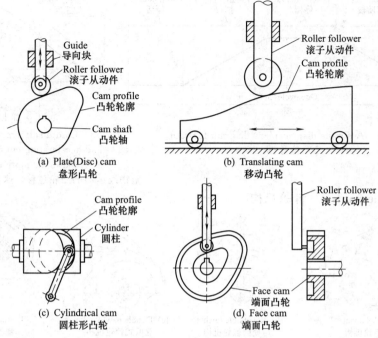

Fig 4.8　Types of cams　凸轮类型

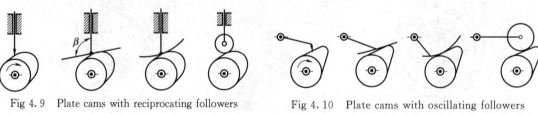

Fig 4.9　Plate cams with reciprocating followers
从动件往复运动的平面凸轮

Fig 4.10　Plate cams with oscillating followers
从动件摆动的平面凸轮

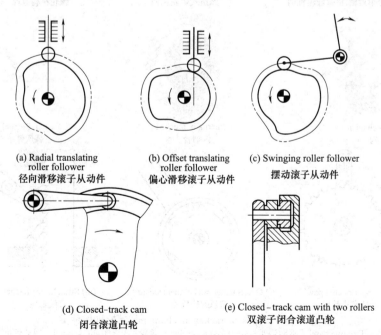

Fig 4.11　Cam follower systems　凸轮从动件系统

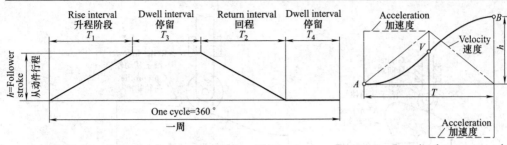

Fig 4.12 A simple displacement diagram for cam 凸轮位移图

Fig 4.13 Cam displacement, velocity and acceleration curves for parabolic motion 抛物线运动的凸轮位移、速度和加速度图

(3) **Ratchet mechanism** 棘轮机构

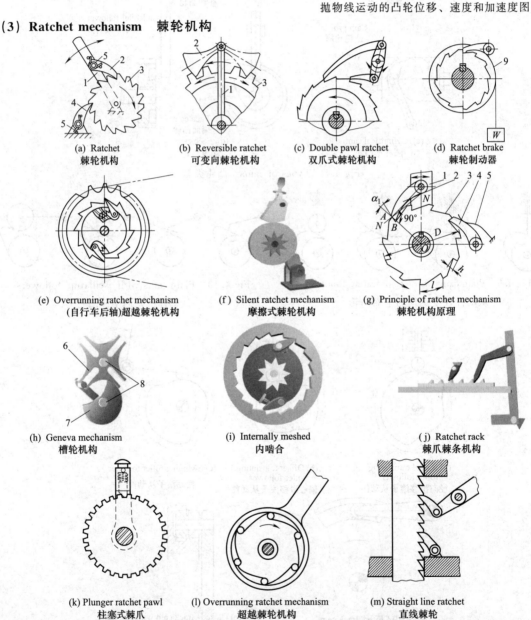

(a) Ratchet 棘轮机构
(b) Reversible ratchet 可变向棘轮机构
(c) Double pawl ratchet 双爪式棘轮机构
(d) Ratchet brake 棘轮制动器
(e) Overrunning ratchet mechanism (自行车后轴)超越棘轮机构
(f) Silent ratchet mechanism 摩擦式棘轮机构
(g) Principle of ratchet mechanism 棘轮机构原理
(h) Geneva mechanism 槽轮机构
(i) Internally meshed 内啮合
(j) Ratchet rack 棘爪棘条机构
(k) Plunger ratchet pawl 柱塞式棘爪
(l) Overrunning ratchet mechanism 超越棘轮机构
(m) Straight line ratchet 直线棘轮

Fig 4.14 Types of racket mechanisms 棘轮机构种类

1—Rocker 摇杆；2—Driving pawl 驱动棘爪；3—Driven ratchet 棘轮；4—Holding pawl 制动棘爪；5—spring 弹簧；6—Driven geneva wheel 从动槽轮；7—Driving plate 主动销轮；8—Rack 机架；9—Barrel 卷筒

(4) Spring 弹簧

Fig 4.15　Typical types of springs　弹簧的典型类别

1—Helical compression types　螺旋压缩弹簧；2—Helical extension types　螺旋拉伸弹簧；3—Torsion types　扭簧；
4—Flat springs, blue-steel and beryllium-copper types　片状弹簧、发蓝钢片或铍青铜类；
5—Slotted spring washers　开槽弹簧垫片；6—Conical compression type　锥形压缩弹簧

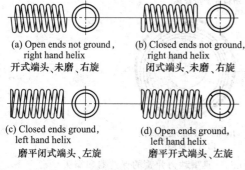

(a) Open ends not ground, right hand helix 开式端头、未磨、右旋
(b) Closed ends not ground, right hand helix 闭式端头、未磨、右旋
(c) Closed ends ground, left hand helix 磨平闭式端头、左旋
(d) Open ends ground, left hand helix 磨平开式端头、左旋

Fig 4.16　Types of helical compression spring ends
螺旋压缩弹簧端头类型

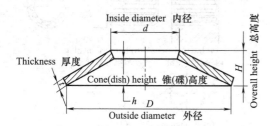

Fig 4.17　Disc spring nomenclature
碟形弹簧术语

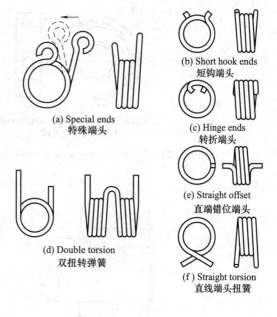

(a) Special ends 特殊端头
(b) Short hook ends 短钩端头
(c) Hinge ends 转折端头
(d) Double torsion 双扭转弹簧
(e) Straight offset 直端错位端头
(f) Straight torsion 直线端头扭簧

Fig 4.18　Common helical torsion-spring end configurations　常用螺旋扭转弹簧的端部构造

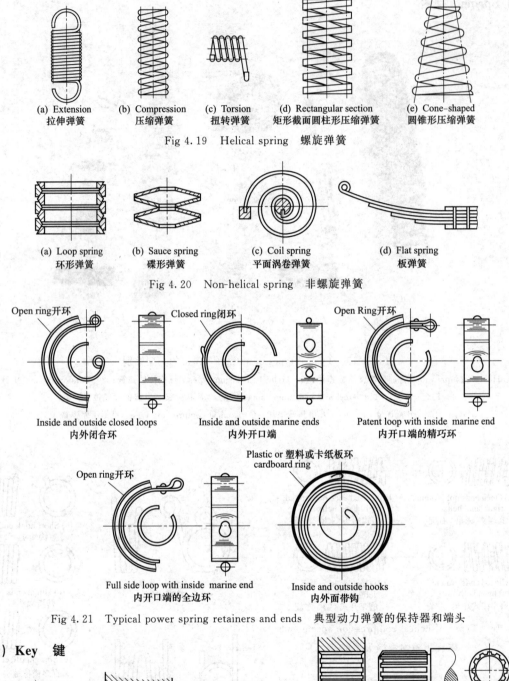

Fig 4.19　Helical spring　螺旋弹簧

Fig 4.20　Non-helical spring　非螺旋弹簧

Fig 4.21　Typical power spring retainers and ends　典型动力弹簧的保持器和端头

(5) Key　键

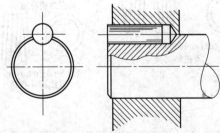

Fig 4.22　Round key　圆柱形键

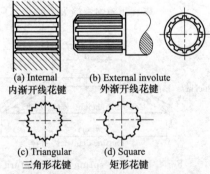

Fig 4.23　Splines　花键

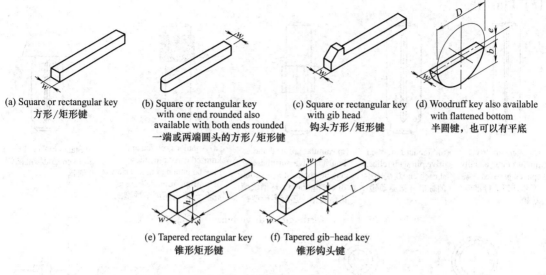

Fig 4.24 Key 键

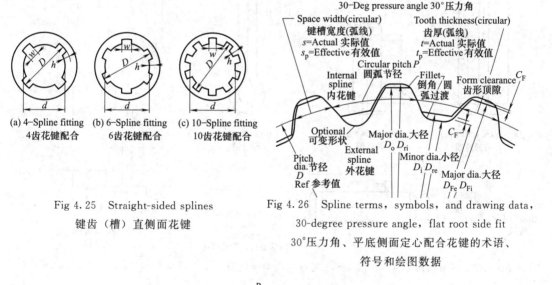

Fig 4.25 Straight-sided splines
键齿（槽）直侧面花键

Fig 4.26 Spline terms, symbols, and drawing data,
30-degree pressure angle, flat root side fit
30°压力角、平底侧面定心配合花键的术语、
符号和绘图数据

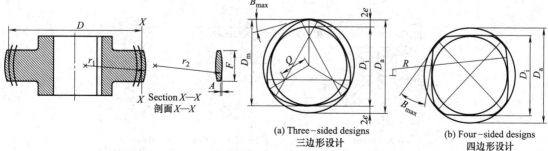

Fig 4.27 Crowned splines for large misalignments
定位误差较大时采用的球冠花键

Fig 4.28 Polygon-type shaft connections
多边形轴的连接

(6) Pin 销

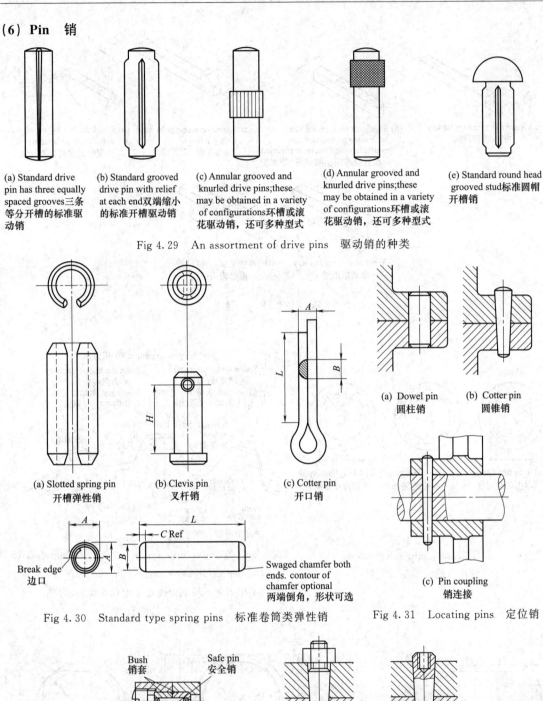

(a) Standard drive pin has three equally spaced grooves 三条等分开槽的标准驱动销

(b) Standard grooved drive pin with relief at each end 双端缩小的标准开槽驱动销

(c) Annular grooved and knurled drive pins; these may be obtained in a variety of configurations 环槽或滚花驱动销，还可多种型式

(d) Annular grooved and knurled drive pins; these may be obtained in a variety of configurations 环槽或滚花驱动销，还可多种型式

(e) Standard round head grooved stud 标准圆帽开槽销

Fig 4.29　An assortment of drive pins　驱动销的种类

(a) Slotted spring pin 开槽弹性销

(b) Clevis pin 叉杆销

(c) Cotter pin 开口销

(a) Dowel pin 圆柱销

(b) Cotter pin 圆锥销

(c) Pin coupling 销连接

Break edge 边口

Swaged chamfer both ends. contour of chamfer optional 两端倒角，形状可选

Fig 4.30　Standard type spring pins　标准卷筒类弹性销

Fig 4.31　Locating pins　定位销

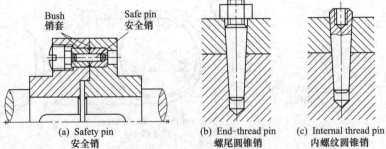

(a) Safety pin 安全销

(b) End-thread pin 螺尾圆锥销

(c) Internal thread pin 内螺纹圆锥销

Bush 销套　Safe pin 安全销

Fig 4.32　Pin with screw head　端部带螺纹的圆锥销

(7) Screw, bolt and nut　螺钉、螺栓及螺母

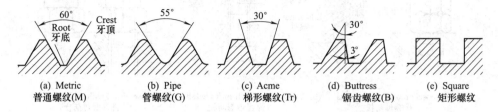

Fig 4.33　Types of helical screw threads　常用螺纹牙型

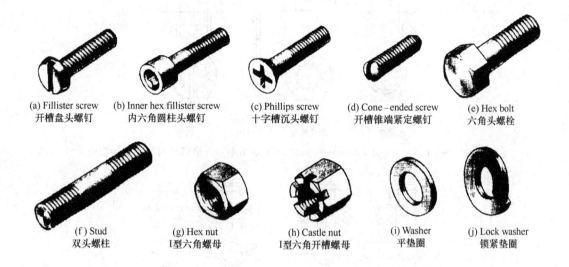

Fig 4.34　Components of bolt coupling　常见螺纹连接构件

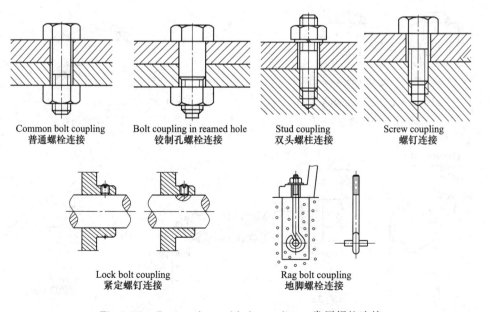

Fig 4.35　Commonly used bolt coupling　常用螺纹连接

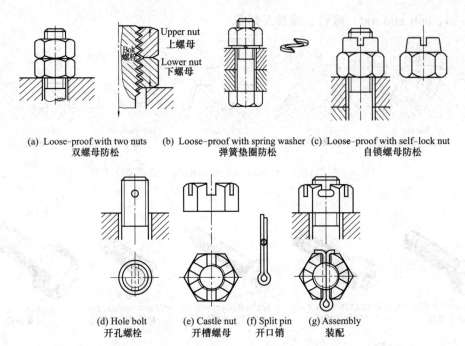

Fig 4.36　Loose-proof with castle nut and hole bolt　开槽螺母与开孔螺栓防松

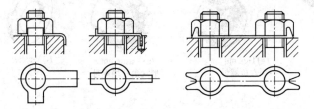

Fig 4.37　Loose-proof with stop washer　止动垫片防松

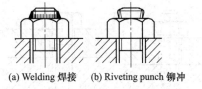

Fig 4.38　Loose-proof with undismantle methods
不可拆卸防松

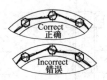

Fig 4.39　Loose-proof by wire connect
串联钢丝防松

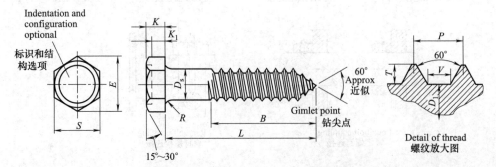

Fig 4.40　Metric hex lag screws　公制六角木螺钉

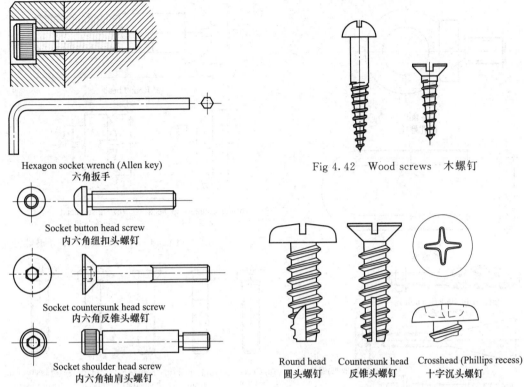

Fig 4.41　Hexagon socket head screw—application　内六角螺钉应用

Fig 4.42　Wood screws　木螺钉

Fig 4.43　Self-tapping screws　自攻螺钉

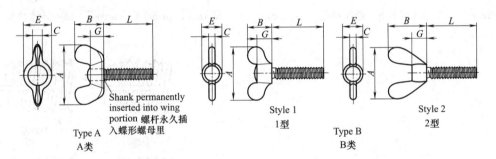

Fig 4.44　Standard wing screws　标准蝶形螺钉

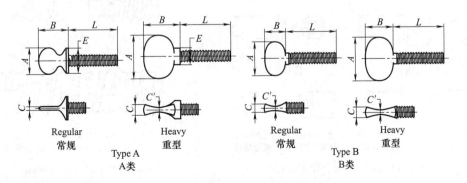

Fig 4.45　Thumb screws　拇指形螺钉

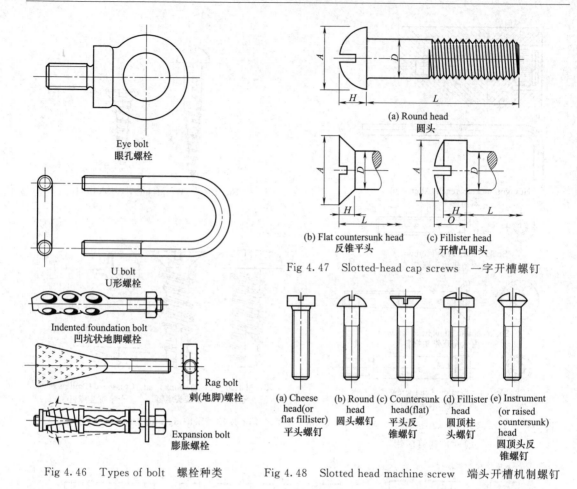

Fig 4.46　Types of bolt　螺栓种类

Fig 4.47　Slotted-head cap screws　一字开槽螺钉

Fig 4.48　Slotted head machine screw　端头开槽机制螺钉

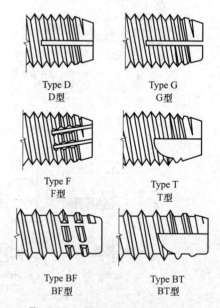

Fig 4.49　Set screw　锁定螺钉

Fig 4.50　Thread-cutting screws 牙形切断螺钉

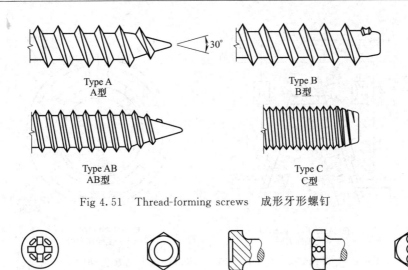

Fig 4.51　Thread-forming screws　成形牙形螺钉

(a) Recessed and hexagon head screws 内沉六角头螺钉

(b) Hexagon machine screw nuts 六角机制螺母

(c) Slotted head screws 头部开槽螺钉

Fig 4.52　British unified machine screws and nuts　英制统一机制螺钉和螺母

(8) Screw drive　螺纹传动

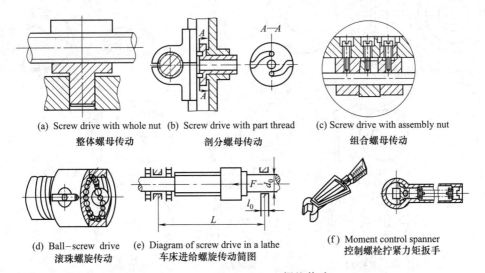

(a) Screw drive with whole nut　(b) Screw drive with part thread　(c) Screw drive with assembly nut
整体螺母传动　　　　　　　剖分螺母传动　　　　　　　组合螺母传动

(d) Ball-screw drive　(e) Diagram of screw drive in a lathe　(f) Moment control spanner
滚珠螺旋传动　　　车床进给螺旋传动简图　　　　控制螺栓拧紧力矩扳手

Fig 4.53　Screw drive　螺纹传动

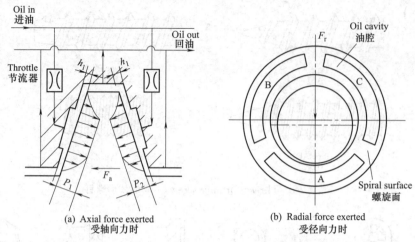

(a) Axial force exerted 受轴向力时

(b) Radial force exerted 受径向力时

Fig 4.54　Principle of static screw driving　静压螺旋传动的工作原理

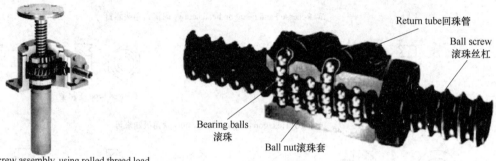

Power screw assembly using rolled thread load screw driven by worm shaft and gear nut
采用蜗杆轴和蜗轮驱动的滚珠丝杠动力丝杠组件

Fig 4.55　Ball screw assembly　滚珠丝杠组件

(9) Washer 垫片

(a) Flush 凸起垫片　　(b) Raised 卷边垫片

Fig 4.56　Finish washers　精密垫片

Fig 4.57　Slotted washers　开槽垫圈

(a) Plain 普通平垫片

(b) Cylindrically curved 圆柱拱曲垫片

(c) Conical or belleville 锥形或钟罩形垫片

(d) Slotted 开槽垫片

(e) Spring 弹簧垫片

(f) Spring-locking 弹簧锁紧垫片

Fig 4.58　Washers　垫片（圈）（一）

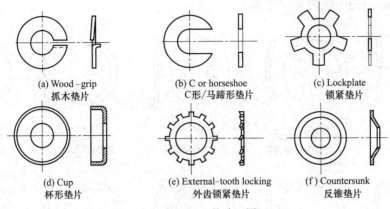

Fig 4.59　Washers　垫片（圈）（二）

Fig 4.60　Stacks of belleville washers
蝶形垫圈的重叠布置

Fig 4.61　Taper washer and application
锥形垫片及应用

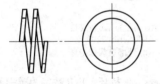

Fig 4.62　Two-coil spring lock washer
双圈弹簧锁紧垫圈

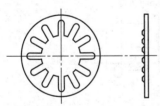

Fig 4.63　Internally serrated lock washer (tooth lock washer)　内错齿锁紧垫圈（齿形锁紧垫圈）

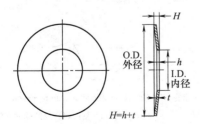

Fig 4.64　Belleville washer
钟罩形垫圈

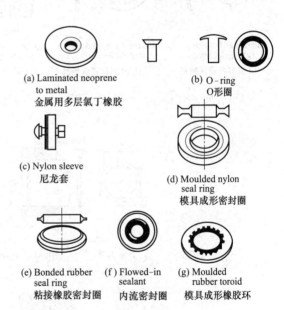

Fig 4.65　Self-sealing fasteners and washers
自封紧固件、垫片

(10) Retaining ring 保持环（卡圈）

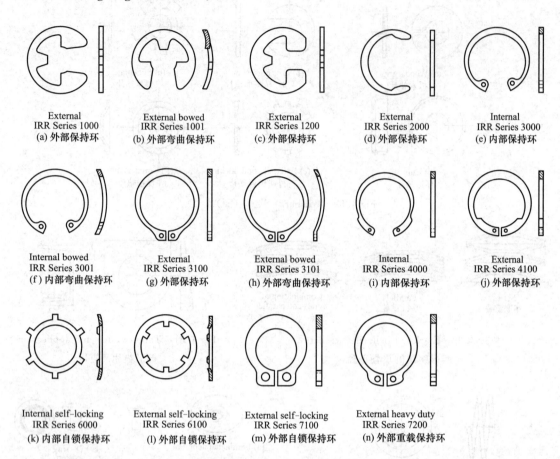

Fig 4.66 Retaining rings, the IRR numbers are catalog numbers 保持环、IRR 数字为类别号

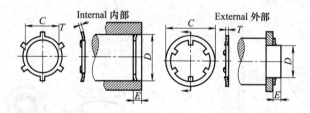

Fig 4.67 Self-locking retaining rings 自锁保持环

(a) Groove profile before loading
加载前的沟槽

(b) Localized yielding of retained part and groove under load 加载后的保持件和沟槽的局部屈服变形

(c) Groove profile after loading beyond thrust capacity 轴向超载处卸载后沟槽形状

Fig 4.68 Localized groove yielding under load 加载下的局部沟槽屈服变形

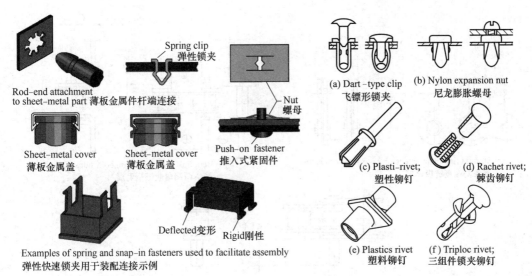

Fig 4.69　Integrated snap fasteners　整体插入式紧固件

Fig 4.70　Various types of plastics fasteners　各种塑料紧固件

(11) Chain drive　链条传动

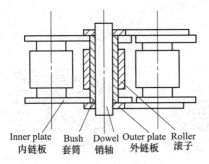

Fig 4.71　Construct of bush-roller chain 套筒滚子链的结构

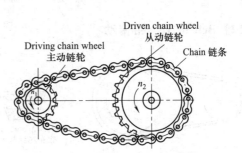

Fig 4.72　Chain driving　链传动

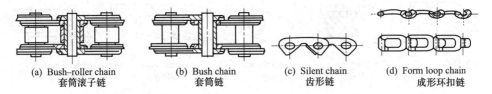

Fig 4.73　Types of chain drive　传动链的类型

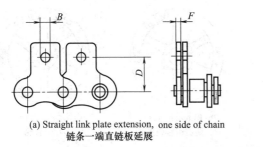

(a) Straight link plate extension, one side of chain
链条一端直链板延展

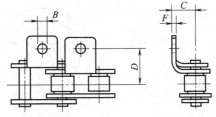

(b) Bent link plate extension, one side of chain
链条一端弯曲链板延展

Fig 4.74

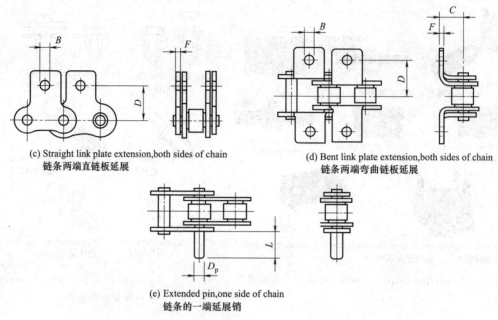

Fig 4.74　Straight and bent link plate extensions and extended pin dimensions
直链板、弯曲链板延展以及延展销尺寸

(12) Belt drive　带传动

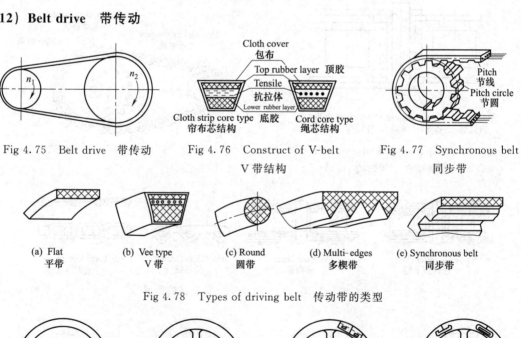

Fig 4.75　Belt drive　带传动　　Fig 4.76　Construct of V-belt　　Fig 4.77　Synchronous belt
　　　　　　　　　　　　　　　　　　　V 带结构　　　　　　　　　　　　同步带

Fig 4.78　Types of driving belt　传动带的类型

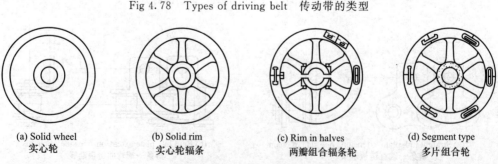

Fig 4.79　Flywheels　飞轮

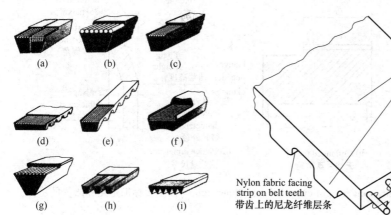

Fig 4.80 V-belt configurations
V 带的构形

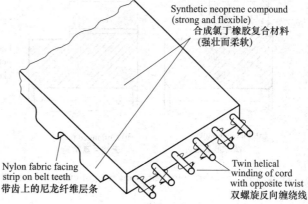

Fig 4.81 Illustrates the typical components of a timing belt
典型正时带结构图解

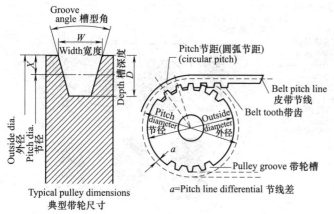

Fig 4.82 Synchronous belt pulley dimensions 同步带轮尺寸

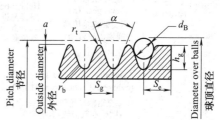

Fig 4.83 V-ribbed belt sheave and groove dimensions
V 形多楔带带轮和沟槽尺寸

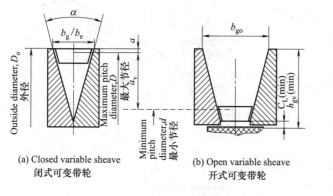
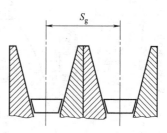

Fig 4.84 Variable sheaves 可变带轮

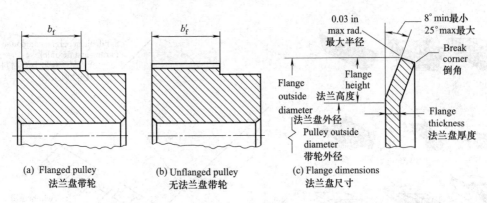

Fig 4.85　Synchronous belt standard pulley and flange dimensions　同步带标准带轮和法兰尺寸

(13) Gear drive　齿轮传动

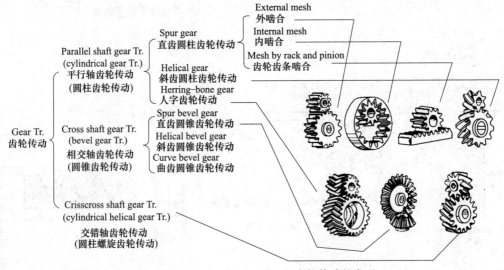

Fig 4.86　Types of gear drive　齿轮传动的类型

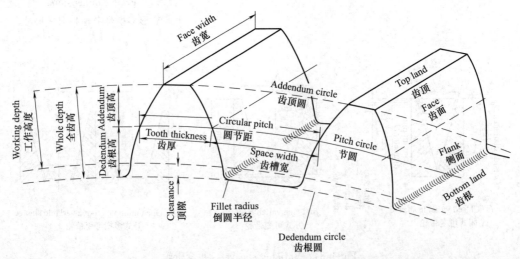

Fig 4.87　Nomenclature for an involute spur gear　渐开线直齿轮术语

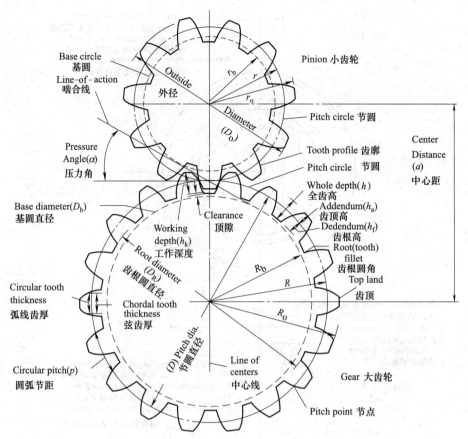

Fig 4.88 Terms used in gear geometry 齿轮啮合术语

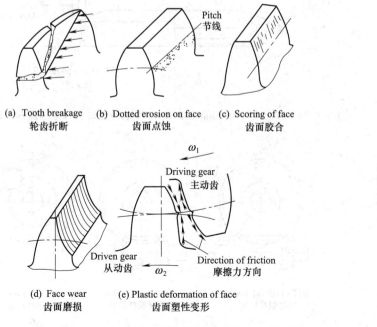

Fig 4.89 Failure forms of gear tooth 齿轮轮齿的失效形式

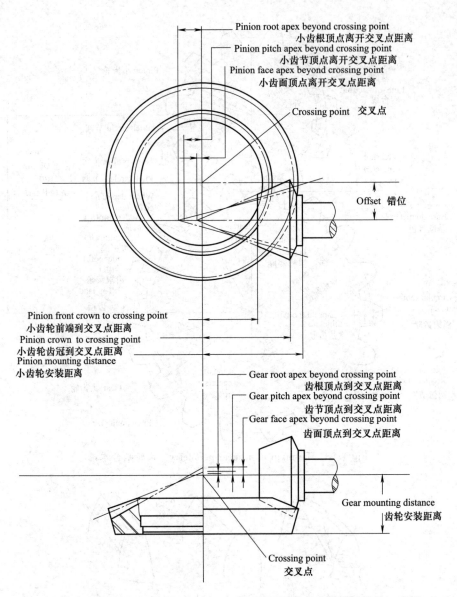

Fig 4.90　Hypoid gear nomenclature　准双曲面齿轮（偏轴圆锥齿轮）术语

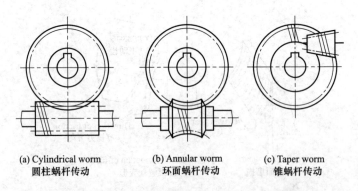

Fig 4.91　Types of worm transmission　蜗杆传动的类型

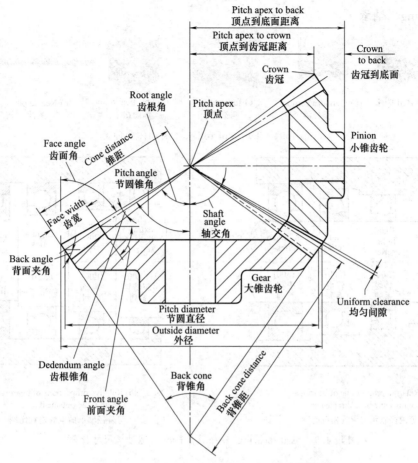

Fig 4.92 Bevel gear nomenclature 锥齿轮术语

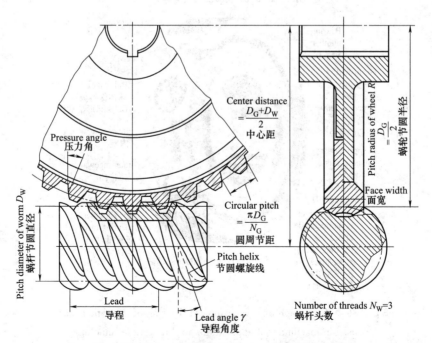

Fig 4.93 Worm gear terminology 蜗轮蜗杆术语

(14) Bearing 轴承

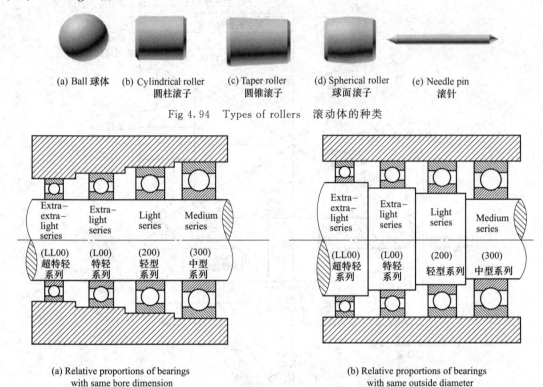

Fig 4.94　Types of rollers　滚动体的种类

(a) Relative proportions of bearings with same bore dimension
等内径轴承的承载相对比例

(b) Relative proportions of bearings with same outside diameter
等外径轴承的承载相对比例

Fig 4.95　Ball-bearing size proportion　球轴承尺寸比例

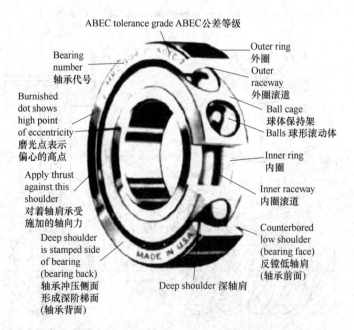

Fig 4.96　Photograph of a precision ball bearing of the type generally used in machine-tool applications to illustrate terminology
机床常用精密轴承术语说明

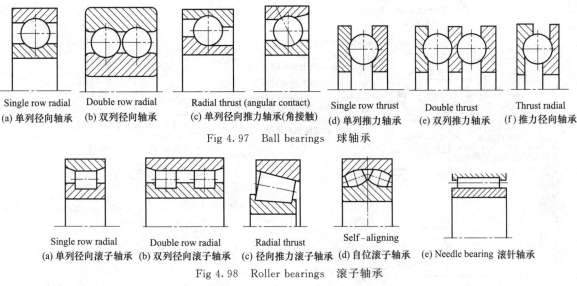

Fig 4.97 Ball bearings 球轴承

(a) Single row radial 单列径向轴承
(b) Double row radial 双列径向轴承
(c) Radial thrust (angular contact) 单列径向推力轴承(角接触)
(d) Single row thrust 单列推力轴承
(e) Double thrust 双列推力轴承
(f) Thrust radial 推力径向轴承

Fig 4.98 Roller bearings 滚子轴承

(a) Single row radial 单列径向滚子轴承
(b) Double row radial 双列径向滚子轴承
(c) Radial thrust 径向推力滚子轴承
(d) Self-aligning 自位滚子轴承
(e) Needle bearing 滚针轴承

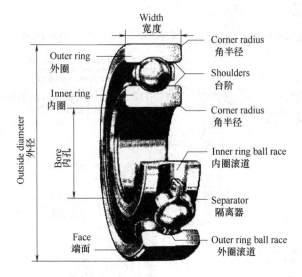

(a) Self-aligning ball bearing 自位球轴承
(b) Split inner ring ball bearing 剖分内圈球轴承
(c) Duplex sets of angular contact ball bearings 成对角接触球轴承
Back-to-back arrangement 背对背布局
Face-to-face arrangement 面对面布局

Fig 4.99 Types of rolling bearing 滚动轴承类别

Fig 4.100 Conrad anti-friction ball bearing parts
深沟防摩擦球轴承部件

Width 宽度; Outer ring 外圈; Inner ring 内圈; Outside diameter 外径; Bore 内孔; Corner radius 角半径; Shoulders 台阶; Inner ring ball race 内圈滚道; Separator 隔离器; Face 端面; Outer ring ball race 外圈滚道

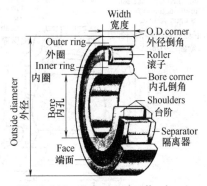

Fig 4.101 Cylindrical roller bearing
柱形滚子轴承

Width 宽度; O.D. corner 外径倒角; Outer ring 外圈; Inner ring 内圈; Roller 滚子; Bore corner 内孔倒角; Shoulders 台阶; Separator 隔离器; Outside diameter 外径; Bore 内孔; Face 端面

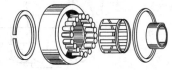

Fig 4.102 Separable inner ring-type cylindrical roller bearings
内圈可拆卸的柱形滚子轴承

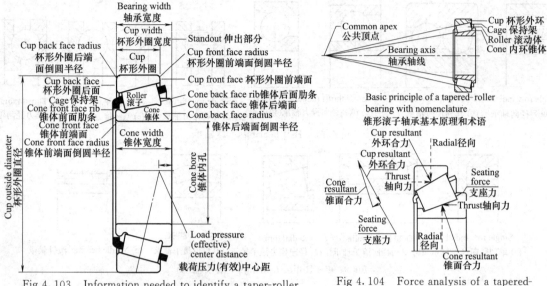

Fig 4.103　Information needed to identify a taper-roller bearing　锥形滚子轴承的识别信息

Fig 4.104　Force analysis of a tapered-roller bearing　锥形滚子轴承受力分析

Fig 4.105　Spherical roller bearings　球形滚子轴承

Fig 4.106　Thrust ball bearing　轴向/推力球轴承

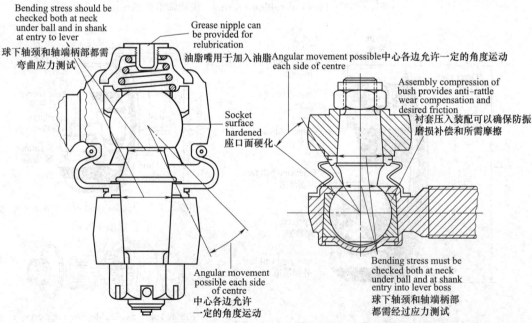

Fig 4.107　Transverse type ball joint with metal surfaces 金属面横向球体连接

Fig 4.108　Transverse steering ball joint 横向转向器球连接

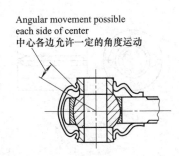
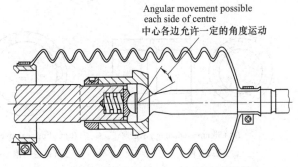

Fig 4.109 Straddle type joint shown with gaiters and associated distance pieces 跨坐式接头可见其罩子及相关隔套件

Fig 4.110 Axial ball joint 轴向球连接

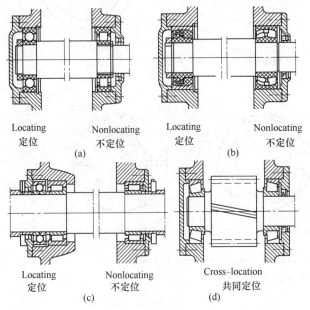
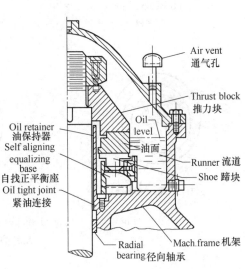

Fig 4.111 Typical bearing mounting 典型轴承安装

Fig 4.112 Half section of mounting for vertical thrust bearing 立式推力轴承安装的半剖图

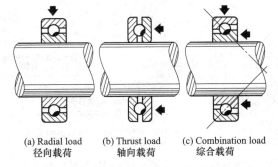

Fig 4.113 Three principal types of ball bearing loads 三种主要的轴承载荷

Fig 4.114 Plain radial or journal bearings or Babbit bearings 普通径向轴承、滑动轴承或巴氏合金衬管轴承

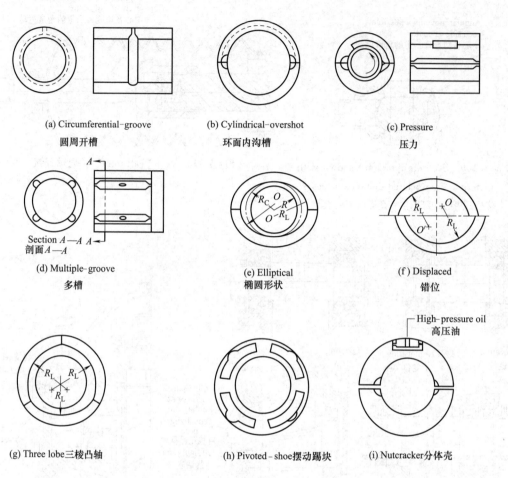

Fig 4.115　Typical shapes of several types of pressure-fed bearings
几种静压轴承的典型结构

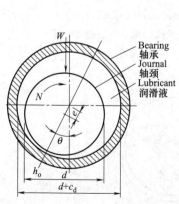

Fig 4.116　Basic components of a journal bearing
滑动轴承基本构成

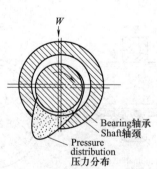

Fig 4.117　Typical pressure profile of journal bearing
滑动轴承典型压力分布

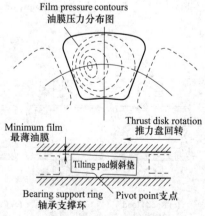

Fig 4.118　Hydrodynamic thrust bearing
动压推力轴承

(15) Shaft 轴

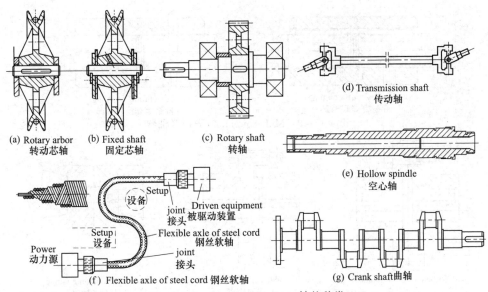

Fig 4.119　Types of shafts　轴的种类

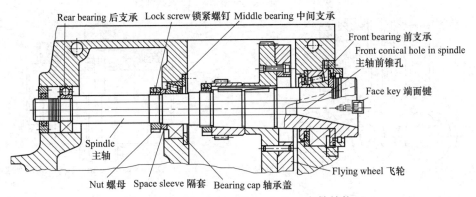

Fig 4.120　Construct of a spindle　主轴结构

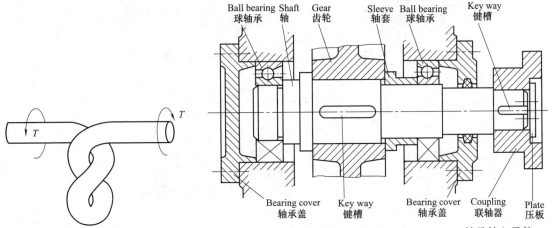

Fig 4.121　"Helixed" flexible shaft made of wire or rope
金属丝或绳制作的"螺旋"柔性轴

Fig 4.122　Shaft and its coupling components　轴及轴上零件

(16) Shaft coupling 联轴器

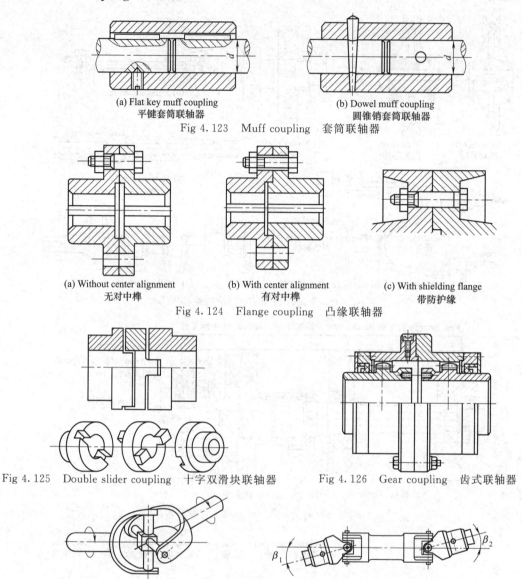

Fig 4.123　Muff coupling　套筒联轴器
(a) Flat key muff coupling　平键套筒联轴器
(b) Dowel muff coupling　圆锥销套筒联轴器

Fig 4.124　Flange coupling　凸缘联轴器
(a) Without center alignment　无对中榫
(b) With center alignment　有对中榫
(c) With shielding flange　带防护缘

Fig 4.125　Double slider coupling　十字双滑块联轴器

Fig 4.126　Gear coupling　齿式联轴器

Fig 4.127　Hooks coupling (universal coupling)　十字轴万向联轴器

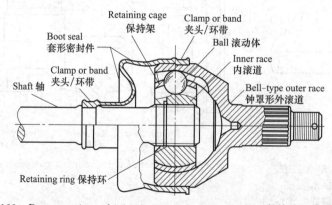

Fig 4.128　Rzeppa universal joint in cross section　Rzeppa 鼠笼式万向节剖视图

(a) Silent-chain coupling 无声链联轴器　(b) Roller-chain coupling 滚子链联轴器　(c) Rotating-link coupling 回转连杆联轴器

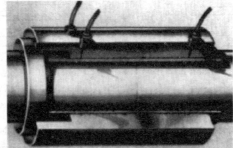

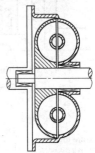

Cutaway shows oil forced between inner and outer tapered sleeves. Note the oil piston chamber at left
剖切图可见压力油在内外锥套间流动,油压活塞缸在左边

(d) Link coupling 连杆联轴器　　(e) Hydraulic coupling 液压联轴器　　Typical hydraulic coupling 典型液压联轴器

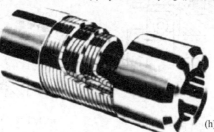

(h) Metallic grid coupling with cover removed to show grid detail
金属格栅联轴器,盖罩移除便于展示格栅细节

(f) A bellows coupling 波纹管联轴器　　(g) Uniflex flexible-spring coupling 万向柔性弹簧联轴器

Fig 4.129　Types of coupling　联轴器种类

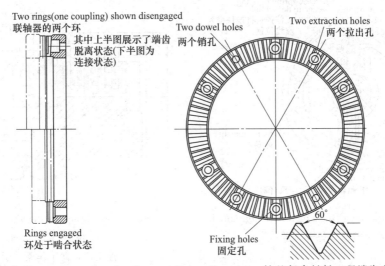

Two rings (one coupling) shown disengaged
联轴器的两个环
其中上半图展示了端齿脱离状态(下半图为连接状态)

Two dowel holes 两个销孔

Two extraction holes 两个拉出孔

Rings engaged 环处于啮合状态

Fixing holes 固定孔

Fig 4.130　A Ti matrix engineering face tooth coupling ring　钛基复合材料工程端齿盘联轴器环

(17) Clutch 离合器

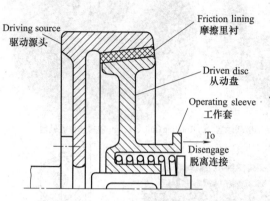

Fig 4.131　Cone-type friction clutch
锥形摩擦离合器

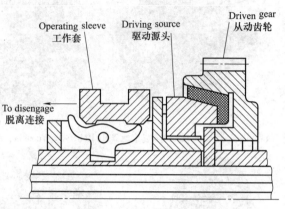

Fig 4.132　Cone clutch used on automatic lathe
自动车床用锥形离合器

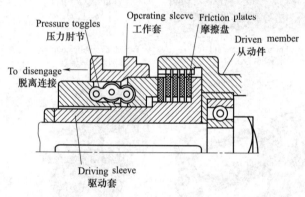

Fig 4.133　Design of multi-plate clutch
多片离合器

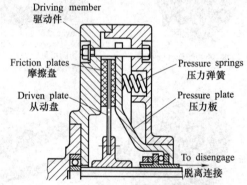

Fig 4.134　Construction of single-plate clutch
单片离合器结构

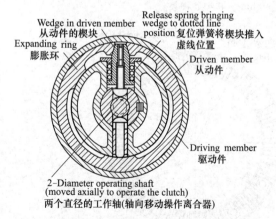

Fig 4.135　Expanding ring type of friction clutch
膨胀环式摩擦离合器

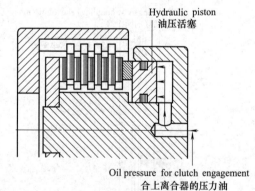

Fig 4.136　Diagram showing operation of hydraulic clutch
油压离合器工作原理图解

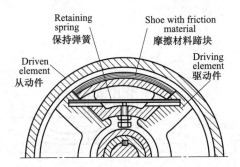

Fig 4.137　Centrifugal clutch with spring control
弹簧控制的离心离合器

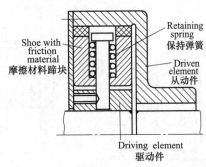

Fig 4.138　Light-duty type of centrifugal clutch
轻载型离心离合器

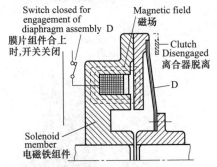

Fig 4.139　Diaphragm type of magnetic clutch
膜片式磁性离合器

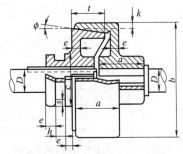

Fig 4.140　Cast-iron friction clutch
铸铁摩擦离合器

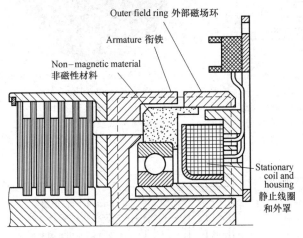

Fig 4.141　Multi-plate type of magnetic clutch
多盘式磁性离合器

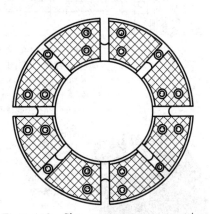

Fig 4.142　Slots to counteract expansion and contraction of plates
摩擦盘开槽以防止膨胀或收缩的变形

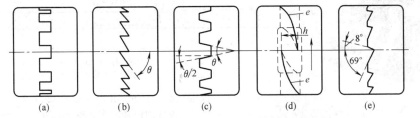

Fig 4.143　Types of clutch teeth　离合器牙形种类

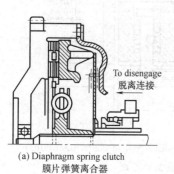
(a) Diaphragm spring clutch
膜片弹簧离合器

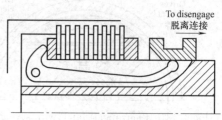
(b) Over–centre clutch, suitable for long engagement periods – no external force is required once clutch is engaged
超越中心离合器，适于长时间合上情形，一旦合上，无需外力

(c) Pivoted lever design for engagement of multi-plate clutch
多盘离合的转枢杠杆设计

Fig 4.144　Alternative operating methods　不同的工作原理

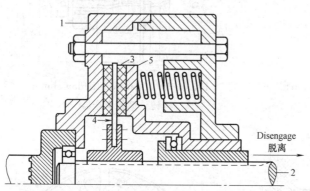

Fig 4.145　Schematic drawing of an axial clutch
轴向离合器示意图
1—Driving member　驱动件；2—Driven shaft　被驱动件；
3—Friction plates　摩擦片；4—Driven plate　从动片；
5—Pressure plate　施压盘

Fig 4.146　An oil-actuated multiple-disk clutch for enclosed operation in an oil spray or bath
油液喷淋或浸泡的闭式工作的油液驱动多片离合器

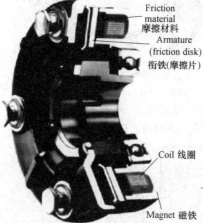

Fig 4.147　Electromagnetic friction clutches and brakes
电磁摩擦离合器和制动器

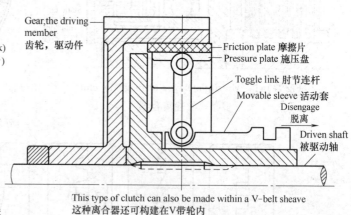

Fig 4.148　Schematic drawing of a radial clutch built within a gear
齿轮内的径向离合器示意图

Unit 4　Mechanical Transmission and Equipments　机械传动与设备装置

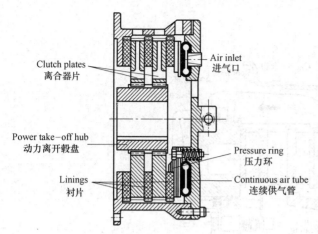

Fig 4.149　Typical air-operated clutch
典型气动离合器

Fig 4.150　Suredrive electromagnetic tooth clutch
可靠连接驱动的电磁齿盘离合器

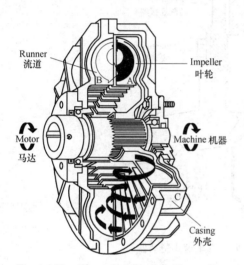

Fig 4.151　The principle of fluid coupling
液力离合器原理

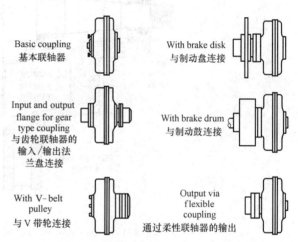

Fig 4.152　Examples of using a fluid coupling in
conjunction with other transmission elements
液力联轴器与其他传动元件的连接

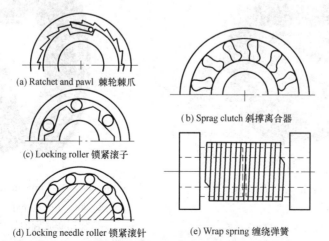

Fig 4.153　Types of one-way clutch（Overrunning clutch）　单向离合器（超越离合器）

(18) Brake 制动器

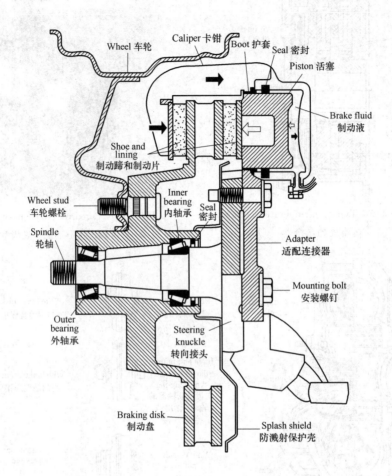

Fig 4.154 Automotive disk brake 汽车盘式制动器

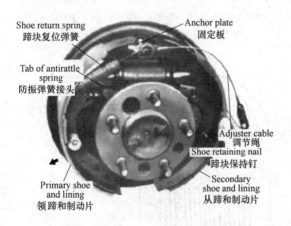

Fig 4.155 Drum brake 鼓式制动器

Fig 4.156 A pneumatically actuated brake using an expandable tube 使用膨胀管的气动制动器

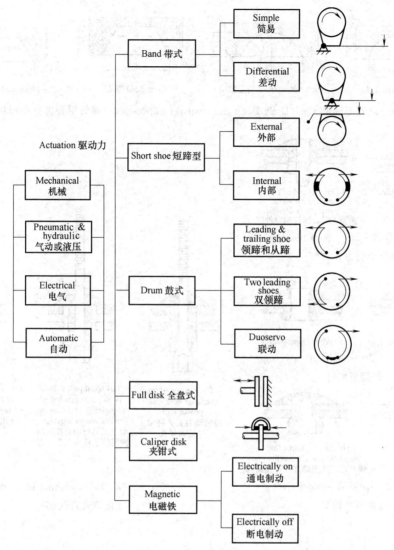

Fig 4.157 Classification of brakes 制动器分类

(19) Rivet 铆钉

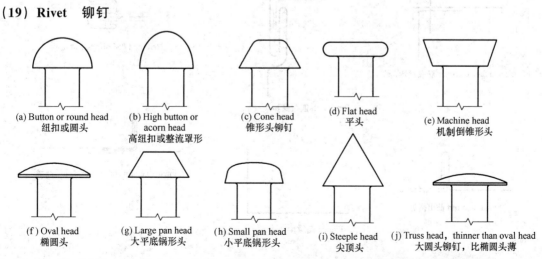

Fig 4.158 Standard rivet heads with flat bearing surfaces 平底支撑面的标准铆钉头

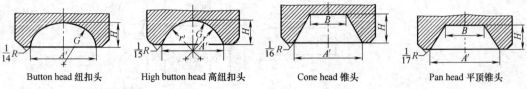

Button head 纽扣头　　High button head 高纽扣头　　Cone head 锥头　　Pan head 平顶锥头

Fig 4.159　Hold-On (Dolly Bar) and rivet set impression　铆钉棍和铆钉座形状

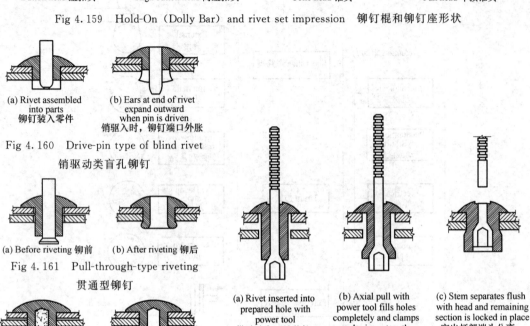

(a) Rivet assembled into parts 铆钉装入零件　　(b) Ears at end of rivet expand outward when pin is driven 销驱入时，铆钉端口外胀

Fig 4.160　Drive-pin type of blind rivet 销驱动类盲孔铆钉

(a) Before riveting 铆前　　(b) After riveting 铆后

Fig 4.161　Pull-through-type riveting 贯通型铆钉

(a) Before explosion 爆炸前　　(b) After, notice that the explosion clamps the join 爆炸后，注意爆炸使连接紧固

Fig 4.162　Explosive blind rivet 爆炸盲孔铆钉

(a) Rivet inserted into prepared hole with power tool 借助动力工具将铆钉插入预孔　　(b) Axial pull with power tool fills holes completely and clamps work pieces together 动力工具拉动孔被填满同时将工件夹紧在一起　　(c) Stem separates flush with head and remaining section is locked in place 突出杆部端头分离，存留段锁紧到位

Fig 4.163　Self-plugging blind rivet 自插式盲孔铆钉

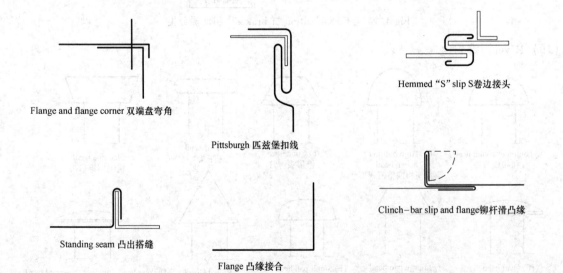

Hemmed "S" slip S卷边接头

Flange and flange corner 双端盘弯角

Pittsburgh 匹兹堡扣线

Clinch-bar slip and flange 铆杆滑凸缘

Standing seam 凸出搭缝

Flange 凸缘接合

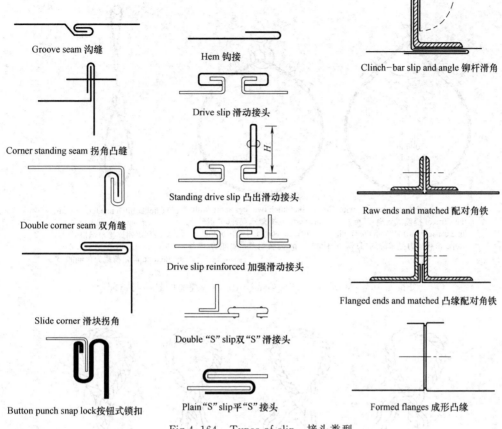

Fig 4.164　Types of slip　接头类型

(20) Fitting　端头

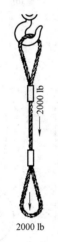

(a) Straight lift one leg vertical
单绳垂直提升
Load capacity is 100% of a single rope
荷载能力为单绳的100%

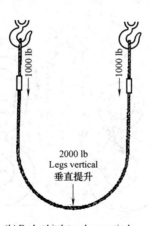

(b) Basket hitch two legs vertical
提篮式双绳垂直提升
Load capacity is 200% of the single rope 荷载能力是单绳的200%

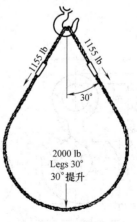

(c) Basket hitch two legs at 30° with the vertical
提篮式双绳30°提升
Load capacity is 174% of the single rope
荷载能力是单绳的174%

Fig 4.165

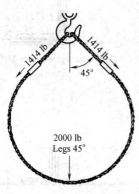 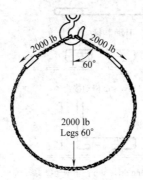 

(d) Basket hitch two legs at 45° with the vertical 提篮式双绳45°提升 Load capacity is 141% of the single rope 荷载能力是单绳的141%

(e) Basket hitch two legs at 60° with the vertical 提篮式双绳60°提升 Load capacity is 100% of the single rope 荷载能力是单绳的100%

(f) Choker hitch one leg vertical, with slip through loop 滑环夹钳连接单绳提升 Rated capacity is 75% of the single rope 额定荷载为单绳的75%

Fig 4.165 Wire rope slings and fittings 缆绳的悬吊与适配

(a)　　(b)　　(c)　　(d)

Fig 4.166 Eye-splice 眼孔接头

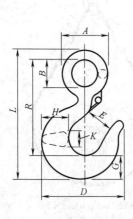  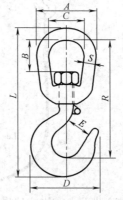 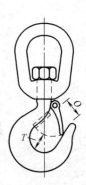

(a) Eye hook 眼孔吊钩

(b) Eye hook with latch assembled 带锁扣眼孔吊钩

(c) Swivel hook 旋转吊钩

(d) Swivel hook with latch assembled 锁扣旋转吊钩

Fig 4.167 Industrial types 工业类

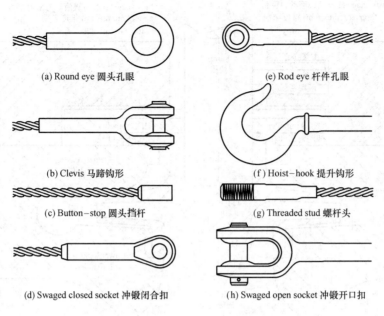

Fig 4.168　Aircraft types　飞行器类

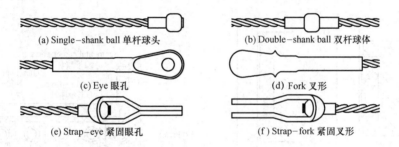

Fig 4.169　Wire rope fittings　缆绳的接头

(21) Sealing　密封

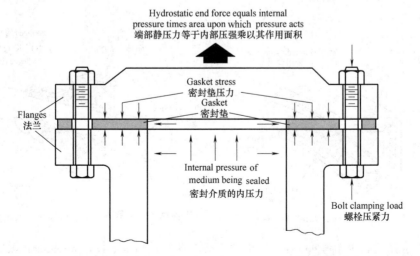

Fig 4.170　Nomenclature of a gasketed joint　密封垫连接术语

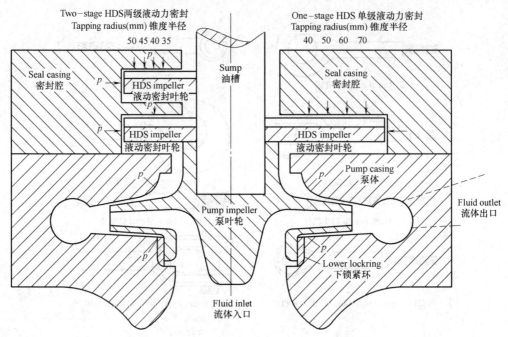

Fig 4.171　Hydrodynamic disk seal (HDS)　液动力盘式密封

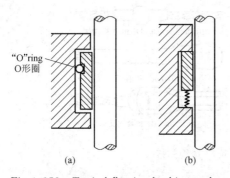

Fig 4.172　Typical floating bushing seals
典型浮动套式密封

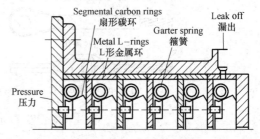

Fig 4.173　Bevel-section carbon gland
锥形碳密封套

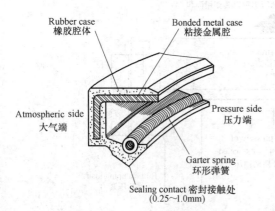

Fig 4.174　Rotary lip seal
回转边缘（唇形）密封

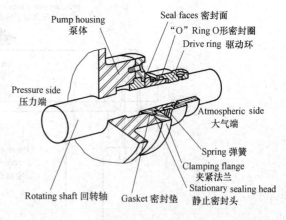

Fig 4.175　Mechanical seal
机械密封

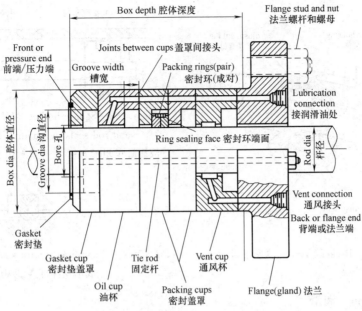

Fig 4.176　General arrangement of a typical mechanical piston rod packing assembly
典型活塞杆机械密封的通用设计

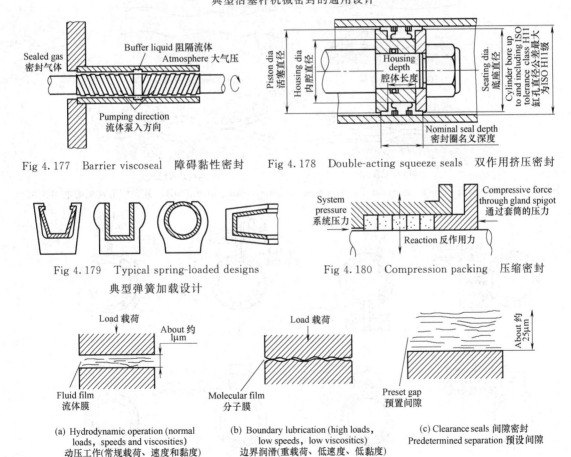

Fig 4.177　Barrier viscoseal　障碍黏性密封　　Fig 4.178　Double-acting squeeze seals　双作用挤压密封

Fig 4.179　Typical spring-loaded designs
典型弹簧加载设计

Fig 4.180　Compression packing　压缩密封

Fig 4.181　Characteristics of dynamic seals　动密封特性

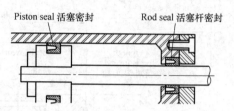

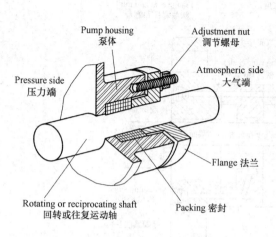

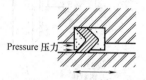

Fig 4.183　Square-backed 'U' seals as piston and rod seals in a hydraulic cylinder
液压缸里矩形背衬 U 形密封用于活塞和活塞杆

Fig 4.182　Packed gland　填塞密封

Fig 4.184　Chevron seal with shaped support rings
成形支撑环 V 芯密封

(22) Lubrication　润滑

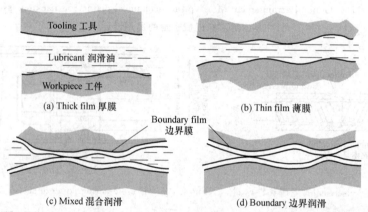

Fig 4.185　Types of lubrication generally occurring in metalworking operations　金属加工常见的润滑类型

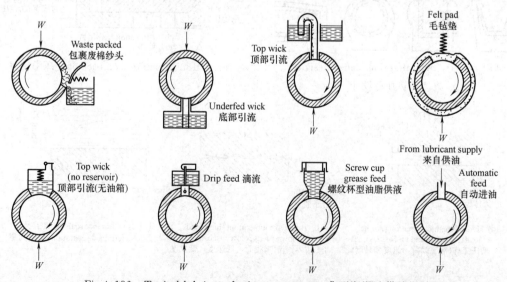

Fig 4.186　Typical lubricant feed arrangement　典型润滑油供给设计

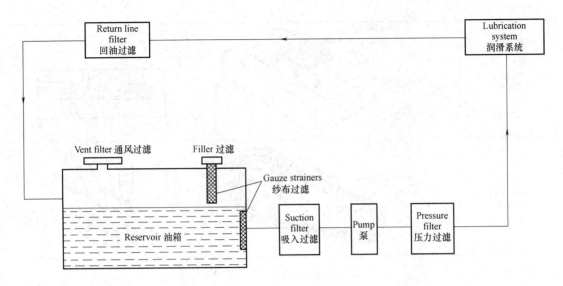

Fig 4.187 Typical circuit showing positions of various filters
各种过滤器的典型回路位置

Table 4.1 Nozzle of positioning for mist systems 油雾润滑系统喷嘴位置的确定

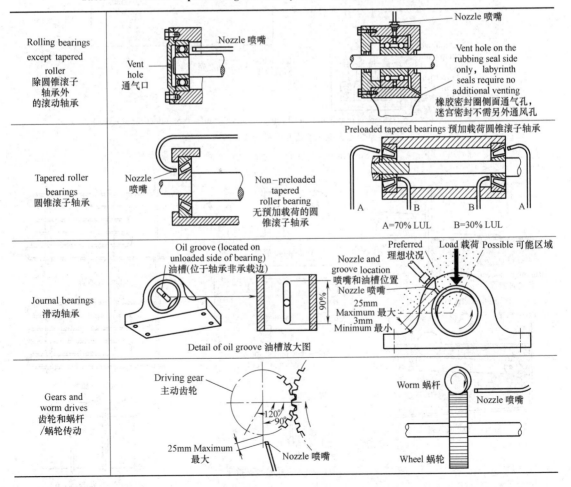

续表

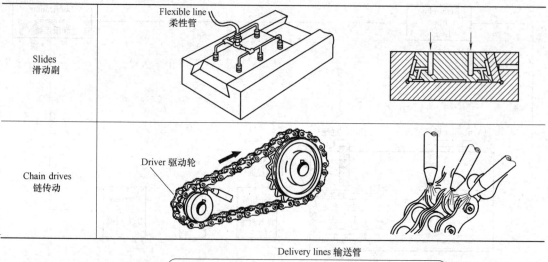

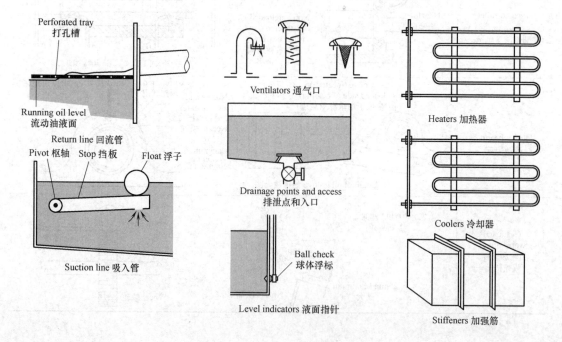

Fig 4.188 Simple multi-point lubricator 简易多点润滑器

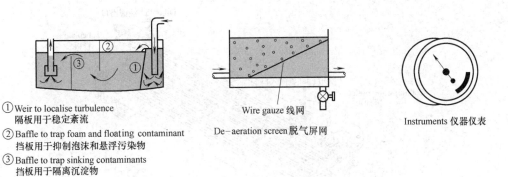

① Weir to localise turbulence 隔板用于稳定紊流
② Baffle to trap foam and floating contaminant 挡板用于抑制泡沫和悬浮污染物
③ Baffle to trap sinking contaminants 挡板用于隔离沉淀物
Baffles and weirs 挡板和隔板

Wire gauze 线网
De-aeration screen 脱气屏网
Instruments 仪器仪表

Fig 4.189　Tank components　油箱组件

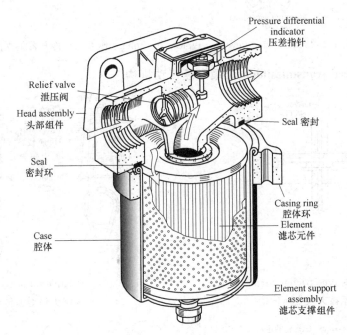

Fig 4.190　Typical full-flow pressure filter with integral bypass and pressure differential indicator
带有整体旁路和压差指示器的典型的全流量压力过滤器

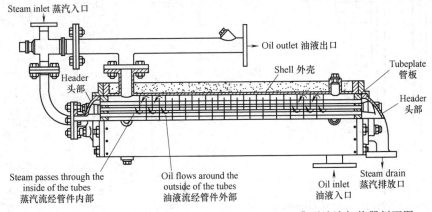

Fig 4.191　Cross section through a typical oil heater　典型油液加热器剖面图

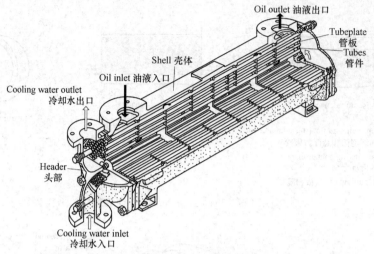

Fig 4.192　Sectional view of a typical oil cooler　典型油液冷却器剖视图

(23) Stepless speed transmission　无级变速传动机构

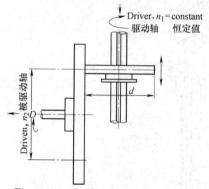

Fig 4.193　Disk-type friction stepless drive
盘式摩擦无级变速传动

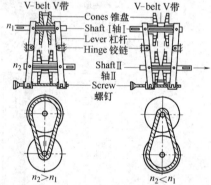

Fig 4.194　Positive infinitely variable drive
强制无级变速传动

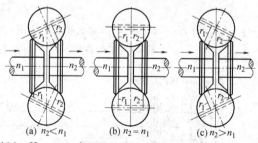

(a) $n_2 < n_1$　(b) $n_2 = n_1$　(c) $n_2 > n_1$

Fig 4.196　Kopp stepless speed mechanism　科比无级变速机构

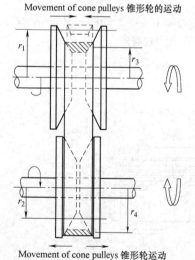

Fig 4.195　Reeves variable speed transmission
皮带接触半径变化的变速传动

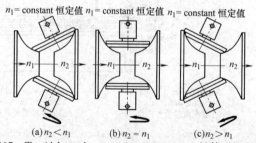

(a) $n_2 < n_1$　(b) $n_2 = n_1$　(c) $n_2 > n_1$

Fig 4.197　Toroidal stepless speed transmission　锥体无级变速传动

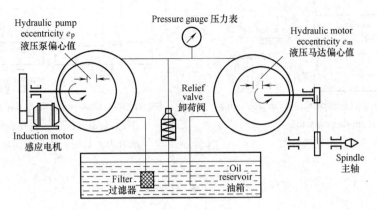

Fig 4.198　Hydraulic stepless speed drive　液压无级变速传动

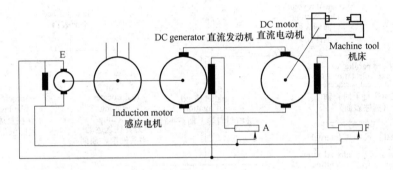

Fig 4.199　Leonard set (electrical stepless speed drive)
发动机电动机组控制装置（电气无级变速传动）

4.2　Various types of machining equipment　各种机械加工设备

(1) Motions of machine and classifications　机床的运动与分类

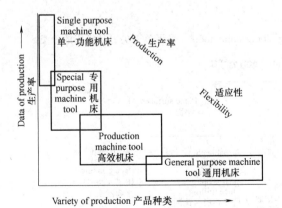

Fig 4.200　Application of machine tools based on their capability
基于生产能力的机床应用

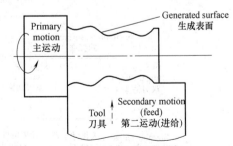

Fig 4.201　Forming a surface with a form tool
成形刀具加工成形表面

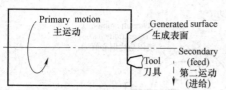

Fig 4.202 Generation of a flat surface using a single point tool
单刀尖刀具生成平面

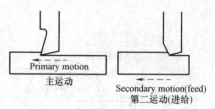

Fig 4.203 Generation of a flat surface with linear motion of a single point tool
单刀尖刀具配合线性运动生成平面

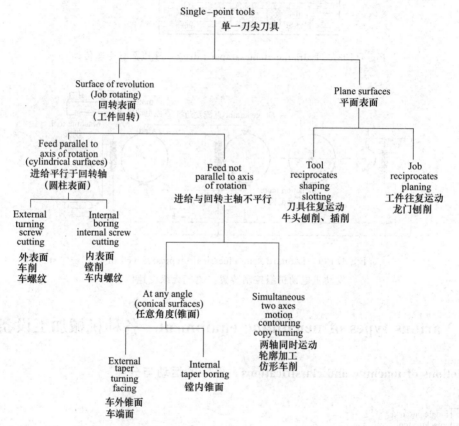

Fig 4.204 Classification of machine tools using single point tools 采用单刀尖刀具机床的分类

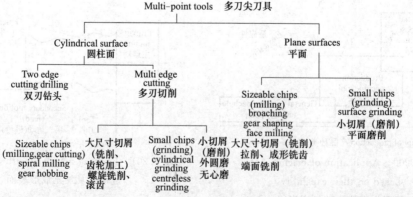

Fig 4.205 Classification of machine tools using multi-point tools 采用多刀尖刀具机床的分类

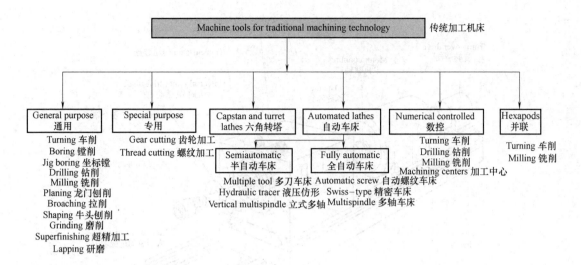

Fig 4.206 Classification of machine tools for traditional machining technology   传统加工机床的分类

Table 4.2 Tool and WP (work piece) motions for machine tools used for traditional machining
传统机械加工机床的刀具和工件的运动

Machining process 加工工艺	Tool and WP movements 刀具和工件运动 v	f	Remarks 备注
Chip removal 切削去除			
Turning 车削	WP 工件 ⌒	Tool 刀具 →	WP stationary 工件静止
Drilling 钻削	Tool 刀具 ⌒	Tool 刀具 →	
Milling 铣削	Tool 刀具 ⌒	WP 工件 →	
Shaping 牛头刨削	Tool 刀具 →	WP 工件 --→	
Planing 龙门刨削	WP 工件 →	Tool 刀具 --→	
Slotting 插削	Tool 刀具 →	WP 工件 --→	
Broaching 拉削	Tool 刀具 / WP 工件	WP 工件 ● / Tool 刀具 ●	Feed motion is built in the tool 进给运动由刀具结构实现
Gear hobbing 滚齿	Tool 刀具 ⌒	WP 工件 ⌒ / Tool 刀具 →	
Abrasion 摩擦去除			
Surface grinding 平面磨削	Tool 刀具 ⌒	WP 工件 →	
Cylindrical grinding 外圆磨削	Tool 刀具 ⌒	WP 工件 ⌒ / Tool or wp 刀具或工件 →	
Honing 珩磨	Tool 刀具 ⌒→	Tool 刀具 ●	WP stationary 工件静止
Superfinishing 超精加工	WP 工件 ⌒	Tool 刀具 →	

Note: ⌒ Rotation; ● stationary; → linear motion; --→ intermittent
注:　　 　回转　　 　静止　　 　线性动动　　 　间隙性运动

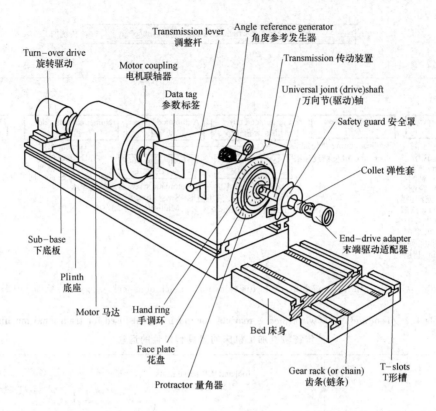

Fig 4.207 V-type headstock with end-drive and bed V形床头箱、末端驱动和床身

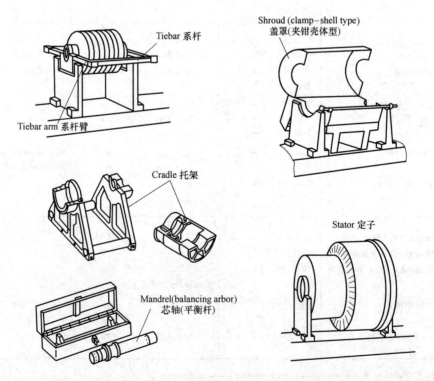

Fig 4.208 Tooling 工装

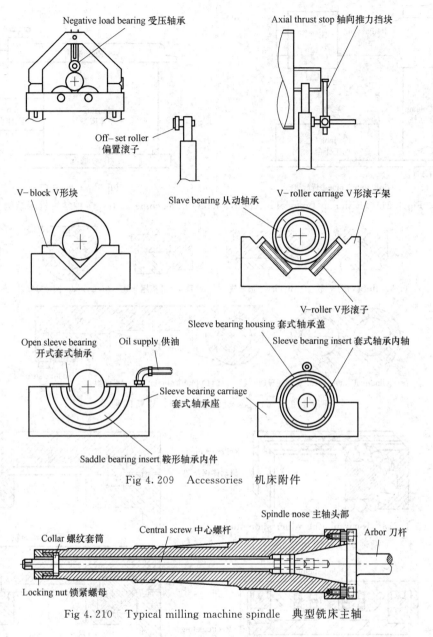

Fig 4.209　Accessories　机床附件

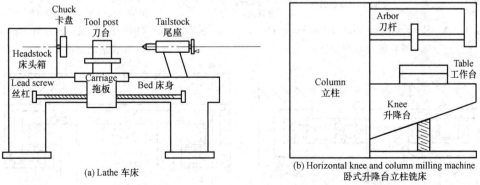

Fig 4.210　Typical milling machine spindle　典型铣床主轴

(a) Lathe 车床

(b) Horizontal knee and column milling machine 卧式升降台立柱铣床

Fig 4.211

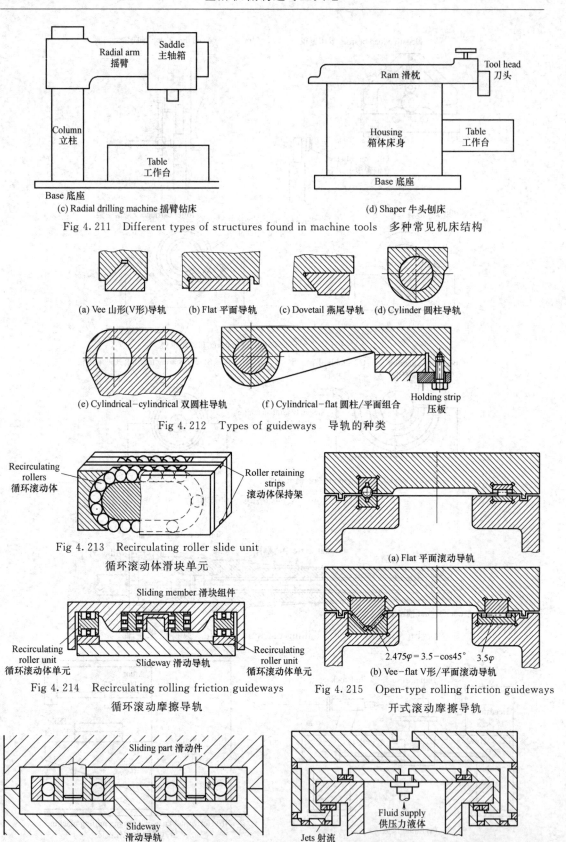

(c) Radial drilling machine 摇臂钻床 　　(d) Shaper 牛头刨床

Fig 4.211　Different types of structures found in machine tools　多种常见机床结构

(a) Vee 山形(V形)导轨　(b) Flat 平面导轨　(c) Dovetail 燕尾导轨　(d) Cylinder 圆柱导轨

(e) Cylindrical-cylindrical 双圆柱导轨　(f) Cylindrical-flat 圆柱/平面组合

Fig 4.212　Types of guideways　导轨的种类

Fig 4.213　Recirculating roller slide unit 循环滚动体滑块单元

(a) Flat 平面滚动导轨

$2.475\varphi = 3.5 \cdot \cos 45°$　3.5φ

(b) Vee-flat V形/平面滚动导轨

Fig 4.214　Recirculating rolling friction guideways 循环滚动摩擦导轨

Fig 4.215　Open-type rolling friction guideways 开式滚动摩擦导轨

Fig 4.216　Ball bearing guideway　球轴承导轨　　Fig 4.217　Externally pressurized guideways　外部施压导轨

(2) lathe 车床

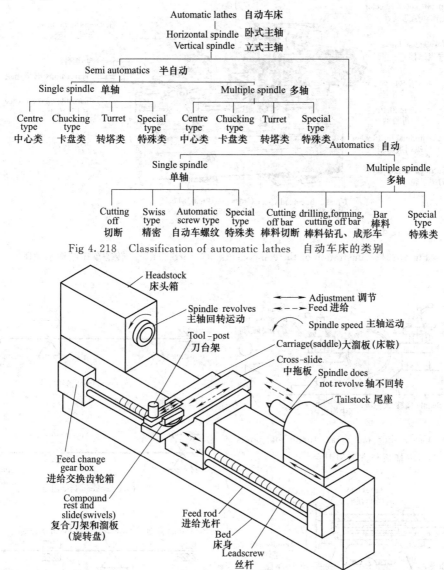

Fig 4.218　Classification of automatic lathes　自动车床的类别

Fig 4.219　General view of a center lathe showing various mechanisms and features　中心车床结构、特征总览

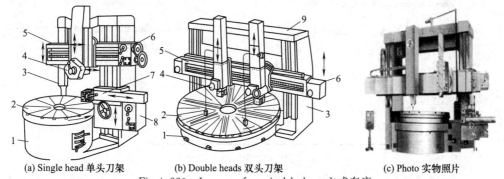

Fig 4.220　Layout of vertical lathe　立式车床

1—Bed　底座；2—Work table　工作台；3—Colunm　立柱；4—Vertical tool head　垂直刀架（头）；5—Cross rail　横梁；6—Feed box　进给箱；7—Side tool post（head）侧刀架（头）；8—Feed box for side head　侧刀架进给箱；9—Arch　顶梁

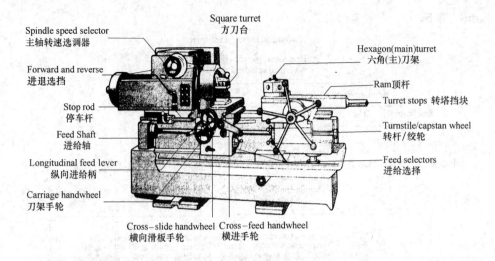

Fig 4.221　Illustration of the components of a turret lathe　转塔车床结构示意图

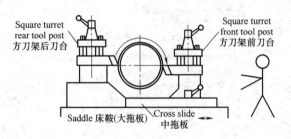

Fig 4.222　Cross slide and square turret tool posts
中拖板与方刀架刀台

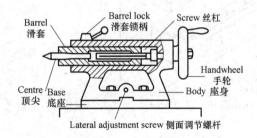

Fig 4.223　Tailstock of central lathe
中心车床的尾座

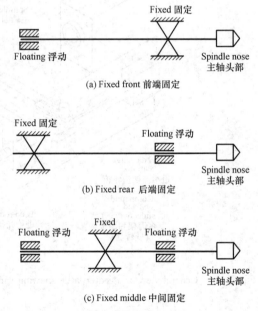

Fig 4.224　Fixed and floating bearing arrangements
固定和浮动轴承的设计

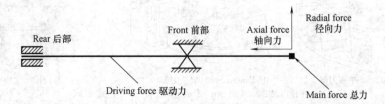

Fig 4.225　Forces acting on machine tool spindles　机床主轴的受力

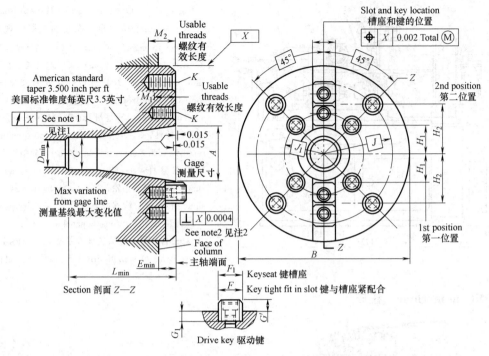

Fig 4.226　Essential dimensions for spindle nose with large flange　大法兰盘主轴端部基本尺寸

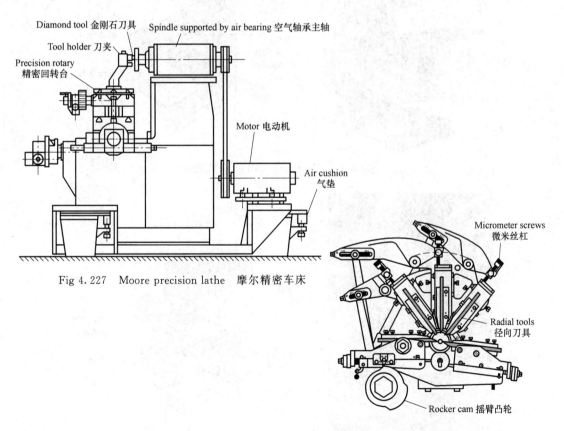

Fig 4.227　Moore precision lathe　摩尔精密车床

Fig 4.228　A Swiss-type automatic screw machine
精密自动螺纹机

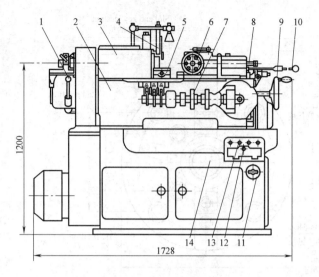

Fig 4.229 General view of the automatic screw machine 自动螺纹加工机外观图
1—Lever to engage auxiliary shaft 辅助轴操控杆；2—Bed 床身；3—Headstock 床头箱；4—Tool slide (vertical) 刀具滑台（立式）；5—Turret-tool slide (horizontal) 转塔刀具滑台（卧式）；6—Turret slide 转塔滑台；7—Main cam shaft 主控凸轮轴；8—Adjustable rod for positioning turret slide with respect to spindle nose 转塔滑台与主轴端调整杆；9—Hand wheel to rotate auxiliary shaft 副轴旋转手轮；10—Lever to traverse turret slide 转塔滑台横移操纵杆；11—Rotary switches 回转开关；12—Console panel for setting up spindle speeds 设置主轴速度操控盘；13—Push button controls of spindle drive 主轴传动控制按钮；14—Base 基座

(3) Milling machine 铣床

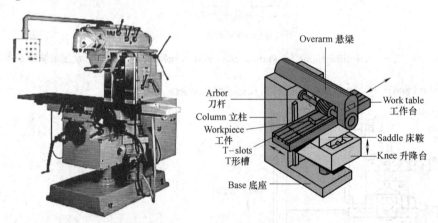

Fig 4.230 Horizontal Mill 卧式铣床

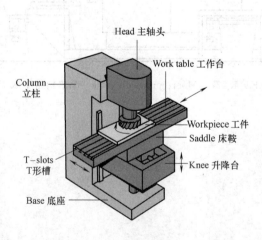

Fig 4.231 Vertical Mill 立式铣床

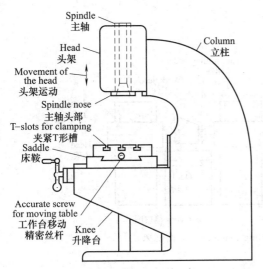

Fig 4.232 Vertical knee and column type milling machine 立式升降台铣床

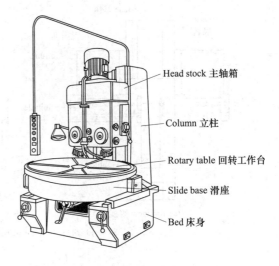

Fig 4.233 Milling machine with rotary table 转台铣床

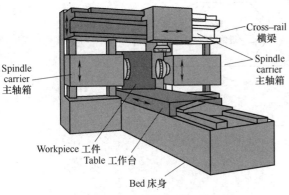

Fig 4.234 A bed-type milling machine 床身式铣床（龙门铣床）

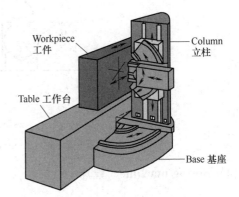

Fig 4.235 A five-axis profile milling machine 五轴轮廓铣床

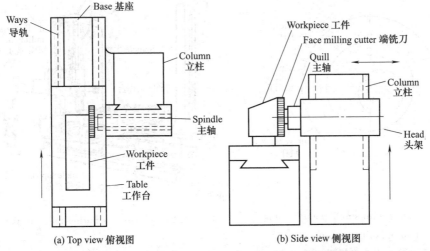

Fig 4.236 Simplex bed-type milling machine 单面铣床

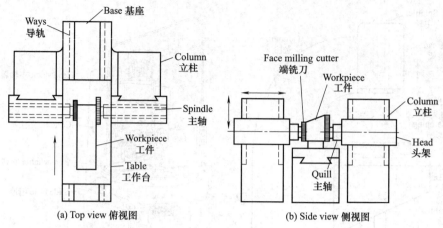

(a) Top view 俯视图　　(b) Side view 侧视图

Fig 4.237　Duplex bed-type milling machine　双面铣床

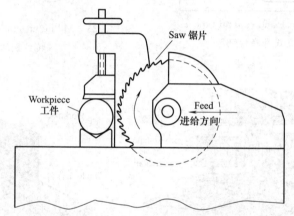

Fig 4.238　A circular sawing machine　圆盘锯床

(4) Boring machine　镗床

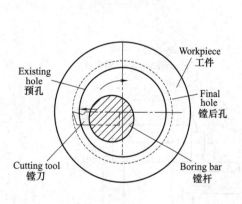

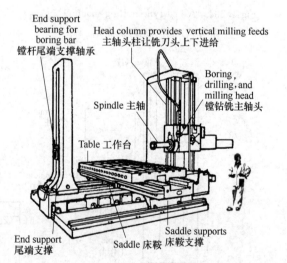

Fig 4.239　Boring with single point turning tools in a boring machine
镗床上单刀尖车刀镗削加工

Fig 4.240　Horizontal boring mill　卧式镗铣床

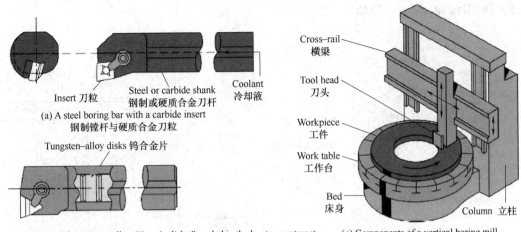

Fig 4.241　Vertical boring mill　立式镗床

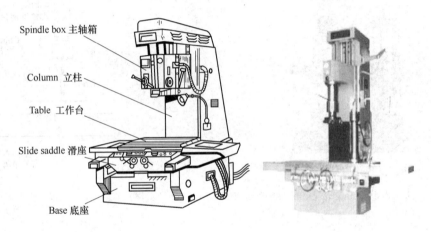

Fig 4.242　Vertical simplex column coordinate boring machine　立式单轴坐标镗床

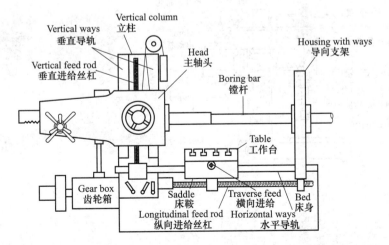

Fig 4.243　Schematic diagram of horizontal boring machine　卧式镗床图解

(5) Drilling machine 钻床

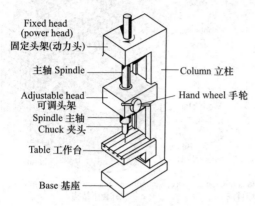

Fig 4.244　A vertical drill press　立式钻床

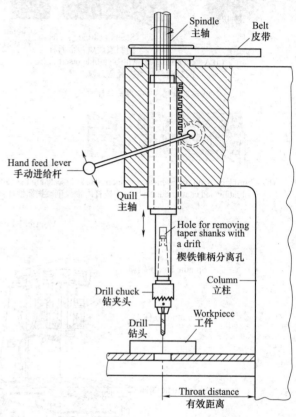

Fig 4.246　The drill press　钻头下压操作

Fig 4.245　A radial drilling machine　摇臂钻床

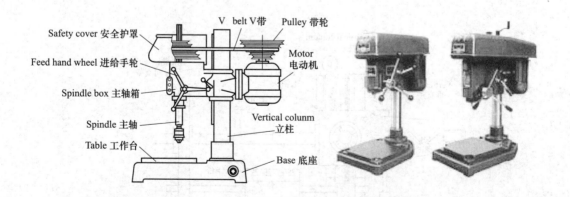

Fig 4.247　Drill press used on bench　台式钻床

(6) Reciprocating machine　往复运动机床

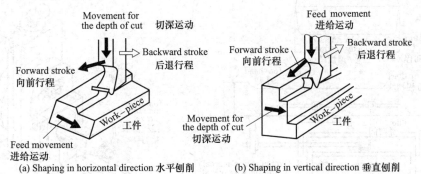

(a) Shaping in horizontal direction 水平刨削　　(b) Shaping in vertical direction 垂直刨削

Fig 4.248　Working principle and operation of a shaper
牛头刨床的工作原理及操作

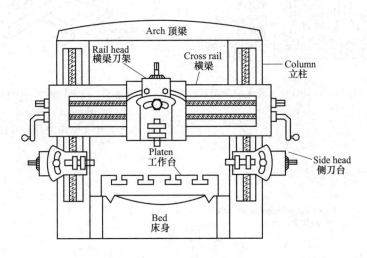

Fig 4.249　The construction of a planning machine with single head
单头龙门刨床结构

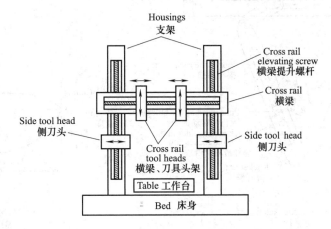

Fig 4.250　Standard or double housing planer
标准/双主轴箱龙门刨床

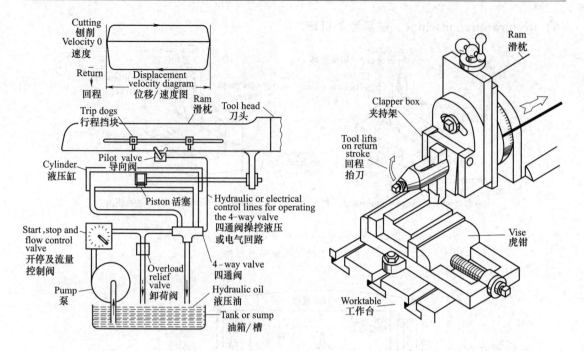

Fig 4.251　Hydraulic shaper　液压牛头刨床

Fig 4.252　Typical arrangement of the workpiece and tool in a shaper　牛头刨床工件和刀具的布置

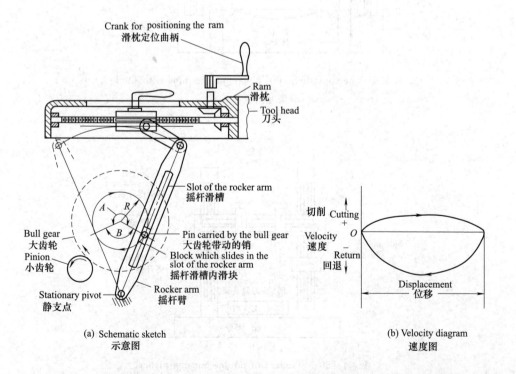

(a) Schematic sketch 示意图

(b) Velocity diagram 速度图

Fig 4.253　The quick return motion in a crank shaper　曲柄式刨床的急回运动

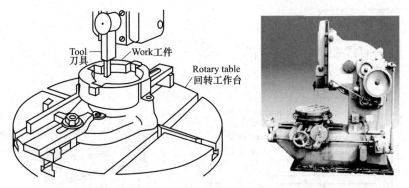

Fig 4.254　A typical component machined in a slotter　典型的插床加工工件

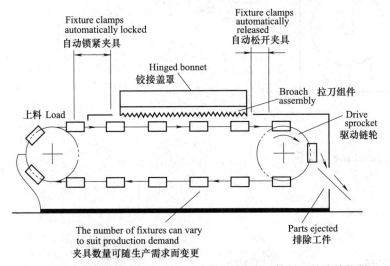

Fig 4.255　Continuous broaching of flats　多个工件平面的连续拉削

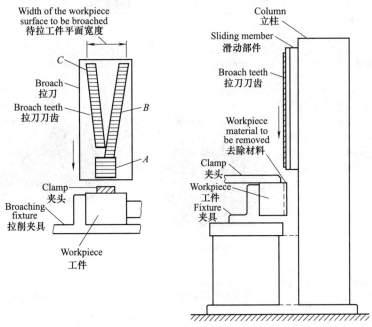

Fig 4.256　A surface broaching machine　平面拉床

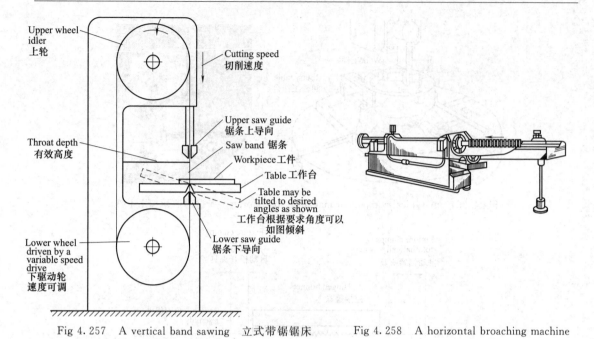

Fig 4.257 A vertical band sawing 立式带锯锯床   Fig 4.258 A horizontal broaching machine 卧式拉床

(7) Grinding machine 磨床

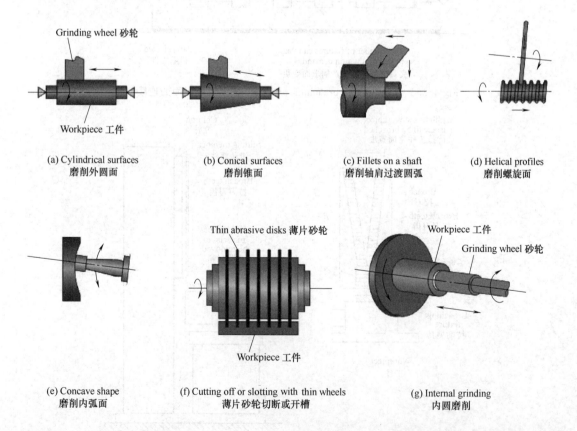

Fig 4.259 The typical types of workpieces and operations of grinding 典型磨削加工及工件类型

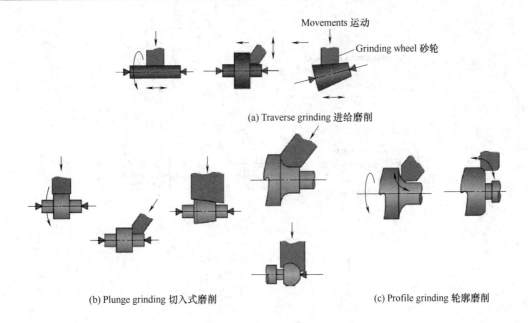

Fig 4.260 Examples of various cylindrical grinding operations 几种外圆磨削操作

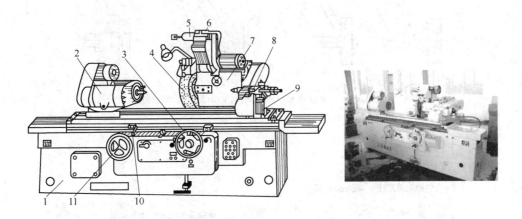

Fig 4.261 Multi-purpose grinding machine for cylinder 万能外圆磨床
1—Bed 床身；2—Headstock 头架；3,11—Hand wheel 手轮； 4—Abrasive (grinding) wheel 砂轮；
5—Inner surface abrasive 内圆磨具；6—Support frame 支架；7—Wheel supporting frame 砂轮架；
8—Tailstock 尾架；9—Work table 工作台；10—Stroke choke 行程挡块

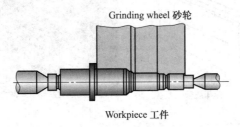

Fig 4.262 Plunge grinding of a workpiece on a cylindrical grinder with the wheel dressed to a stepped shape 外圆磨床上阶梯修整砂轮的切入式磨削

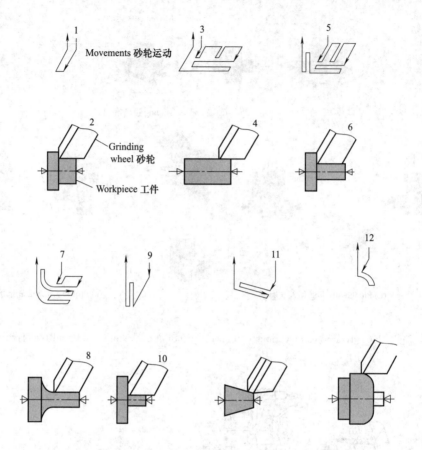

Fig 4.263　Cycle patterns in cylindrical grinding　外圆磨削循环图

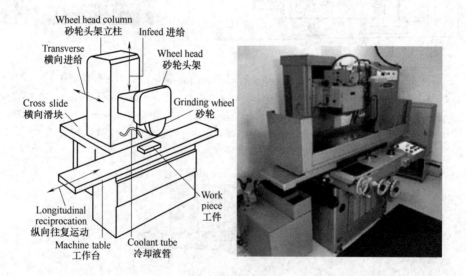

Fig 4.264　Horizontal Grinding　卧式磨床

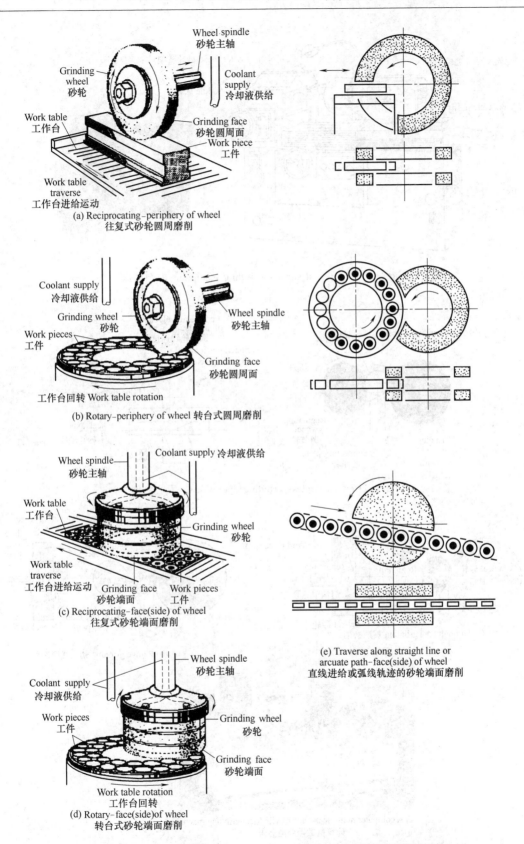

Fig 4.265 Principal systems of surface grinding 主要的平面磨削系统

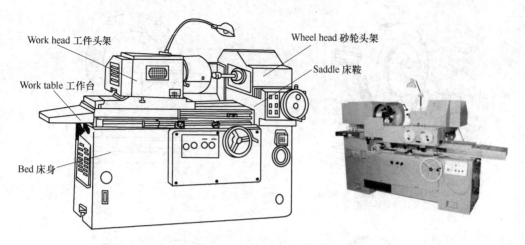

Fig 4.266 Internal surface grinding machine 内圆磨床

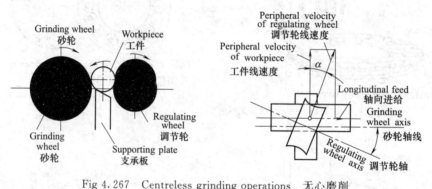

Fig 4.267 Centreless grinding operations 无心磨削

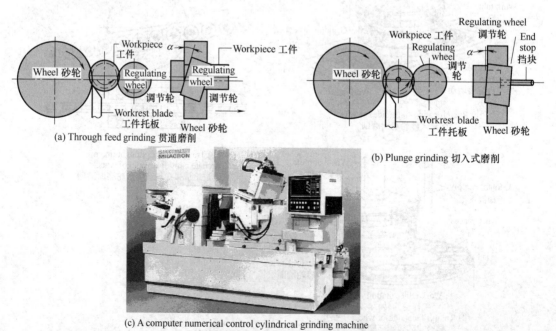

(a) Through feed grinding 贯通磨削

(b) Plunge grinding 切入式磨削

(c) A computer numerical control cylindrical grinding machine
计算机数控外圆磨床

Fig 4.268 Schematic illustration of centreless grinding operations 无心磨削工作示意图

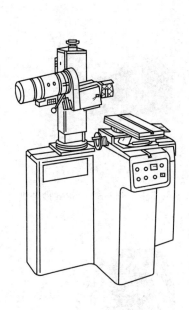

Fig 4.269 Multi-purpose grinding machine for tools 万能工具磨床

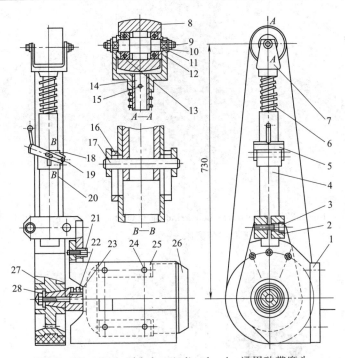

Fig 4.270 General belt grinding head 通用砂带磨头
1—Clamp base 夹座；2—Revolution frame 转架；3—Bolt 螺栓；4,14—Supporting rod 支承杆；5—Knob 手把；6—Spring 弹簧；7—Support 支承叉；8—Tension wheel 张紧轮；9—Shaft 轴；10,28—Nut 螺母；11—Washer 垫片；12—Sleeve 衬套；13—Bearing 轴承；15,17,19—Pin 销；16—Slot frame 叉架；18,21,24—Screw 螺钉；20—Belt 砂带；22—Tapper bushing 锥套；23—Key 键；25—Rubber cushion 橡胶垫；26—Motor 电机；27—Contact wheel 接触轮

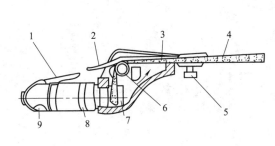

Fig 4.271 Pneumatic pistol-like portable belt grinder 气动手枪式砂带机
1—Switch 开关；2—Tension adjusting bar 张紧调节杆；3—Belt 砂带；4—Contact arm 接触臂；5—Adjusting snob 调节旋钮；6—Idle wheel 惰轮；7—Driving wheel 驱动轮；8—Pneumatic propel wheel 气动叶轮；9—Revolution speed adjust snob 速度调节旋钮

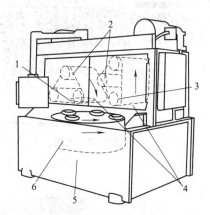

Fig 4.272 Flat surface grinding machine 平面砂带磨床
1—Wide belt 宽砂带；2—Tension roller 张紧辊；3—Contact roller 接触辊；4—Grinding area 磨削区域；5—Bed 床身；6—Rotary table 回转工作台

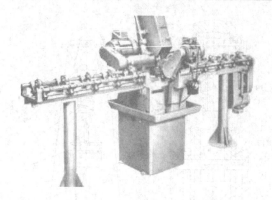

Fig 4.273　Centreless belt grinding machine
无心砂带磨床

Fig 4.274　Portable belt grinder　手提式砂带机

Fig 4.275　Portable welding seam polisher
手提式焊缝打磨机

Fig 4.276　Flap（page）wheel
（千）页轮

Fig 4.277　Abrasive disc precision polisher
圆盘精密抛光机

Fig 4.278　Abrasive disc grinder
圆盘打磨机

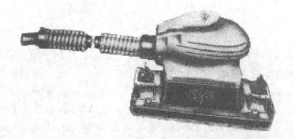

Fig 4.279　Reciprocating vibration flat grinder　往复振动平面磨光机

Unit 4　Mechanical Transmission and Equipments　机械传动与设备装置

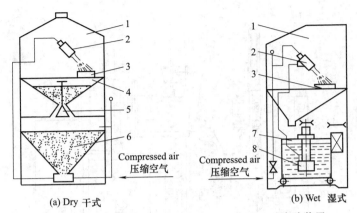

(a) Dry 干式　　(b) Wet 湿式

Fig 4.280　Sand blasting (abrasive-jet) setup　喷砂装置

1—Blasting chamber　喷射室；2—Nozzle　喷嘴；3—Workpart　工件；4—Funnel　漏斗；5—Automation valve　自动阀；6—Abrasive tank　磨料箱；7—Fluidized abrasive (slurry) tank　流化磨料箱；8—Pump　泵

(8) Gear cutting machine　齿轮加工机床

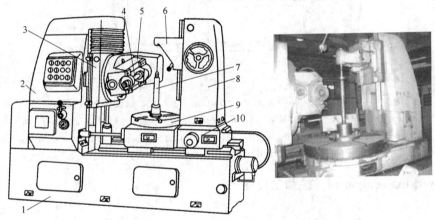

Fig 4.281　Gear hobbing machine　滚齿机

1—Bed　床身；2—Column　立柱；3—Tool post slide　刀架溜板；4—Tool arbor　刀杆；5—Tool post　刀架；6—Support　支架；7—Mandrel　芯轴；8—Rear column　后立柱；9—Table　工作台；10—Saddle　床鞍

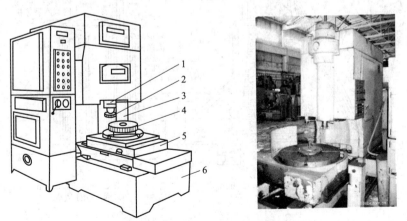

Fig 4.282　A gear shaper　插齿机

1—Spindle　主轴；2—Pinion cutter　插齿刀；3—Column　立柱；4—Workpiece　工件；5—Table　工作台；6—Bed　床身

113

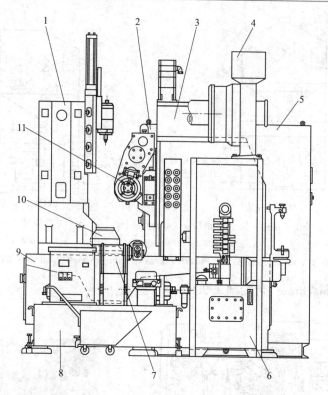

Fig 4.283 NC high speed gear cutting machine 数控高速滚齿机
1—Rear column 后立柱；2—Slide 滑板；3—Main column 主立柱；4—Oil frog absorber 抽油烟机；
5—Electrical apparatus box 电气柜；6—Bed 床身；7—Chip excavator 排屑器；8—Cooling box 冷却箱；9—Hydraulic oil tank 液压油箱；10—Table 工作台；11—Cutter head 刀架

(9) Hot working equipment 热加工设备

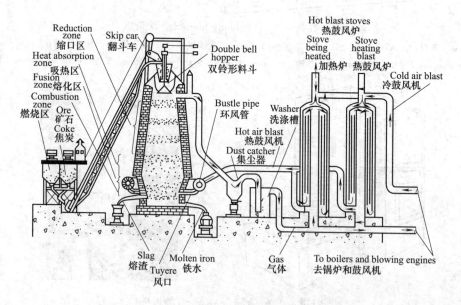

Fig 4.284 Schematic diagram of a blast furnace and its associated equipment
冲天炉及其相关装置

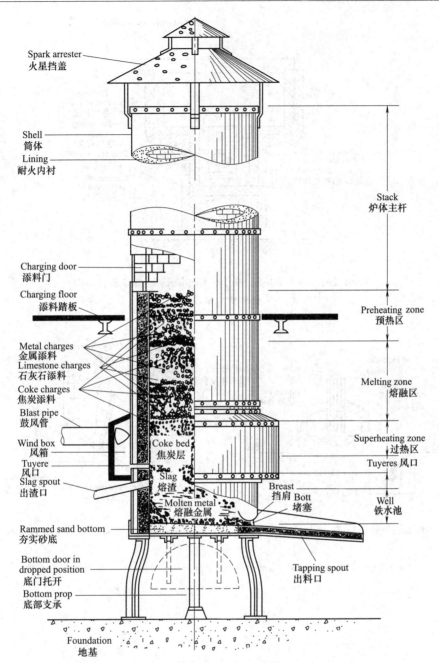

Fig 4.285　External and internal view of a cupola　冲天炉内外结构

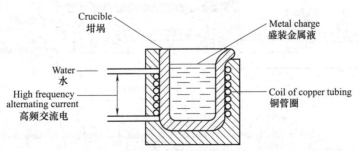

Fig 4.286　Cross-sectional view of a high-frequency induction furnace　高频感应炉剖面图

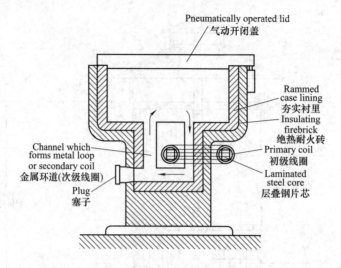

Fig 4.287　Principle of the low-frequency induction furnace
低频感应炉原理

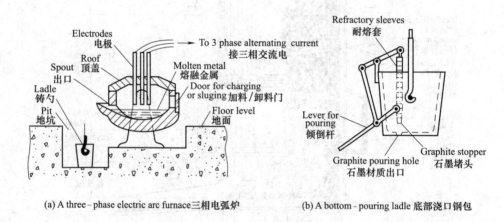

(a) A three-phase electric arc furnace 三相电弧炉　　(b) A bottom-pouring ladle 底部浇口钢包

Fig 4.288　Principle of the low-frequency induction furnace　低频感应炉原理

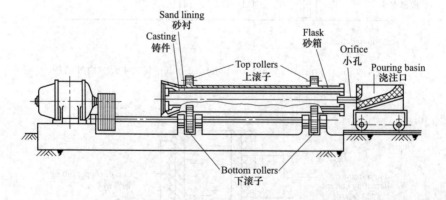

Fig 4.289　Schematic representation of a horizontal centrifugal casting machine
水平离心铸造机图解

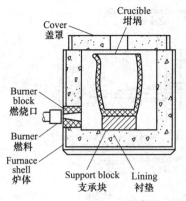

Fig 4.290 Section of a stationary type crucible furnace 固定式坩埚剖面图

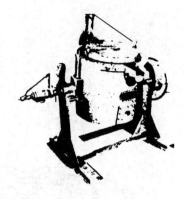

Fig 4.291 Tilting type crucible furnace 可倾斜式坩埚

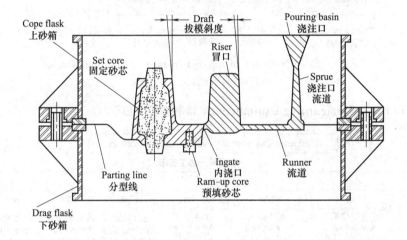

Fig 4.292 Sectional view of a casting mold 铸造砂箱剖面图

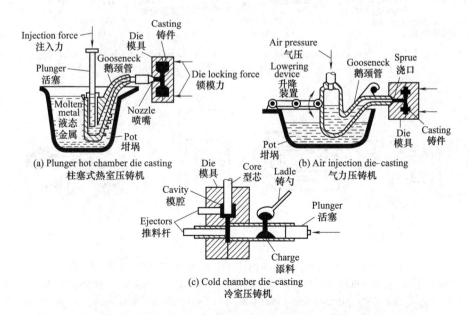

Fig 4.293 Types of die casting machines 压铸机类型

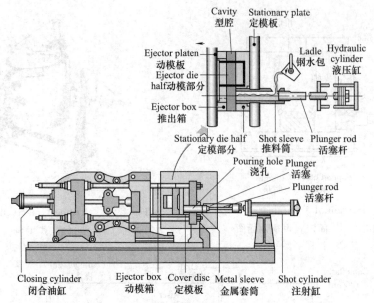

Fig 4.294 Illustration of the cold-chamber die-casting process
冷室压铸机及其工艺示意图

(10) Non-traditional machining equipments 特种加工机床

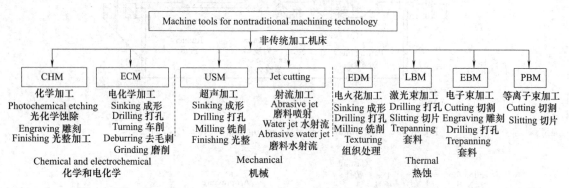

Fig 4.295 Classification of machine tools for nontraditional machining technology
非传统加工技术机床类别

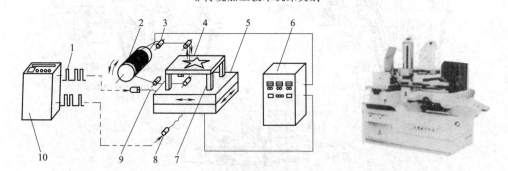

Fig 4.296 Principle of NC wire EDM process 数控线切割工作原理
1—Electric pulse signal 电脉冲信号；2—Wire spool 储丝筒；3—Guide wheel 导轮；4—Work 工件；
5—Table 工作台；6—Pulse power 脉冲电源；7—Pad 垫铁；8—Stepping motor 步进电机；
9—Leading screw 丝杆；10—Computer controller 计算机控制器

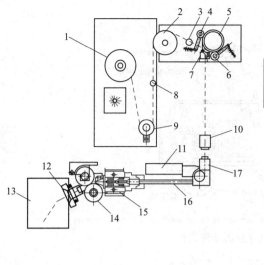
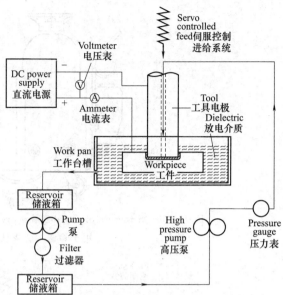

Fig 4.297　Lower speed wire feeding mechanism　低速走丝机构

1—Wire spool　丝筒；2—Pulley　滑轮；3—Felt roller 毡轮；4,6—Press wheel　压轮；5—Tension controller 张紧机构；7—Wire breakage detector　断丝检测器；8—Guide hook　导向钩；9—Spindle bushing　轴套；10—Upper wire guide　上导向器；11—Wire dismantling arm　线丝拆除臂；12—Exit of used wire 废丝排除口；13—Used wire spool　废丝筒；14—Roller　滚轮；15—Pull part　牵引部件；16—Guide tube for wire exit　出丝导管；17—Lower wire guide　下导向器

Fig 4.298　A diagram of the components that form a typical EDM machine　典型电火花机床结构

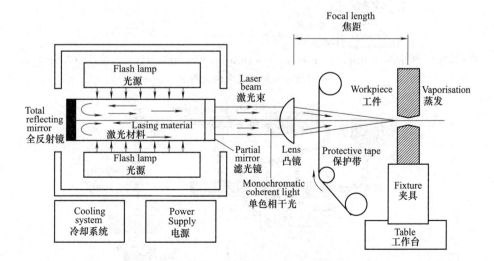

Fig 4.299　Schematic set up of a laser drilling operation　激光钻孔加工装置

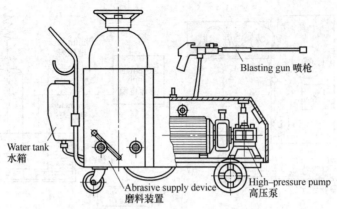

Fig 4.300 Structure of a hydro-abrasive suspension jet system for rust removal
用于除锈的磨浆悬浮射流系统结构

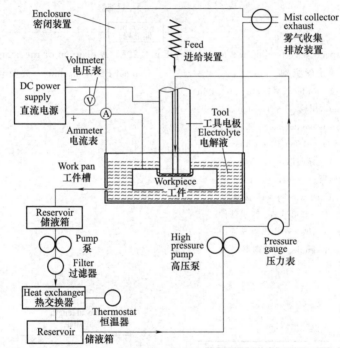

Fig 4.301 Schematic diagram of the various elements present in a commercial ECM machine
商用电解加工机床构成图解

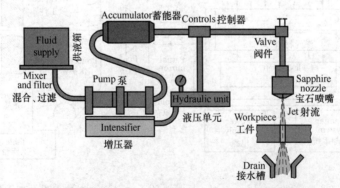

Fig 4.302 Water jet machining (WJ) 水射流加工

(11) Stamping sets 冲压设备

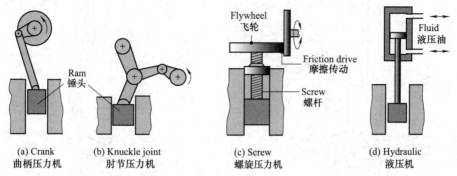

Fig 4.303　Illustration of the principles of various forging machines　锻压机床的工作原理

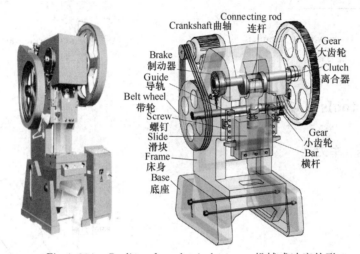

Fig 4.304　Outline of mechanical press　机械式冲床外形

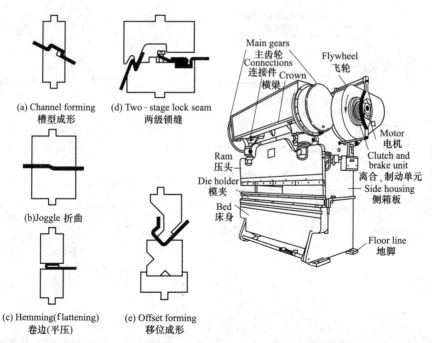

Fig 4.305　Various bending operations and a press brake　几种弯曲工艺及折弯机

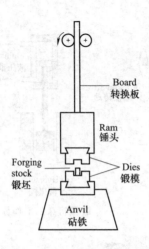

Fig 4.306　Gravity drop hammer
　　　　　重力锤

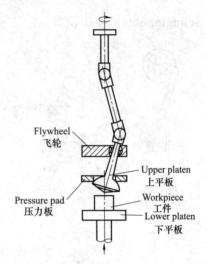

Fig 4.307　Orbital forging arrangement
　　　　　摆辗成形布局

4.3　Cutting tools　切削刀具

(1)　Turning tools　车刀

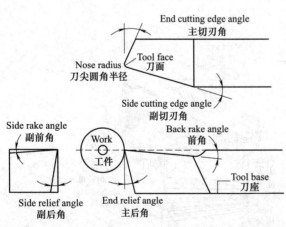

Fig 4.308　Turning tool geometry　车刀几何参数

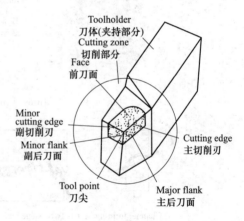

Fig 4.309　Construct of a cutting tool
　　　　　刀具结构

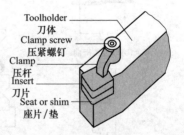

Fig 4.310　Carbide insert held by clamp screw for cutting tool　螺钉压板固定刀粒

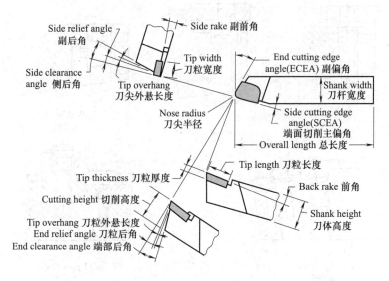

Fig 4.311　A typical single-point carbide tipped cutting tool
典型单刀尖硬质合金刀具

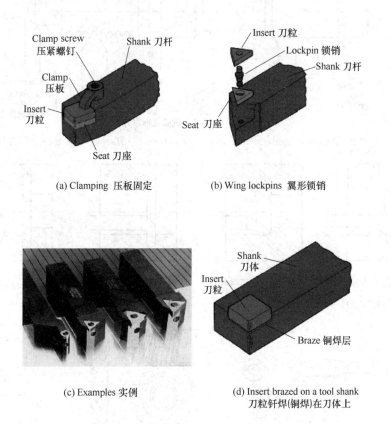

(a) Clamping 压板固定　　(b) Wing lockpins 翼形锁销

(c) Examples 实例　　(d) Insert brazed on a tool shank
　　　　　　　　　　　刀粒钎焊(铜焊)在刀体上

Fig 4.312　Methods of attaching inserts to toolholders　刀粒固定的方法

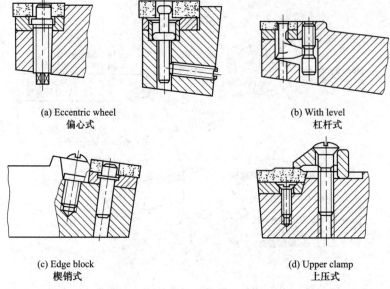

Fig 4.313　Various types of fixing inserts into tool body　可转位车刀的结构

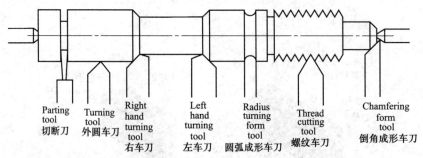

Fig 4.314　Different kinds of tools used for external surface　外表面加工车刀种类

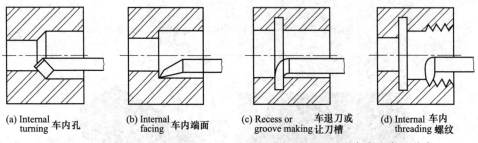

Fig 4.315　Different kinds of tools used for internal surface　内表面车刀种类

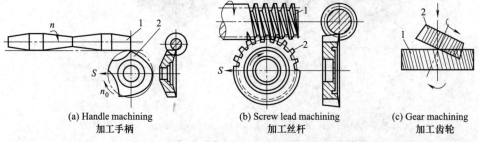

Fig 4.316　Applications of generating turning cutter　展成车刀的应用

1—Workpiece　工件；2—Generating turning cutter　展成车刀

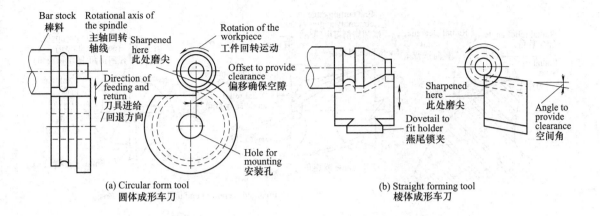

Fig 4.317 Form tool typed used in center lathe 中心车床采用的成形车刀种类

(2) Milling tools 铣刀

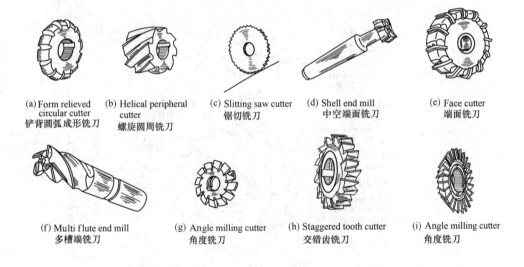

Fig 4.318 Various types of milling cutters 各种形式的铣刀

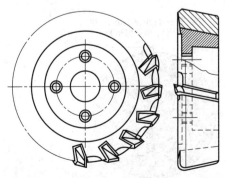

Fig 4.319 Inserted tooth cutter
刀粒嵌入铣刀

Fig 4.320 Face milling
端面铣削

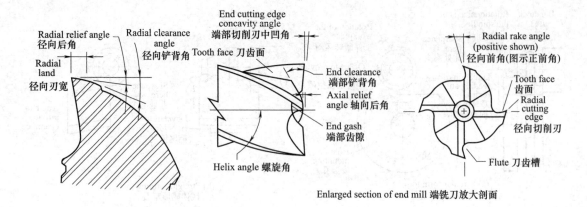
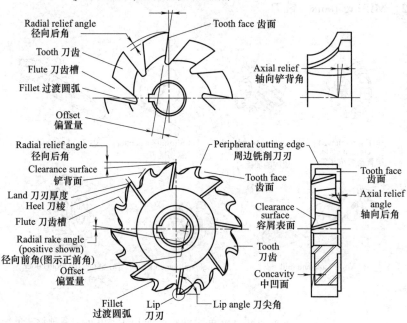
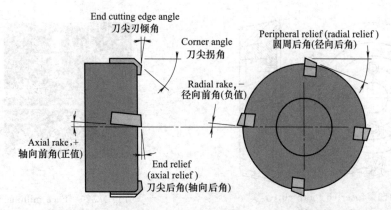

Fig 4.321　Terminology for a face-milling cutter　端面铣刀术语

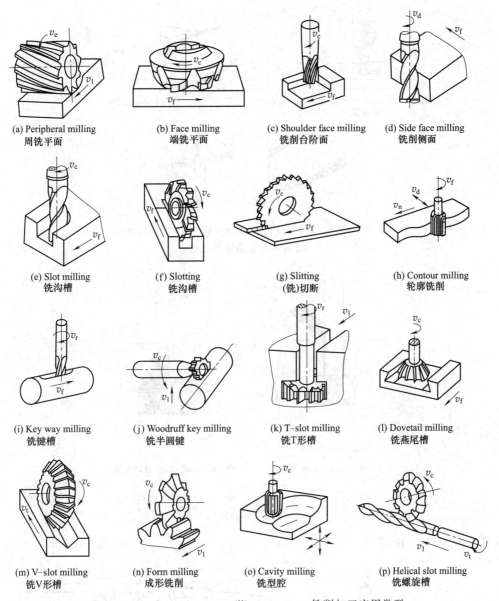

Fig 4.322 Operations on milling process 铣削加工应用类型

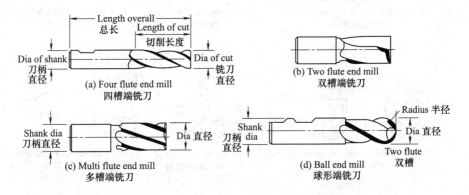

Fig 4.323

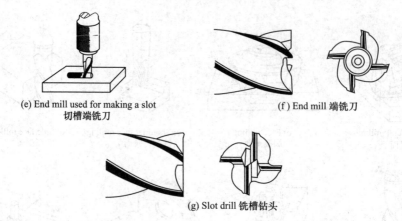

(e) End mill used for making a slot 切槽端铣刀

(f) End mill 端铣刀

(g) Slot drill 铣槽钻头

Fig 4.323　Shank mounted milling cutters and various types of end mills
带柄铣刀及端铣刀类别

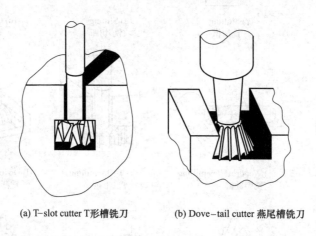

(a) T-slot cutter T形槽铣刀　　(b) Dove-tail cutter 燕尾槽铣刀

Fig 4.324　Special milling cutters for specific application
特型铣刀的应用

(3) Boring tools　镗刀

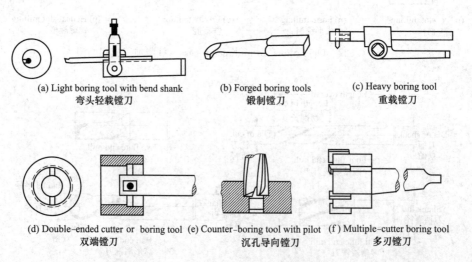

(a) Light boring tool with bend shank 弯头轻载镗刀

(b) Forged boring tools 锻制镗刀

(c) Heavy boring tool 重载镗刀

(d) Double-ended cutter or boring tool 双端镗刀

(e) Counter-boring tool with pilot 沉孔导向镗刀

(f) Multiple-cutter boring tool 多刃镗刀

Fig 4.325　Types of boring tools　镗刀种类

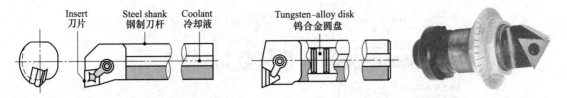

Fig 4.326　Boring bar structure　镗刀杆结构（一）

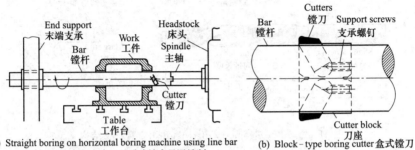

(a) Straight boring on horizontal boring machine using line bar and support 使用刀杆和支承的卧式镗床贯通镗削　　(b) Block-type boring cutter 盒式镗刀

(c) A modern removable insert boring head 可换刀粒的现代镗刀头

Fig 4.327　Boring bar structure　镗刀杆结构（二）

(4) Hole-making tools　钻扩铰孔加工刀具

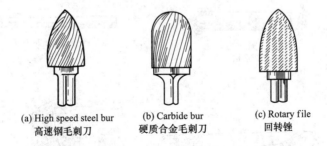

(a) High speed steel bur 高速钢毛刺刀　　(b) Carbide bur 硬质合金毛刺刀　　(c) Rotary file 回转锉

Fig 4.328　Various types of burs　去毛刺刀类别

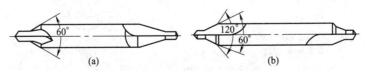

Fig 4.329　Center drill　中心钻

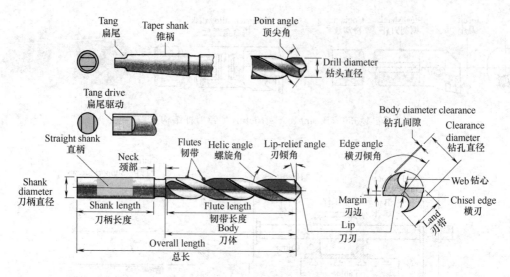

Fig 4.330 Geometry of twist drill 麻花钻结构

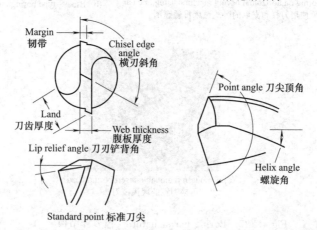

The principal elements of tool geometry on twist drills 麻花钻几何要素

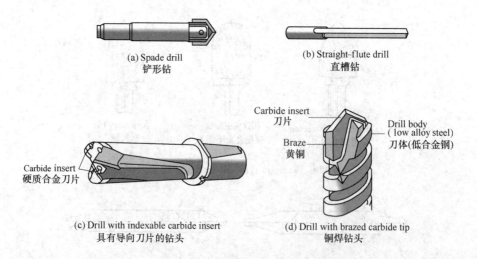

Fig 4.331 Various types of drills 钻头种类

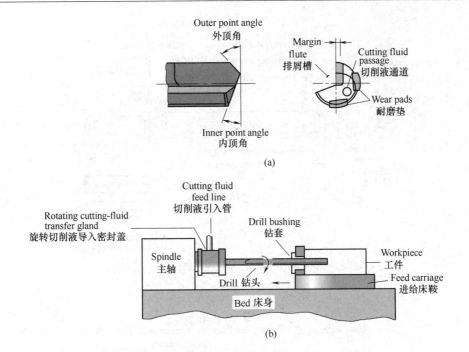

Fig 4.332　A gun drill features and gun-drilling operation　枪钻特点及其加工应用

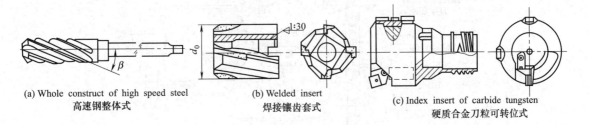

Fig 4.333　Construct of expanding drill (bit)　扩孔钻的结构

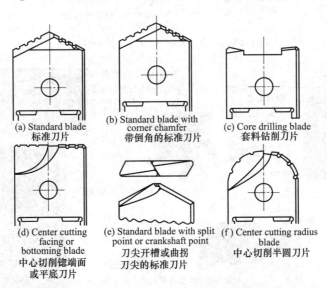

Fig 4.334　Typical spade drill blades　典型铲形钻刀片

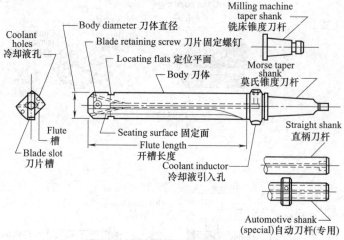

Fig 4.335　Spade drill blade holder　铲形钻刀片固定器

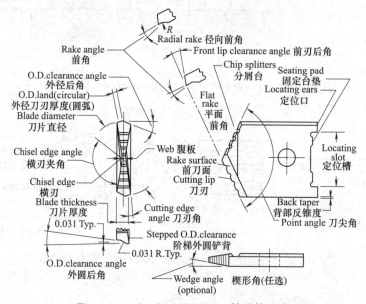

Fig 4.336　Spade drill blade　铲形钻刀片

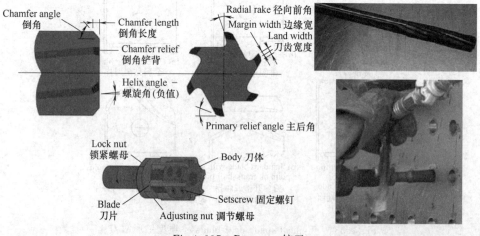

Fig 4.337　Reamer　铰刀

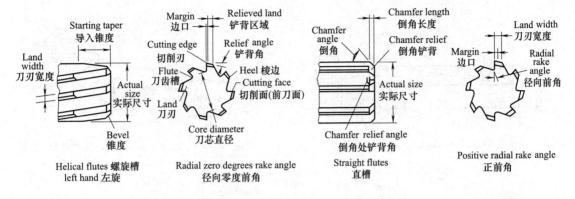

Fig 4.338　Hand reamer　手动铰刀

Fig 4.339　Machine reamer　机动铰刀

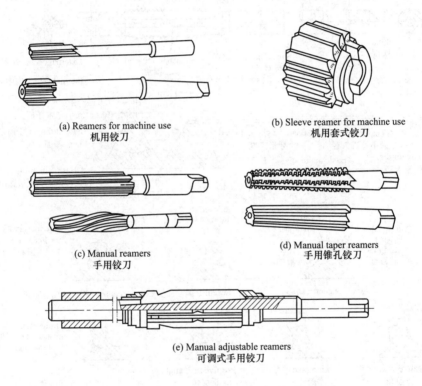

Fig 4.340　Types of reamers　铰刀种类

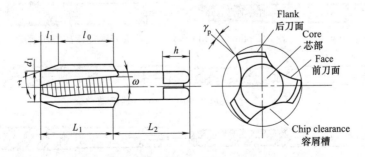

Fig 4.341　Taper geometry　丝锥结构

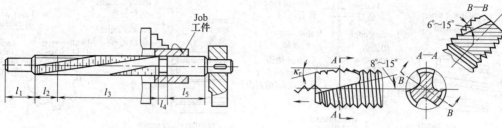

Fig 4.342　Broaching taper　拉削丝锥　　　　Fig 4.343　Non-groove taper　无槽丝锥

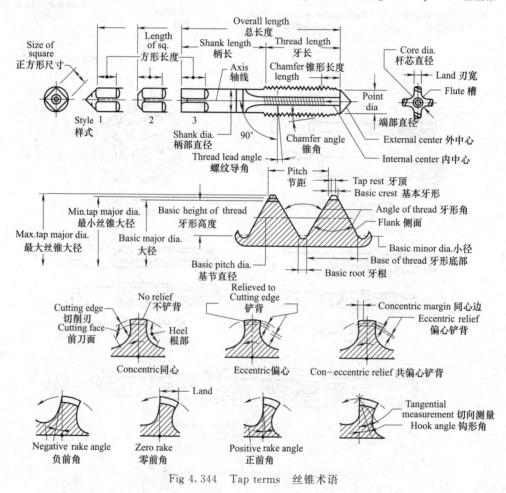

Fig 4.344　Tap terms　丝锥术语

Fig 4.345　Spiral pointed only taps　仅端部开螺旋槽的挤压丝锥

Fig 4.346　Spiral fluted taps　螺旋槽丝锥

Fig 4.347　Spiral fluted taps　快速螺旋槽丝锥

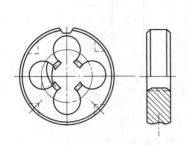

Fig 4.348　Circular die　圆板牙

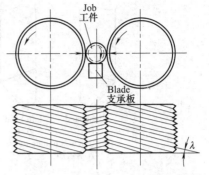

Fig 4.349　Rolled tap　滚丝轮滚压螺纹

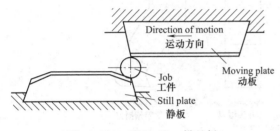

Fig 4.350　Plate die　搓丝板

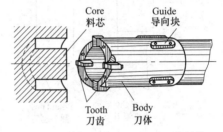

Fig 4.351　Trepanning tool　套料钻（又称环孔钻）

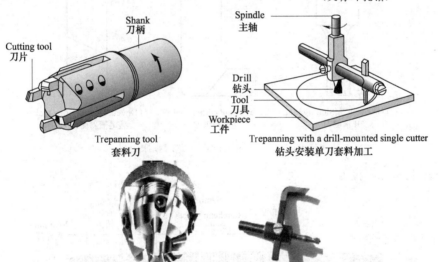

Fig 4.352　Trepanning machining　套料加工刀具

(5) Reciprocating process tools　往复运动加工刀具

① Shaping tool　刨刀

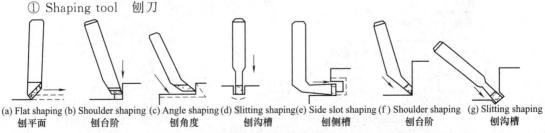

(a) Flat shaping　(b) Shoulder shaping　(c) Angle shaping　(d) Slitting shaping　(e) Side slot shaping　(f) Shoulder shaping　(g) Slitting shaping
刨平面　　　　刨台阶　　　　　刨角度　　　　　刨沟槽　　　　　刨侧槽　　　　　刨台阶　　　　　刨沟槽

Fig 4.353　Shaping tools and various shaping types　刨刀与刨削加工类型

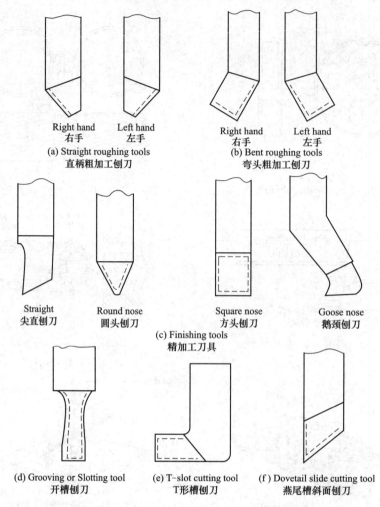

Fig 4.354　Planer tools　龙门刨床刀具

② Pull broach　拉刀

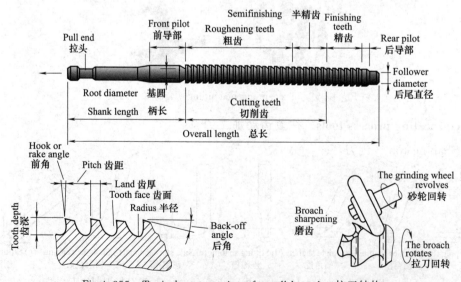

Fig 4.355　Typical construction of a pull broach　拉刀结构

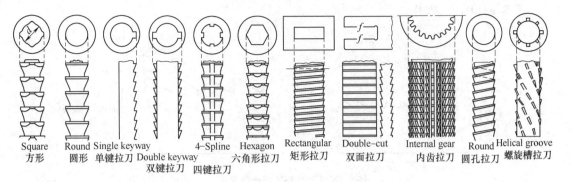

Fig 4.356　Types of broaches　拉刀类型

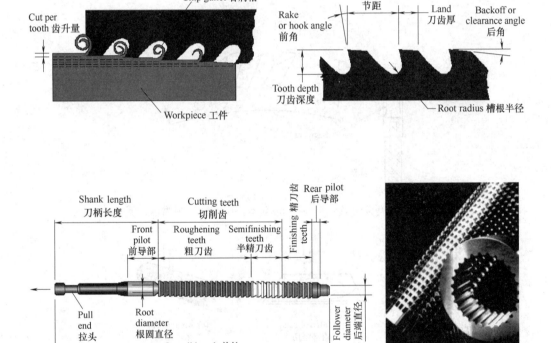

Fig 4.357　Broach　拉刀

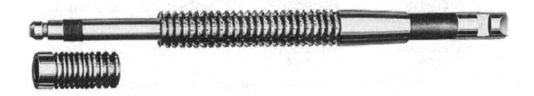

Fig 4.358　Shell broach　套式拉刀

③ Saw blade 锯片

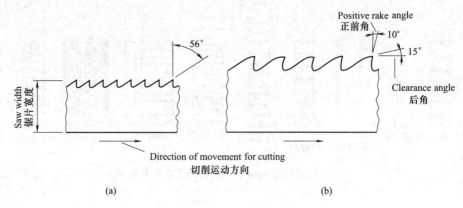

Fig 4.359　Commonly used saw tooth forms　常用锯齿形貌

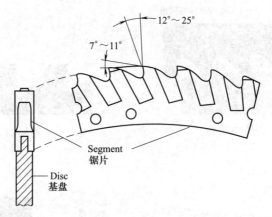

Fig 4.360　A typical circular saw blade construction　典型圆盘锯结构

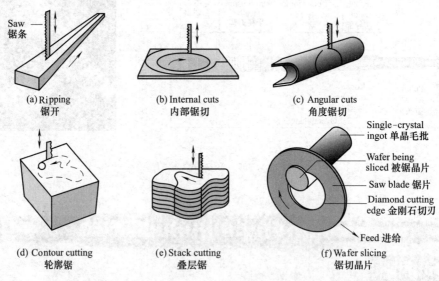

Fig 4.361　Various examples of sawing operations　锯切操作

(6) **Abrasives** 磨具

① Solid abrasives　固结磨具

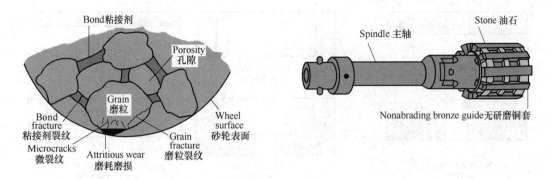

Fig 4.362　Grinding wheel surface　砂轮表面

Fig 4.363　A honing tool used to improve the surface finish of bored or ground holes
珩磨工具用于改善镗孔或磨孔的表面粗糙度

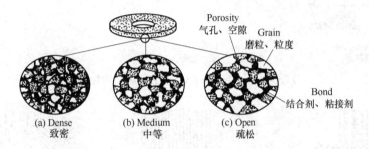

Fig 4.364　Grinding wheel construct　砂轮组织

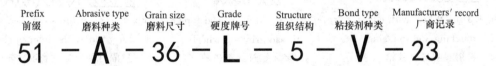

Fig 4.365　Standard grinding wheel markings　标准的砂轮标识

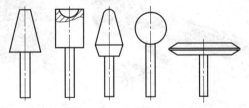

Fig 4.366　Contour grinding wheels　成形磨削砂轮

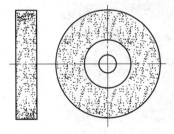

Fig 4.367　Standard grinding wheel
标准砂轮

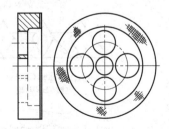

Fig 4.368　Steel wheel coated with abrasive
钢制涂覆磨料砂轮

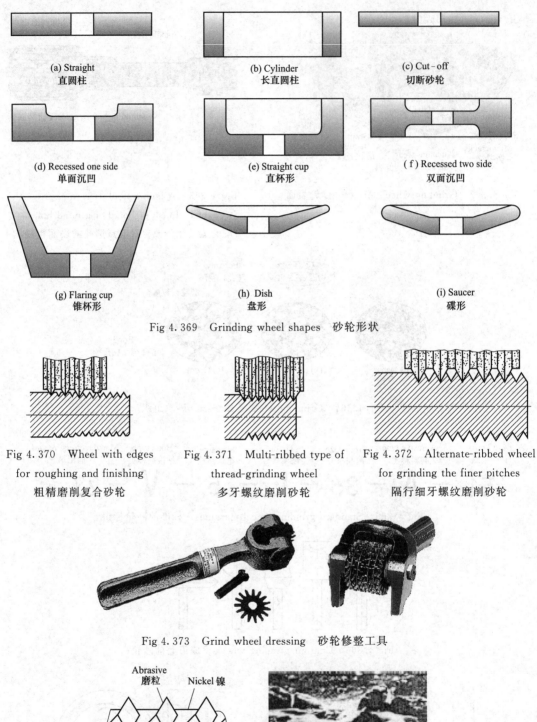

(a) Straight 直圆柱　　(b) Cylinder 长直圆柱　　(c) Cut-off 切断砂轮

(d) Recessed one side 单面沉凹　　(e) Straight cup 直杯形　　(f) Recessed two side 双面沉凹

(g) Flaring cup 锥杯形　　(h) Dish 盘形　　(i) Saucer 碟形

Fig 4.369　Grinding wheel shapes　砂轮形状

Fig 4.370　Wheel with edges for roughing and finishing　粗精磨削复合砂轮

Fig 4.371　Multi-ribbed type of thread-grinding wheel　多牙螺纹磨削砂轮

Fig 4.372　Alternate-ribbed wheel for grinding the finer pitches　隔行细牙螺纹磨削砂轮

Fig 4.373　Grind wheel dressing　砂轮修整工具

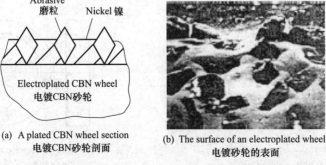

(a) A plated CBN wheel section 电镀CBN砂轮剖面　　(b) The surface of an electroplated wheel 电镀砂轮的表面

Fig 4.374　An electroplated wheel　电镀砂轮

(a) Schematic 示意图　　(b) The surface of a brazed wheel 砂轮表面

Fig 4.375　A brazed wheel　镀铜砂轮

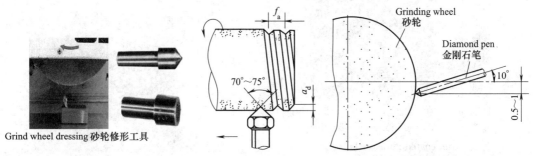

Fig 4.376　Grinding dressing with diamond pen　金刚石笔修整砂轮

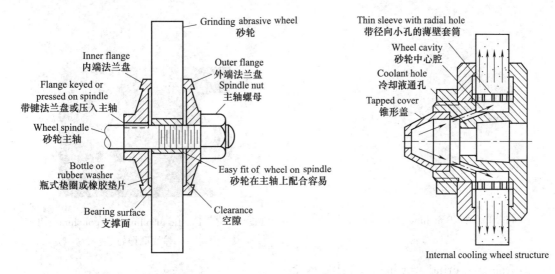

Fig 4.377　Correctly mounted wheel　砂轮的正确安装　　Fig 4.378　内部冷却砂轮结构

② Coated abrasives　涂覆磨具

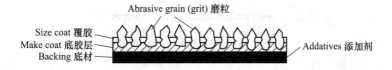

Fig 4.379　Cross section structure of abrasive belt　砂带截面图

Fig 4.381 Coated abrasive belt 砂带产品

Fig 4.380 Various forms of abrasives from coated abrasive belt
各种形式的涂覆磨具

Fig 4.382 Grinding disc 磨盘、砂盘

Fig. 4.383 Polishing cloth wheel
抛光布轮

Fig. 4.384 Elastic grinding and polishing wheel
弹性磨抛轮

③ Diamond grinding wheel 金刚石砂轮

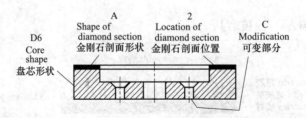

Fig. 4.385 A typical diamond wheel shape designation symbol 典型金刚石砂轮形状设计符号

Table 4.3 Designations for location of diamond section on diamond wheel
金刚石砂轮上金刚石剖面的位置设计

Designation No. and location 设计号和位置	Description 描述	Illustration 图解
8—Throughout 完全金刚石	Designates wheels of solid diamond abrasive section without cores 整个实体为金刚石磨料，没有轮毂	
9—Corner 角落	Designates a location which would commonly be considered to be on the periphery except that the diamond section shall be on the corner but shall not extend to the other corner 金属石层位于剖面一角落，但不宜延伸到另一个角落	
10—Annular 内环面	Designates a location of the diamond abrasive section on the inner annular surface of the wheel 金刚石层位于轮毂内环面上	

Table 4.4 Designation letters for modifications of diamond wheels
金刚石砂轮改型标识字母

Designation letter 标识字母	Description 描述	Illustration 图解
B—Drilled and counterbored 钻孔并锪沉孔	Holes drilled and counterbored in core 轮毂基体上钻孔并锪沉孔	
C—Drilled and countersunk 钻孔并锪锥孔	Holes drilled and countersunk in core 轮毂基体上钻孔并锪锥孔	
H—Plain hole 钻通孔	Straight hole drilled in core 轮毂基体上钻通孔	
M—Holes plain and threaded 钻通孔和螺纹孔	Mixed holes, some plain, some threaded, are in core 轮毂基体上钻孔、螺纹孔	
P—Relieved one side 单面内沉	Core relieved on one side of wheel. Thickness of core is less than wheel thickness 砂轮单面内沉，轮中心厚度小于砂轮厚度	
R—Relieved two sides 双面内沉	Core relieved on both sides of wheel. Thickness of core is less than wheel thickness 砂轮双面内沉，轮中心厚度小于砂轮厚度	
S—Segmented-diamond section 金刚石层开槽分片	Wheel has segmental diamond section mounted on core (clearance between segments has no bearing on definition) 轮毂上安装开槽分片的金刚石层（片间无支撑）	
SS—Segmental and slotted 金刚石层分片基体开槽	Wheel has separated segments mounted on a slotted core 开槽轮毂基体上安装金刚石片层	
T—Threaded holes 设置螺纹孔	Threaded holes are in core 轮毂基体上设置螺纹孔	
Q—Diamond inserted 金刚石嵌入	Three surfaces of the diamond section are partially or completely enclosed by the core 金刚石断面的三个面部分或全部为基本材料所覆盖	

续表

Designation letter 标识字母	Description 描述	Illustration 图解
V—Diamond inverted 圆周面金刚石层内凹	Any diamond cross section, which is mounted on the core so that the interior point of any angle, or the concave side of any arc, is exposed shall be considered inverted 各种内凹尖角或弧面断面金刚石层外向地安装在轮毂上可以认为是反向安装	

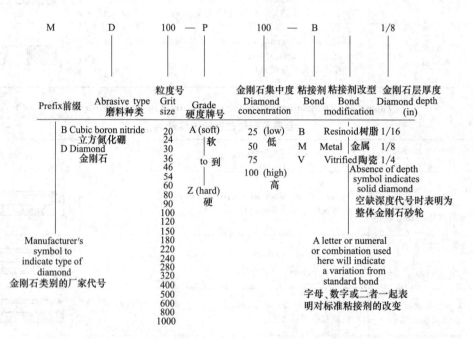

Fig. 4.386　Standard marking system for cubic boron nitride and diamond bonded abrasives
立方氮化硼和金刚石砂轮的标准标识系统

(7) **Gear cutting tools**　齿轮刀具

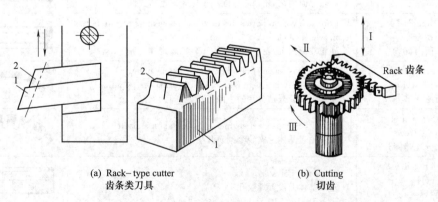

(a) Rack-type cutter
齿条类刀具

(b) Cutting
切齿

Fig. 4.387　Cutting gears with rack-type cutters
齿条类刀具加工齿轮

Fig. 4.388 Cutting gears with shaping cutter 插齿刀插齿
1—Tool-alloy-steel cutter 合金工具钢刀具；2—Carbon-steel shim 碳钢刀垫

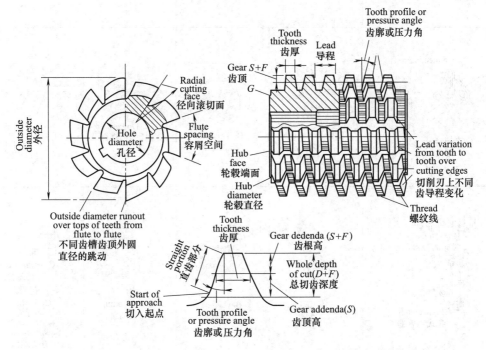

Fig. 4.389 A typical gear hob with its elements 典型齿轮滚刀及其要素

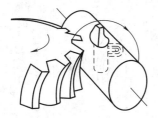

Fig. 4.390 Worm wheel cutting with flying cutter
飞刀加工蜗轮

Fig. 4.391 Milling cutter bevel-gear of curved tooth
弧齿锥齿铣刀盘

4.4 Collection of commonly used machinery parts and tools 机械零部件和工具列表

(1) Commonly used machinery parts 机械零部件

Table 4.5 Commonly used machinery parts 机械零部件

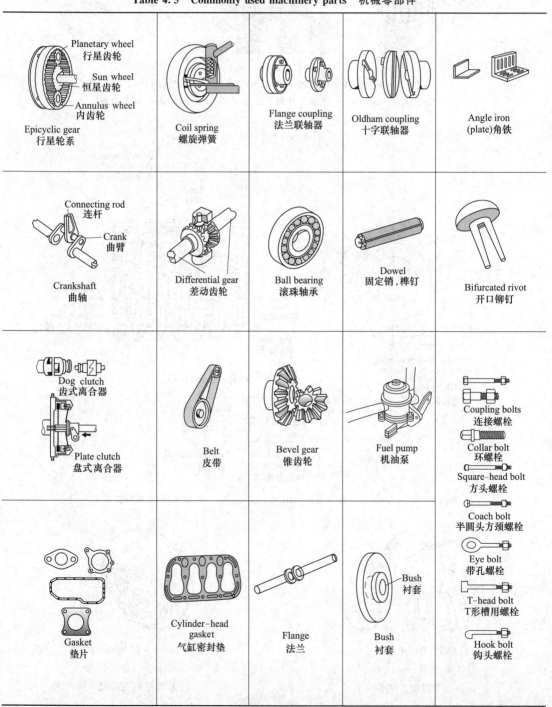

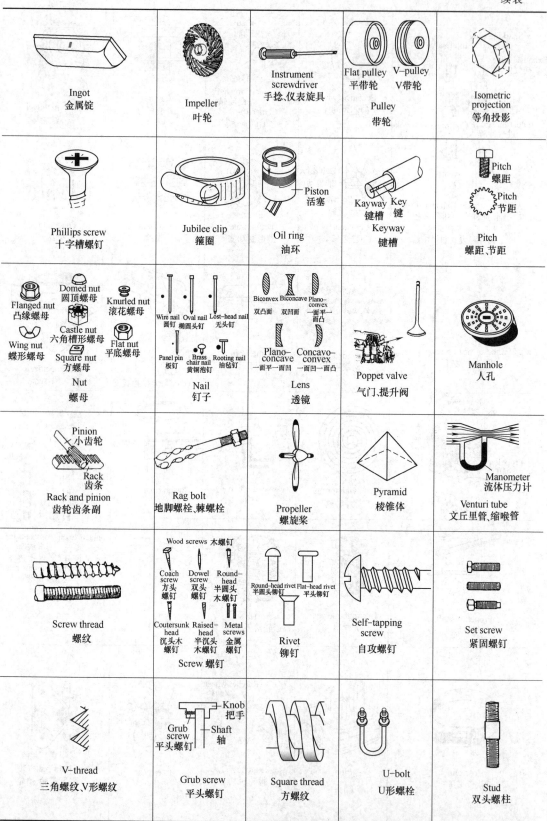

(2) Commonly machinery tools   机械工具

Table 4.6   Commonly machinery tools   机械工具

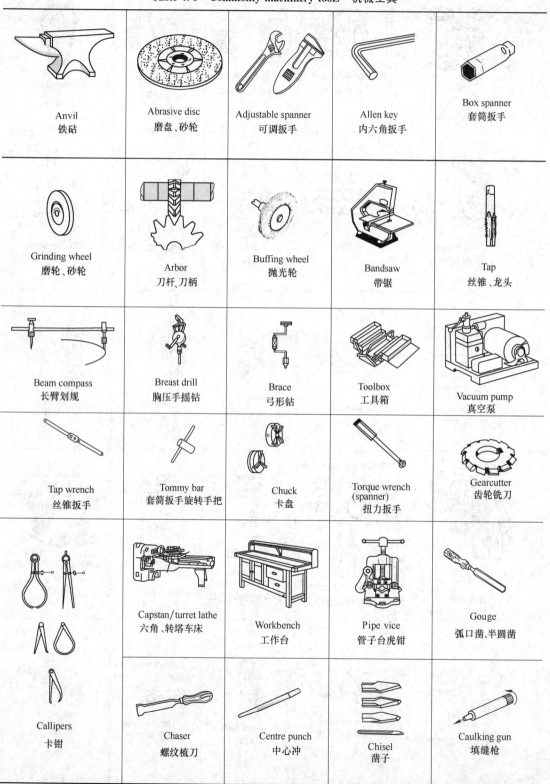

续表

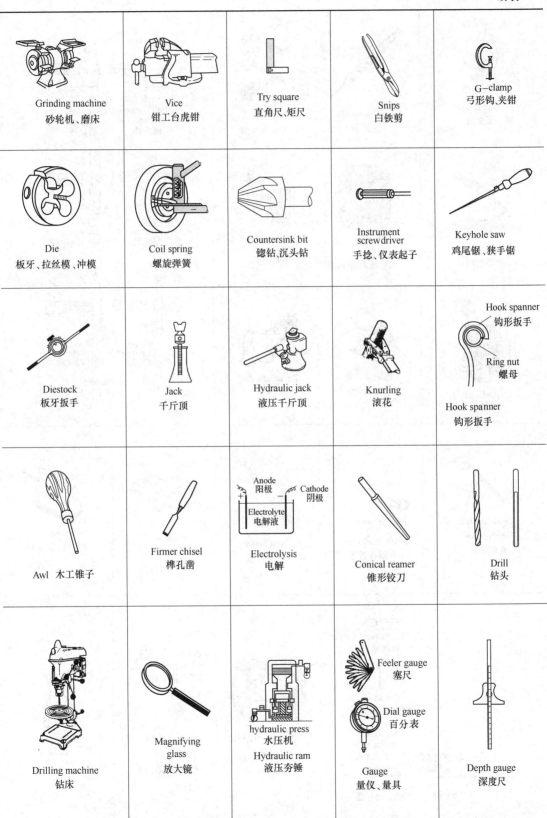

(3) Manual tools 手动工具

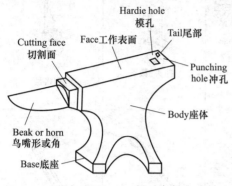

Fig. 4.392 Anvil 砧座

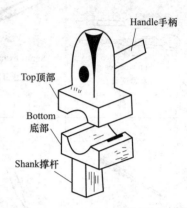

Fig. 4.393 Swages 旋锻工具

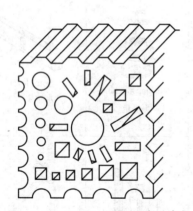

Fig. 4.394 Swage block 陷型砧座

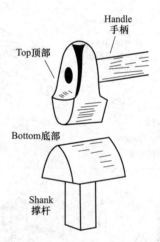

Fig. 4.395 Fullers 套柄铁锤

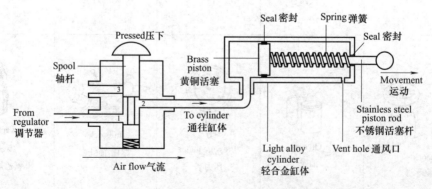

Fig. 4.396 Pneumatic system 风动系统

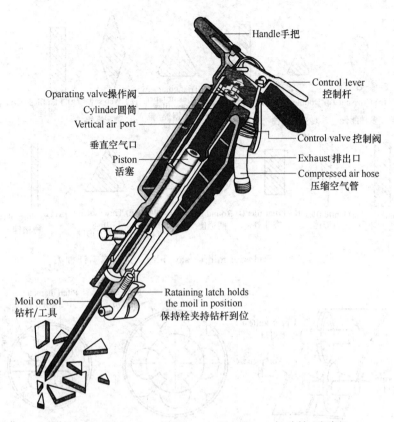

Fig. 4.397　Pneumatic drill or road breaker　气动钻/破路机

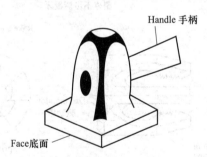

Fig. 4.398　Flatter　平锤

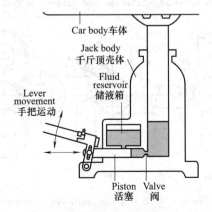

Fig. 4.399　Hydraulic jack　液压千斤顶

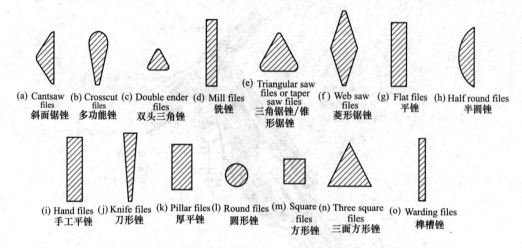

Fig. 4.400　Styles of mill or saw files　铣锉或锯锉种类

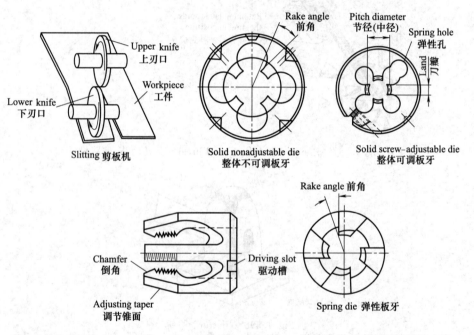

Fig. 4.401　Spring type collet-adjustable die and holder　弹性类收口式可调板牙和夹套

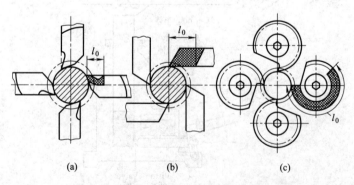

Fig. 4.402　Threading die heads：l_0 = Maximum layer of stock available for sharpening
螺纹加工板牙工具头：l_0 为可重磨的最大刀具材料厚度

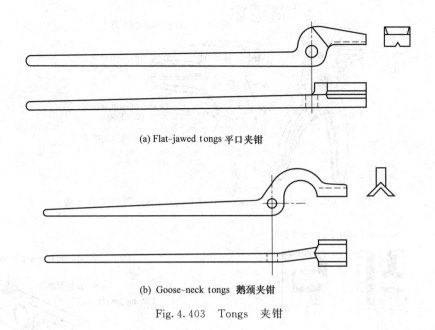

Fig. 4.403　Tongs　夹钳

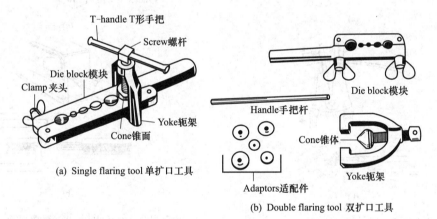

Fig. 4.404　Flaring tool　扩口工具

Fig. 4.405　Circular blade saws　圆盘锯

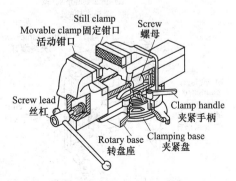

Fig. 4.406　Vice　台虎钳

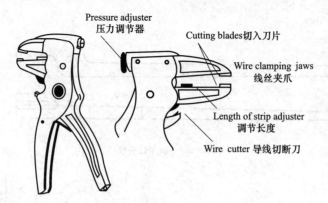

Fig. 4.407　Non-adjustable wire stripper　不可调节的剥线钳

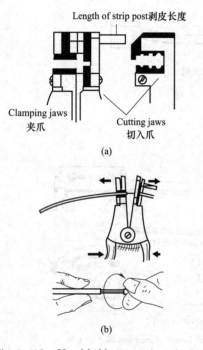

Fig. 4.408　Hand-held automatic stripper
手持自动剥线钳

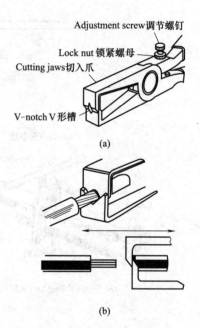

Fig. 4.409　Adjustable hand-operated strippers
可调手动剥线钳

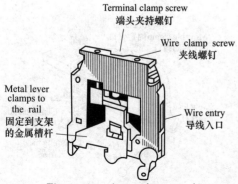

Fig. 4.410　An earth terminal
接地端子

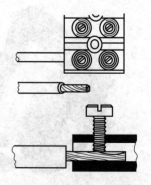

Fig. 4.411　Screw terminals
螺钉压紧端子

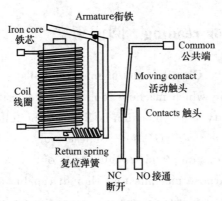

Fig. 4.412　Mechanical switching devices controlled by an electromagnet
电磁铁控制的机械式开关装置

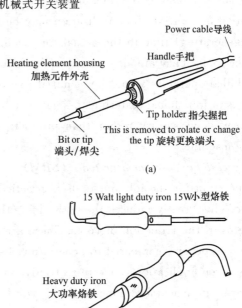

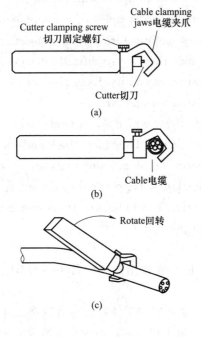

Fig. 4.413　Cable strippers
电缆剥线钳

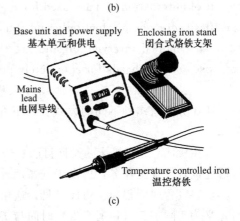

Fig. 4.414　The soldering iron　电焊烙铁

4.5　Short passage for reading　阅读短文

Classification of machine tools

There are many ways in which machine tools can be classified. One such classification based on production capability and application is given in the following lines.

General purpose machine tools（GPM）　These tools are those designed to perform a variety of machining operations on a wide ranging type of components. By its very nature of generalization, a general purpose machine tool though capable of carrying out a variety of tasks, would not be suitable for large production, since the setting time for any given operation is large. Thus the idle time on the general purpose machine tool is more and the machine utilization is poor. Machine utilization may be termed as the percentage of actual machining (chip generating) time to the actual time available. This is much lower for general purpose machine tools. They are also termed as basic machine tools.

Skilled operators would be required to run general purpose machine tools. Hence their utility is in job shops (catering to small batch, large variety job production) where the requirement is versatility rather than production capability. Examples are lathe, shaper and milling machine.

Special purpose machine tools（SPM）　These are those machine tools where the setting operation for the job and tools is practically eliminated and complete automation is achieved. This greatly reduces the cycle time (the actual manufacturing time) of a component and helps in the reduction of costs. These are used for mass manufacturing. These machine tools are expensive compared to general purpose machine since they are specifically designed for the given application, and are restrictive in their application capability. Examples are cam shaft grinding machine, connecting rod twin boring and piston turning lathe.

Single purpose machine tools　These machine tools are those which are designed specifically for doing single operation on a class of jobs or on a single job. They have the highest amount of automation and are used for high rates of production. These machine tools are used specifically for one product only and thus have the least flexibility. However they do not require any manual intervention and are the most cost effective. Examples are transfer lines composed of unit heads for completely machining any given product.

机床的分类

机床分类有多种不同的方式，以下介绍的是基于生产能力和应用范围的其中一种分类方式。

通用机床：通用机床的设计目的在于对各种零件完成一系列的加工操作。尽管这类机床能够完成各种加工任务，但由于其通用属性，它不适合于大量生产方式，因为对于给定的加工其调整设置时间很长。由此可见，通用机床的空闲时间多而其利用时间较少。机床利用率可定义为实际加工（切屑产生）时间与实际耗用时间的百分比。通用机床的利用率非常低。所以，这类机床被称为基本机床。

通用机床的运行要求操作工技能熟练。由此它主要用在那些有万能性而非生产能力要求的修理车间（适合于小批量、多品种生产情形），典型的通用机床有车床、牛头刨床和铣床。

专用机床：在专用机床上，工件和刀具的布局设定时间基本消除并完全实现自动化。这会减少零件循环时间（实际的制造时间）并有助于降低成本，它们用于大批量生产。与通用机床相比，专用机床更为昂贵，应用范围有限，因为它们是针对具体用途而专门设计。典型的专用机床有凸轮轴磨床、连杆双孔镗床和活塞车床。

单一用途机床：这种机型特别针对某一类或某一个工件的某一道工序而专门设计，其自动化程度最高，并用于高效率生产情形。单一用途机床仅用于某一种特定产品，因而其柔性（适应性）最差。尽管如此，这类机床不需任何的人工干预，而且其生产成本最低。例如，对于给定产品能完全加工的由各种床头单元构成的传输生产线（流水线）。

Unit 5 Hydraulic and Pneumatic Drives
液压与气动传动

5.1 Hydraulic and pneumatic elements 液压气动元件

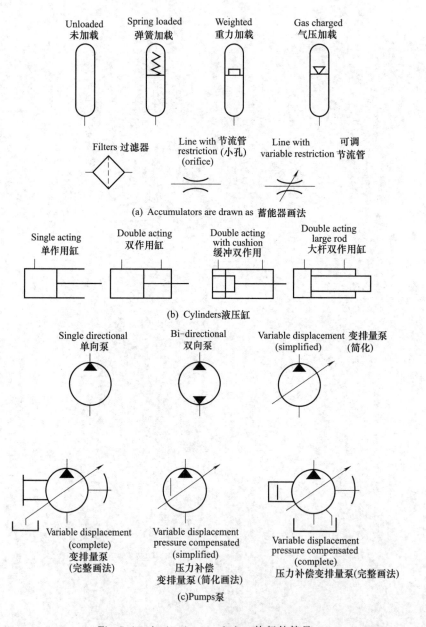

Fig. 5.1 Activation symbols 执行件符号

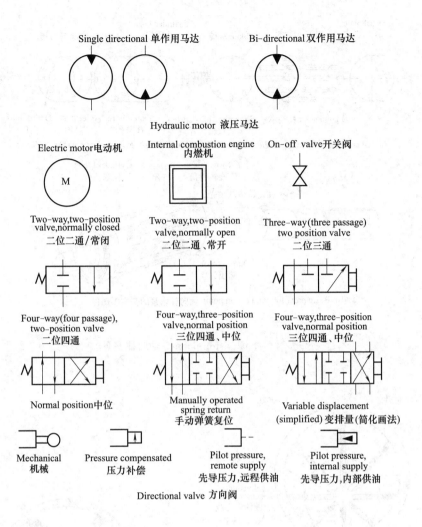

Fig. 5.2　Other activation symbols　其他执行件符号

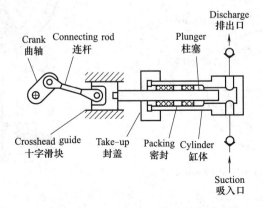

Fig. 5.3　Plunger pump　柱塞泵

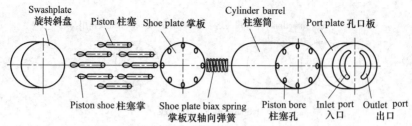

(a) Overcenter axial pump without drive shaft shown 驱动轴未画出的过中心的轴向泵

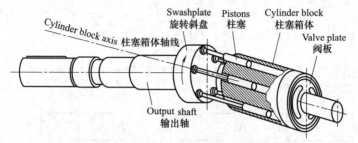

(b) Basic parts for axial piston pump 轴向柱塞泵的基本零部件

Fig. 5.4　Axial piston pump　轴向柱塞泵

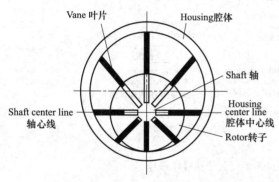

(a) Cross section shown schematically 横截面示意图解

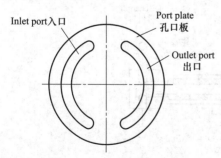

(b) Port plate with inlet port and outlet port 出入口油盘

Fig. 5.5　Vane pump　叶片泵

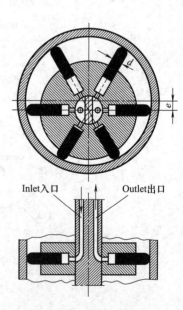

Fig. 5.6　Sectional views of radial piston pump
径向柱塞泵截面图

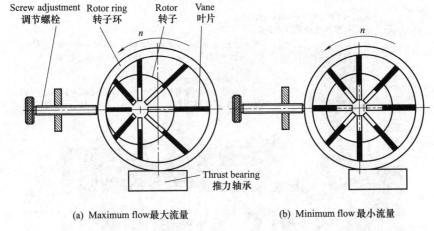

(a) Maximum flow 最大流量　　(b) Minimum flow 最小流量

Fig. 5.7　Cross-sectional schematic for variable vane　变量叶片泵横截面示意图

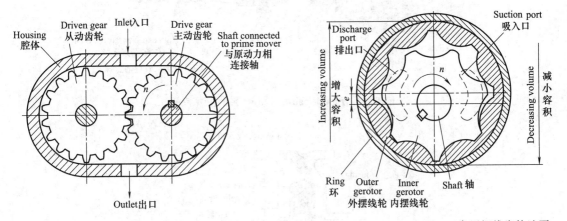

Fig. 5.8　Gear pump　齿轮泵　　　　Fig. 5.9　Gerotor pump　常压摆线齿轮油泵

Fig. 5.10　Double-volute pump　双蜗壳泵

Fig. 5.11　A variety of vane types that might be used on a centrifugal fan　离心泵上可能应用的叶片类别

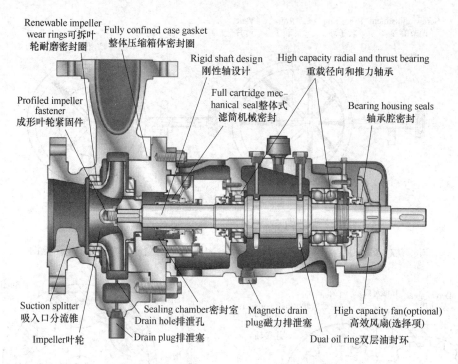

Fig. 5.12 Pump main feature 泵的主要特征

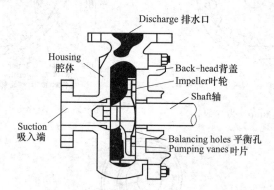

Fig. 5.13 Cross-section of a typical end-suction centrifugal 典型端部吸入离心泵剖开图

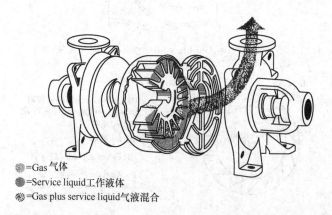

Fig. 5.14 Operating principle of liquid vacuum pumps 液体真空泵原理

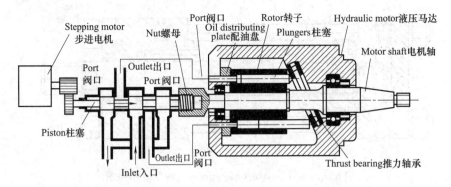

Fig. 5.15　Hydraulic motor　液压马达

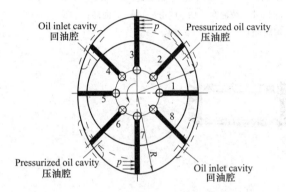

Fig. 5.16　Hydraulic vane motor
叶片式液压马达工作原理图

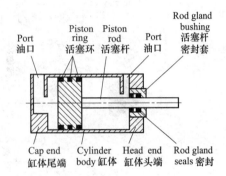

Fig. 5.17　Major components of hydraulic cylinder
液压缸主要部件

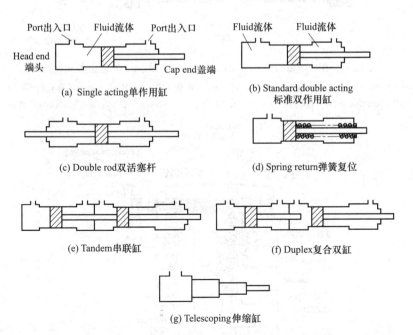

Fig. 5.18　Types of hydraulic cylinders　液压缸种类

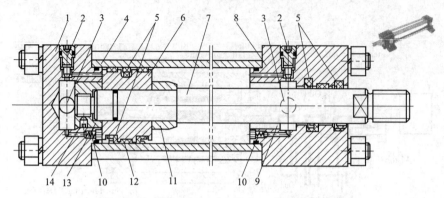

Fig. 5.19 Construct of cylinder 液压缸结构图

1—Backcover 后端盖；2—Throttle valve 缓冲节流阀；3—Oil inlet/outlet 进/出油口；4—Cylinder tube 缸筒；5—Seals 密封件；6—Piston 活塞；7—Piston bar 活塞杆；8—Front cover 前端盖；9—Guide bush 导向套；10—One-way valve 单向阀；11—Buffer bush 缓冲套；12—Guide ring 导向环；13—Buffer ring 无杆端缓冲套；14—Bolt 螺栓

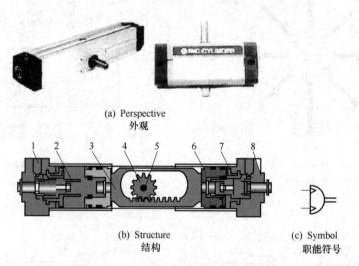

(a) Perspective
外观

(b) Structure
结构

(c) Symbol
职能符号

Fig. 5.20 Swing air cylinder with rack and pinion 齿轮齿条式摆动气缸

1—Buffer throttle 缓冲节流阀；2—Buffer plunger 缓冲柱塞；3—Rack 齿条组件；4—Pinion 齿轮；5—Output shaft 输出轴；6—Piston 活塞；7—Cylinder 缸体；8—Side plate 端盖

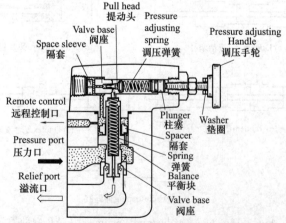

Fig. 5.21 Pilot operated relief valve 先导型溢流阀

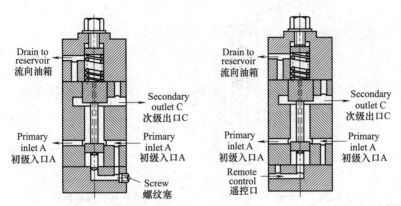

Fig. 5.22   Sequence valve   顺序阀

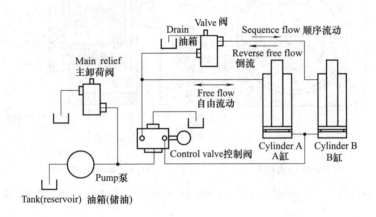

Fig. 5.23   Sequence valve for reverse free flow   顺序阀用于自由回流

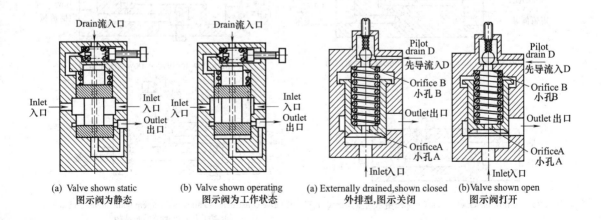

Fig. 5.24   Pressure-reducing valve   减压阀   Fig. 5.25   Compound relief valve   复合卸荷阀

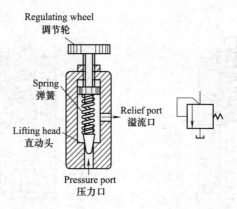

Fig. 5.26　Spring loaded type relief valve　弹簧直动型溢流阀

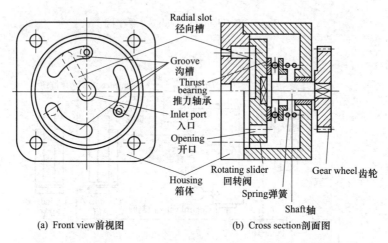

(a) Front view 前视图　　(b) Cross section 剖面图

Fig. 5.27　Hydraulic valve as a master controller　用作主控制器的液压阀

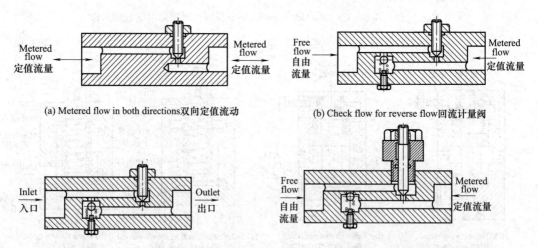

(a) Metered flow in both directions 双向定值流动　　(b) Check flow for reverse flow 回流计量阀

(c) Reverse flow check valve shown open 图示回流计量阀打开　　(d) Valve constructed to allow adjustment while under pressure 承载压力时可调整的阀结构

Fig. 5.28　Single-needle valve flow control　单一针阀的流量控制

5.2 Hydraulic and pneumatic auxilary component 液压气动附件

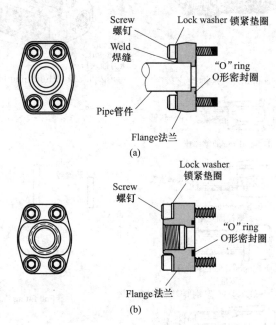

Fig. 5.29　Two types of bolted flange connectors　两种螺栓孔法兰连接器

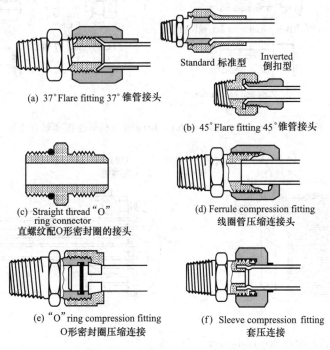

Fig. 5.30　Flared tube fitting　锥管头连接

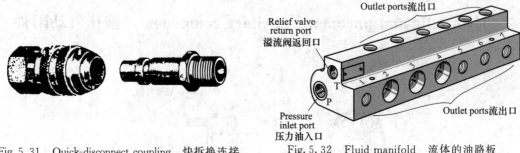

Fig. 5.31　Quick-disconnect coupling　快拆换连接

Fig. 5.32　Fluid manifold　流体的油路板

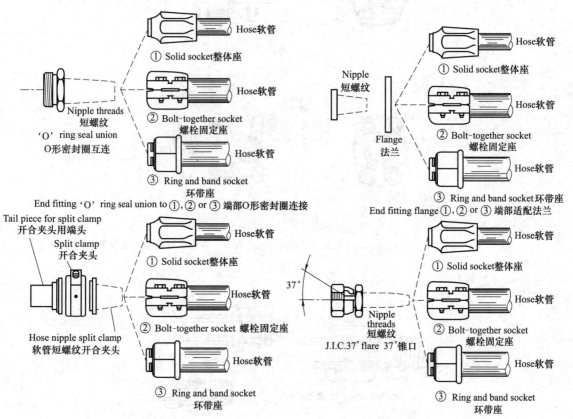

Fig. 5.33　End fittings and hose fittings　端部连接和软管连接

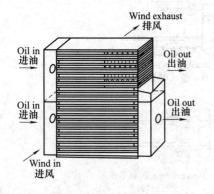

Fig. 5.34　Wing shaped plate heat exchanger 板翅式换热器

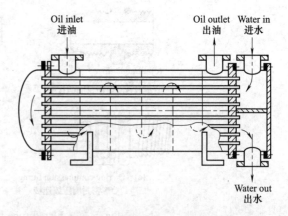

Fig. 5.35　Multi-pipe cooler　多管式冷却器

Optional cooling for over 315℃ 用于超过 315℃ 的冷却

Fig. 5.36　Fin tube oil cooler　鳍板式油液冷却器

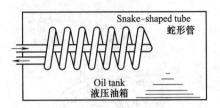

Fig. 5.37　Cooler of snake-shaped tube 蛇形管冷却器

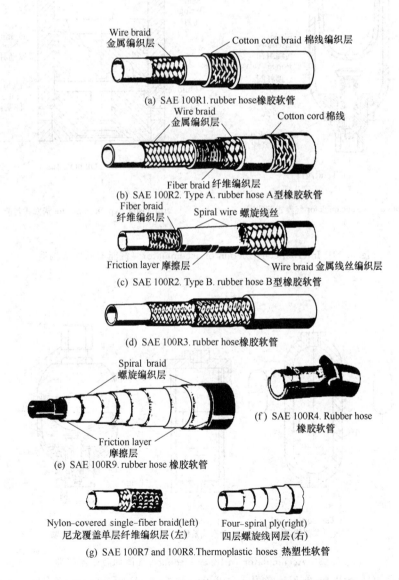

(a) SAE 100R1. rubber hose 橡胶软管

(b) SAE 100R2. Type A. rubber hose A型橡胶软管

(c) SAE 100R2. Type B. rubber hose B型橡胶软管

(d) SAE 100R3. rubber hose 橡胶软管

(e) SAE 100R9. rubber hose 橡胶软管

(f) SAE 100R4. Rubber hose 橡胶软管

(g) SAE 100R7 and 100R8. Thermoplastic hoses 热塑性软管

Fig. 5.38　Types of flexible hose　软管的种类

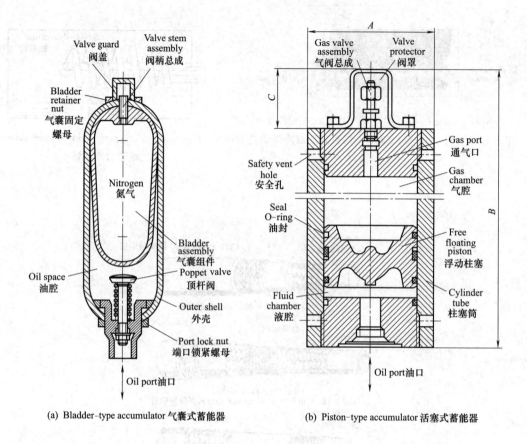

Fig. 5.39　Internal construction of accumulator　蓄能器的内部构造

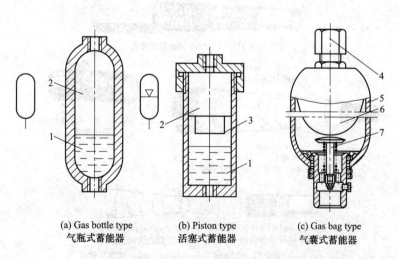

Fig. 5.40　Accumulator with gas loading　气体加载式蓄能器
1—Oil　液压油；2—Gas　气体；3—Piston　活塞；4—Valve for air in　充气阀；
5—Shell　壳体；6—Bag　皮囊；7—Valve for oil in　进油阀

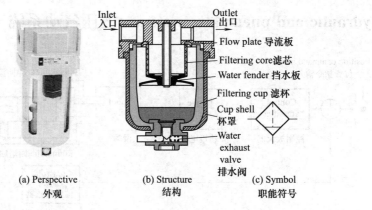

Fig. 5.41 Standard air filter 标准气体过滤器

Fig. 5.42 Vacuum sucker 真空吸盘

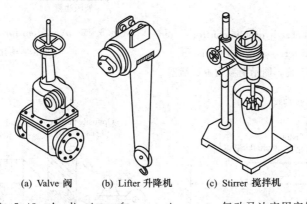

Fig. 5.43 Applications of pneumatic motor 气动马达应用实例

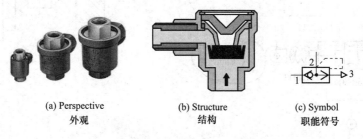

Fig. 5.44 Quick exhaust valve 快速排气阀

5.3　Hydraulic and pneumatic system　液压气动系统

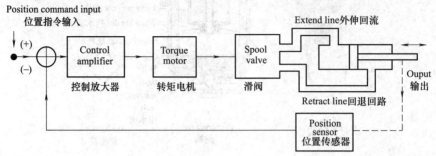

Fig. 5.45　A pneumatic closed-loop linear control system　气动闭环线性控制系统

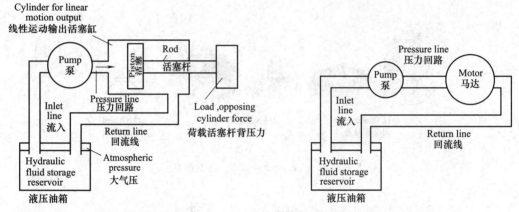

Fig. 5.46　A simple linear hydraulic control system in which the load force returns the piston
简易线性液压控制系统，图示荷载力退回活塞

Fig. 5.47　A system for driving a rotating load
回转驱动比较系统

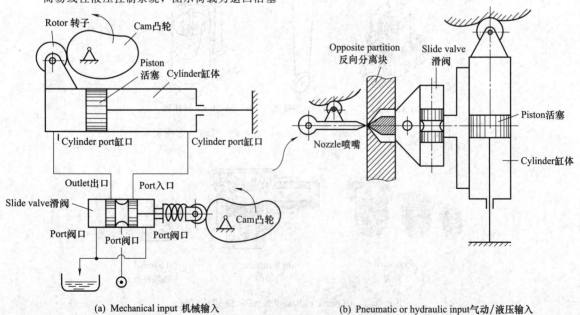

(a) Mechanical input　机械输入　　　　　　　(b) Pneumatic or hydraulic input　气动/液压输入

Fig. 5.48　Layout of a hydraulic amplifier　液压放大器设计

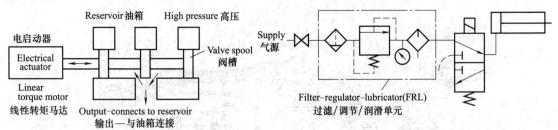

Fig. 5.49 Proportional control systems
比例控制系统

Fig. 5.50 A pneumatic direction control circuit
气动方向控制回路

Fig. 5.51 Representive hydraulic circuit 典型液压回路

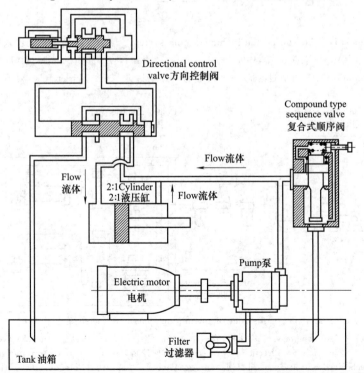

Fig. 5.52 Schematic for regenerative cylinder circuit 可重构的液压缸回路简图

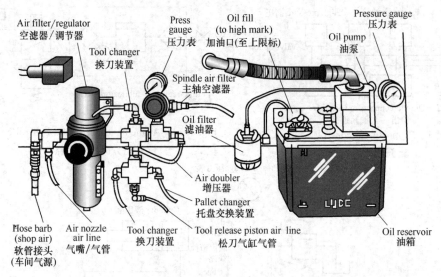

Fig. 5.53　Lubricant way for pneumatic system　气动系统润滑回路

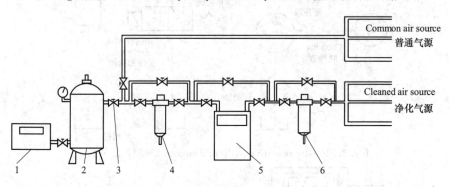

Fig. 5.54　Air source and its air cleaning system　气源及空气净化处理系统
1—Air compressor　空压机；3—Gas tank　气体罐；3—Valve（switch）阀门；
4—Main tube filter　主管过滤器；5—Air drier　干燥机；6—Filter of main tube　主管过滤器

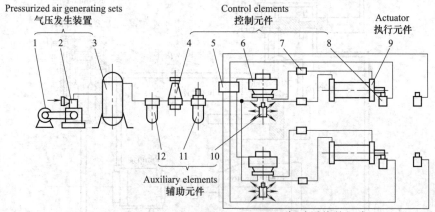

Fig. 5.55　Construct of pneumatic system　气动系统的组成
1—Motor　电机；2—Air compressor　空压机；3—Gas tank　储气罐；4—Pressure control valve　压力控制阀；
5—Logic element　逻辑元件；6—Direction control valve　方向控制阀；7—Flowrate control valve　流量控制阀；
8—Mechanical control valve　机控阀；9—Air cylinder　气缸；10—Noise absorber　消声器；
11—Oil spray　油雾器；12—Air filter　空气滤清器

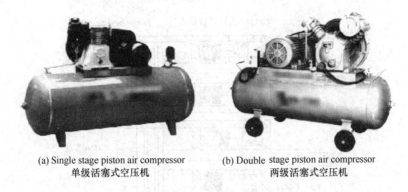

Fig. 5.56　Piston air compressor　活塞式空压机

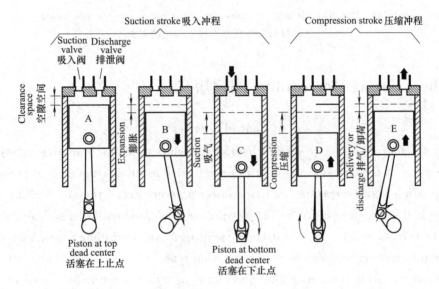

Fig. 5.57　Two-cycle, or single-action, air compressor cylinders
双循环单作用空气压缩机缸体

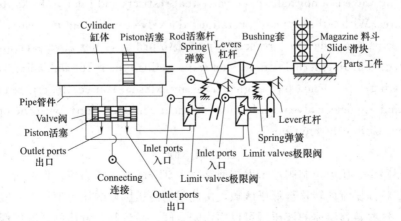

Fig. 5.58　Pneumatic circuit controlled by a limit valve　极限阀控制的气动回路

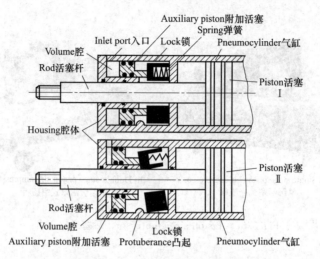

Fig. 5.59 Pneumatic jam for stopping the piston rod at any point in its stroke
活塞杆行程中任意点停止用气动夹头

5.4 Short passage for reading 阅读短文

Control Valves

Pressure control valves are used in hydraulic circuits to maintain desired pressure levels in various parts of the circuits. A pressure-control valve maintains the desired pressure level by (1) diverting higher-pressure fluid to a lower-pressure area, thereby limiting the pressure in the higher pressure area, or (2) restricting flow into another area. Valve that divert fluid can be safety, relief, counter-balance, sequence, and unloading types. Valves that restrict flow into another area can be of the reducing type.

A pressure-control valve may also be defined as either a normally closed or normally open two-way valve. Relief, sequence, unloading and counter-balance valves are normally closed, two-way valves that are partially or fully opened while performing their design function. A reducing valve is a normally open valve that restricts and finally blocks fluid flow into a secondary area. With either type of operation, the valve can be said to create automatically an orifice to provide the desired pressure control. An orifice is not always created when the valve is piloted from an external source. One valve of this type is the unloading valve——it is not self-operating; it depends on a signal from an external source. Relief, reducing, counterbalance, and sequence valves can be fully automatic in operation, with the operating signal taken from within the envelop.

控 制 阀

在液压回路中，压力控制阀用于保持回路各个部分的要求压力值。保持所需压力通过两种途径：(1) 将高压流体转移至低压区域，由此限制高压区域的压力值；(2) 限制流入另一区域的流量。这些转移流体的液压阀可以用作安全阀、溢流阀、背压阀、顺序阀和卸荷阀等不同类别。限制流入另一区域的流量的阀属于减压阀类型。

压力控制阀可定义为既可以是常闭的，也可为常开的双向阀。溢流阀、顺序阀、卸荷阀和背压阀在完成其设定功能时是部分或完全打开的双向阀。减压阀通常为常开阀，它限制或阻止流体流入另一区域。可以说以上两种情况都是靠阀形成的孔口来自动保证所需压力控制。阀在靠外部引导时，通常情况不需要形成孔口。卸荷阀就属于此类，它不是自己操控，而是取决于外部信号。借助来自工作区域的操控信号，溢流阀、减压阀、背压阀和顺序阀就可以实现全自动的运行。

Unit 6　Mechanical Manufacturing Technologies
机械制造技术与方法

6.1　Outline of manufacturing processes 各种制造工艺技术简图要览

Table 6.1　Casting processes　铸造工艺

Expendable pattern and mold and other 消失模具及其他	Expendable mold, permanent pattern 消失模具、永久性铸模	Permanent mold 金属永久性模具
Investment casting 熔模（失蜡）铸造	Sand casting 砂型铸造	Permanent-mold casting 永久性铸型
Lost foam casting 失沫铸造	Shell-mold casting 壳型造型	Die casting 压铸
Single-crystal casting 单晶铸造	Ceramic-mold casting 陶瓷模具铸造	Centrifugal casting 离心铸造
Melt-spinning process 熔旋快速固化		Squeeze casting 压实铸造

Table 6.2 Bulk deformation process 体积变形加工

Rolling 滚压、轧制	Forging 锻压	Extrusion and drawing 挤出与拉制
Flat rolling 平板轧制	Open die forging 自由锻	Direct extrusion 定向挤出
Shape rolling 型材轧制	Closed die forging 模锻	Cold extrusion 冷挤出
Ring rolling 环件轧制	heading 锻头	Drawing 棒料拉制
Roll forging 辊锻	Piercing 锻孔	Tube drawing 管材拉制

Table 6.3 Sheet metal processes 金属板材加工

Shearing 剪切	Bending and drawing 弯曲、拉制	Forming 成形
Blanking 落料	Bending 弯曲	Stretch forming 延展
Slitting 切开	Hemming 卷边	Hydroforming 液力挤压

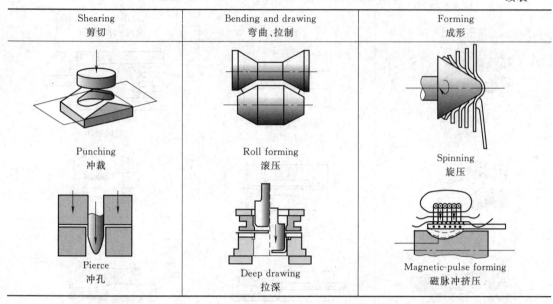

Table 6.4 Polymer processing 聚合物成型加工

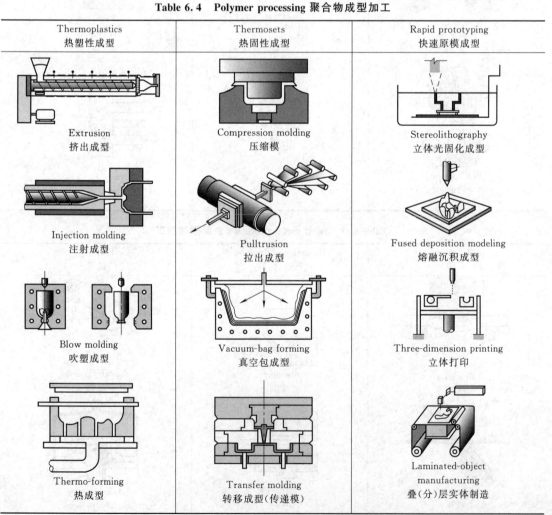

Table 6.5 Machining and finishing processes 去除加工和光整加工工艺

Table 6.6 Joining processes 连接工艺方法

续表

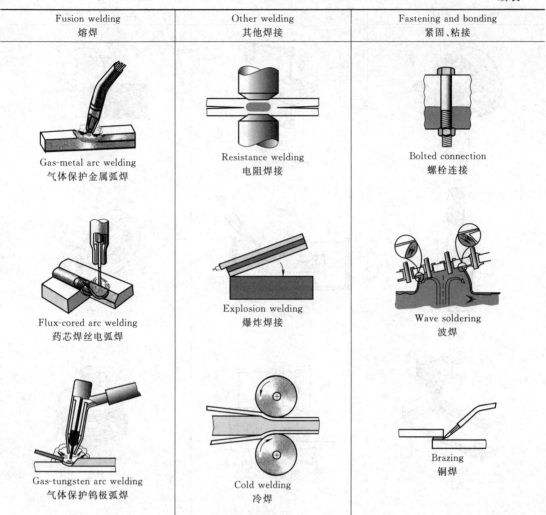

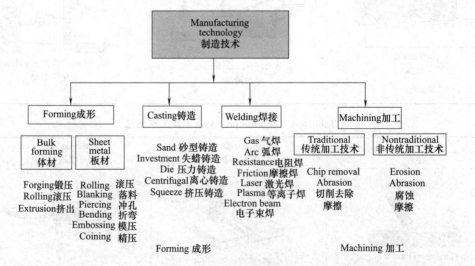

Fig. 6.1 Classification of manufacturing processes 制造技术分类

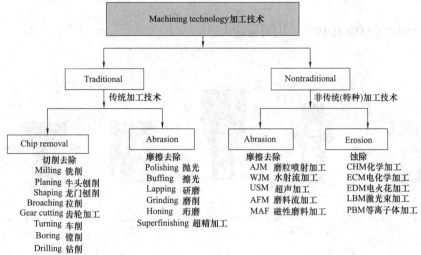

AJM,abrasive jet machining磨料喷射加工;WJM,water jet machining水射流加工;USM,ultrasonic machining 超声加工 AFM,abrasive flow machining磨料流加工;MAF,magnetic abrasive finishing磁性磨料加工;CHM,chemical machining 化学加工;ECM, electrochemical machining 电化学加工；EDM,electrodischarge machining 电火花加工;LBM,laser beam machining激光束加工； PBM plasma beam machining 等离子体加工

Fig. 6.2 Classification of machining processes 加工工艺分类

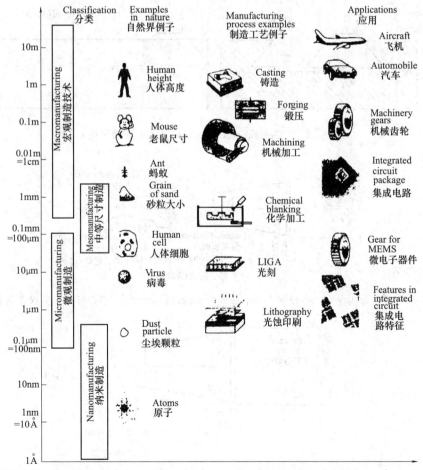

Fig. 6.3 Illustration of the regime of macro-，meso-，micro, and nano-manufacturing
宏观、中等尺寸、微观和纳米制造技术领域图解

6.2 Cutting principle 切削原理

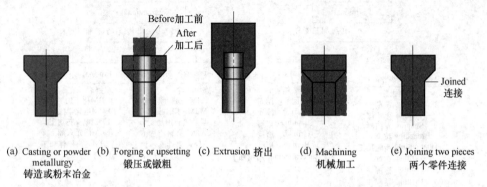

Fig. 6.4 Various methods of making a simple part 制造简单零件的几种方法

(1) Cutting 切削

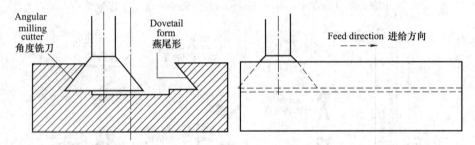

Fig. 6.5 Generation of surfaces 加工表面的形成

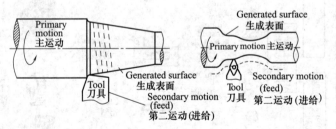

Fig. 6.6 Generation of cylindrical surface by a single point tool 单刀尖刀具生成外圆表面

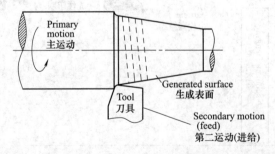

Fig. 6.7 Generation of a conical surface by a single point tool 单刀尖刀具生成外圆锥面

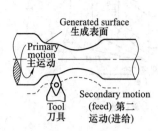

Fig. 6.8　Generation of a contoured surface with a single point tool
单刀尖刀具生成外轮廓面

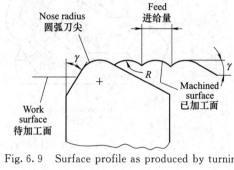

Fig. 6.9　Surface profile as produced by turning with a cutting tool having a nose radius
圆弧车刀车削表面形貌

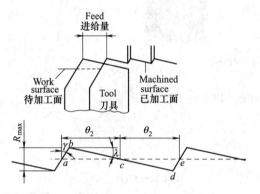

Fig. 6.10　Surface profile as produced by turning with a sharp cutting tool
普通尖角车刀车削表面形貌

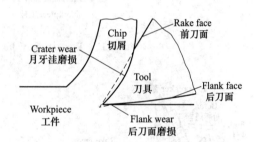

Fig. 6.11　Typical wear pattern present in cutting tools　刀具典型磨损形态

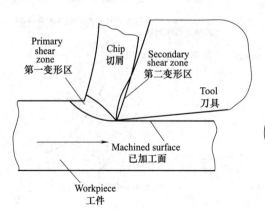

Fig. 6.12　The possible deformation in metal cutting
金属切削过程可能的变形

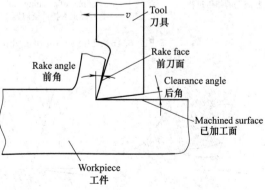

Fig. 6.13　The general characteristics of a metal cutting tool
金属切削刀具的通用特征

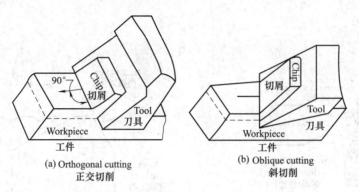

Fig. 6.14 Cutting methods 切削方式

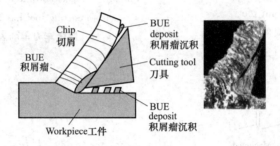

Fig. 6.15 Formation of built-up edge (BUE) 积屑瘤的形成

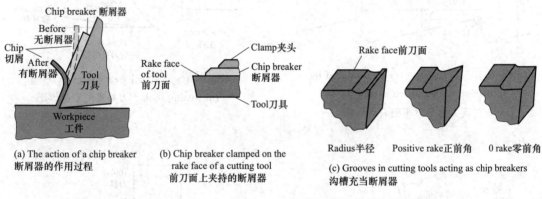

Fig. 6.16 The action of a chip breaker 断屑器的作用过程

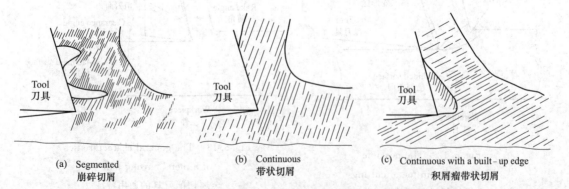

Fig. 6.17 Three main types of chips 三种主要的切屑

(2) Grinding 磨削

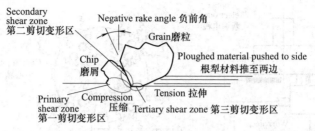

Fig. 6.18　The concept of shear zones applied to an abrasive grain　磨粒作用时剪切区的概念

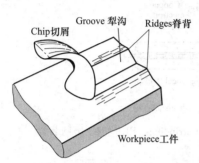

Fig. 6.19　Chip formation and plowing of the workpiece surface by an abrasive grain
磨粒对工件表面的根犁和切屑的形成

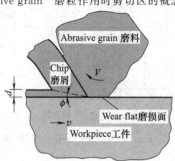

Fig. 6.20　Grinding chips　磨屑

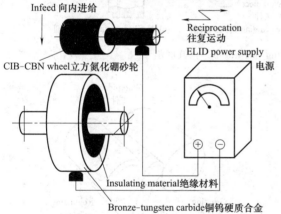

Fig. 6.21　ELID truing mechanism
在线电解修形磨削的机理

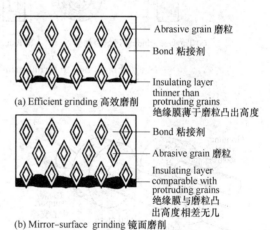

(a) Efficient grinding 高效磨削

(b) Mirror-surface grinding 镜面磨削

Fig. 6.22　Ideal wheel conditions
理想的砂轮状况

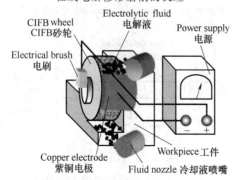

Fig. 6.23　Basic arrangement for ELID grinding
在线电解修形磨削的基本设计

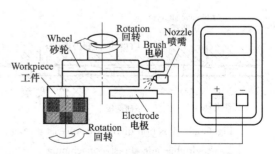

Fig. 6.24　Principle of ELID face-grinding
ELID 端面磨削的原理

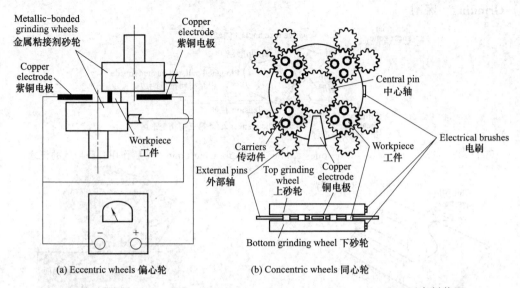

Fig. 6.25　Set-up for ELID duplex (double-sided) grinding　ELID 双面磨削装置

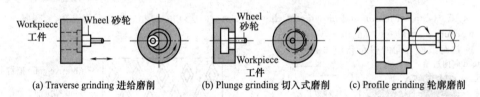

Fig. 6.26　Internal grinding operations　内圆磨削

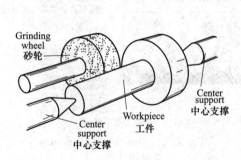

Fig. 6.27　Centered grinding　中心磨削

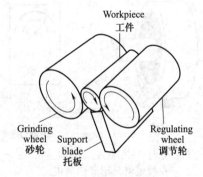

Fig. 6.28　Centerless grinding　无心磨削

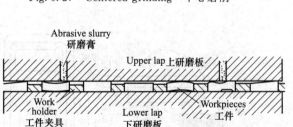

Fig. 6.29　Position of the workpieces during double-side abrasive machining
双面研磨加工的工件位置

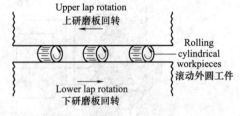

Fig. 6.30　Schematic showing cylindrical lapping method
外圆研磨方法

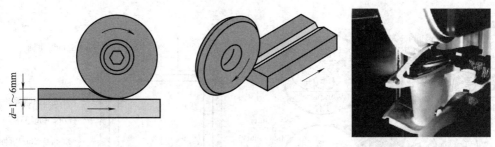

(a) Low work speed 低工件速度, v　(b) A shaped groove produced on a flat surface by creep-feed grinding in one pass 缓进给大吃深一次通过平面磨成形沟槽　(c) An example of creep-feed grinding with a shaped wheel 成形砂轮缓进给大吃深磨削例子

Fig. 6.31　Creep-feed grinding process　缓进给大吃深磨削

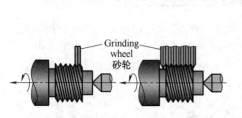

(a) Traverse 进给磨削　(b) Plunge grinding 切入式磨削

Fig. 6.32　Thread grinding　螺纹磨削

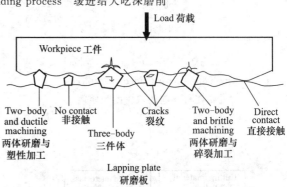

Fig. 6.33　Schematic showing two-body and three-body abrasion　两体和三体研磨

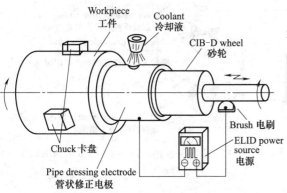

Fig. 6.34　Schematic of interval ELID grinding 间隙性 ELID 磨削布局

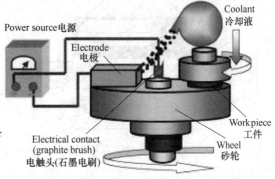

Fig. 6.35　Principle of ELID lap-grinding ELID 研磨原理

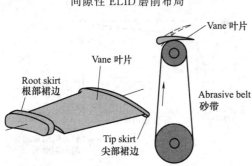

Fig. 6.36　Belt grinding of turbine nozzle vanes 砂带磨削涡轮喷嘴叶片

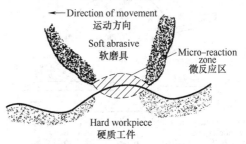

Fig. 6.37　The chemo-mechanical action between abrasive, work material, and environment 磨粒、工件及环境间的化学-机械作用

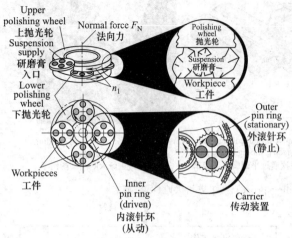

Fig. 6.38 Principle of two-wheel polishing with guided workpieces 带工件导向的双轮抛光原理

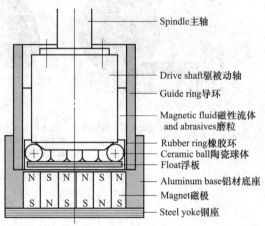

Fig. 6.39 The magnetic floating polishing apparatus used for polishing Si_3N_4 balls 用于抛光 Si_3N_4 球体的磁力浮动抛光装置

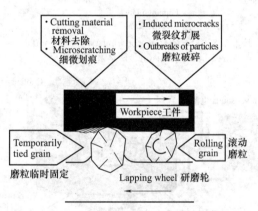

Fig. 6.40 Polishing of a plane surface 平面抛光

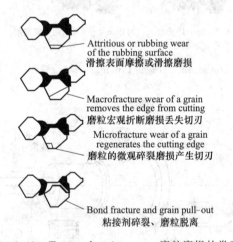

Fig. 6.41 Types of grain wear 磨粒磨损的类型

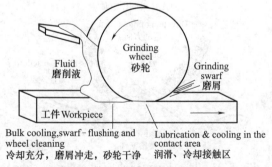

Fig. 6.42 The role of a process fluid in grinding 磨削时切削液的作用

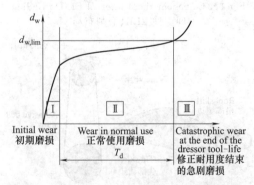

Fig. 6.43 Stages of grinding wheel wear 砂轮磨损的不同阶段

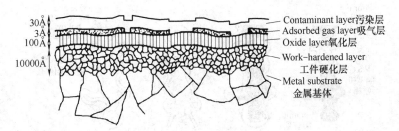

Fig. 6.44 Representation of a workmaterial complex structure on the cross section of the workpiece 工件截面上的材料复合结构

6.3 Heat process for metals 金属的热加工工艺

(1) Casting 铸造

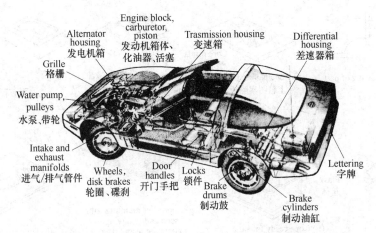

Fig. 6.45 Cast parts in a typical automobile 典型汽车中的铸件

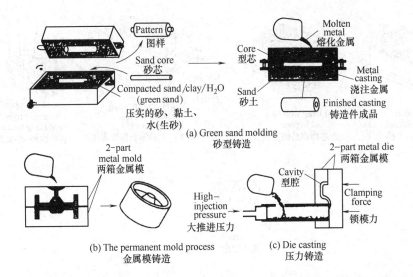

(a) Green sand molding 砂型铸造

(b) The permanent mold process 金属模铸造

(c) Die casting 压力铸造

Fig. 6.46

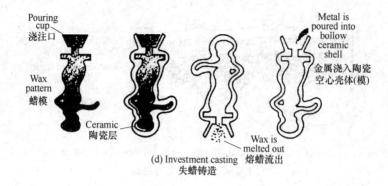

(d) Investment casting 失蜡铸造

Fig. 6.46 Four of the typical casting process 四类典型铸造工艺

(m) Casting ready for shippement 铸件待出厂

Fig. 6.47 Schematic illustration of the sequence of operations for sand casting 砂型铸造操作顺序

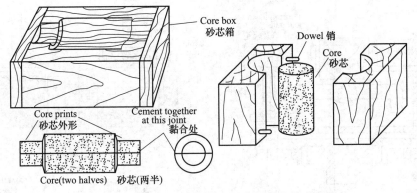

Fig. 6.48　Typical core boxes　典型砂芯铸造砂箱

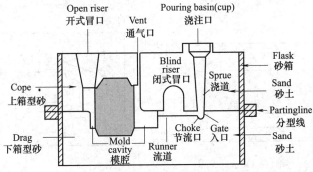

Fig. 6.49　Schematic illustration of a sand mold, showing various features　砂型模具结构特征

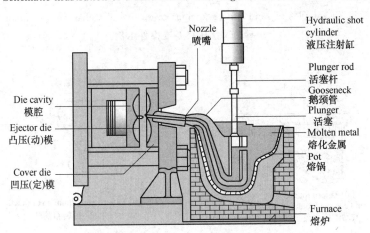

Fig. 6.50　Illustration of the hot-chamber　热室压铸工艺

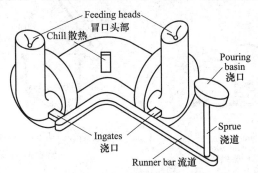

Fig. 6.51　Components of a running and feeding system　浇口和流道系统组件

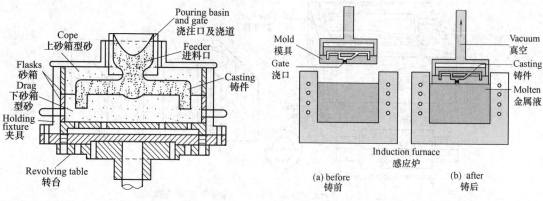

Fig. 6.52　Semi-centrifugal casting　半离心铸造工艺

Fig. 6.53　Vacuum casting process　真空铸造

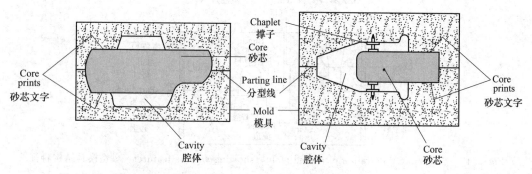

Fig. 6.54　Examples of sand cores showing core prints and chaplets to support core
砂芯文字图样及支撑件示例

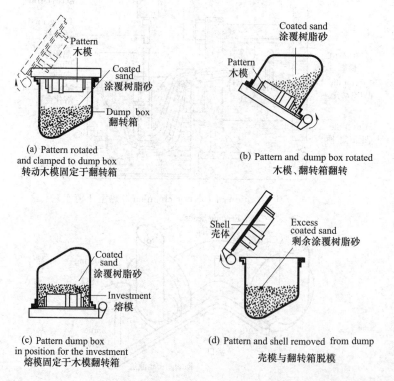

Fig. 6.55　A common method of making shell molds　壳模制备的常用方法

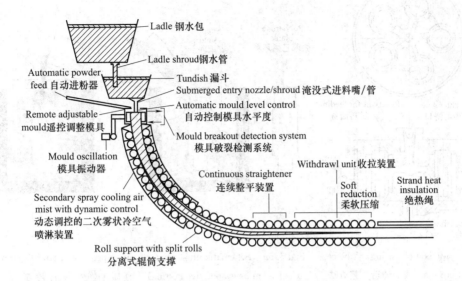

Fig. 6.56 Layout of a continuous slab casting machine with hot connection facility
具有热连接设施的平板连铸机构造

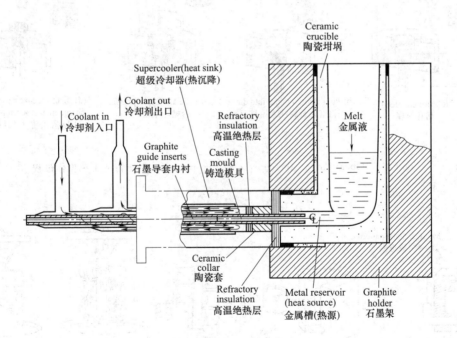

Fig. 6.57 Supercooler and containment for large diameter casting
大直径连铸的超级冷却器和容器

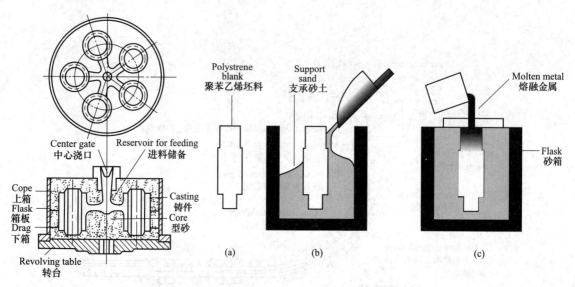

Fig. 6.58　Method of casting by the centrifugal process　离心铸造工艺方法

Fig. 6.59　Schematic illustration of the expendable pattern casting process (lost foam or evaporative casting)　消失模铸造（失沫铸造、蒸发铸造）

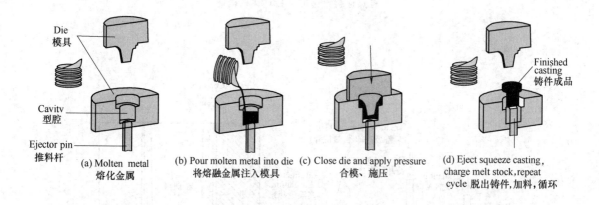

Fig. 6.60　Operations of the squeeze casting process　挤压铸造工艺操作过程

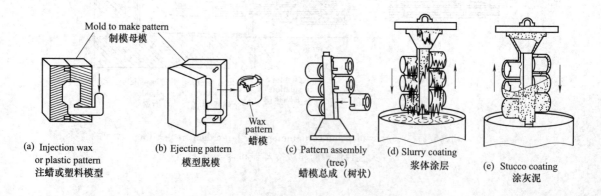

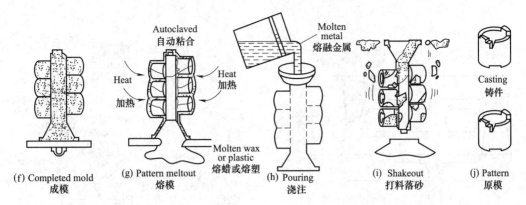

Fig. 6.61　Schematic illustration of investment casting (lost-wax process)　消失模铸造（失蜡浇铸）

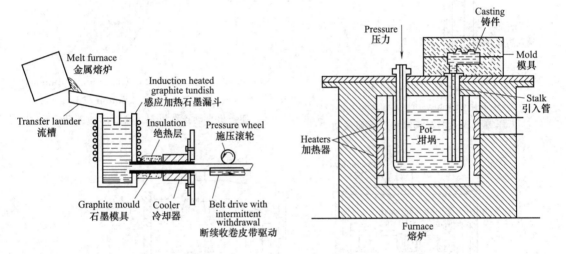

Fig. 6.62　Strip caster for copper base alloy
连续铸造铜基合金带材

Fig. 6.63　Diagram of low-pressure casting
低压铸造示意图

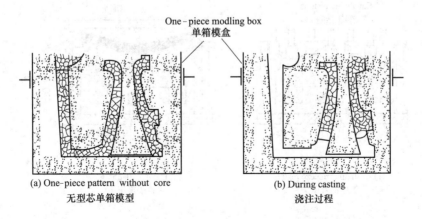

Fig. 6.64　The full-mold process utilizes a styrofoam pattern that is vaporized by the molten metal
利用熔融金属汽化聚苯乙烯发泡材料模芯的单箱模铸造工艺

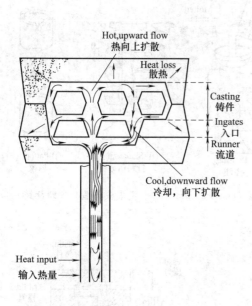

Fig. 6.65　Convection-driven, flow within a solidifying low-pressure casting
低压铸件固化的对流驱动的金属流动

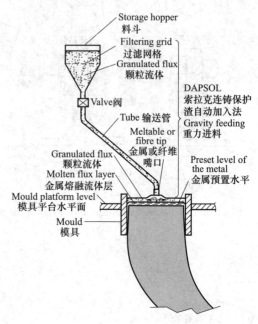

Fig. 6.66　Automatic flux feeder for continuous caster showing distribution of flux
连铸机自动连续进料装置展示的流量分布

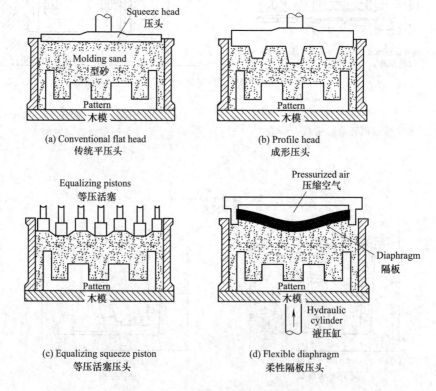

Fig. 6.67　Various designs of squeeze heads for mold making
砂型制模的几种压头设计

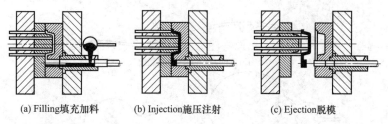

(a) Filling 填充加料　　(b) Injection 施压注射　　(c) Ejection 脱模

Fig. 6.68　Working principles of horizontal cold chamber high-pressure die casting machine
卧式冷室高压压力铸造机及工作原理

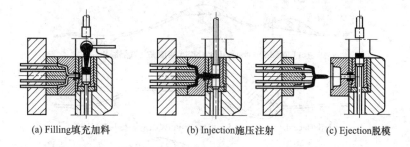

(a) Filling 填充加料　　(b) Injection 施压注射　　(c) Ejection 脱模

Fig. 6.69　Working principles of vertical cold chamber high-pressure die casting machine
立式冷室高压压力铸造机及工作原理

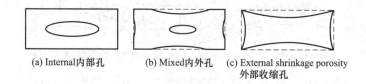

(a) Internal 内部孔　　(b) Mixed 内外孔　　(c) External shrinkage porosity 外部收缩孔

Fig. 6.70　The three regimes of shrinkage porosity　三种类别的收缩孔

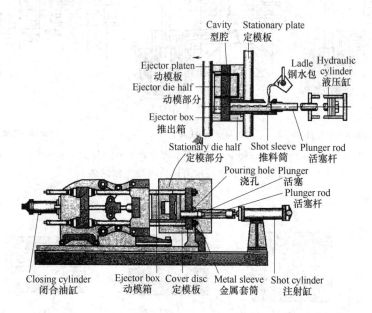

Fig. 6.71　Illustration of the cold-chamber die-casting process　冷室压铸机及其工艺示意图

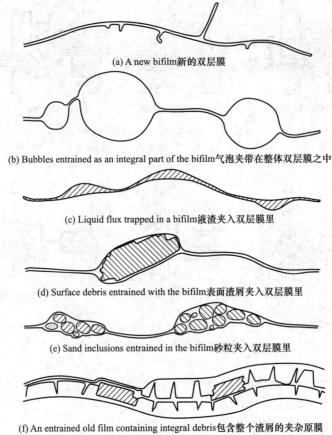

(a) A new bifilm 新的双层膜

(b) Bubbles entrained as an integral part of the bifilm 气泡夹带在整体双层膜之中

(c) Liquid flux trapped in a bifilm 液渣夹入双层膜里

(d) Surface debris entrained with the bifilm 表面渣屑夹入双层膜里

(e) Sand inclusions entrained in the bifilm 砂粒夹入双层膜里

(f) An entrained old film containing integral debris 包含整个渣屑的夹杂原膜

Fig. 6.72　Entrainment defects　夹杂缺陷

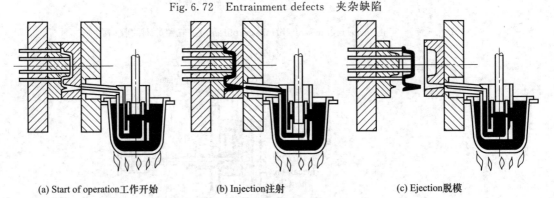

(a) Start of operation 工作开始　　(b) Injection 注射　　(c) Ejection 脱模

Fig. 6.73　Working principles of piston operated hot chamber high-pressure die casting machine 柱塞式热室高压压力铸造机及工作原理

(2) Forging　锻压

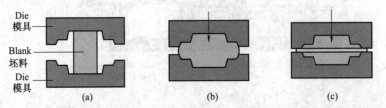

Fig. 6.74　Stages of impress-die forging of a solid round billet　整体圆形坯料的锻打过程

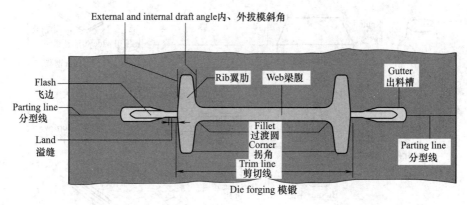

Fig. 6.75 Standard terminology of various features of a forging die 模锻标准术语

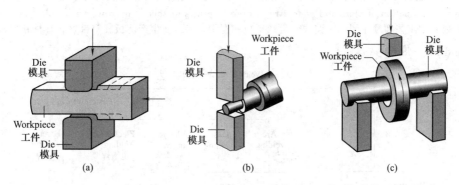

Fig. 6.76 Various operations of forging process with open-die 自由锻压加工操作

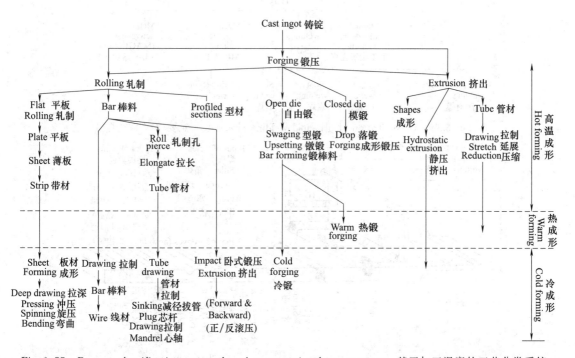

Fig. 6.77 Process classification system based on operational temperature 基于加工温度的工艺分类系统

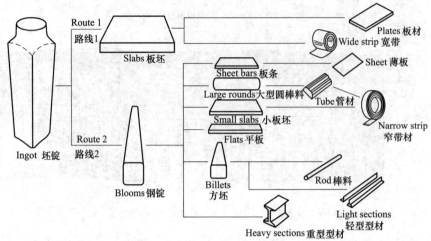

Fig. 6.78　Schematic, simplified representation of the sequences of the basic rolling processes. Route 1 leads to the production of plate and wide strip. Route 2 results in sheet, narrow strip, tube and sections.　轧制基本工艺和顺序图解：路线 1 生产平板和宽带，路线 2 生产薄板、窄带材、管材和型材

(3) Welding　焊接

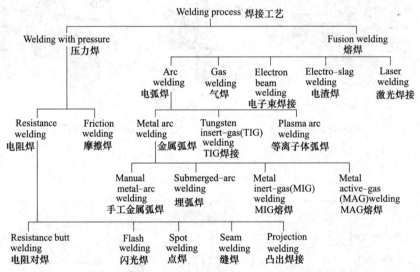

Fig. 6.79　Classification of principal welding processes　主要焊接工艺类别

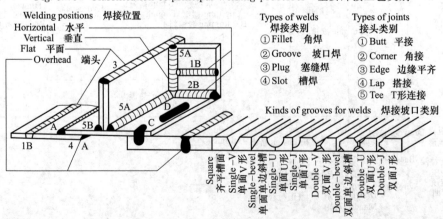

Fig. 6.80　Types of welded joints　焊接接口种类

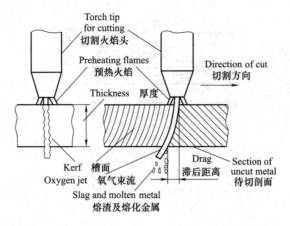

Fig. 6.81　Principles of flame cutting　火焰切割原理

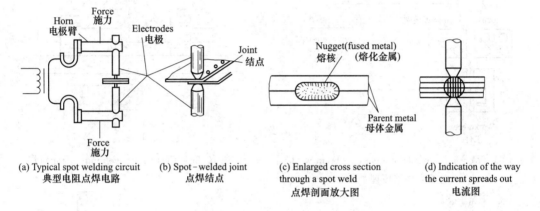

Fig. 6.82　Process of spot resistance welding　电阻点焊工艺

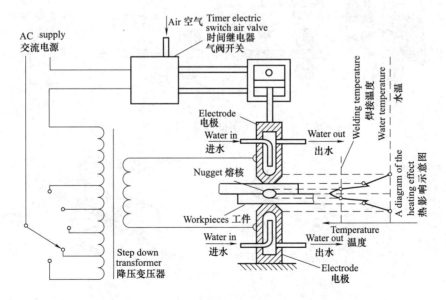

Fig. 6.83　Principle of resistance welding　电阻焊接原理

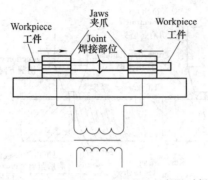

Fig. 6.84　Upset-butt welding　电阻对焊

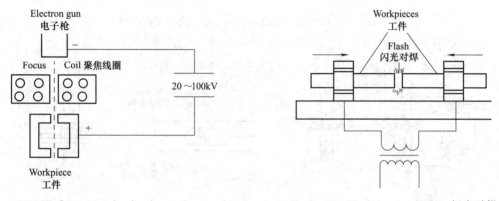

Fig. 6.85　Working principle of a electron beam welder
电子束焊接原理

Fig. 6.86　Flash-butt welding　闪光对焊

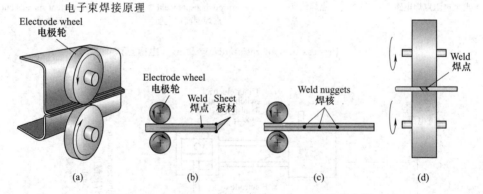

Fig. 6.87　Seam spot-welding process　缝隙的点焊

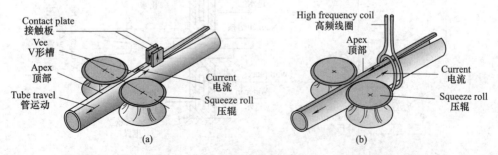

Fig. 6.88　Two methods of high-frequency continuous butt welding of tube
管的两种高频连续对焊方法

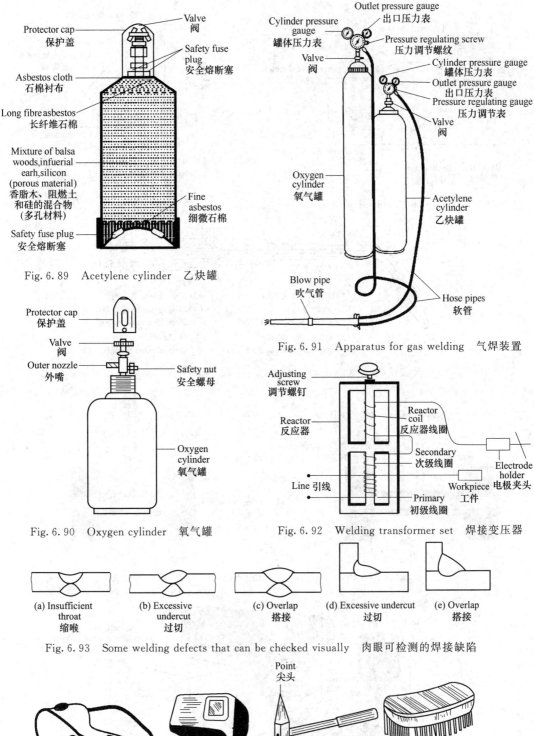

Fig. 6.89　Acetylene cylinder　乙炔罐

Fig. 6.90　Oxygen cylinder　氧气罐

Fig. 6.91　Apparatus for gas welding　气焊装置

Fig. 6.92　Welding transformer set　焊接变压器

Fig. 6.93　Some welding defects that can be checked visually　肉眼可检测的焊接缺陷

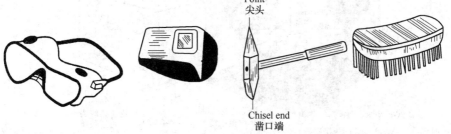

(a) Goggles 护目镜　　(b) Face shield 面罩　(c) Chipping hammer 除渣锤　　(d) Wire brush 钢丝刷

Fig. 6.94　Accessories　焊接用附件

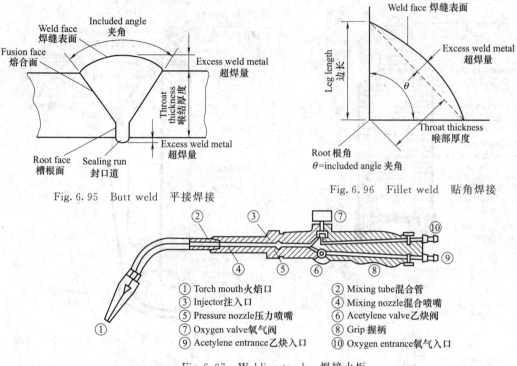

Fig. 6.95　Butt weld　平接焊接

Fig. 6.96　Fillet weld　贴角焊接

① Torch mouth 火焰口　② Mixing tube 混合管
③ Injector 注入口　④ Mixing nozzle 混合喷嘴
⑤ Pressure nozzle 压力喷嘴　⑥ Acetylene valve 乙炔阀
⑦ Oxygen valve 氧气阀　⑧ Grip 握柄
⑨ Acetylene entrance 乙炔入口　⑩ Oxygen entrance 氧气入口

Fig. 6.97　Welding torch　焊接火炬

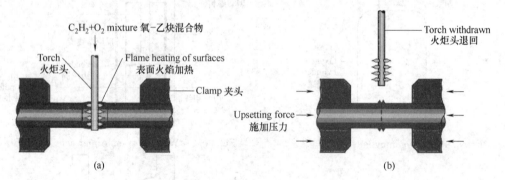

Fig. 6.98　Pressure-gas welding process　压力气体焊接工艺

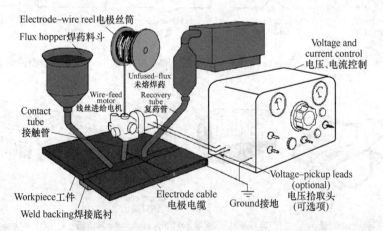

Fig. 6.99　Submerged-arc welding process and equipment　埋弧焊接工艺和设备

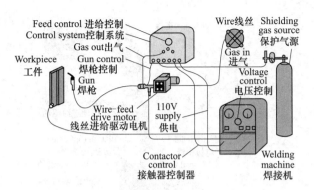

Fig. 6.100 Basic equipment used in gas metal-arc welding operations 惰性气体金属保护焊的基本设备

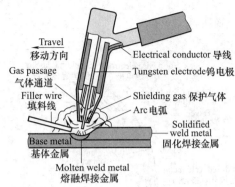

Fig. 6.101 The gas tungsten-arc welding process: formerly known as TIG (for tungsten inert gas) welding 钨电极气体保护焊，以前称为 TIG 焊接（钨电极惰性气体保护焊）

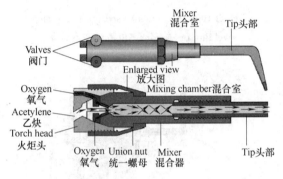

Fig. 6.102 General view of and cross-section of a torch used in oxyacetylene welding 氧乙炔焊接用火炬头的外观图和剖面图

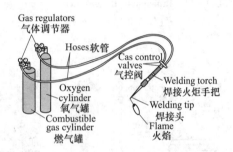

Fig. 6.103 Basic equipment used in oxyfuel-gas welding 氧乙炔焊接基本设备

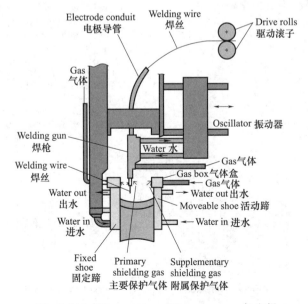

Fig. 6.104 Electrogas welding process 气电焊

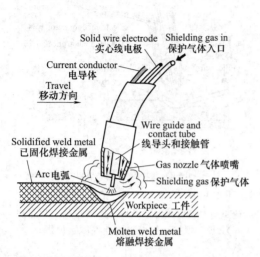

Fig. 6.105　Principle of the gas metal-arc process　气体保护金属电弧焊

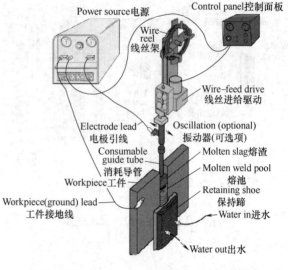

Fig. 6.106　Equipment used for electroslag welding operations　电渣焊基本设备

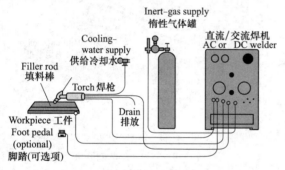

Fig. 6.107　Equipment for gas tungsten-arc welding operations　钨电极气体保护焊基本设备

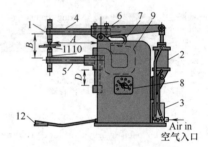

Fig. 6.108　An air-operated rocker-arm spot welding machine　气动摇臂式点焊机
D—Lower arm adjustment　下臂调整范围；A—Throat depth　喉部深度；B—Horn spacing　电极头开度；1—Centerline of rocker arm　摇杆中心线；2—Air cylinder　气缸；3—Air valve　气阀；4—Upper horn 上臂；5—Lower horn　下臂；6—Rocker arm　摇臂；7—Secondary flexible conductor　第二柔性导体；8—Current regulator (tap switch)　电流调节（旋钮）；9—Transformer secondary　变压器次级线圈；10—Electrode holder　电极夹头；11—Electrode　电极；12—Foot control　脚踏

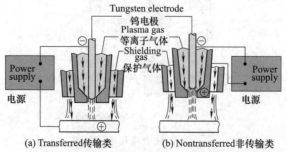

Fig. 6.109　Two types of plasma-arc welding processes　两类等离子弧焊接

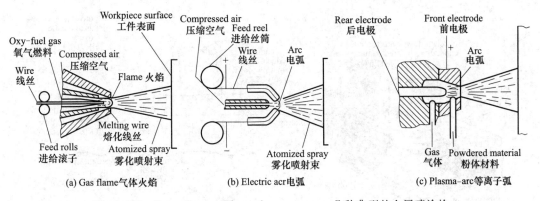

Fig. 6.110　Several types of metal spray guns　几种典型的金属喷涂枪

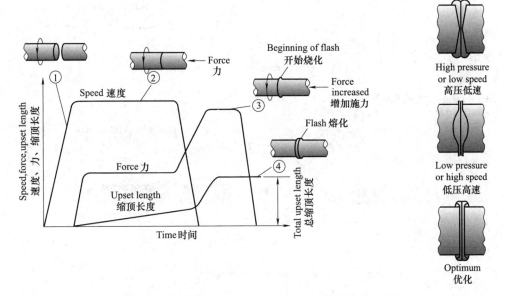

Fig. 6.111　Friction welding process　摩擦焊接工艺过程

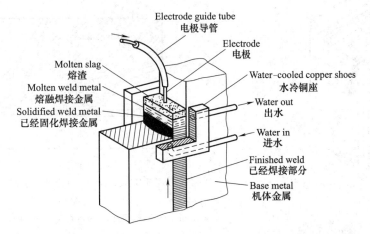

Fig. 6.112　Schematic sketch of electroslag welding　电熔渣焊接图解

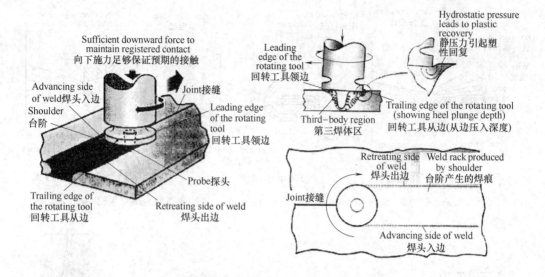

Fig. 6.113　Friction stir welding　摩擦激励焊接

(4) Soldering　低温焊接

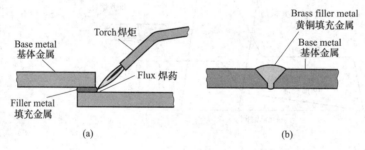

Fig. 6.114　Soldering and brazing　低温焊接和铜焊

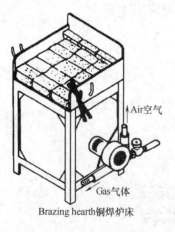

Fig. 6.115　Above about 800℃ the process is called 'brazing' (or hard soldering)
温度超过 800℃ 的焊接称为铜焊
(或硬低温焊接)

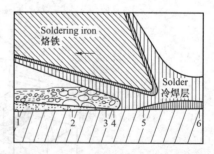

Fig. 6.116　Section of soldering　冷焊断面
1—Flux over oxidized metal　氧化层上的焊剂；2—Boiling flux removes oxide　熔化焊剂隔绝氧气；3—Base metal in contact with molten flux　基体金属与熔化焊剂接触；4—Molten solder displaces molten flux　熔焊材料排除熔化焊剂；
5—Solder alloys with base metal　冷焊合金与基体金属；
6—Solder solidifies　冷焊固化层

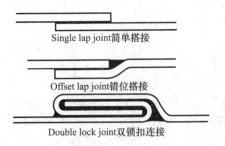

Fig. 6.117　Soldered joints　低温焊接连接

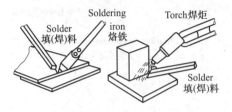

Fig. 6.119　Gas-air brazing torch
燃气/空气铜焊焊炬

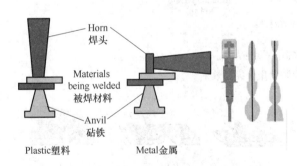

Fig. 6.121　Ultrasonic welding　超声波焊接

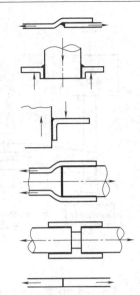

Fig. 6.118　Brazed joints　铜焊接头

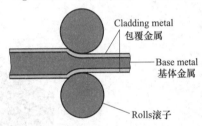

Fig. 6.120　Roll bonding or cladding process
滚压粘接或包覆工艺

Fig. 6.122　Pipe solder joint　低温焊接的管件

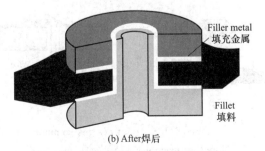

Fig. 6.123　An example of furnace brazing. Note that the filler metal is a shaped wire
炉内铜焊，注意填充金属就是成形金属线丝

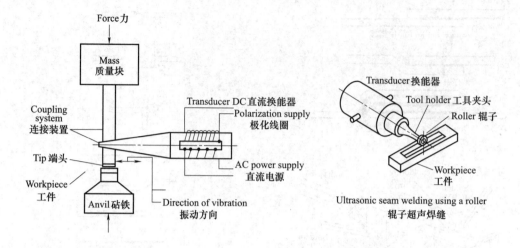

Fig. 6.124 Components of an ultrasonic welding machine for lap welds 搭接件的超声焊接装置

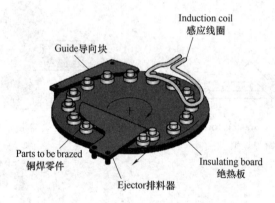

Fig. 6.125 A continuous induction-brazing setup: for increased productivity
连续感应加热铜焊装置用于提高效率

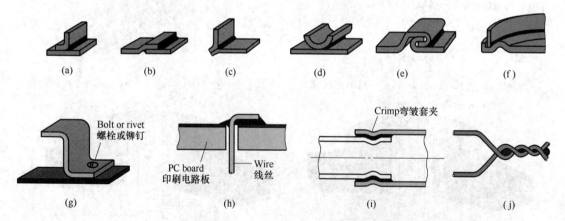

Fig. 6.126 Joint designs commonly used for soldering 低温焊接常用接头设计
[Note that examples (e), (g), (i), and (j) are mechanically joined prior to being soldered, for improved strength 例 (e), (g), (i), 和 (j) 焊前机械连接目的是增加强度]

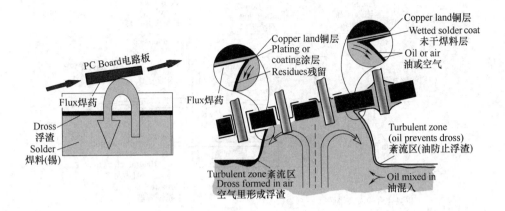

Fig. 6.127 Wave soldering process 波焊工艺

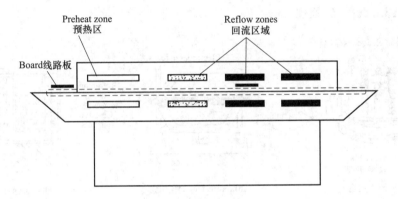

(a) An IR oven 红外炉

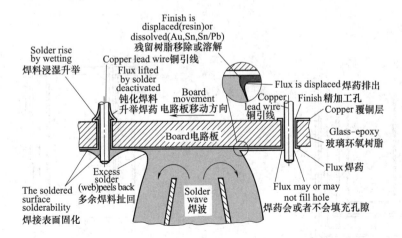

(b) Wave soldering 波焊

Fig. 6.128

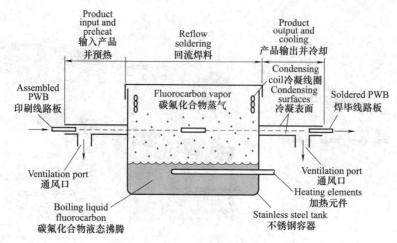

(c) Vapor phase condensation soldering 气相冷凝焊接

Fig. 6.128　Three commonly used soldering (or reflow soldering) facilities
三种常用（低温）焊接（回流焊接）设备

(5) Heat treatment　热处理

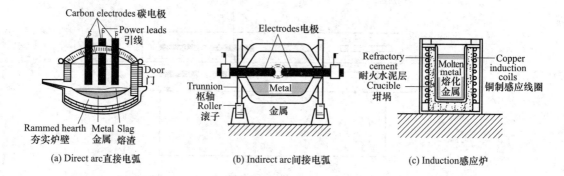

(a) Direct arc 直接电弧　　(b) Indirect arc 间接电弧　　(c) Induction 感应炉

Fig. 6.129　Types of electric furnaces　电炉类型

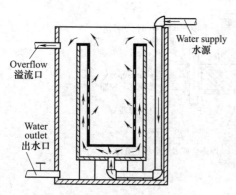

Fig. 6.130　A water or brine tank for quenching baths
淬火用的水箱或盐水箱

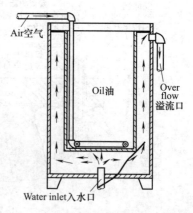

Fig. 6.131　An oil-quenching tank in which water is circulated in an outer surrounding tank to keep the oil bath cool　淬火用油箱，水绕油箱外围循环冷却油液

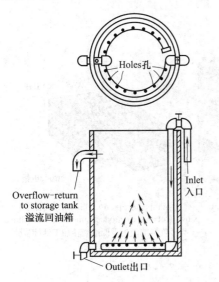

Fig. 6.132 Water or brine is pumped from the storage tank and continuously returned to it 水/盐水从储液箱泵入并流回箱体

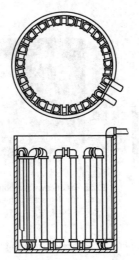

Fig. 6.133 Ordinary type of quenching tank cooled by water forced through a coil of pipe 水强制循环通过的普通淬火箱

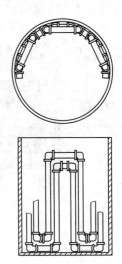

Fig. 6.134 Quenching tank with two coils of pipe 两套冷却管的淬火箱

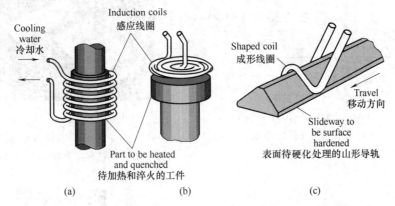

Fig. 6.135 Types of coils used in induction heating of various surfaces of parts
几种工件表面感应加热线圈型式

6.4 Non-traditional processes 非传统加工（特种加工）工艺方法

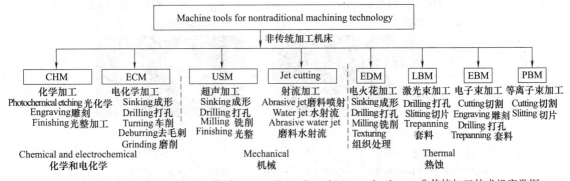

Fig. 6.136 Classification of machine tools for nontraditional machining technology 非传统加工技术机床类别

(1) EDM 电火花加工

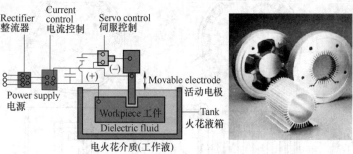
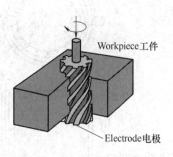

Examples of cavities produced by the electrical-discharge machining process 电火花加工型腔示例

A spiral cavity produced by EDM using a slowly rotating electrode, similar to a screw thread 类似攻螺纹的电极低速旋转加工螺旋型腔

Fig. 6.137 Electrical-discharge machining process 电火花加工工艺

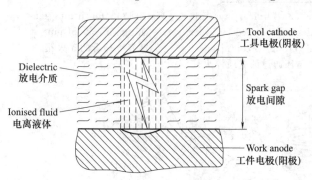

Fig. 6.138 Schematic diagram of arc formation in EDM process 电火花弧的形成

Fig. 6.139 Stepped cavities produced with a square electrode by the EDM process (EDM milling) 方形电极电火花加工的阶梯型腔（电火花铣切）

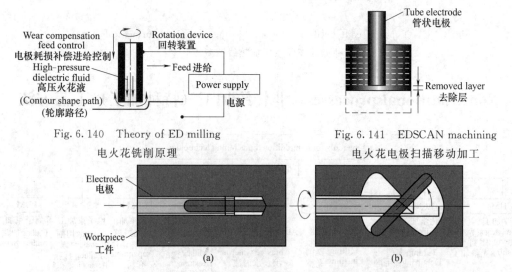

Fig. 6.140 Theory of ED milling 电火花铣削原理

Fig. 6.141 EDSCAN machining 电火花电极扫描移动加工

Fig. 6.142 Producing an inner cavity by EDM, using a specially designed electrode with a hinged tip, which is slowly opened and rotated to produce the large cavity
电火花加工内部空腔：电极特殊设计的端部铰链活动头进入孔后慢慢打开并回转形成大的空腔

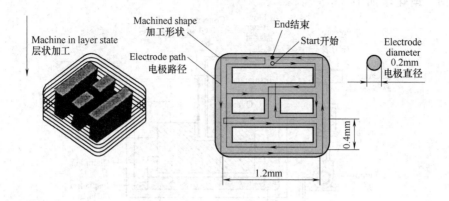

Fig. 6.143　Micro EDM　细微电火花加工

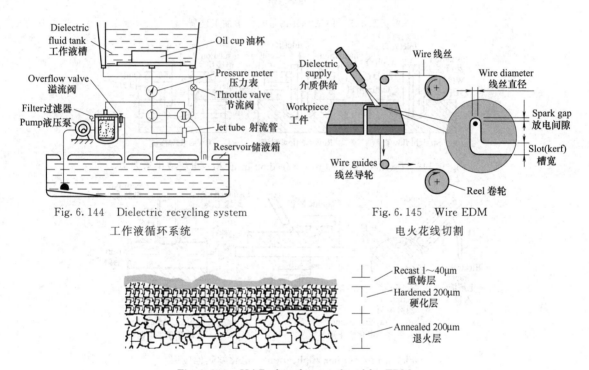

Fig. 6.144　Dielectric recycling system
工作液循环系统

Fig. 6.145　Wire EDM
电火花线切割

Fig. 6.146　HAZ of surface produced by EDM
电火花加工产生表面热烧伤层

Fig. 6.147　Wire EDM parts
电火花线切割工件

(2) ECM 电化学加工

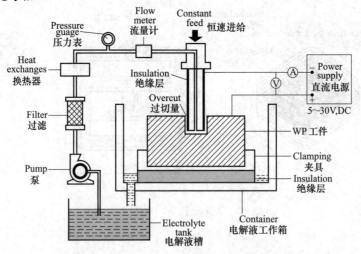

Fig. 6.148　ECM setup　电化学加工装置

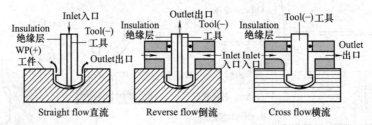

Fig. 6.149　Methods of electrolyte feeding in ECM　电解液供给方法

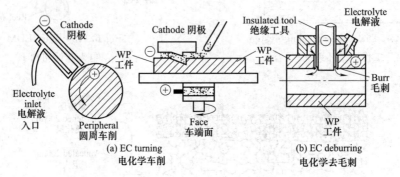

Fig. 6.150　Other applications　电化学其他应用

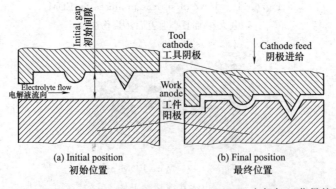

Fig. 6.151　Complimentary shape produced by ECM　电解加工获得的形状

(a) Hole sinking with insulated tool 绝缘工具沉孔

(b) EC sinking of stepped through hole 阶梯沉孔

(c) EC trepanning 套料

(d) ECM of internal cavity by stationary electrode 工具静止孔内部扩孔

(e) ECM of turbine blade 涡轮叶片加工

(f) EC deep hole drilling 深孔加工

(g) EC surfacing 平面加工

(h) EC hogging 拱起加工

Fig. 6.152　Typical ECM applications　典型电化学加工

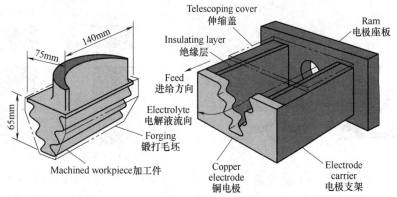

(a) Turbine blade made of a nickel alloy 360HB 镍合金(360HB)涡轮叶片

Fig. 6.153

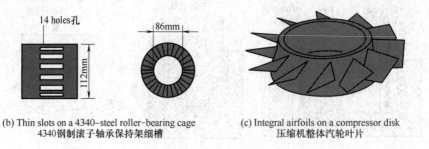

(b) Thin slots on a 4340-steel roller-bearing cage
4340钢制滚子轴承保持架细槽

(c) Integral airfoils on a compressor disk
压缩机整体汽轮叶片

Fig. 6.153　Typical parts made by electrochemical machining　电化学加工的典型零件

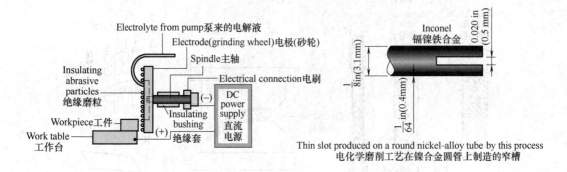

Fig. 6.154　Electrochemical-grinding process　电化学磨削工艺

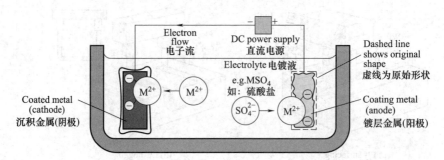

Fig. 6.155　Electroplating process　电镀工艺

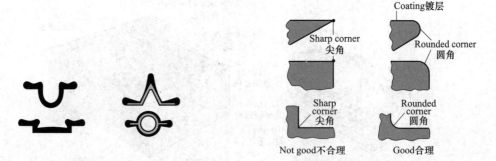

Fig. 6.156　Nonuniform coatings (exaggerated) in electroplated parts
电镀件不均匀的镀层（夸张放大）

Fig. 6.157　Design guidelines for electroplating
电镀工艺设计要点

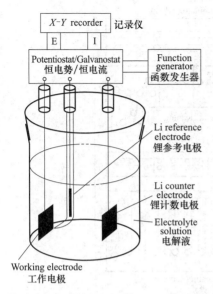

Fig. 6.158 Schematic illustration of an electrochemical cell 电化学电池图解

Fig. 6.159 Electroplated 3D stator winding for microgenerator 电镀微发电机的 3D 定子绕组

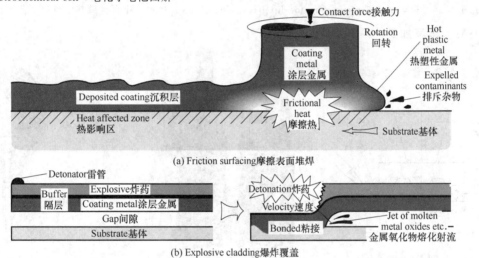

Fig. 6.160 Coating processes based on deposition in the solid state 基于固体状态沉积的涂层工艺

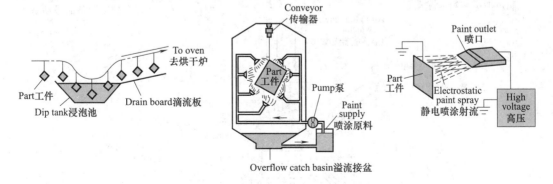

(a) Dip coating 浸泡涂层　　(b) Flow coating 流动喷涂　　(c) Electrostatic spraying 静电喷涂

Fig. 6.161 Methods of paint application 喷涂实施方法

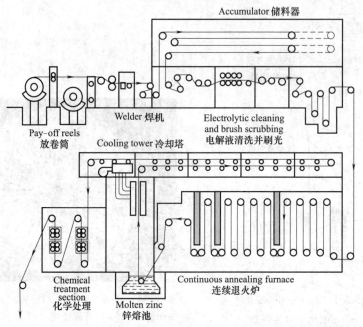

Fig. 6.162　Flowline for continuous hot-dip galvanizing of sheet steel　钢板连续热浸镀锌工艺流程

(3) USM　超声加工

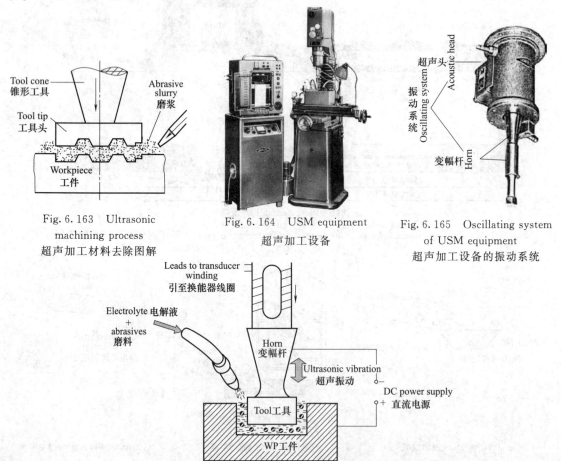

Fig. 6.163　Ultrasonic machining process 超声加工材料去除图解

Fig. 6.164　USM equipment 超声加工设备

Fig. 6.165　Oscillating system of USM equipment 超声加工设备的振动系统

Fig. 6.166　The ECUSM hybrid process　电解超声复合加工

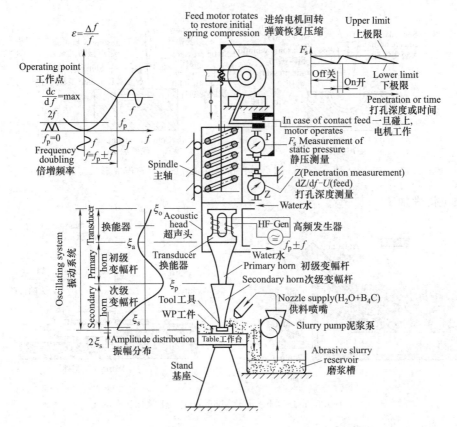

Fig. 6.167　Schematic of complete vertical USM equipment　立式超声加工机图解

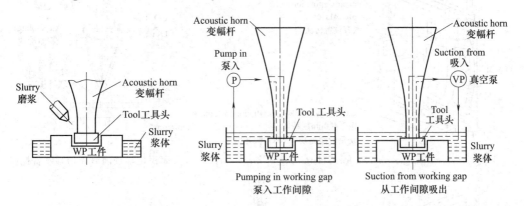

(a) Nozzle supply system 喷嘴系统　　(b) Pumping in or suction from working gap 泵入工作间隙或从工作间隙吸出

Fig. 6.168　Slurry supplying system　磨浆供给系统

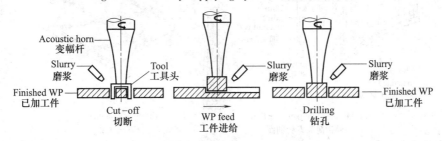

Fig. 6.169　Rotary ultrasonic machining (RUM)　回转超声加工

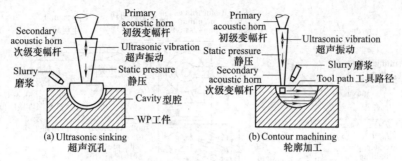

Fig. 6.170 Sinking (conventional) and contouring USM 超声成形加工和轮廓加工

(4) CM 化学加工

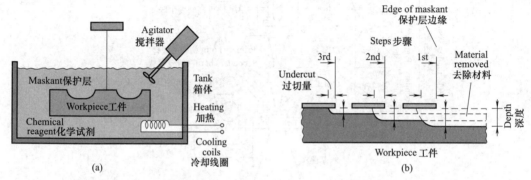

Fig. 6.171 Chemical Machining 化学加工

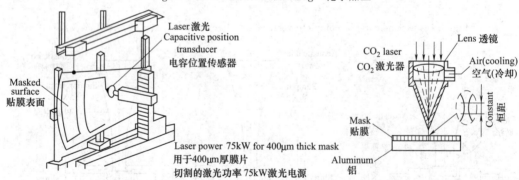

Fig. 6.172 Laser cutting of masks for CH-milling of large surfaces 大面积化学铣削激光切割制备掩膜

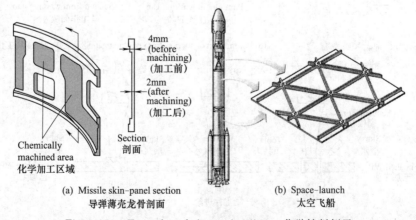

Fig. 6.173 Examples of chemical milling 化学铣削例子

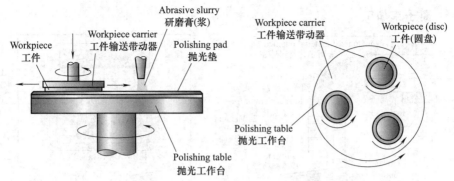

Fig. 6.174　Chemical-mechanical polishing process (CMP)　化学机械抛光

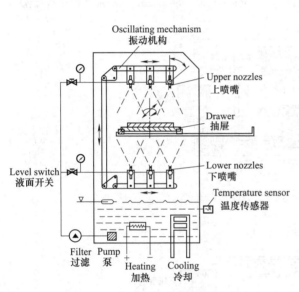

Fig. 6.175　Schematic of PCM equipment
光化学加工设备图解

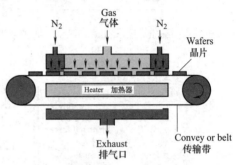

Fig. 6.176　Continuous, atmospheric-pressure CVD reactor　连续大气压力化学气相沉积反应器

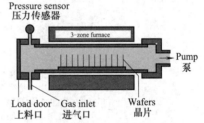

Fig. 6.177　low-pressure CVD
低压化学气相沉积

(5) EBM　电子束加工

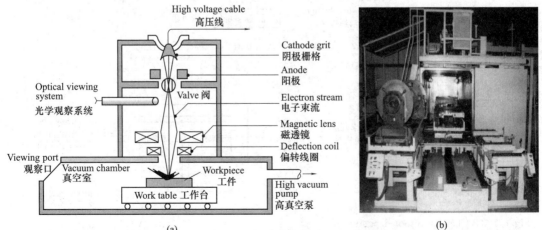

Fig. 6.178　electron-beam process　电子束加工

(6) IBM 离子束加工

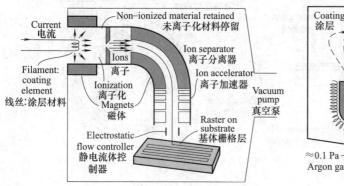

Fig. 6.179　Ion implantation process　离子注入工艺

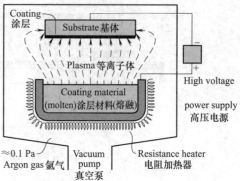

Fig. 6.180　Ion-plating process　离子镀过程

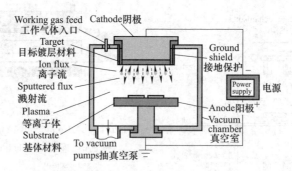

Fig. 6.181　Sputtering process　阴极真空喷镀工艺

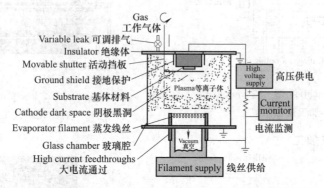

Fig. 6.182　An ion-plating apparatus　离子镀装置

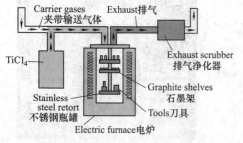

Fig. 6.183　Chemical vapor deposition process (CVD)　化学气相沉积工艺

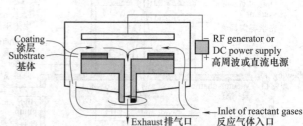

Fig. 6.184　PECVD process　等离子体增强化学气相沉积工艺

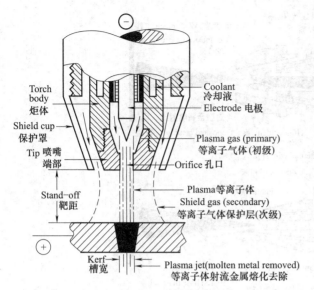

Fig. 6.185 Constructional assembly of transferred plasma torch 约束等离子炬装置图解

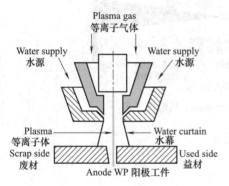

Fig. 6.186 Water-shielded plasma 水套保护等离子体

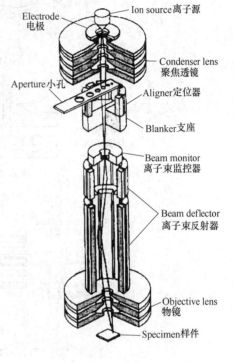

Fig. 6.187 Schematic diagram of the FIB (focused ion beam) system 聚焦离子束系统图解

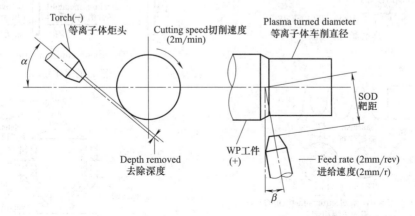

Fig. 6.188 Plasma arc turning (PAT) 等离子弧车削

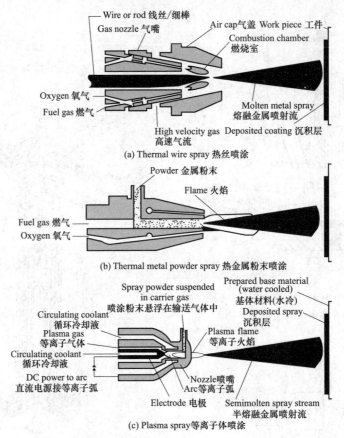

Fig. 6.189　Thermal spray operations　热喷涂工艺

(7) LBM　激光束加工

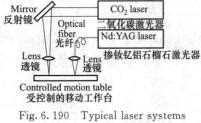

Fig. 6.190　Typical laser systems
典型激光系统

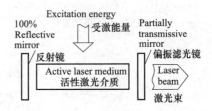

Fig. 6.191　Basic components of a laser
激光的基本组成

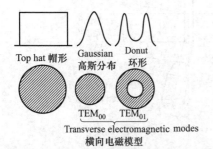

Fig. 6.192　Spatial intensity distribution in laser beams　激光束的空间能量密度分布

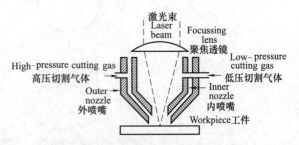

Fig. 6.193　Laser gas cutting nozzle for steel　激光气体切割钢材喷嘴

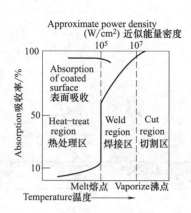

Fig. 6.194 Laser energy absorption intensity vs. temperature 激光能量吸收强度与温度的关系

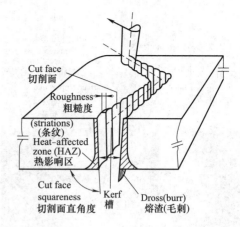

Fig. 6.195 Factors in laser cutting 激光切割要素

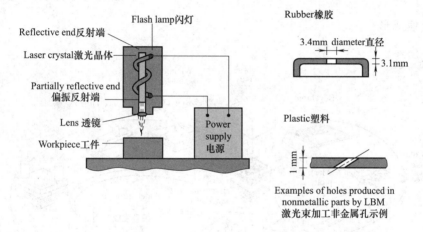

Fig. 6.196 Laser-beam machining process 激光束加工工艺

(a) Cutting sheet metal with a laser beam 激光切割板材

(b) Microscopic gear with a diameter on the order of 100μm, made by a special etching process 特殊的蚀出工艺加工的直径为100μm量级的显微齿轮

Fig. 6.197 Examples of parts made by advanced machining processes 先进制造技术加工的零件示例

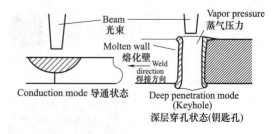

Fig. 6.198 Types of laser welds 激光焊接种类

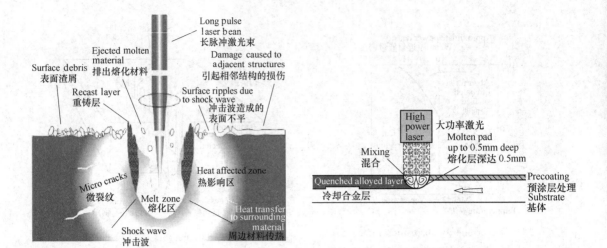

Fig. 6.199　Laser ablation　激光烧蚀加工

Fig. 6.200　Laser surface alloying process　激光表面合金化处理工艺

(8) RP 快速成形

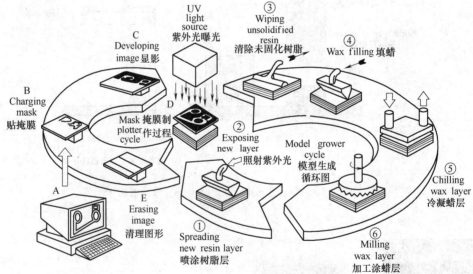

Fig. 6.201　Solid-base-curing process　固态基体凝固过程

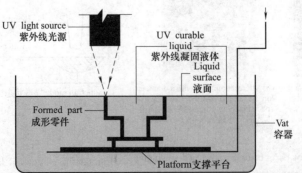

Fig. 6.202　Stereolithography process　液相立体固化成形工艺

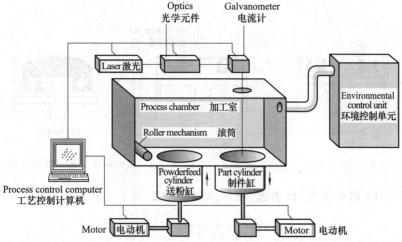

Fig. 6.203　Selective-laser-sintering process (SLS)　选择性激光烧结成形工艺

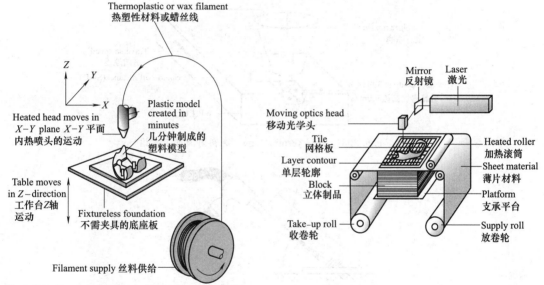

Fig. 6.204　Fused-deposition-modeling process (FDM)
熔丝堆积成形工艺

Fig. 6.205　Laminated-object-manufacturing process (LOM)
薄片分层叠层制造

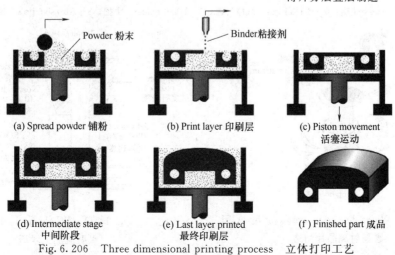

Fig. 6.206　Three dimensional printing process　立体打印工艺

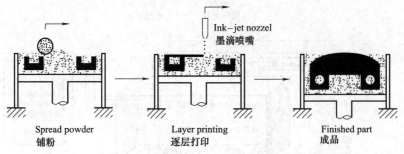

Fig. 6.207 Ink-jet binding process (3D printing) 喷绘粘接工艺（立体打印）

（9）AJ/WJ/AWJ 磨料射流/水射流/磨料水射流加工

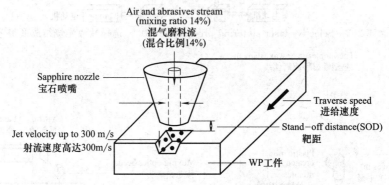

Fig. 6.208 AJM terminology 磨料射流加工术语

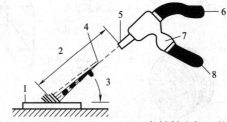

Fig. 6.209 AJM inclination angle 磨料射流加工的倾斜角度

1—WP 工件；2—Stand-off distance（SOD）靶距；3—Jet angle 喷射角度；4—AJ 磨料射流；5—Nozzle 喷嘴；6—Carrier gas 载体气源；7—Hand holder 手把；8—Abrasive flow 磨料流

Fig. 6.210 Wafer disc edge trimming by AJM 磨料射流晶片切边

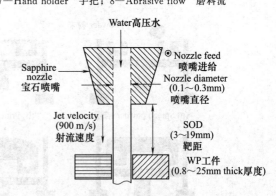

Fig. 6.211 WJM terminology 水射流加工术语

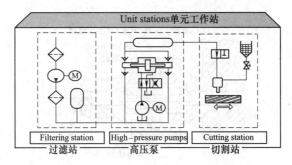

Fig. 6.212　Simplified layout of WJM equipment　水射流加工设备简易布局

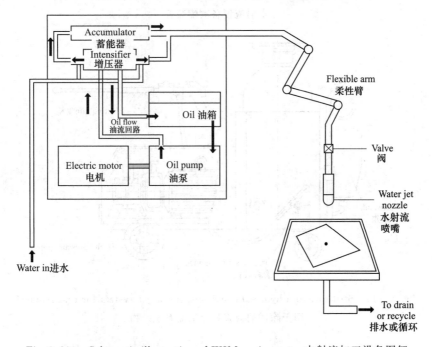

Fig. 6.213　Schematic illustration of WJM equipment　水射流加工设备图解

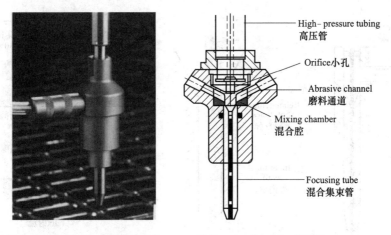

(a) Ingersoll-Rand(1996)英格索兰产品　　(b) Cross-sectional view 剖面图

Fig. 6.214　Jet former　喷嘴结构

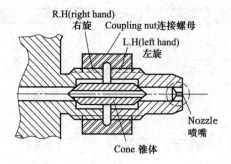

Fig. 6.215　Nozzle assembly of WJM equipment
水射流设备喷嘴装置

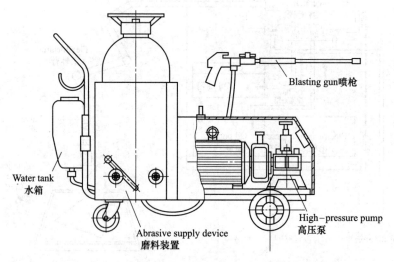

Fig. 6.216　Structure of a hydro-abrasive suspension jet system for rust removal
用于除锈的磨浆悬浮射流系统结构

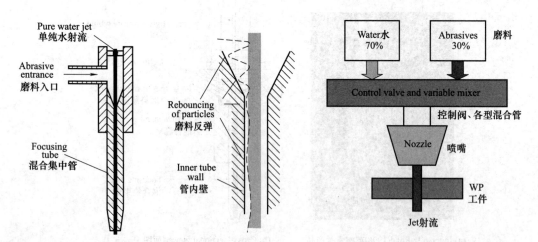

Fig. 6.217　Abrasive acceleration in the focusing tube
混合集中管内磨料加速

Fig. 6.218　AWJM elements terminology
磨料水射流元件术语

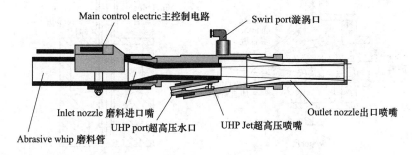

Fig. 6.219 Two-stage acceleration process of abrasive particles in an injection system
磨料水射流的两级加速过程

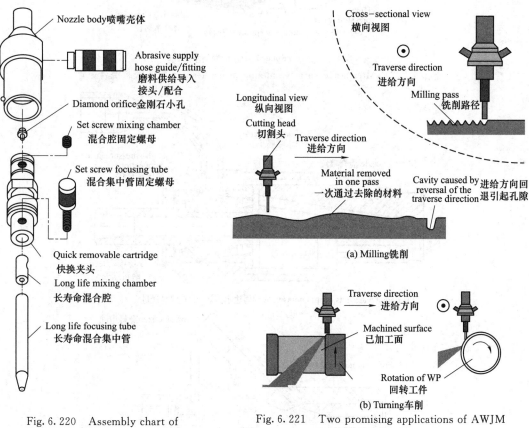

Fig. 6.220 Assembly chart of jet former AWJM
磨料水射流喷嘴前端组件图

Fig. 6.221 Two promising applications of AWJM
磨料水射流未来十分看好的两种应用

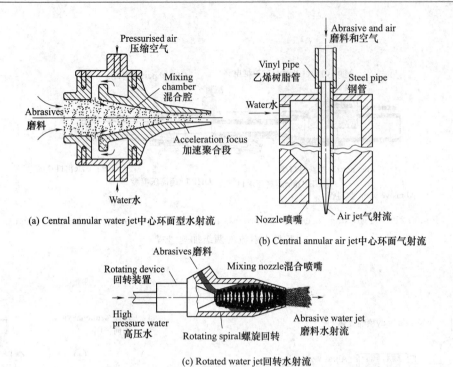

Fig. 6.222 Alternative abrasive mixing principles 不同的磨料混合原理

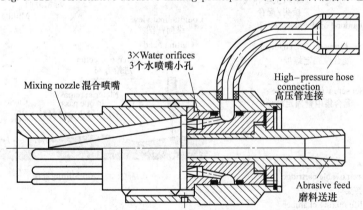

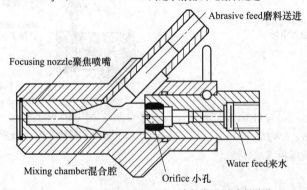

Fig. 6.223 Abrasive mixing devices for injection jet formation 注入式射流形成的磨料混合装置

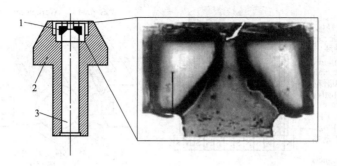

Fig. 6.224　Typical hydroblasting nozzle　典型高压水喷射喷嘴
1—Sapphire inlet　宝石喷嘴；2—Nozzle holder　喷嘴座；3—Flow stabilizer　流体稳定器

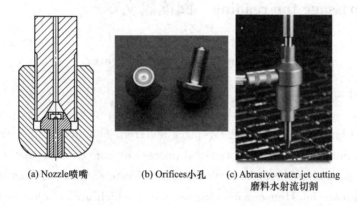

(a) Nozzle 喷嘴　　(b) Orifices 小孔　　(c) Abrasive water jet cutting 磨料水射流切割

Fig. 6.225　Water jet cutting nozzle　水射流切割喷嘴

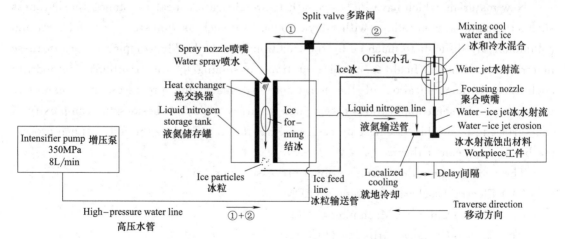

Fig. 6.226　Schematic diagram of an ice formation system, based on spray cooling
基于喷雾冷却的制冰系统图解

(10) MAM 磁性磨料加工

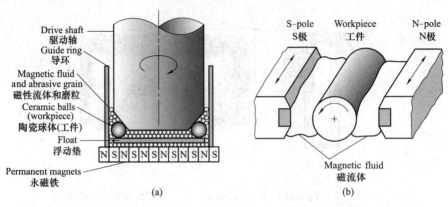

Fig. 6.227　Magnetic fluid and abrasive polishing　磁流体和磨粒抛磨球体和辊柱

6.5　Short passage for reading　阅读短文

Need for Unconventional Process

　　Conventional machining processes utilize the ability of the cutting tool to stress the material beyond the yield point to start the material removal process. This requires that the cutting tool material be harder than the workpiece material. The advent of harder materials for aerospace applications have made the removal process by conventional methods very difficult as well as time consuming since the material removal rate reduces with an increase in hardness of the work material. Hence machining processes which utilize other methods such as electro-chemical processes for material removal have been developed. These processes are termed as unconventional or non-traditional machining methods.

　　New materials which have high strength to weight ratio, heat resistance and hardness such as nimonic alloys, alloys with alloying elements such as tungsten, molybdenum and columbium are difficult to machine by the traditional methods. The complex shapes in these materials are either difficult to machine or time consuming by the traditional methods. In such cases, the application of the non-traditional machining processes finds extensive use. Further, in some applications a very high accuracy is desired besides the complexity of the surface to be machined. These processes are not meant to replace the conventional processes but to supplement them.

　　There are a number of unconventional processes. They are:
　　(ⅰ) Electric Discharge Machining (EDM)
　　(ⅱ) Electro Chemical Machining (ECM)
　　(ⅲ) Electro Chemical Grinding (ECG)
　　(ⅳ) Ultrasonic Machining (USM)
　　(ⅴ) Laser Beam Machining (LBM)
　　(ⅵ) Chemical Machining (CHM)

(Ⅶ) Abrasive Jet Machining (AJM)
(Ⅷ) Water Jet Machining (WJM)
(Ⅸ) Plasma Arc Machining (PAM)

The conventional metal cutting processes make use of the shearing process as the basis for material removal. However, non-traditional processes depend on a number of other factors such as the vaporization of the metal, electrolytic displacement, chemical reaction and mechanical erosion. The main reasons for using non-traditional machining processes are high strength alloys, complex surfaces and higher accuracies and surface finish.

High strength alloys The hardness of the work material is often higher than the cutting tool material and sometimes it becomes unnecessary to use the machining process on hardened material. In such cases the electro-chemical processes would be required.

Complex surfaces There are times when very complex surfaces in three dimensions need to be produced, such as those in moulds and dies where the workpiece surface being the hardened tool steel would be difficult to be processed by conventional means.

Higher accuracies and surface finish The accuracy and surface finish desired in hard workpiece materials cannot be obtained through conventional machining as it is done at a very slow pace, making it uneconomical.

In addition to the complex geometries, sometimes it is required to produce difficult geometries such as long holes with length to diameter ratio approaching that of 100, or very small size holes such as those with less than 0.1 mm in diameter which are almost impossible to be produced by conventional methods.

非传统工艺的必要性

传统加工工艺是利用刀具能够施加于超过工件材料屈服点的应力而达到材料去除，这就要求刀具材料的硬度比工件材料更硬。航空领域硬质材料的出现使传统方法去除材料十分困难，并且费工费时，因为材料去除率随工件硬度的增加而降低。由此使用诸如电化学加工去除材料的其他工艺方法应运而生。这些工艺被称为非常规或非传统的加工方法。

传统方法难于加工的新材料有高强度重量比材料、高抗热材料、高硬度材料，诸如镍合金或含有合金元素为钨、钼、铌的合金。采用传统方法加工这些材料的复杂形状要么困难重重，要么费工费时。如此情况，非传统工艺获得广泛应用。更有甚者，某些场合的待加工面不仅形状复杂，而且精度要求极高。（需要说明的是）非传统方法并非一定要取代传统方法，但是它们是传统方法的必要补充。

非传统加工方法多种多样，分别是：
ⅰ. 电火花加工；ⅱ. 电化学加工；ⅲ. 电化学磨削加工；ⅳ. 超声加工；ⅴ. 激光束加工；ⅵ. 化学加工；ⅶ. 磨料喷射加工；ⅷ. 水射流加工；ⅸ. 等离子弧加工

常规的金属切削工艺以剪切为基础去除材料。而非传统工艺依靠其他要素（去除材料），诸如金属的汽化、电解移除、化学反应和机械蚀出。采用非传统工艺的主要原因有高强度合金、复杂表面、更高的精度和较低的表面粗糙度（高的表面光洁度）。

高强度合金：工件材料硬度常常高于刀具材料，有时对于硬化材料再无必要采用机械加工方法。这种情况可以考虑电化学方法。

复杂表面：有时需要加工三维的复杂表面，如模具表面，其表面的硬化工具钢材料很难用常规方法加工。

高精度和低的粗糙度：硬质工件材料在要求高精度和低粗糙度时，常规方法不能达到，因为其加工节拍太慢而成本增加。

除了几何形状复杂情况之外，有时还会要求加工难于达到的几何尺寸，例如长径比达到100的深长孔或直径小于0.01mm的极小孔，这些孔的加工采用常规方法几乎是不可能的事。

Unit 7　NC Machining and NC Machine Tools
数控加工与数控机床

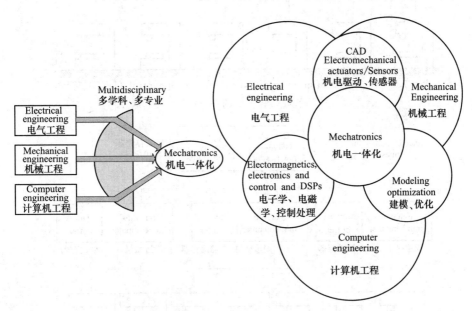

Fig. 7.1　Mechatronics integrates electrical, mechanical and computer engineering
机电一体化集成了电气工程、机械工程和计算机工程

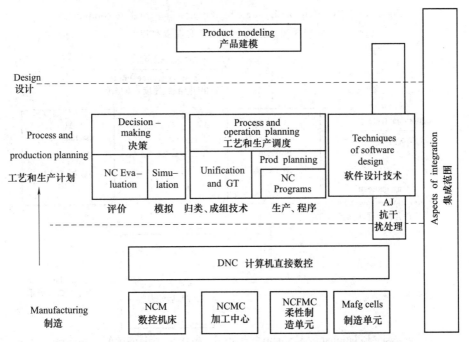

Fig. 7.2　The general scope of CAM　计算机辅助制造的通用范围

7.1 Basic knowledge on numerical control 数控基本知识

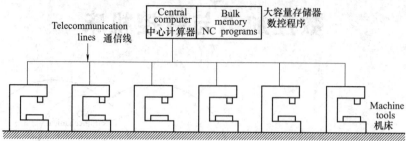

Fig. 7.3　General configuration of a direct numerical control (DNC) system
直接数控系统的一般构建

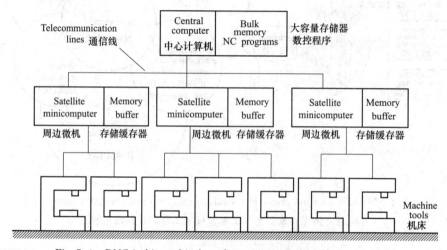

Fig. 7.4　DNC in hierarchical configuration using satellite computers
使用周边计算机分级构建的直接数控

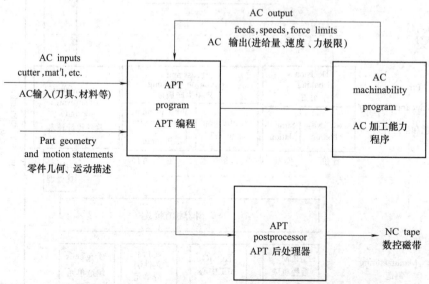

Fig. 7.5　Relationship of adaptive control (AC) software to APT program
自适应控制软件与自动编程的关系

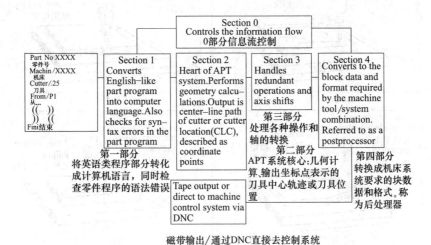

Fig. 7.6 APT (automatically programmed tool) system
APT（自动编程工具）系统

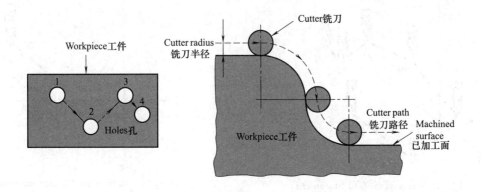

(a) Point-to-point 点到点　　(b) Continuous path by a milling cutter 铣刀连续运动轨迹(路径)

Fig. 7.7 Movement of tools in numerical-control machining
数控加工刀具的运动

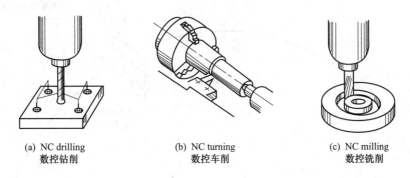

(a) NC drilling　　(b) NC turning　　(c) NC milling
　　数控钻削　　　　数控车削　　　　数控铣削

Fig. 7.8 Types of NC (numerical control) machining
数控加工的类型（一）

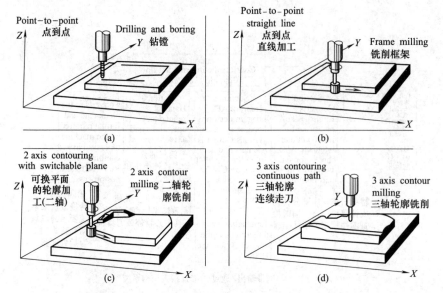

Fig. 7.9　Types of NC（numerical control）machining
数控加工的类型（二）

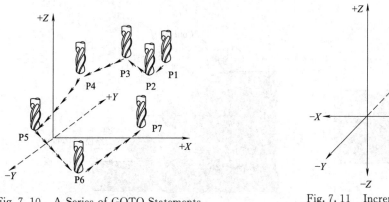

Fig. 7.10　A Series of GOTO Statements
系列 GOTO 指令

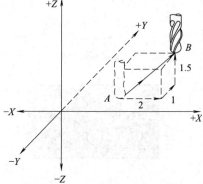

Fig. 7.11　Incremental cutter movements
增量刀具运动

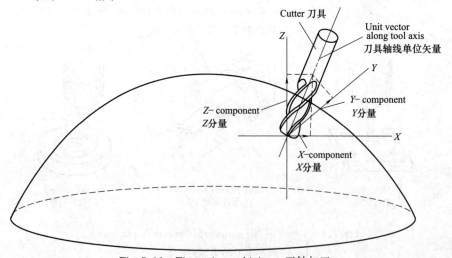

Fig. 7.12　Five-axis machining　五轴加工

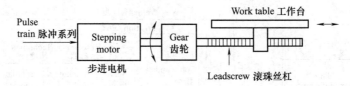

(a) An open-loop control system 开环控制系统

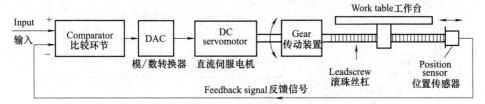

(b) A closed-loop control system 闭环控制系统

Fig. 7.13　An open-loop and a closed-loop control system for a numerical-control machine
数控机床的开环控制系统和闭环控制系统

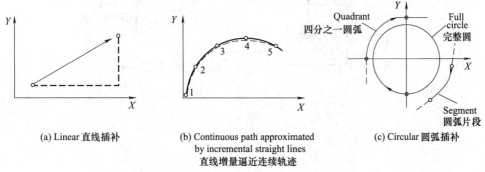

(a) Linear 直线插补　　(b) Continuous path approximated by incremental straight lines 直线增量逼近连续轨迹　　(c) Circular 圆弧插补

Fig. 7.14　Types of interpolation in numerical control
数控插补类型

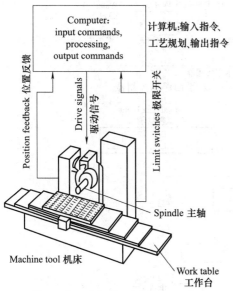

Fig. 7.15　Major components of a numerical-control machine tool
数控机床的主要部件

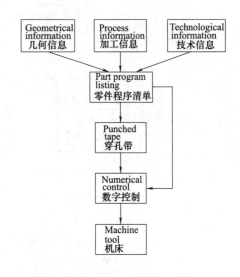

Fig. 7.16　Principle of operation of an NC machine tool
数据机床操作原理

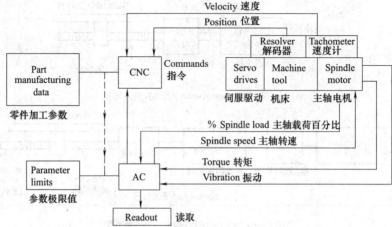

Fig. 7.17　Application of adaptive control (AC) for a turning operation　适应控制应用于车削加工

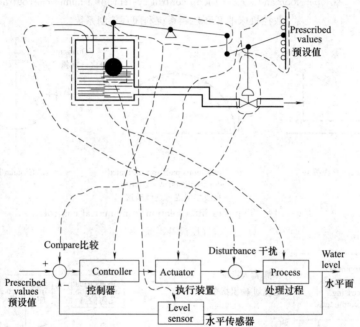

Fig. 7.18　Water-level float regulator　水平面浮标控制器

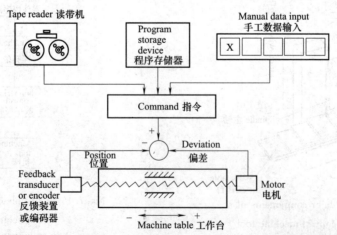

Fig. 7.19　Data processing in CNC machining tool in a closed loop control　闭环 CNC 机床的数据处理

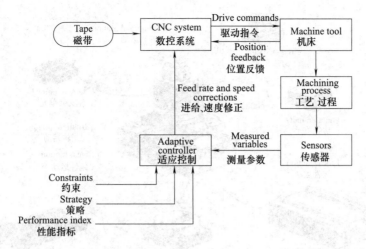

Fig. 7.20　Typical adaptive control configuration for a machine tool　典型机床自适应控制构成

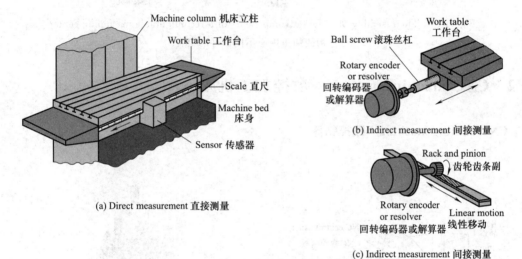

Fig. 7.21　Direct measurement and indirect measurement methods of the linear displacement of a machine-tool work table
机床工作台线性位移的直接测量和间接测量方法

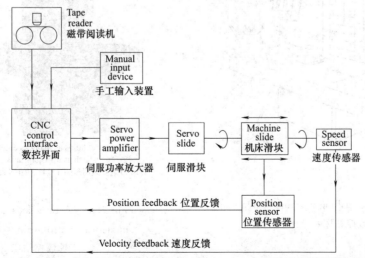

Fig. 7.22　Machine tool slide control interface　机床滑块控制界面

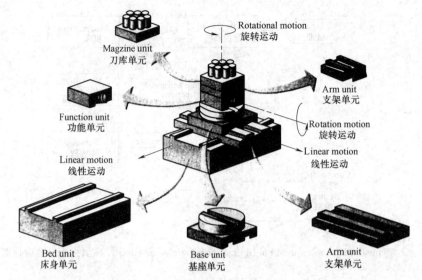

Fig. 7.23 The assembly of different components of a reconfigurable machining center
可重构的加工中心不同部件的组合

7.2　CNC machining tools　数控加工机床

（1）CNC drilling machine　数控钻床

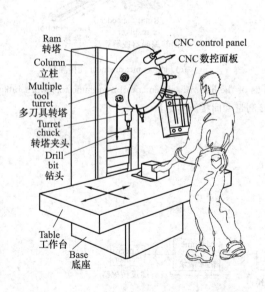

Fig. 7.24　CNC drilling machine sketch map
数控钻床示意图

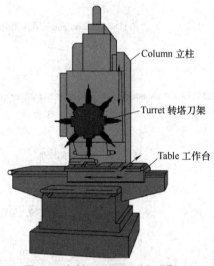

Fig. 7.25　A three-axis computer numerical control drilling machine
三轴数控钻床

(2) CNC milling machine 数控铣床

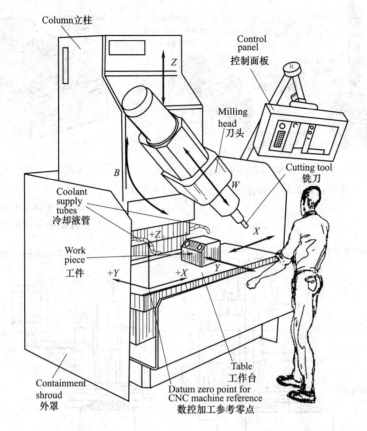

Fig. 7.26　CNC milling machine　数控铣床

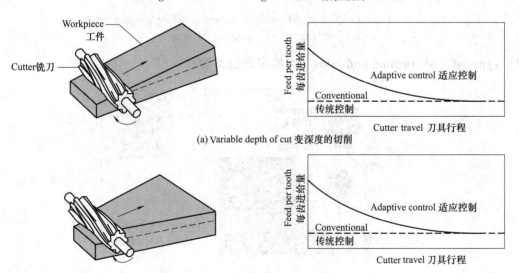

(a) Variable depth of cut 变深度的切削

(b) Variable width of cut 变宽度切削

Fig. 7.27　An example of adaptive control in milling
铣削适应控制示例

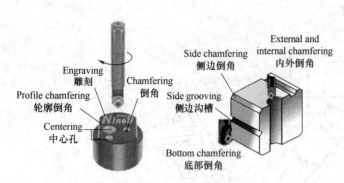

Fig. 7.28　Operations CNC milling machine
数控铣床的加工操作

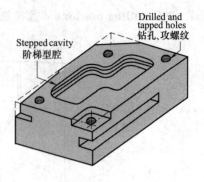

Fig. 7.29　A typical part that can be produced on a milling machine equipped with computer controls
计算机控制的铣床能加工的典型零件

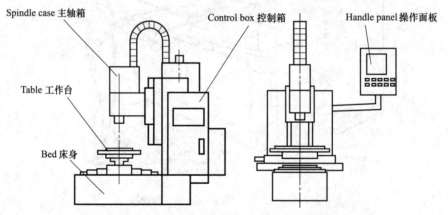

Fig. 7.30　Layout of vertical NC milling, boring, drilling complex machine
立式数控铣、镗、钻复合机床布局

(3) Types of CNC turning and lathe　数控车床的类型

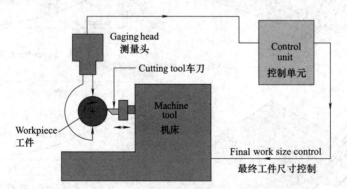

The system automatically adjusts the radial position of the cutting tool in order to produce the correct diameter
系统自动调整刀具径向位置以获得正确的直径值

Fig. 7.31　In-process inspection of workpiece diameter in a turning operation
车削工件直径在线检测

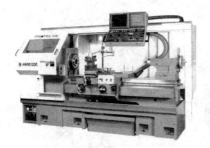

Fig. 7.32 CNC horizental lathe 卧式数控车床

Fig. 7.33 CNC vertical lathe 立式数控车床

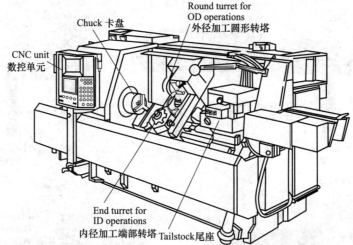

Fig. 7.34 A computer numerical control lathe 计算机数控车床

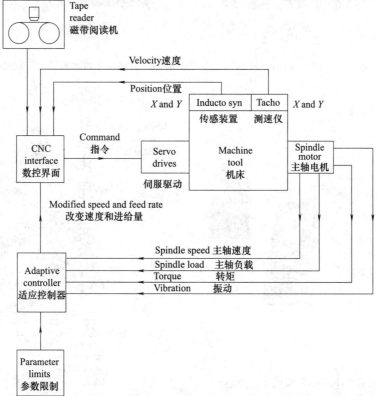

Fig. 7.35 Adaptive control on a NC turning machine 数控车床适应控制

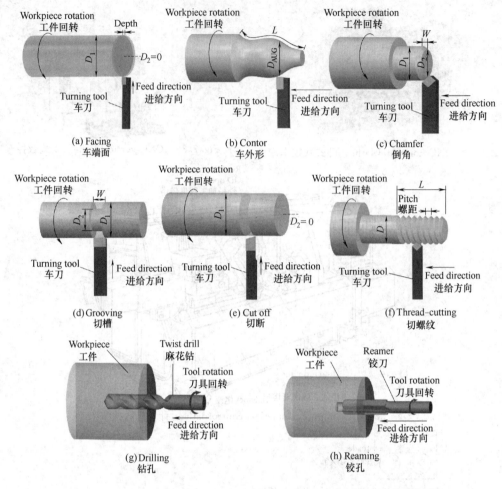

Fig. 7.36 Possible operations on a NC lathe 数控车床可实施的加工操作

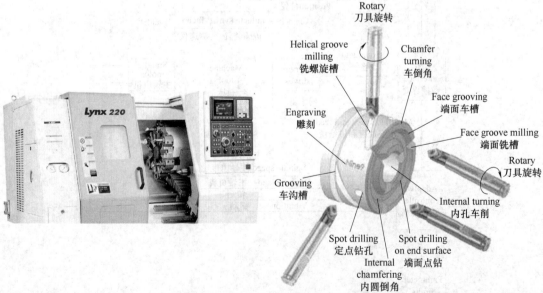

Fig. 7.37 Turning center 车削加工中心

Fig. 7.38 Applications on a lathe machining center 车削加工中心的各种操作

(4) NC grinding machine 数控磨床

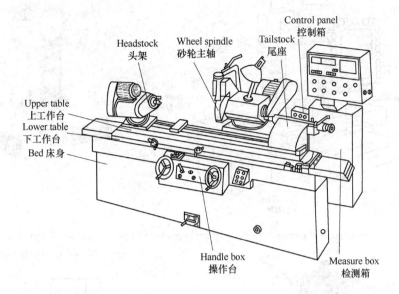

Fig. 7.39　NC cylindrical grinding machine 数控外圆磨床

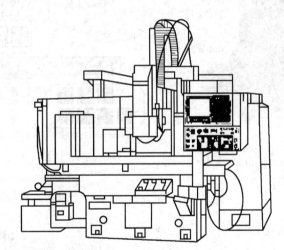

Fig. 7.40　NC flat grinding machine　数控平面磨床

(5) Machining center 加工中心

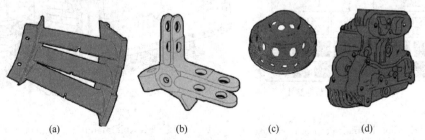

Fig. 7.41　Examples of parts that can be machined on machining centers
可以在加工中心上加工的零件

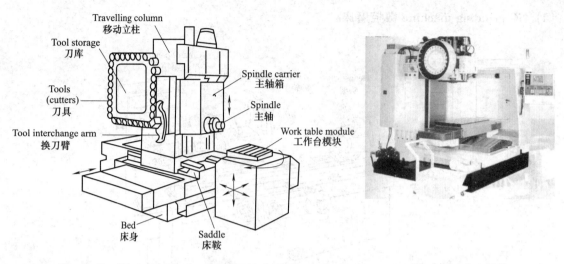

Fig. 7.42 Schematic illustration of a horizontal spindle machine center 卧式加工中心结构

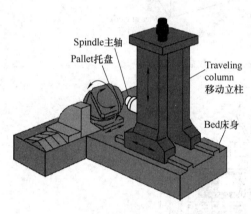

Fig. 7.43 A five-axis machining center
五轴加工中心

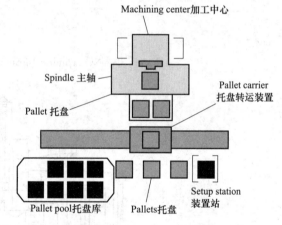

Fig. 7.44 The top view of a horizontal-spindle machining center
卧式加工中心俯视图

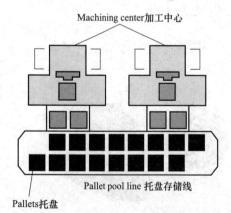

Fig. 7.45 Schematic illustration of two machining centers with a common pallet pool
共用托盘库的两台加工中心视图

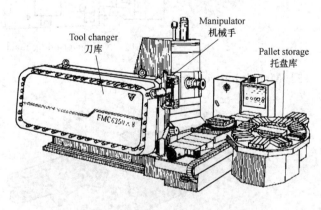

Fig. 7.46 Flexible manufacturing cell consisting of single machining center with pallets
由托盘和单台加工中心构成的柔性制造单元

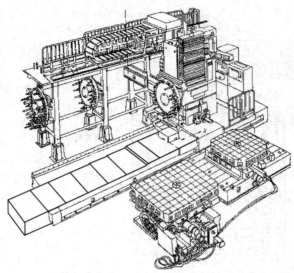

Fig. 7.47 Horizontal machining center with exchangeable tool changer 有可换刀库的卧式加工中心

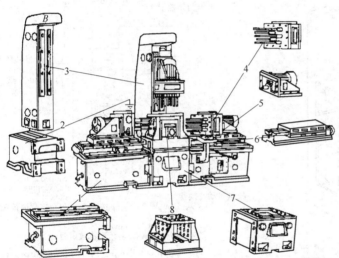

1—Left base 左底座；
2—Base for column 立柱底座；
3—Column 立柱；
4—Spindles box 主轴箱；
5—Power driving box 动力箱；
6—Sliding table 滑台；
7—Central base 中央底座；
8—Jig and fixture 夹具

Fig. 7.48 Components of modular machine 模块组合机床的组成

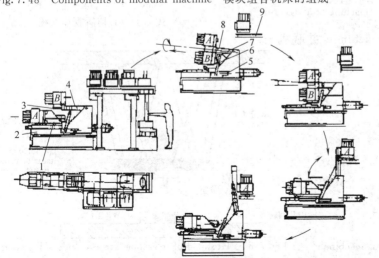

1—Driving box 动力箱；
2—Sliding table 滑台；
3—Clamp 抓手；
4—Lifting set 升降装置；
5—Hydraulic cylinder 液压缸；
6—Side lifting hydraulic cylinders 侧面升降油缸；
7—Rotary hydraulic cylinder 四转液压缸；
8—Clamping head 夹头；
9—Storage for multi-spindle box 多轴箱库

Fig. 7.49 Modular machine with changeable driving box 动力头可换式组合机床

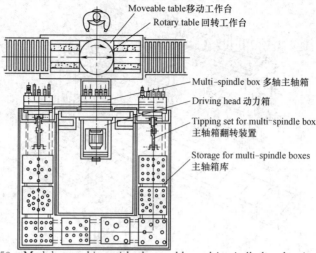

Fig. 7.50 Modular machine with changeable multi-spindle box by tipping set
带翻转装置的卧式多轴可换箱组合机床

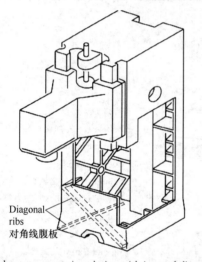

The boxtype, one-piece design with internal diagonal ribs significantly improves the stiffness of the machine
对角线腹板的盒式整体设计明显改善机床刚性

Fig. 7.51 An example of a machine tool structure
机床结构示例

Fig. 7.52 A chip-collecting system in a horizontal spindle machining center
卧式加工中心切屑收集系统

(6) Parallel kinematic machine 并联机床

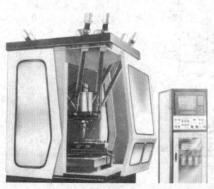

Fig. 7.53 Parallel kinematic machine
并联机床

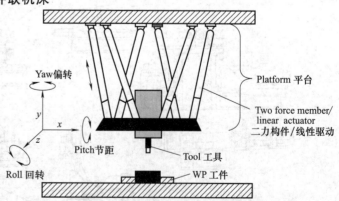

Fig. 7.54 Hexapod of telescopic struts, Ingersoll system
英格索兰伸缩构件的六底座机构

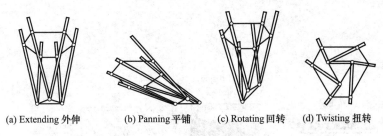

(a) Extending 外伸　　(b) Panning 平铺　　(c) Rotating 回转　　(d) Twisting 扭转

Fig. 7.55　Models of hexapod movements　六底座运动模型

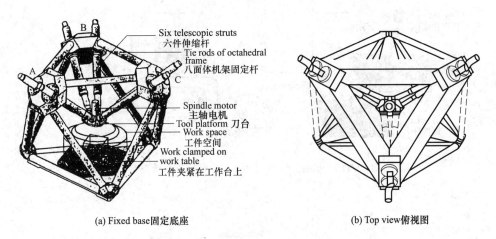

(a) Fixed base 固定底座　　(b) Top view 俯视图

Fig. 7.56　Hexapod with rigid frame
刚性结构的六面底座

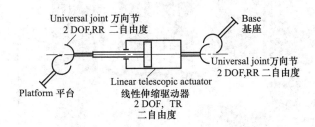

Fig. 7.57　Telescopic struts with universal joints　万向节伸缩杆件

7.3 CNC functional components and appendix 数控机床功能部件及附件

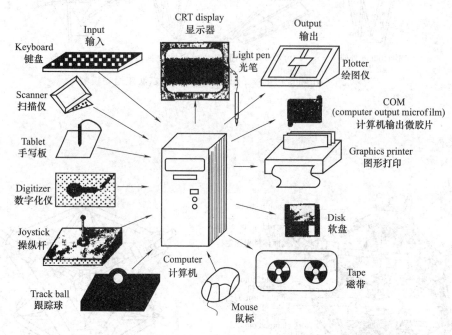

Fig. 7.58 I/O Devices of a CAD system CAD 系统输入/输出装置

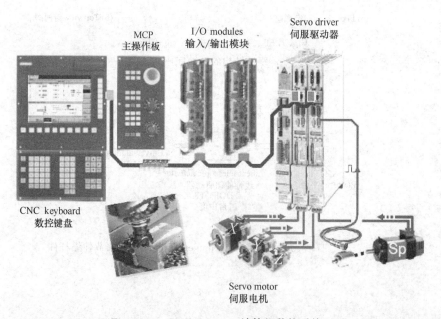

Fig. 7.59 CNC system 计算机数控系统

Fig. 7.60　The control panel from CNC machine center　加工中心控制面板

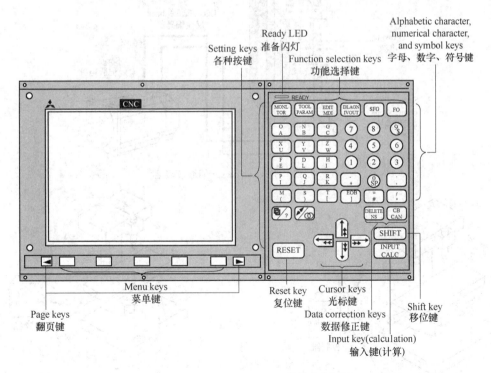

Fig. 7.61　CNC control panel 数控控制面板

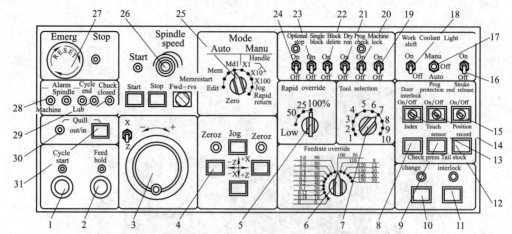

Fig. 7.62　Manual panel of NC machine　数控机床操作面板

1—Cycle start　程序启动按钮；2—Feed hold　进给保持按钮；3—Pulse generator by hand wheel　手摇脉冲发生器；4—Jog　点动按钮；5—Rapid override　快速倍率旋转开关；6—Feedrate override　进给倍率旋转开关；7—Tool selection　刀具选择旋转开关；8—Index　刀架转位按钮；9—Touch sensor　对刀仪按钮；10—Chuck press change 卡盘压力转换按钮；11—Tail stock interlock　尾座夹紧按钮；12—Position record　位置记录按钮；13—Door interlock　门联锁钥匙开关；14—Prog protection　程序保护钥匙开关；15—Stroke end release　超程解除钥匙开关；16—Light　机床灯开关；17—Coolant　冷却液开关；18—Work shift 工件坐标系偏置开关；19—Machine lock　机床锁定开关；20—Prog check　程序检查开关；21—Dry run　空运行开关；22—Block delete　程序段跳开关；23—Single block　单步运行开关；24—Optional stop　选择停止开关；25—Mode　方式选择旋转开关；26—Spindle　主轴功能按钮；27—Emerg stop　紧急停止按钮；28—Alarm　报警指示灯；29—Cycle end　程序结束指示灯；30—Chuck closed　卡盘夹紧指示灯；31—Quill out/in　套筒伸/缩按钮

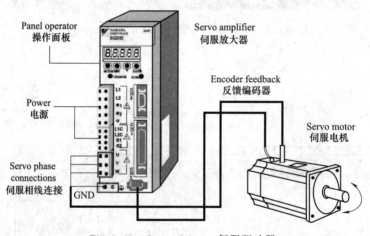

Fig. 7.63　Servo driver　伺服驱动器

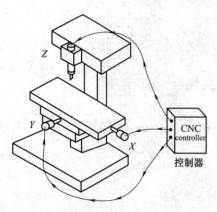

Fig. 7.64　Open loop system　开环系统

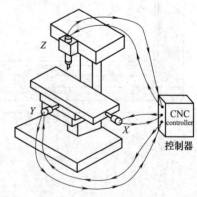

Fig. 7.65　Closed loop system　闭环系统

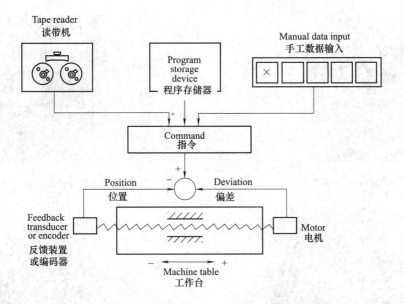

Fig. 7.66 Data processing in CNC machining tool in a closed loop control
闭环 CNC 机床的数据处理

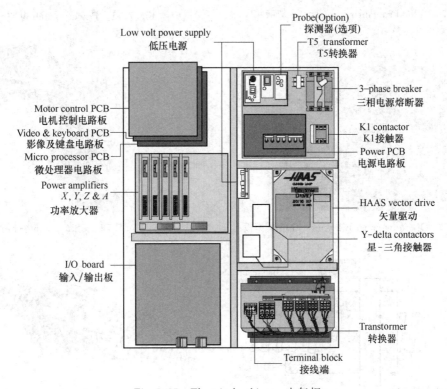

Fig. 7.67 Electrical cabinet 电气柜

Fig. 7.68　Oil reservoir　储油器

Fig. 7.69　Barometer　气压表

Fig. 7.70　Flood coolant reservoir　冷却液箱

Fig. 7.71　Power switch　电源开关

Fig. 7.72　Operator panel B layout　B层操作板

Fig. 7.73　Chip auger　排屑螺旋

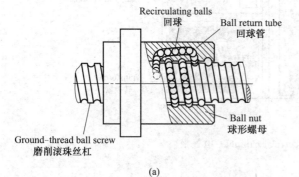

(a)　　　　　　　　　　　(b)

Fig. 7.74　External recirculating ball screw　外循环滚珠丝杠

Fig. 7.75　Tooth belt drive 同步齿形带传动

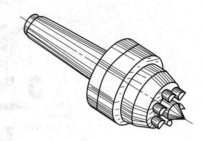

Fig. 7.76　Face driving center 端面拨动顶尖

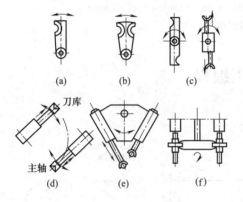
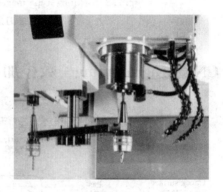

Fig. 7.77　Various forms of manipulators for tool changing 各种形式的换刀机械手

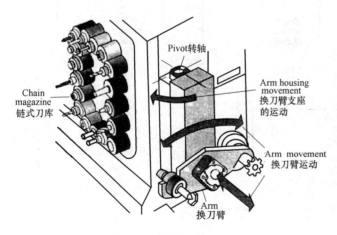

Fig. 7.78　Chain-type magazine with automatic tool changer 带自动换刀的链式刀库

Fig. 7.79　Automatic tool changer (ATC) 自动换刀装置

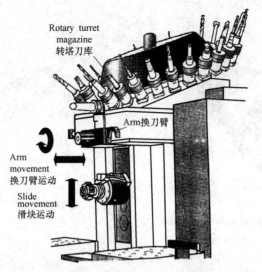

Fig. 7.80　Rotary-type magazine with automatic tool changer
带自动换刀装置的回转刀库

7.4　CNC programming　数控加工编程

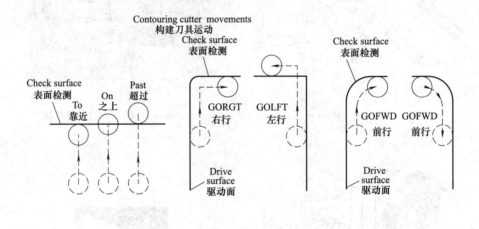

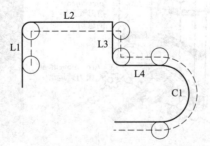

Fig. 7.81　Motion statements for movements around a workpiece
工件周边移动的运动描述

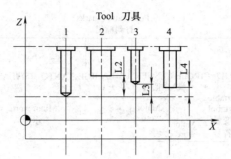

Fig. 7.82　Tool length compensation　刀具长度补偿

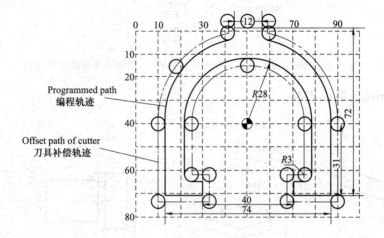

Fig. 7.83　Cutter radius compensation　刀具半径补偿

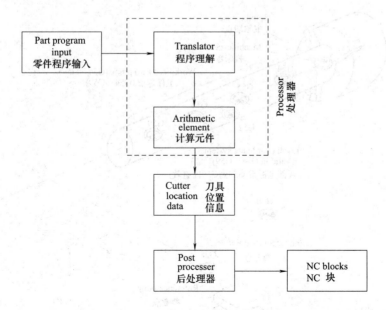

Fig. 7.84　Computer aided part programming system configuration
计算机辅助编程系统构成

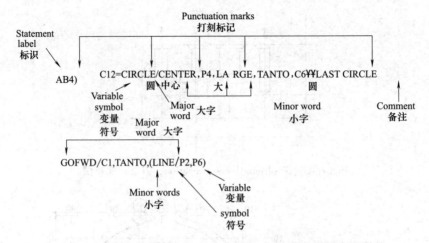

Fig. 7.85 Structure of statements in APT 自动编程系统标识结构

(1) CNC turning 数控车削

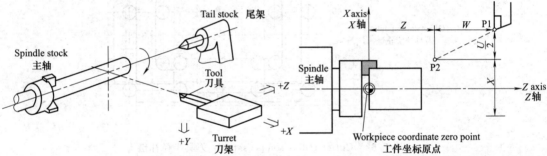

Fig. 7.86 Coordinate axes and polarities 坐标轴和极性

Fig. 7.87 Incremental and absolute value commands 增量值指令和绝对值指令

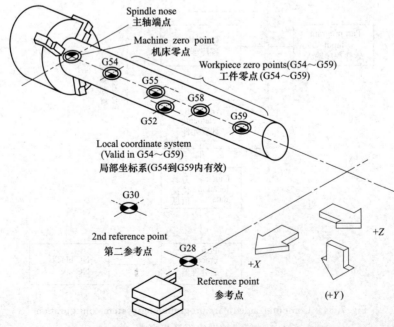

Fig. 7.88 Relationship between coordinates 各坐标的关系

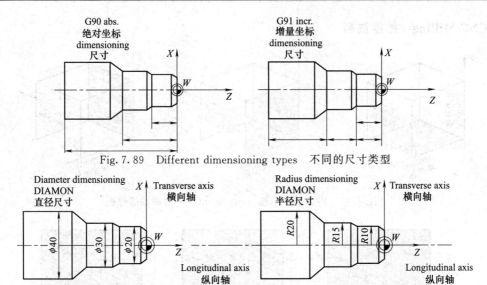

Fig. 7.89　Different dimensioning types　不同的尺寸类型

Fig. 7.90　Diameter and radius dimensioning for the transverse axis　移动轴的直径与半径尺寸

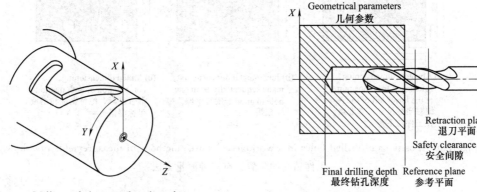

Fig. 7.91　Milling of the peripheral surface on turning machines　在车床上铣削柱面

Fig. 7.92　Drilling cycles　钻孔循环

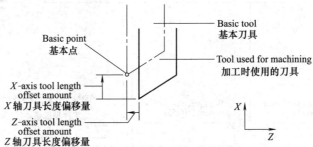

Fig. 7.93　Tool length offsets in different directions　不同方向的刀具长度偏移量

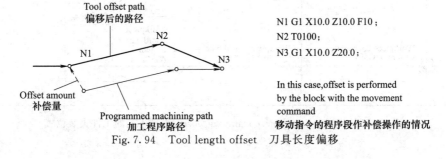

N1 G1 X10.0 Z10.0 F10；
N2 T0100；
N3 G1 X10.0 Z20.0；

In this case, offset is performed by the block with the movement command
移动指令的程序段作补偿操作的情况

Fig. 7.94　Tool length offset　刀具长度偏移

(2) CNC Milling 数控铣削

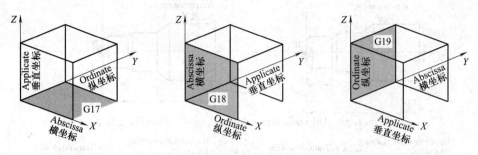

Fig. 7.95 Plane and axis assignment 平面和轴的分配

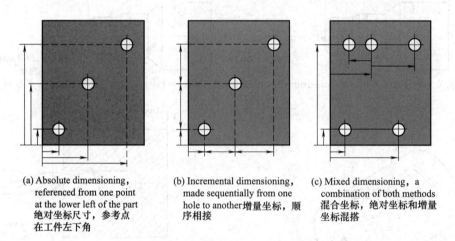

(a) Absolute dimensioning, referenced from one point at the lower left of the part 绝对坐标尺寸，参考点在工件左下角

(b) Incremental dimensioning, made sequentially from one hole to another 增量坐标，顺序相接

(c) Mixed dimensioning, a combination of both methods 混合坐标，绝对坐标和增量坐标混搭

Fig. 7.96 Positions of drilled holes in a workpiece. Three methods of measurements are shown 工件钻孔的位置：有三种测量方法

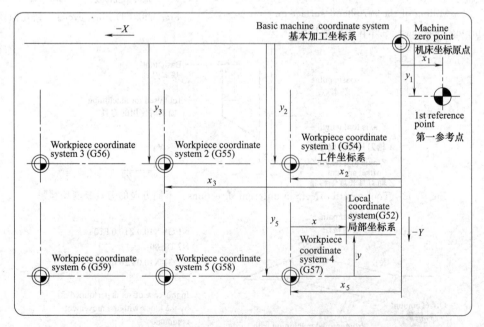

Fig. 7.97 Various workpiece clamping positions 不同的工件夹装位置

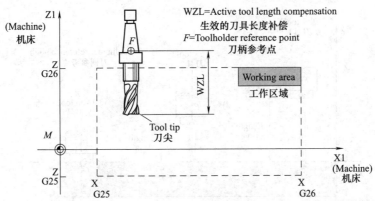

Fig. 7.98　Programmable working area limitation　可编程工作区域限制

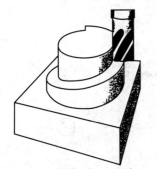

Fig. 7.99　Helical interpolation
螺旋线插补

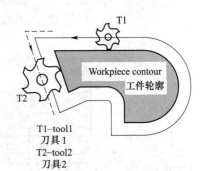

Fig. 7.100　Machining of a workpiece with different tool radius　使用各种刀具半径加工一个工件

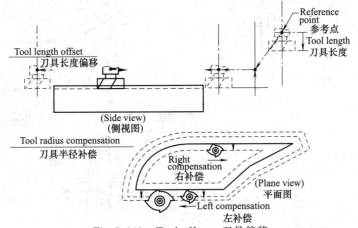

Fig. 7.101　Tool offset　刀具偏移

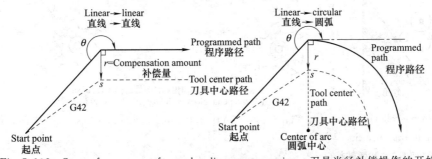

Fig. 7.102　Start of movement for tool radius compensation　刀具半径补偿操作的开始

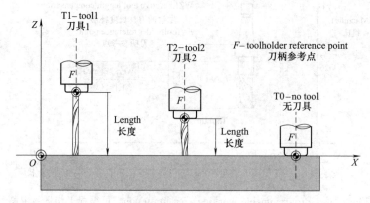

Fig. 7.103　Approaching the workpiece position Z0 different length compensations
接近工件位置 Z0 的不同长度补偿

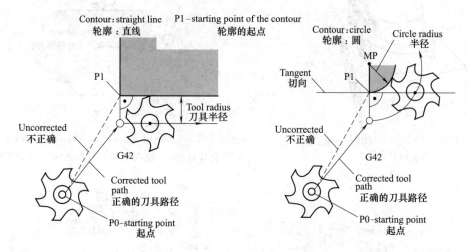

Fig. 7.104　Start of the tool radius compensation with G42　以 G42 进行刀具半径补偿

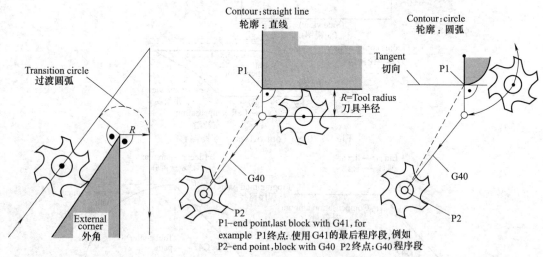

Fig. 7.105　Acute contour angle and switching to transition circle
尖的轮廓角和过渡圆弧转换

Fig. 7.106　Quitting the tool radius compensation　关闭刀具半径补偿

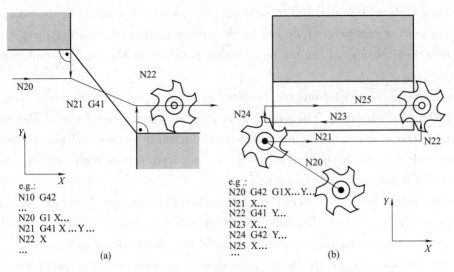

Fig. 7.107 Change of the compensation direction 补偿方向的转换

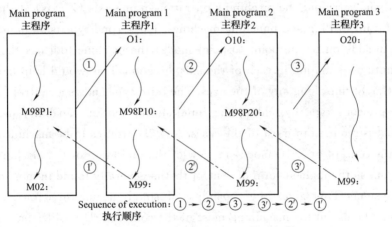

Fig. 7.108 Subprogram 子程序

7.5 Short passage for reading 阅读短文

NC Machine Tools

At present, the CNC machining center appears to be the most capable and versatile automatic machine tool that can perform drilling, milling, boring, reaming and tapping operations. The general objective behind the development of NC machine tools continues to remain the reduction of cost of production by reducing the production time. This in turn is directed towards the avoidance of non-productive time which is mainly due to the number of setups, setup time, workpiece handling time, tool change time and lead time. The performance of a variety of machining operations on the same machining center eliminates the non-productive waiting time that occurs if such operations are performed on different machines. Provision of automatic tool changing, indexing of tables and several pallets add to the productivity of the machining centers.

The basic information that has to be input into the system consists of the part geometry and cutting process parameters followed by the cutting tools used. This part program is then entered into the controller of the machine, which in turn runs the machine tool to make the part.

The command received from the operator is communicated to the corresponding axis driving system for execution. The axis motion control system operates in a feed back loop with suitable transducers such as linear scales and/or rotary encoders to get the appropriate position or velocity feed back. Most of these systems have a very high response with good resolution of the order of 1 micron or less.

The controllers have a number of modes in which they operate. There can be four possible modes in which the controller can function in relation to a machining center. The first shows a typical drilling machine operation, termed as point-to-point mode. In this, the control has the capability to operate all the three axes, but not necessarily simultaneously. As a result, it would be possible to move the tool to any point (in X and Y-axes) in the fastest possible speed and carry out the machining operation in one axis (Z-axis) at that point. This would be useful for drilling and punching machines. The second type is an improvement over this in which in addition to the point to point mode, the machine tool has the capability to carry out a continuous motion in each of the axis direction. This would help in obtaining the milling in a straight line along any of the axes. The third type shows a control system, which improves the previous type by adding the simultaneous motion capability in any two axes. This is what is required in most of the cases. Any 3D profiles to be machined can be completed using the concept of 2.5D mode, in view of the limitation of the machine.

The last one is the highest form of control that is generally found in most of the current day control systems. This gives the capability of simultaneous three or more axes motion. This would be useful for machining most of the complex 3D profiles encountered in industrial practice such as aerospace components, moulds and dies.

数 控 机 床

目前，计算机数控加工中心似乎是最万能和通用的自动机床，它能完成钻削、铣削、镗孔、铰孔、攻螺纹等加工操作。开发加工中心背后的通用目的是通过减少加工时间来持续保持降低成本。减少加工时间直接目标指向避免非加工时间，其因素有安装次数、安装时间、工件布置时间、换刀时间和导刀时间。同一台加工中心上能够完成不同的加工工序，这根除了如果采用多台不同机床完成所必需的非加工等待时间。自动换刀、工作台自动分度和多个托盘的配备可进一步提升加工中心的生产率。

系统输入的基本信息包括工件几何要素、所用刀具遵循的切削工艺参数。工件程序输入机床控制器后，它会按照顺序运行控制刀具加工工件。

操作者传来的指令与相应的轴驱动系统通信而执行动作。轴的运动控制系统工作方式为闭环反馈，借助于适当的转化器（如线性或回转编码器）获得适当的位置或速度反馈信息。这些系统多数响应速度快，分辨率高达微米级或更细。

控制器可有多种工作模式，与加工中心相关的控制器功能模式大体有四种。第一种为典型的钻床加工模式，即所谓点对点模式；这种模式的控制器能控制三轴，但未必同时进行。

这样就有可能以它能达到的最快速度将刀具移至任何位置点（X 轴和 Y 轴方向），并在该点单轴（Z 轴）执行加工操作。这种模式最适合于钻床和冲床。第二种模式是第一种的改进，除了点对点模式外，机床还能执行每个轴方向的连续运动。这就可以完成沿任何轴方向的直线铣削运动。第三种模式为前面模式的改进系统，它增加了任何两轴的同时运动能功能，这正是多数加工情形所需的。采用 2.5D 模式理念可以完成三维轮廓的加工，视机床工作范围而定。

最后一种为控制器的最高形式，也是当今最常见的控制系统。它能完成同时驱动三轴或更多轴的运动。这适合于工业生产中遇到的最为复杂的三维形貌加工情形，如航空零件、模具。

Unit 8 Manufacturing Processes and Procedures
机械加工工艺过程

8.1 Various commonly used processes 多种常用的工艺方法和过程

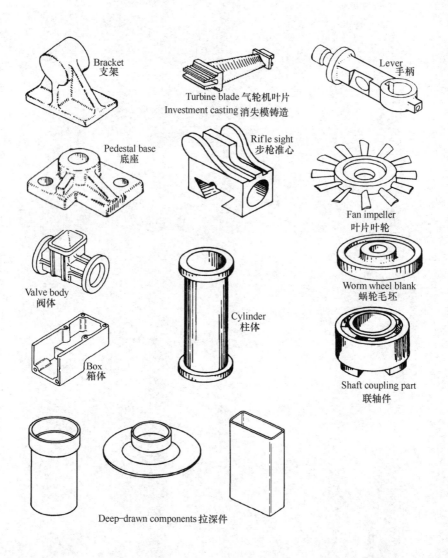

Fig. 8.1 Types of blanks 毛坯类型

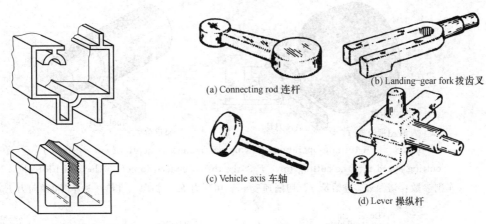

Fig. 8.2　Aluminum architectural sections　铝型材结构截面

Fig. 8.3　Forgings　锻压件

(1) Turning and lathe　车削加工

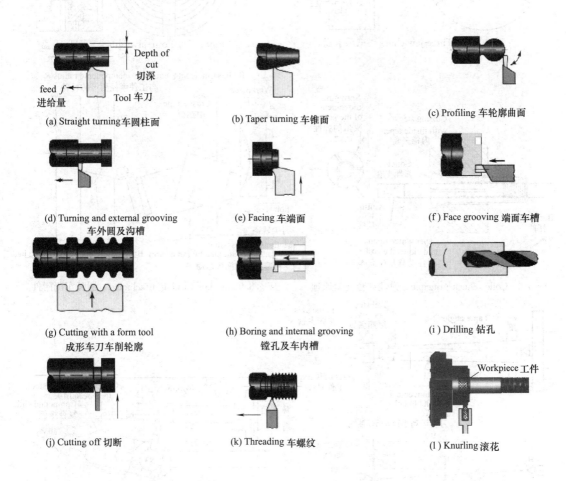

Fig. 8.4　Various cutting operations that can be performed on a lathe　车床上可实施的各种操作

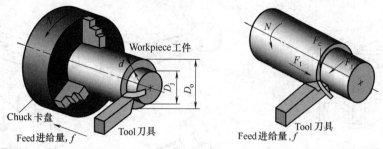

Fig. 8.5　A turning operation showing parameters as depth of cut d, feed f, cutting speed v_c. the cutting force F_c. the thrust or feed force F_t, the radial force F_r
车削参数：切深 d、进给量 f、切削速度 v_c、切削力 F_c、轴向（进给）力 F_t 和径向力 F_r

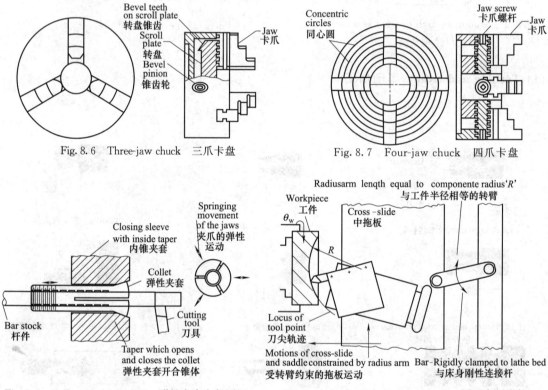

Fig. 8.6　Three-jaw chuck　三爪卡盘

Fig. 8.7　Four-jaw chuck　四爪卡盘

Fig. 8.8　Collet chuck principle　弹性夹套夹紧原理

Fig. 8.9　Radius turning attachment　圆弧车削附件

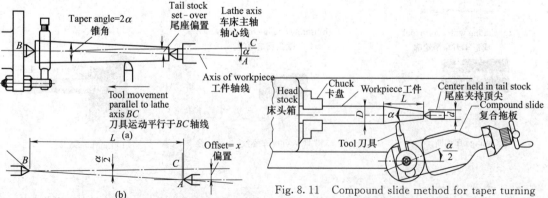

Fig. 8.10　Tail stock offset　尾座偏移车削锥度

Fig. 8.11　Compound slide method for taper turning
复合拖板车削锥度

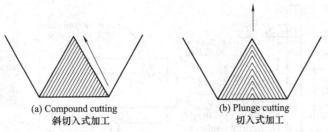

Fig. 8.12　Depth of cut in screw cutting　车制螺纹的切削深度

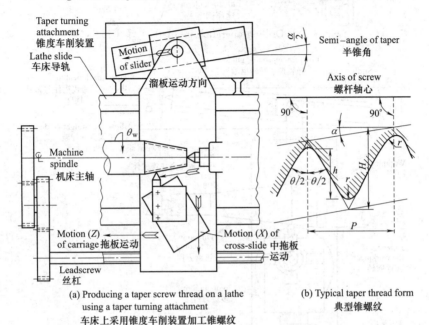

Fig. 8.13　Set-up for thread cutting on a taper　锥面上车削螺纹装置

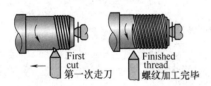

Fig. 8.14　Cutting screw threads on a lathe with a single-point cutting tool
单刀尖车刀车床上车螺纹

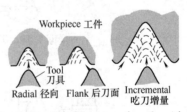

Fig. 8.15　Cutting screw threads with a single-point tool in several passes
单刀尖车刀车床上车多次走刀螺纹

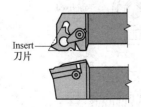

Fig. 8.16　A typical carbide insert and toolholder for cutting screw threads
典型硬质合金刀片和刀体用于车螺纹

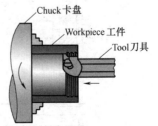

Fig. 8.17　Cutting internal screw threads with a carbide insert
硬质合金刀片车内螺纹

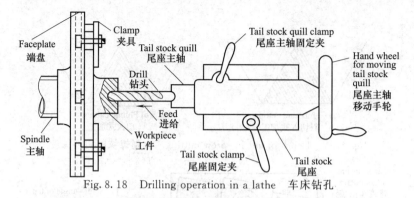

Fig. 8.18　Drilling operation in a lathe　车床钻孔

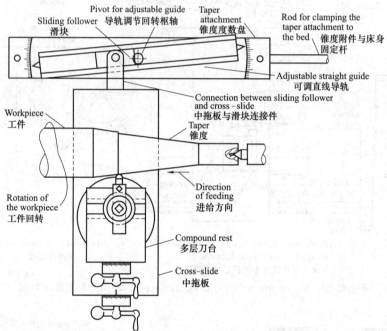

Fig. 8.19　Taper turning attachment　锥度车削附件

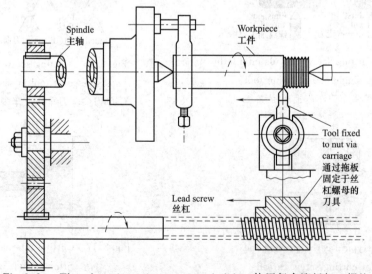

Fig. 8.20　Thread cutting using compound slide　使用复合溜板加工螺纹

Unit 8　Manufacturing Processes and Procedures　机械加工工艺过程

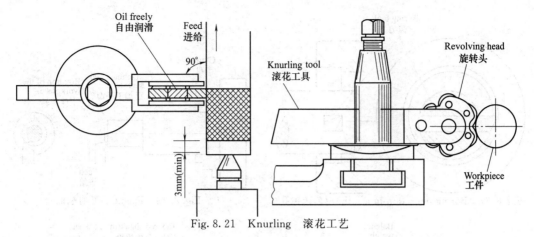

Fig. 8.21　Knurling　滚花工艺

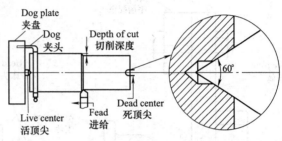

Fig. 8.22　Reverse jaw usage　反卡爪应用　　　Fig. 8.23　center hole, locating between centers
顶尖中心孔定位

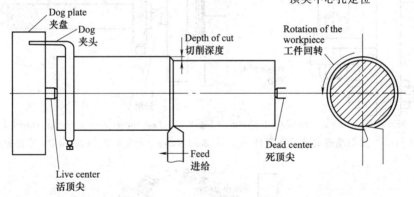

Fig. 8.24　Cylindrical turning operation in a lathe　车削外圆工艺

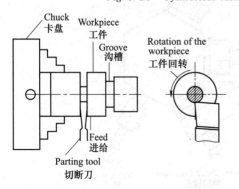　　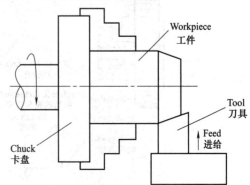

Fig. 8.25　Parting tool in operation　切断工具　　　Fig. 8.26　Taper turning using form tools
成形刀具车削锥度

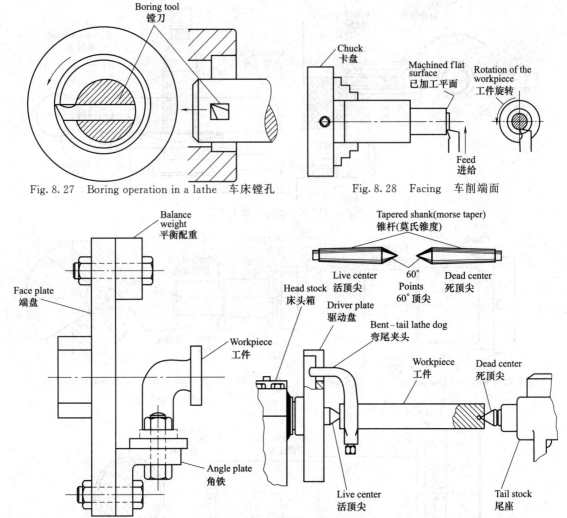

Fig. 8.27 Boring operation in a lathe 车床镗孔

Fig. 8.28 Facing 车削端面

Fig. 8.29 Fixturing using a face plate for odd shaped parts 使用端盘夹持异形零件

Fig. 8.30 Dog carrier and revolving center, half center, dead center 夹头支架、回转顶尖、半顶尖及死顶尖

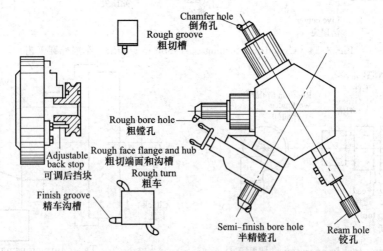

Fig. 8.31 Tooling layout of cast iron V-belt pulley casting
V 带轮铸件的加工工装布局

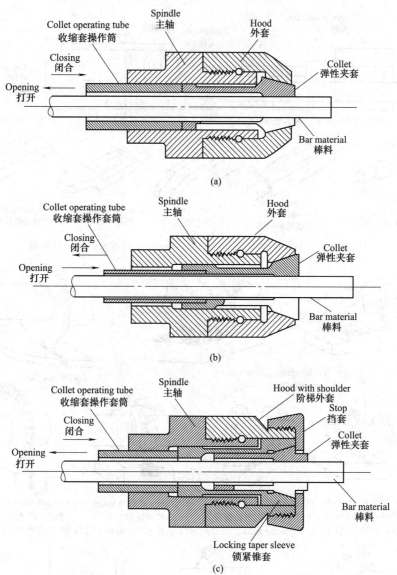

Fig. 8.32 Different forms of collet chucks used in turret lathe
转塔车床采用的多种弹性夹套

(2) Milling 铣削加工

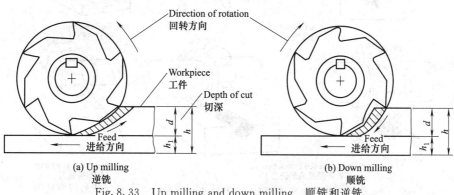

Fig. 8.33 Up milling and down milling 顺铣和逆铣

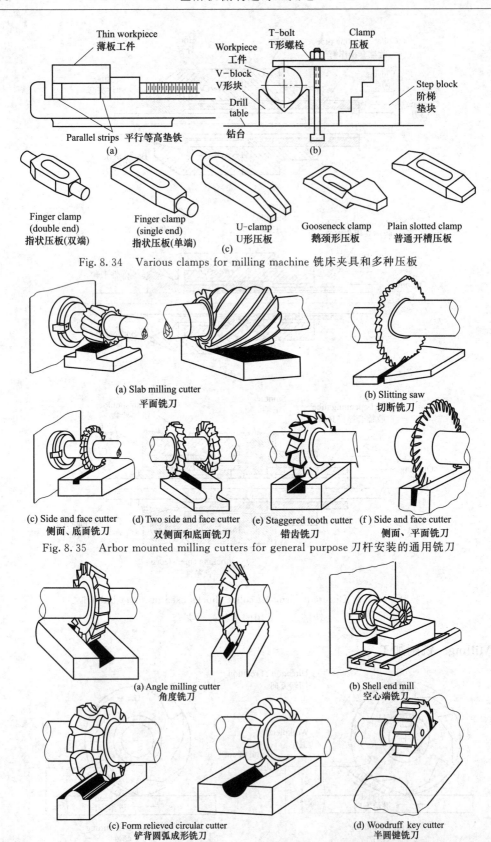

Fig. 8.34 Various clamps for milling machine 铣床夹具和多种压板

Fig. 8.35 Arbor mounted milling cutters for general purpose 刀杆安装的通用铣刀

Fig. 8.36 Special forms of arbor mounted milling cutter 刀杆安装的特型铣刀

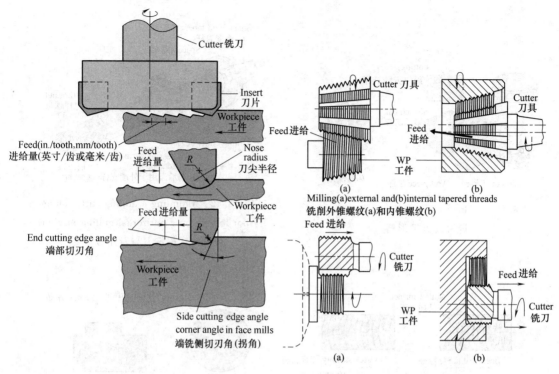

Fig. 8.37　Feed marks due to various insert shapes
不同刀片形状的进给痕迹

Fig. 8.38　Milling straight (a) external and (b) internal threads,
铣削外螺纹（a）和内螺纹（b）

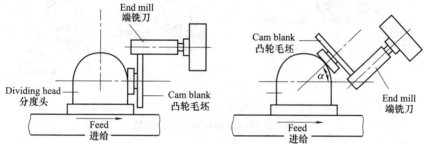

Fig. 8.39　Cam milling set-up at two different angles　两个不同角度铣削凸轮装置

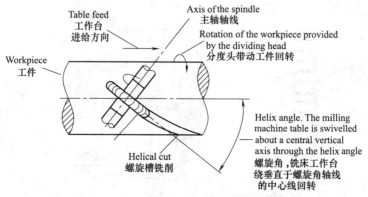

Fig. 8.40　Helical milling operation　螺旋槽铣削工艺

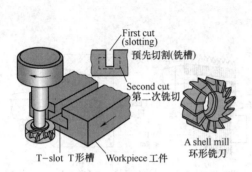

Fig. 8.41　T-slot cutting with a milling cutter
铣刀铣切 T 形槽

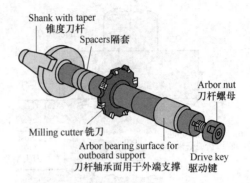

Fig. 8.42　Mounting a milling cutter on an arbor for use on a horizontal milling machine
卧式铣床用铣刀与刀杆的安装

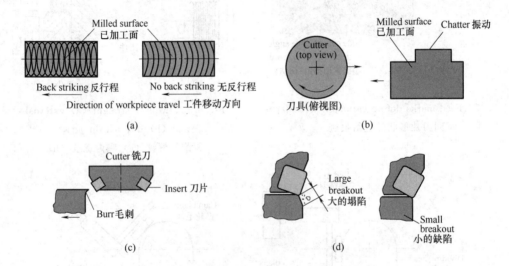

Fig. 8.43　Surface features and corner defects in face milling operations
端面铣削的表面特征和拐角缺陷

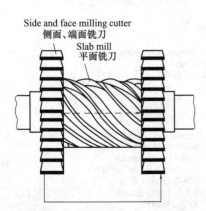

Fig. 8.44　Gang milling　组合铣削

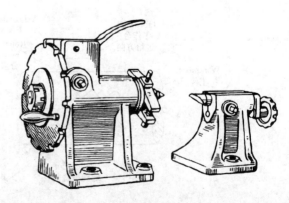

Fig. 8.45　Plain milling dividing head　普通铣削分度头

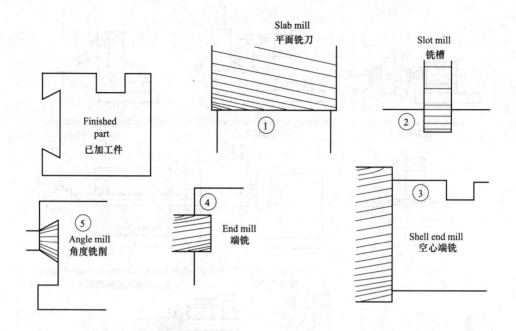

Fig. 8.46 Typical process sequence in milling 典型铣削工序

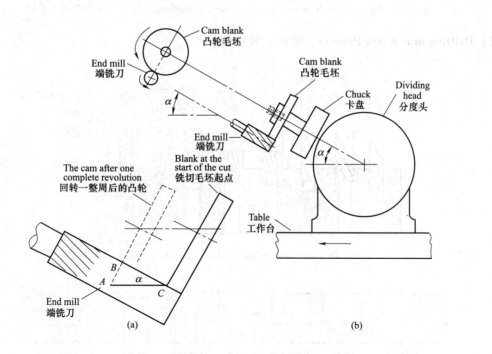

Fig. 8.47 Cam milling set-up 凸轮铣削装置

（3）Boring process 镗削加工

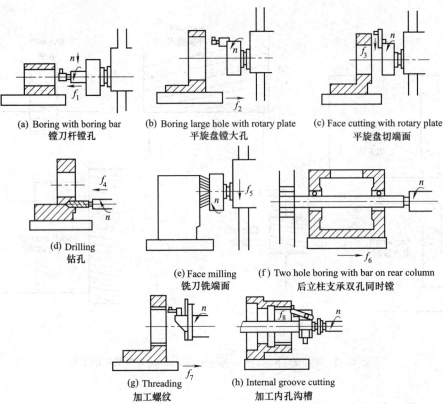

Fig. 8.48 Main operations for horizontal boring machine 卧式镗床主要加工方法

（4）Drilling and Ream Process 钻削、铰削加工

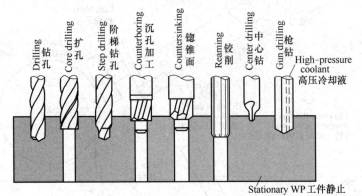

Fig. 8.49 Drilling and drilling allied operations 钻削及关联操作

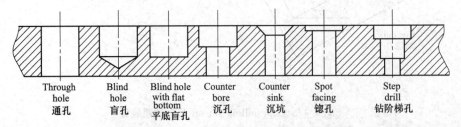

Fig. 8.50 Various types of holes 孔的类型

(5) Reciprocating machining processes 往复式加工

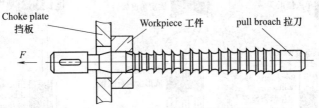

Fig. 8.51 Broach process 拉削过程

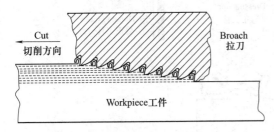

Fig. 8.52 Cutting action of individual teeth in a broach 拉刀单齿的切削过程

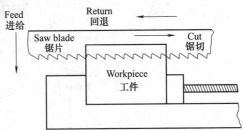

Fig. 8.53 Power hack saw in action 机动钢锯的切削过程

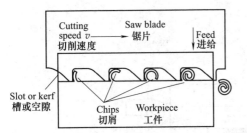

Fig. 8.54 Saw blade in action 锯片的切削过程

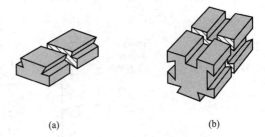

Fig. 8.55 Typical parts that can be made on a planer 可以在刨床上加工的典型零件

(6) Abrasives Process 磨削加工

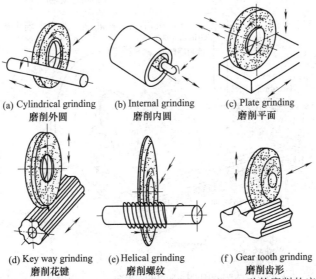

(a) Cylindrical grinding 磨削外圆
(b) Internal grinding 磨削内圆
(c) Plate grinding 磨削平面
(d) Key way grinding 磨削花键
(e) Helical grinding 磨削螺纹
(f) Gear tooth grinding 磨削齿形

Fig. 8.56 Various applications of wheel grinding 砂轮磨削的应用

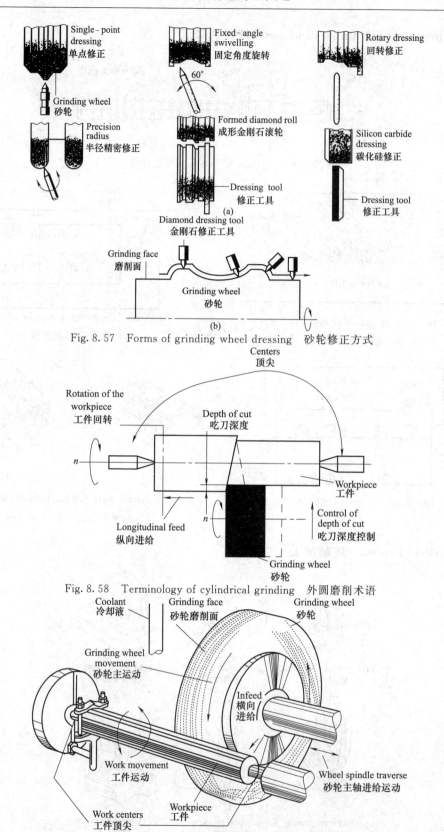

Fig. 8.57 Forms of grinding wheel dressing 砂轮修正方式

Fig. 8.58 Terminology of cylindrical grinding 外圆磨削术语

Fig. 8.59 Cylindrical grinding process 外圆磨削加工

Unit 8 Manufacturing Processes and Procedures 机械加工工艺过程

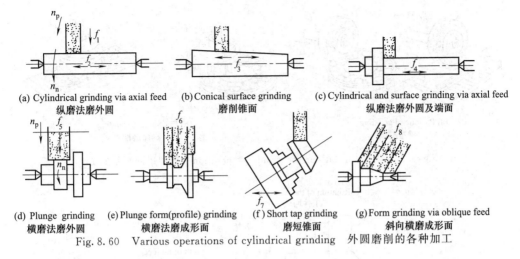

(a) Cylindrical grinding via axial feed 纵磨法磨外圆
(b) Conical surface grinding 磨削锥面
(c) Cylindrical and surface grinding via axial feed 纵磨法磨外圆及端面
(d) Plunge grinding 横磨法磨外圆
(e) Plunge form(profile) grinding 横磨法磨成形面
(f) Short tap grinding 磨短锥面
(g) Form grinding via oblique feed 斜向横磨成形面

Fig. 8.60 Various operations of cylindrical grinding 外圆磨削的各种加工

Fig. 8.61 Cutting principles and main variables of a surface grinding process 平面磨削工艺加工原理和主要参数

Fig. 8.62 Revolving-disk wheel balancing stand 转盘式砂轮平衡台

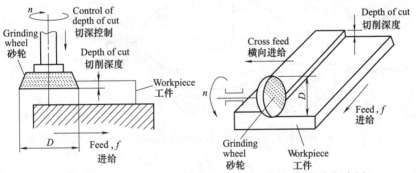

Fig. 8.63 Terminology of flat surface grinding 平面磨削术语

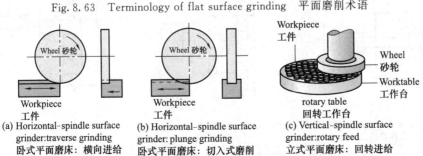

(a) Horizontal-spindle surface grinder: traverse grinding 卧式平面磨床：横向进给
(b) Horizontal-spindle surface grinder: plunge grinding 卧式平面磨床：切入式磨削
(c) Vertical-spindle surface grinder: rotary feed 立式平面磨床：回转进给

Fig. 8.64 Various surface-grinding operations 平面磨削操作

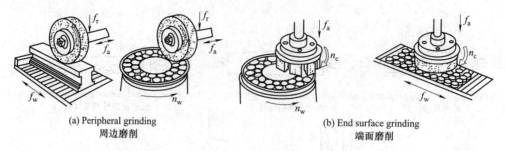

(a) Peripheral grinding 周边磨削 　　(b) End surface grinding 端面磨削

Fig. 8.65　Typical flat surface grinding operation　典型平面磨削加工

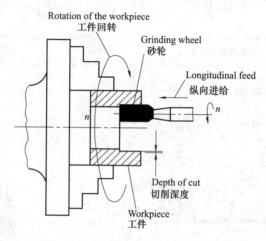

Fig. 8.66　Terminology of internal grinding　内圆磨削术语

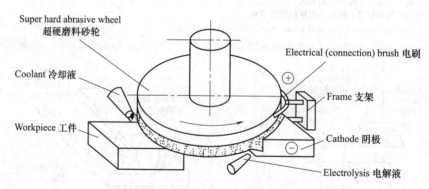

Fig. 8.67　Electrolytic in-process dressing (ELID)　电解在线砂轮修正

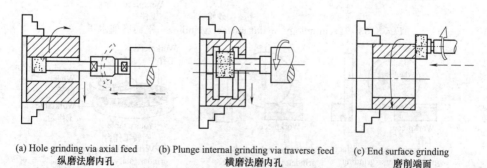

(a) Hole grinding via axial feed　　(b) Plunge internal grinding via traverse feed　　(c) End surface grinding
纵磨法磨内孔　　　　　　　　　　横磨法磨内孔　　　　　　　　　　　　磨削端面

Fig. 8.68　Operations for inner surface grinding machine　内圆磨削方法

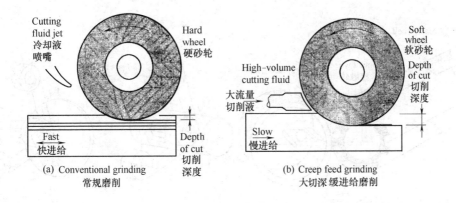

Fig. 8.69 Creep feed grinding operation   大切深缓进给磨削

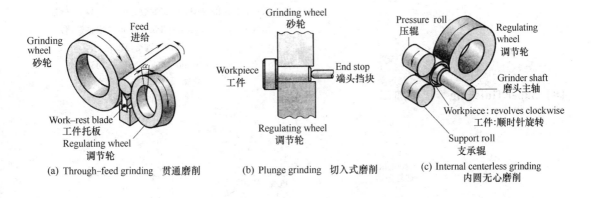

Fig. 8.70 Forms of centerless grinding   无心磨削形式

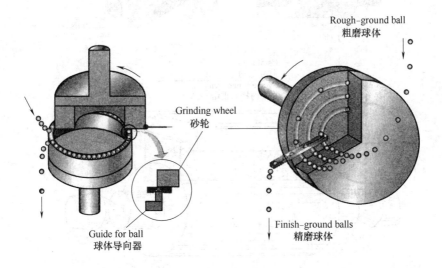

Fig. 8.71 Steel-ball grinding   钢球磨削

(7) Coated abrasive process 涂覆磨具磨削加工

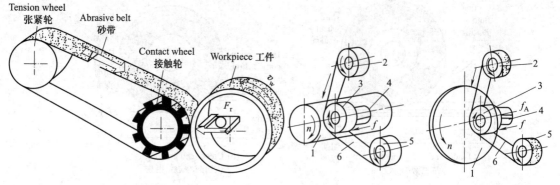

Fig. 8.72　Coated abrasive belt grinding set structure　砂带磨削装置构成

Fig. 8.73　Open-loop belt precision lapping　开式砂带精密研抛

1—Workpiece 工件；2—Belt coil 砂带卷；
3—Contact wheel 接触轮；4—Vibrator 激振器；
5—Belt pulling wheel 砂带收卷轮；6—Belt 砂带；
n—Revolution speed of spindle 主轴转速；
f—Feed 进给速度；
f_A—Vibration frequency 振动频率

(8) Super finishing 超精加工

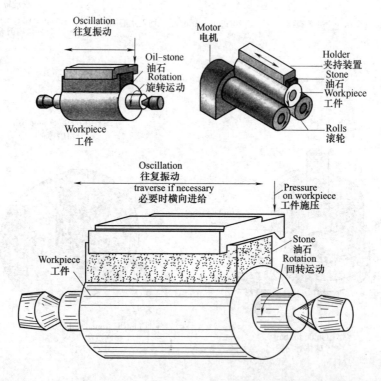

Fig. 8.74　Typical motions in a super finishing operation 典型的超精加工运动

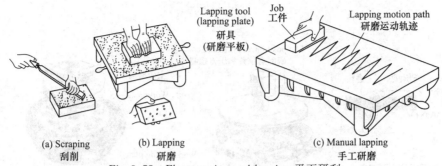

Fig. 8.75　Flat scraping and lapping　平面研刮

Fig. 8.76　Honing operation　珩磨加工

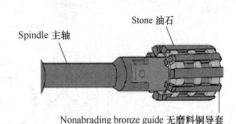

Fig. 8.77　Honing head　珩磨头

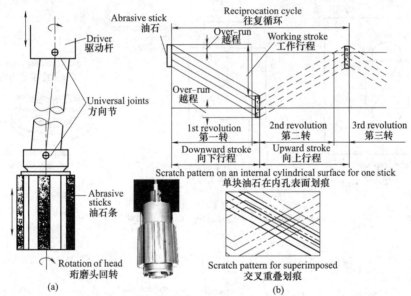

Fig. 8.78　Honing operation and its scratch pattern　珩磨工艺及表面划痕形貌

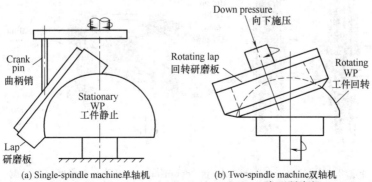

Fig. 8.79　Lapping of spherical surfaces　球面研磨机

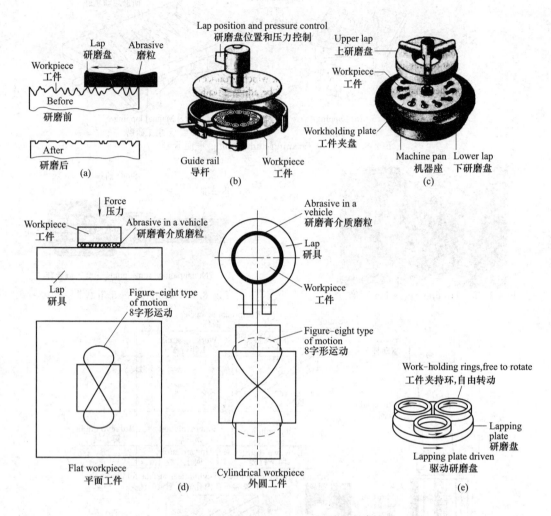

Fig. 8.80 Flat lapping process 平面研磨工艺

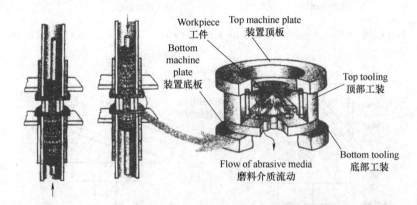

Fig. 8.81 Abrasive-flow lapping (deburing) 流动磨粒研磨（去毛刺）

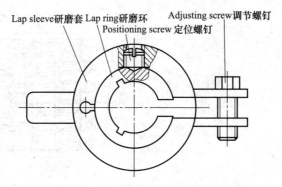

Fig. 8.82 Cylindrical lapping operation 研磨外圆

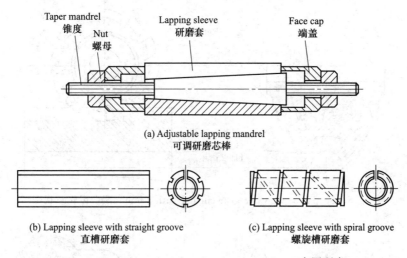

Fig. 8.83 Internal surface lapping operation 内圆研磨

(9) Gear cutting 齿轮加工

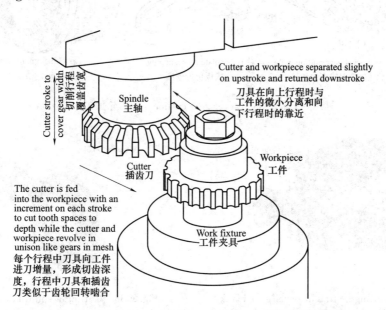

Fig. 8.84 Operation zone of a gear shaper 插齿刀工作区域

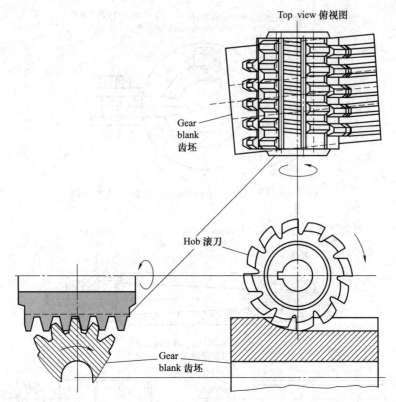

Fig. 8.85　Three views of gear cutting with a hob　滚切齿轮三视图

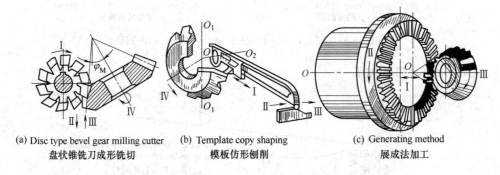

(a) Disc type bevel gear milling cutter 盘状锥铣刀成形铣切　　(b) Template copy shaping 模板仿形刨削　　(c) Generating method 展成法加工

Fig. 8.86　Bevel gear cutting　锥齿轮加工

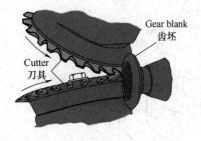

Fig. 8.87　Cutting a straight bevel-gear blank with two cutters　双刀切削直齿锥齿齿坯

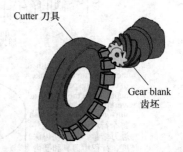

Fig. 8.88　Cutting a spiral bevel gear with a single cutter　单刀切削螺旋锥齿轮

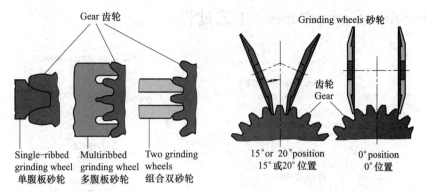

(a) Form grinding with shaped grinding wheels 成形砂轮成形磨齿

(b) Grinding by generating with two wheels 双砂轮展成磨齿

Fig. 8.89　Finishing gears by grinding　齿轮磨削精加工

(a) Spur gear 直齿齿轮

(b) Helical gear 斜齿齿轮

Fig. 8.90　Gear shaving　剃齿

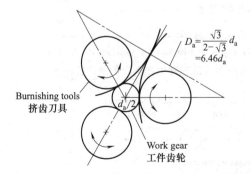

Fig. 8.91　Burnishing operation and maximum limit of addendum diameters of burnishing tools 挤齿加工及挤齿刀具的齿顶直径最大极限值

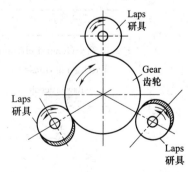

Fig. 8.92　Gear lapping　研磨齿轮

8.2　Machining procedures　工艺过程

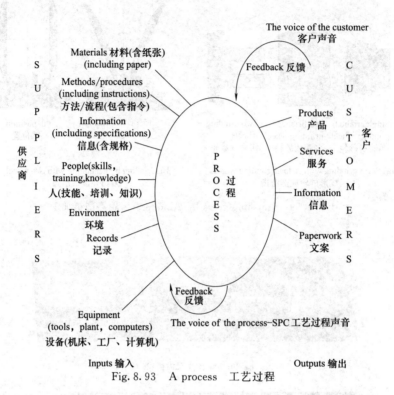

Fig. 8.93　A process　工艺过程

Fig. 8.94　General characteristics of three types of production methods: job shop, batch, and mass production　单件、成批和大量三种生产类型的通用特征

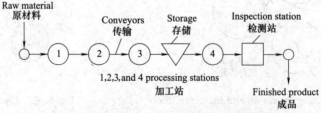

Fig. 8.95　Schematic of an automated production line (flood shop MS)
自动化生产线（流水线车间）布局

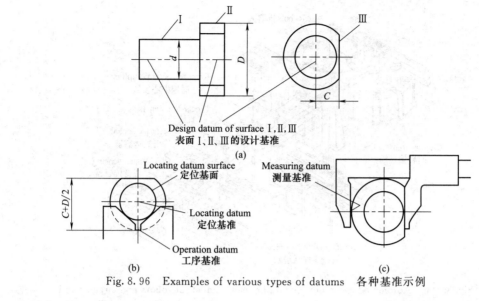

Fig. 8.96　Examples of various types of datums　各种基准示例

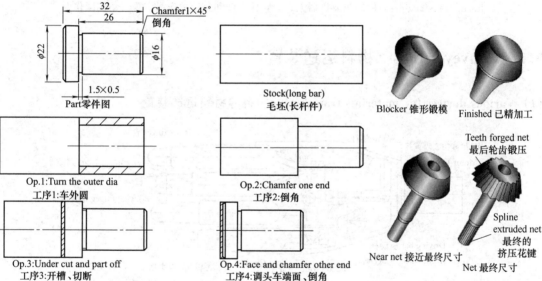

Fig. 8.97　Typical process pictures for machining a pin from a cylindrical bar on a lathe involving only external features
车床上将圆柱体棒料加工滚针外部的典型工艺图

Fig. 8.98　The steps involved in forging a bevel gear with a shaft　带轴锥齿轮锻压步骤

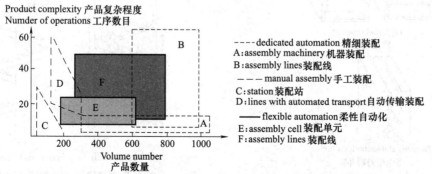

Fig. 8.99　Classification of assembly systems　装配系统的分类

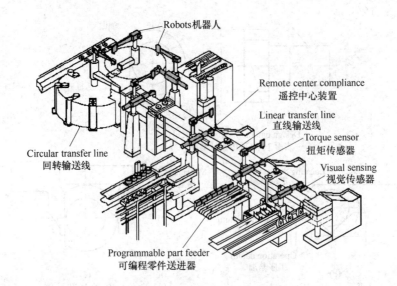

Fig. 8.100 Automated assembly operations using industrial robots and circular and linear transfer lines 使用工业机器人、回转输送线和直接输送线实现自动装配作业

8.3 Convey setups 物料运送装置

(1) Various devices for materials transferring 各种材料运送装置

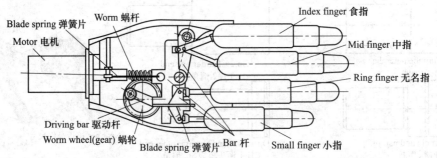

Fig. 8.101 Imitating jaw of human hand 仿人手手爪

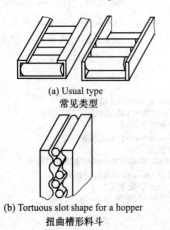

Fig. 8.102 Tray hoppers 槽形料斗

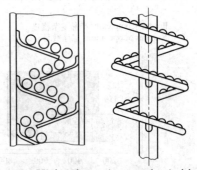

Fig. 8.103 High-volume zigzag and spiral hoppers 大容量交错输送槽和螺旋输送槽

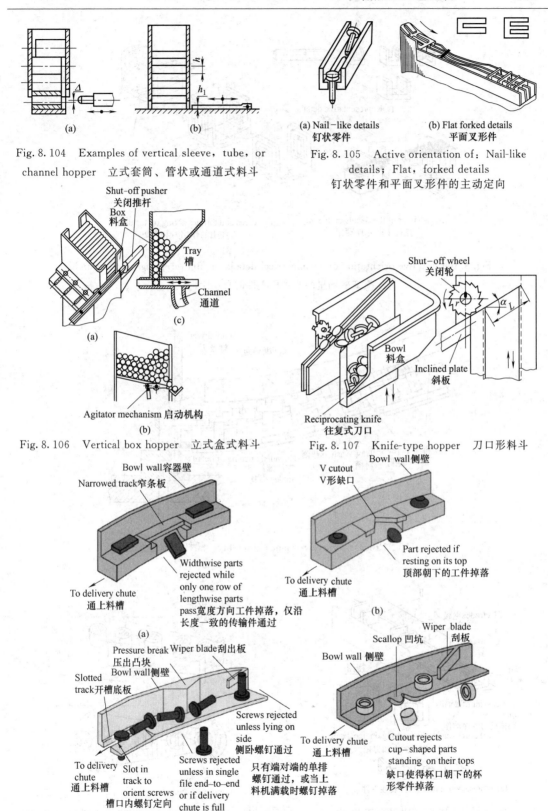

Fig. 8.104　Examples of vertical sleeve, tube, or channel hopper　立式套筒、管状或通道式料斗

Fig. 8.105　Active orientation of: Nail-like details; Flat, forked details　钉状零件和平面叉形件的主动定向

Fig. 8.106　Vertical box hopper　立式盒式料斗

Fig. 8.107　Knife-type hopper　刀口形料斗

Fig. 8.108　Various guides that ensure that parts are properly oriented for automated assembly　自动装配保证零件合理定向的各种导向器

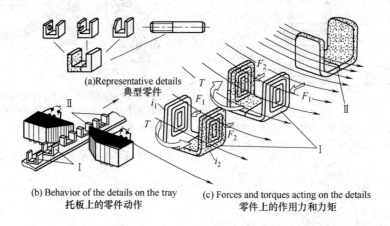

Fig. 8.109　Active orientation of asymmetrical details in an alternating magnetic field
交变磁场里的非对称零件的自动定向

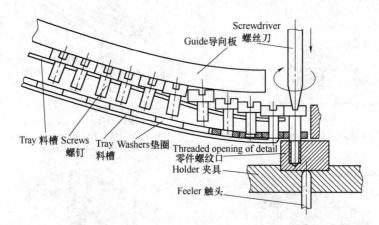

Fig. 8.110　Process of screw-washer assembly　螺杆垫圈装配过程

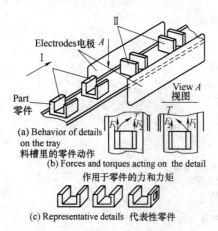

Fig. 8.111　Active orientation in an electrostatic field　静电场里主动定向

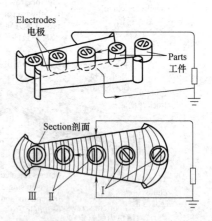

Fig. 8.112　Active orientation in an electrostatic field of a cylindrical detail having internal features
具有内部特征的圆柱体零件在电场里主动定向

(2) Convey mechanism and system 传输机构和系统

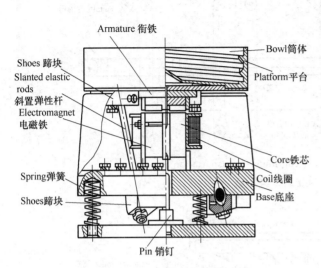

Fig. 8.113 Vibrofeeder 振动进给装置

Fig. 8.114 General view of a vibrofeeder with its controller 振动进料机及控制器外观图

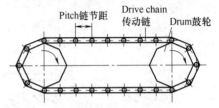

Fig. 8.115 Chain-type conveyor for periodic automatic processing
周期性自动处理装置的链式传动

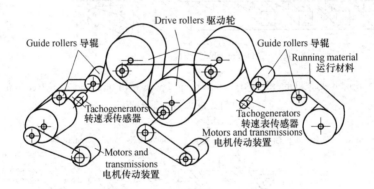

Fig. 8.116 Constant transportation speed system 恒速传输系统

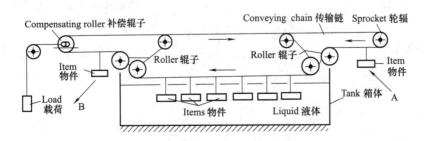

Fig. 8.117 Continuous transportation device 连续传输装置

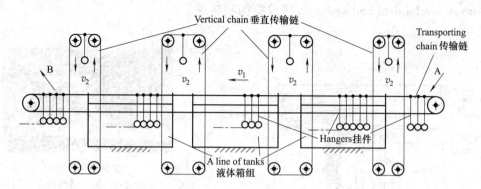

Fig. 8.118 Time-saving continuous transportation device
节时连续传输装置

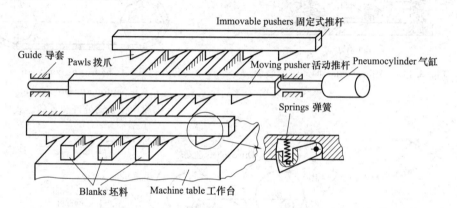

Fig. 8.119 Chainless transportation device with one degree of freedom
单自由度无链传输装置

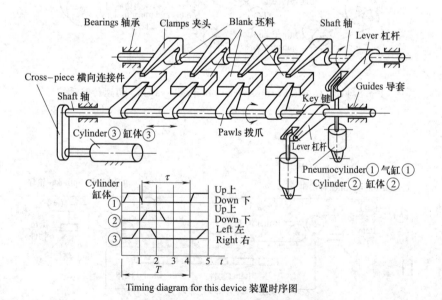

Fig. 8.120 Chainless transportation device with two degrees of freedom
两自由度无链传输装置

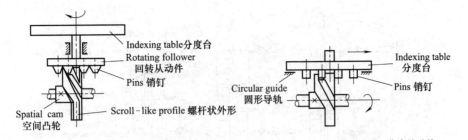

Fig. 8.121 Spatial cam drives for a circular transporting device 圆形传输装置的空间凸轮驱动机构

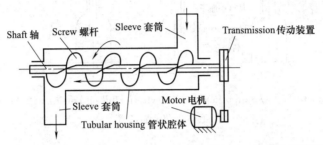

Fig. 8.122 Screw conveyor for feeding granular material 颗粒材料螺杆送进装置

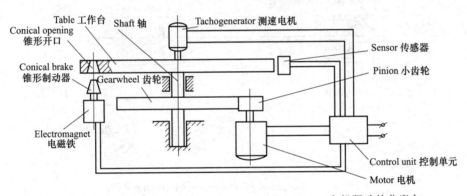

Fig. 8.123 Indexing table driven by an electric motor 电机驱动的分度台

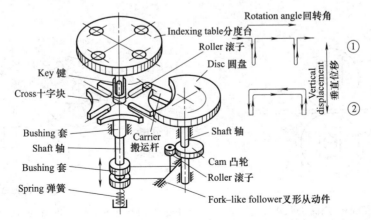

Fig. 8.124 Indexing mechanism with two degrees of freedom 两自由度分度机构
(①and②: two variations of the indexing mechanism movement 分度机构运动的两个变量)

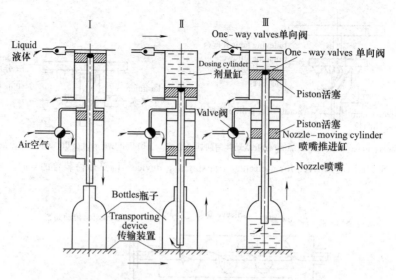

Fig. 8.125　Design of automatic device for filling bottles with liquid

液体自动装瓶装置

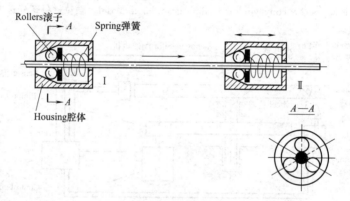

Fig. 8.126　Layout of portionwise wire feeding device

分段线材进给装置

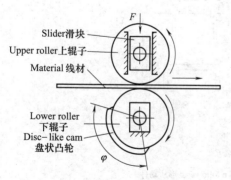

Fig. 8.127　Frictional roller device for continuous feeding of wires

线材连续送进摩擦辊装置

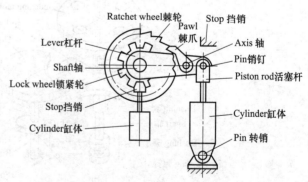

Fig. 8.128　Pneumatically driven indexing table

气动分度台

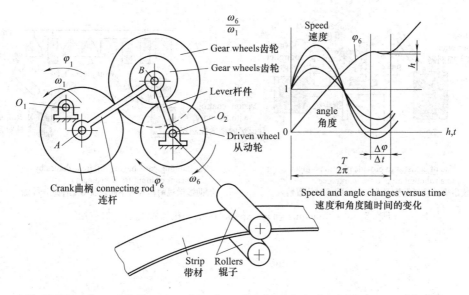

Fig. 8.129 Geared linkage as a drive for roller friction feeder for interrupted feeding
间隙进给摩擦滚子驱动进给机构的齿轮连杆

(3) Robot applications 机器人应用

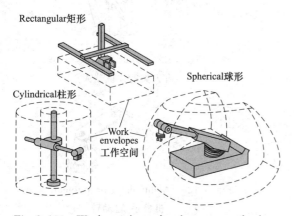

Fig. 8.130 Work envelopes for three types of robots
三种类型机器人的工作空间

Fig. 8.131 A robot gripper with tactile sensors
触觉传感器机器人夹头

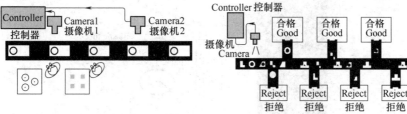

(a) In-line inspection of parts
工件在线检测

(b) Identification of parts with various shapes, and inspection and rejection of defective parts
各种形状工件的识别、检验和不合格件的拒收

Fig. 8.132

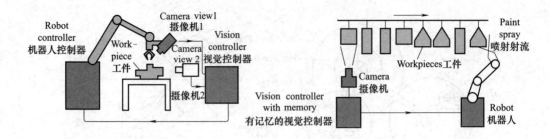

(c) Use of cameras to provide positional input to a robot relative to the workpiece
使用摄像机提供机器人与工件的相对位置输入

(d) Painting parts having different shapes by means of input from a camera
借助摄像机的输入对不同形状的工件进行喷涂

Fig. 8.132　Machine-vision applications　机器视觉系统的应用

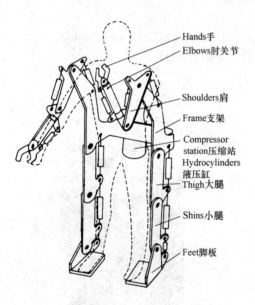

Fig. 8.133　Layout of an exoskeleton
（机器人）外骨骼设计

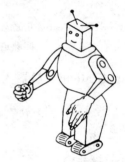

Fig. 8.134　Android-type robot
有人类特征机器人

Fig. 8.135　Manipulator or automatic arm
机械手/自动臂

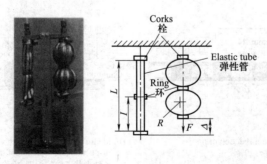

Fig. 8.136　Artificial "muscle"　人造"肌肉"

(4) Various vehicles 各种运输小车

Fig. 8.137 A self-guided vehicle carrying a machining pallet 搬运加工托盘的自导向小车

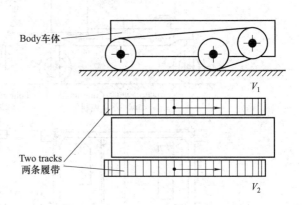

Fig. 8.138 Caterpillar-driven vehicle 履带驱动车辆

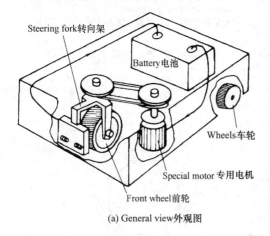

(a) General view 外观图

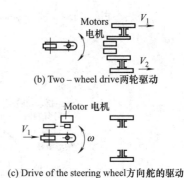

(b) Two-wheel drive 两轮驱动

(c) Drive of the steering wheel 方向舵的驱动

Fig. 8.139 Three-wheeled bogie 三轮小车

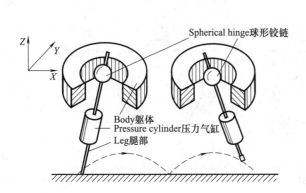

Fig. 8.140 One-legged hopper 单腿跳跃器

This is a vehicle for transportation in very rough terrain conditions which uses legged locomotion 这是一种适于高低不平地面行走，采用腿杆驱动的装置

Fig. 8.141 The adaptive suspension vehicle 适应性悬架行走装置

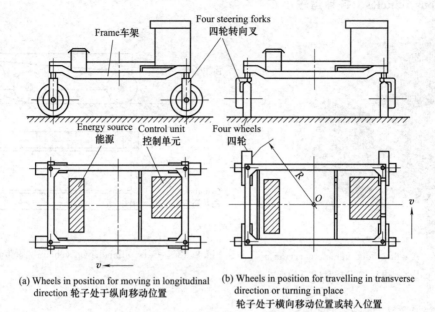

Fig. 8.142 Four-wheeled bogie （车轮可调转90°的）四轮小车

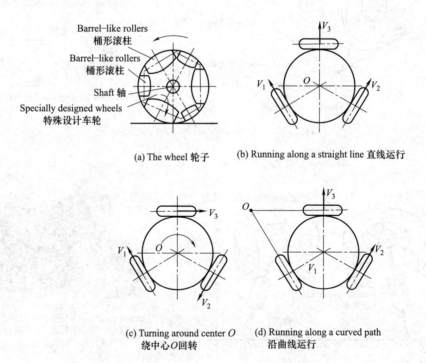

Fig. 8.143 Stanford three-wheeled bogie 斯坦福三轮小车

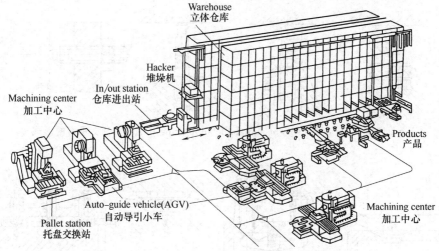

Fig. 8.144　Typical FMS　典型的柔性制造系统

8.4　Jig and fixture, tooling　工装夹具

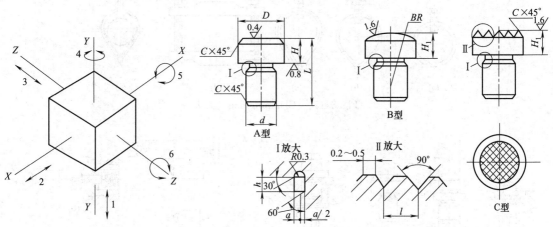

ig. 8.145　The six degrees of freedom 六个自由度

Fig. 8.146　Various forms of supporting pins　支承钉的形式

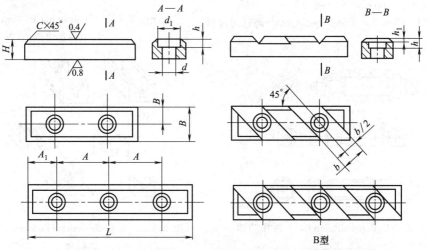

Fig. 8.147　Various forms of supporting plates　支承板的形式

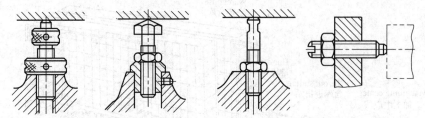

Fig. 8.148　Various forms of adjustable supporting pins　可调支承钉的形式

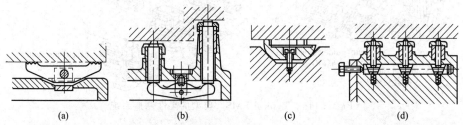

(a)　(b)　(c)　(d)

Fig. 8.149　Various forms of self-positioning supporting pins　自位支承钉的形式

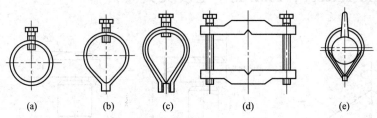

(a)　(b)　(c)　(d)　(e)

Fig. 8.150　Clamping dog　夹头

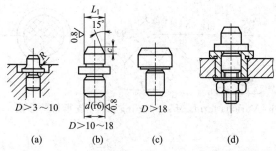

(a)　(b)　(c)　(d)

Fig. 8.151　Cylindrical positioning pin　圆柱定位销

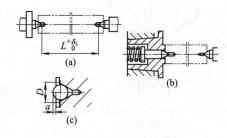

Fig. 8.152　Positioning by center hole
中心孔定位

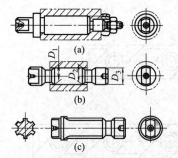

Fig. 8.153　Cylindrical mandrel　圆柱芯轴

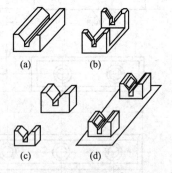

(a)　(b)　(c)　(d)

Fig. 8.154　V-positioning (locating) block
V形块

Fig. 8.155 Various types of mandrels to hold workpieces for turning. These mandrels are usually mounted between centers on a lathe 几种芯轴车削夹具；芯轴通常安装在车床的两个顶尖上
[note that in (a), both the cylindrical and the end faces of the workpiece can be machined, whereas in (b) and (c), only the cylindrical surfaces can be machined 注意图（a）的工件外圆和端面都可车削。图（b）、(c) 只能车外圆面]

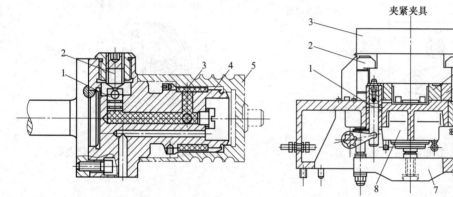

Fig. 8.156 Positioning and clamping fixture with liquidized plastics 液性塑料定心
1—Slide pin 滑柱；2—Clamp bolt 压钉；3—Liquidized plastics 液性塑料；4—Thin-wall bushing 薄壁套筒；5—Workpiece 工件

Fig. 8.157 Follower jig and fixture on automation line 自动线上随行夹具
1—Slide positioning pin 活动定位销；2—Hook clamping plate 钩形压板；3—Follower jig 随行夹具；4—Convey support 输送支承；5—Positioning support plate 定位支承板；6—Lubricating pump 润滑液压泵；7—Lever 杠杆；8—Hydraulic cylinder 液压缸

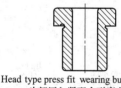

(a) Head type press fit wearing bushings 头部压入紧配合耐磨套 　(b) Headless type press fit wearing bushings 无端头压入紧配合耐磨套 　(c) Slip type renewable wearing bushings 滑移配合可拆卸耐磨套

(d) Fixed type renewable wearing bushings 固定式可拆卸耐磨套　(e) Headless type liner bushings 无端头直线型钻套　(f) Head type liner bushings 带端头直线型钻套

Fig. 8.158 Types of jig bushings 夹具衬套（钻套）类别

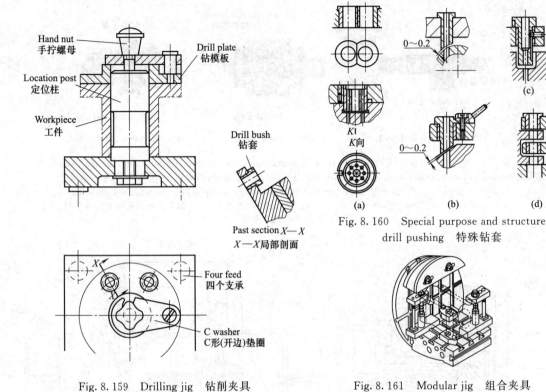

Fig. 8.159　Drilling jig　钻削夹具

Fig. 8.160　Special purpose and structure drill pushing　特殊钻套

Fig. 8.161　Modular jig　组合夹具

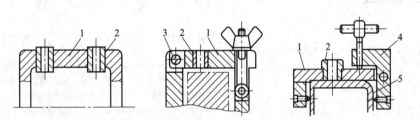

Fig. 8.162　Drill jig plate　钻模板
1—Drill jig plate　钻模板；2—Drill bushing　钻套；3—Pivot　转轴；
4—Clamping plate　压板；5—Workpiece　工件

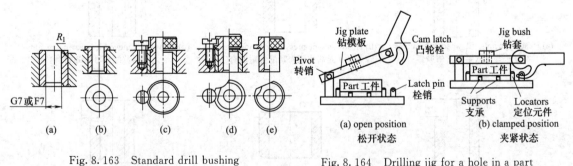

Fig. 8.163　Standard drill bushing
标准钻套

Fig. 8.164　Drilling jig for a hole in a part
钻孔夹具

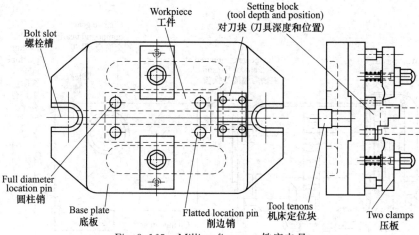

Fig. 8.165 Milling fixture 铣床夹具

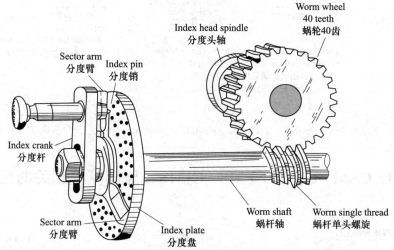

Fig. 8.166 Indexing method of a dividing head 分度头分度方法

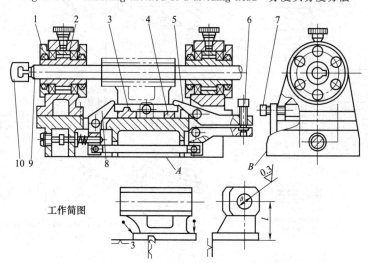

Fig. 8.167 Boring jig for tail stock machining 尾座镗削夹具

1—Jig frame 镗模架; 2—Boring bushing 镗套; 3,4—Positioning plate 定位板; 5,8—Clamping bar 压杆;
6—Clamping screw 夹紧螺钉; 7—Adjustable supporting 可调支承; 9—Tool bar 镗刀杆;
10—Floating couple 浮动接头

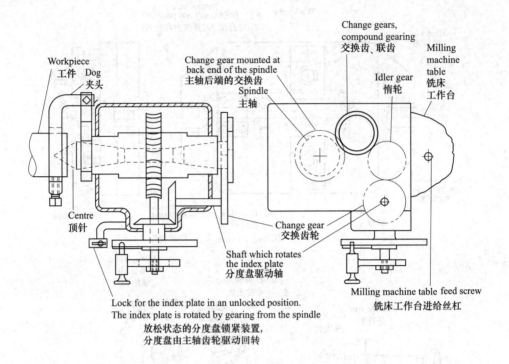

Fig. 8.168 Dividing head setup for differential indexing 差分分度头装置

8.5 CAD/CAM/CAPP/FMS/CIMS 与计算机相关的先进系统

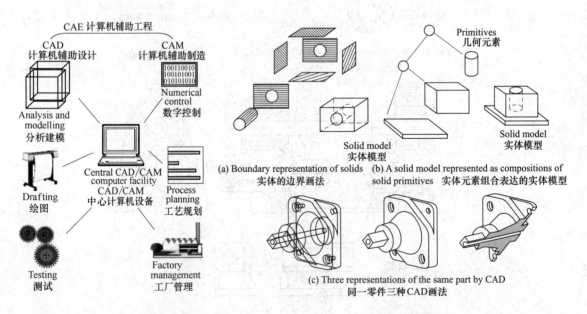

Fig. 8.169 CAE, CAD and CAM

Fig. 8.170 CAD Representations CAD 画法

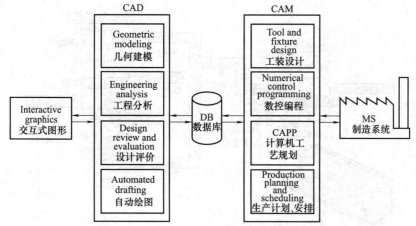

Fig. 8.171　Database to CAD/CAM　CAD/CAM 数据库

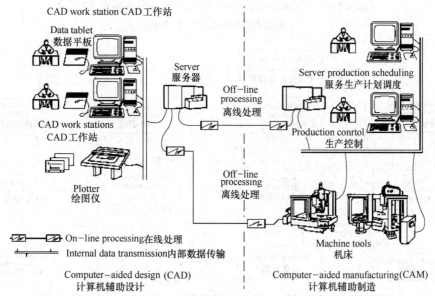

Fig. 8.172　Information flow chart in CAD/CAM application　CAD/CAM 信息流程图

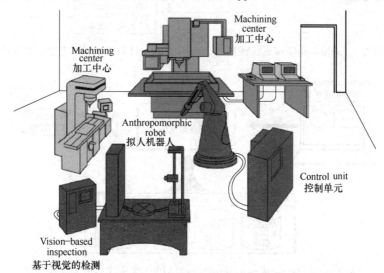

Fig. 8.173　A flexible manufacturing cell(FMC)　柔性制造单元

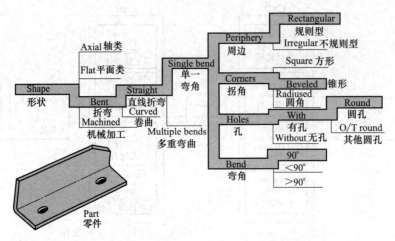

Fig. 8.174 Decision-tree classification for a sheet-metal bracket
板金支架零件的决策树分类

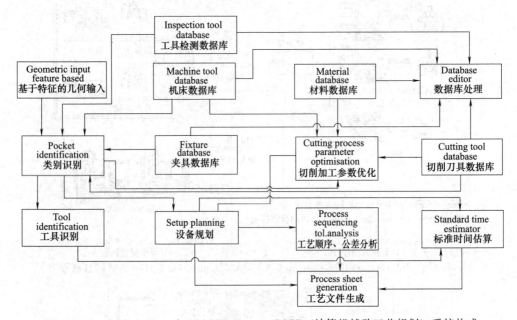

Fig. 8.175 Architecture of a CAPP system　CAPP（计算机辅助工艺规划）系统构成

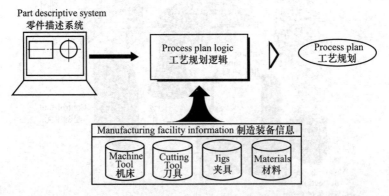

Fig. 8.176 Generative approach to CAPP　生成式 CAPP 系统构建

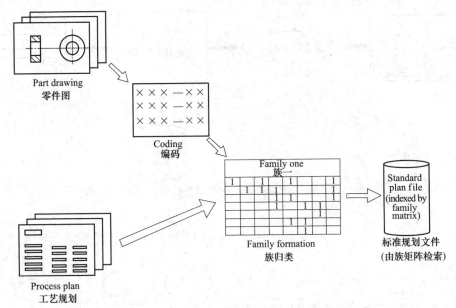

Fig. 8.177 Essential elements of a retrieval type CAPP system
搜索型 CAAPP 系统的基本构成要素

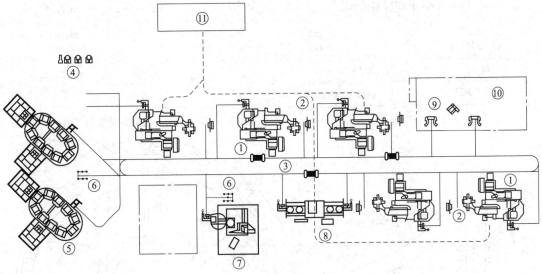

① Five CNC machine centers, 90 tools each 五台加工中心，每台 90 把刀
② Five tool interchange stations, one per machine, accepting tool delivery via cart 五个工具交换站，每台加工中心一个，接受小车来的工具交换
③ Three computer-controlled carts, with wire-guided path 三台计算机控制小车，及线导轨道
④ Cart maintenance station 小车维修站
⑤ Two automatic workchangers, 10 pallets each, with dual load/unload position with 90°tilt, 360°rotation 两台工件交换机，每台 10 个托盘，两个装/卸工位，可以 90°倾斜，360°旋转
⑥ Two material review stands, for on-demanding part inspection 两个材料检测站，用于检测所需工件
⑦ Inspection module, with horizontal arm coordinate measuring machine 检查模块，配卧式悬臂坐标测量机
⑧ Automatic part washing station 工件自动清洗站
⑨ Tool chain load/unload tool gage, and calibration gage stand 工具链式装卸检测仪，检查站
⑩ Elevated computer room, with DEC VAX 8200 central computer 升高电脑房，配 DEC AX 8200 中心计算机
⑪ Centralized chip/coolant collection/recovery system, with dual flume. …Flume path 切屑集中、冷却液收集循环系统，两个火警通道，防火设施等

Fig. 8.178 Typical FMS and its major identifiable components 典型柔性制造系统及其主要类同部件构成

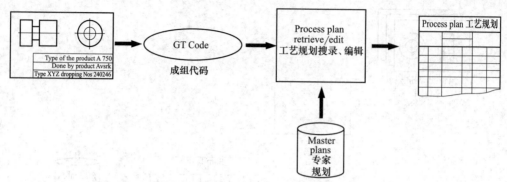

Fig. 8.179 Variant approach to CAPP CAPP 的派生式构建

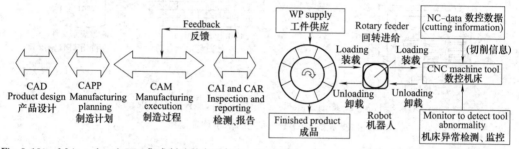

Fig. 8.180 Main tasks of CIM 集成制造的主要任务　　Fig. 8.181 Unmanned manufacturing cell 无人制造单元

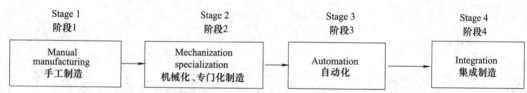

Fig. 8.182 Historical development of integrated manufacturing 集成制造发展历程

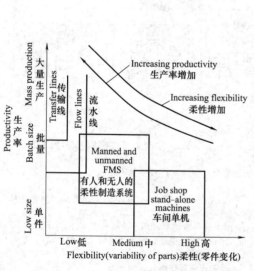

Fig. 8.183 Flexibility against production rate of different MSs 各种柔性系统的生产率与柔性对比

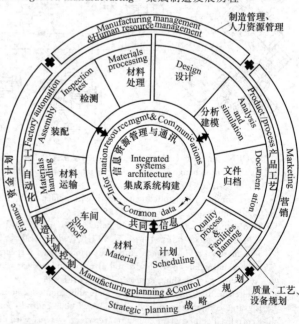

Fig. 8.184 CIM wheel 集成制造系统构成轮图

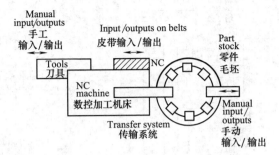

Fig. 8.185 Elementary cell 基本单元

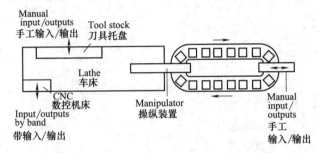

Fig. 8.186 Simple turning cell for small work piece
小件加工的简单车削单元

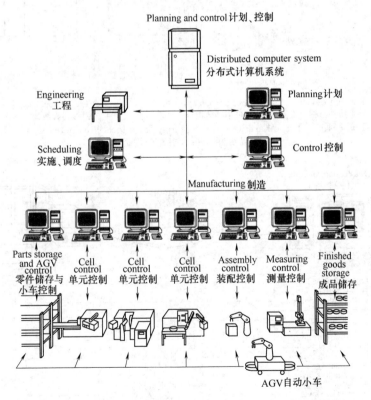

Fig. 8.187 A computer integrated manufacturing system (CIMS)
计算机集成制造系统

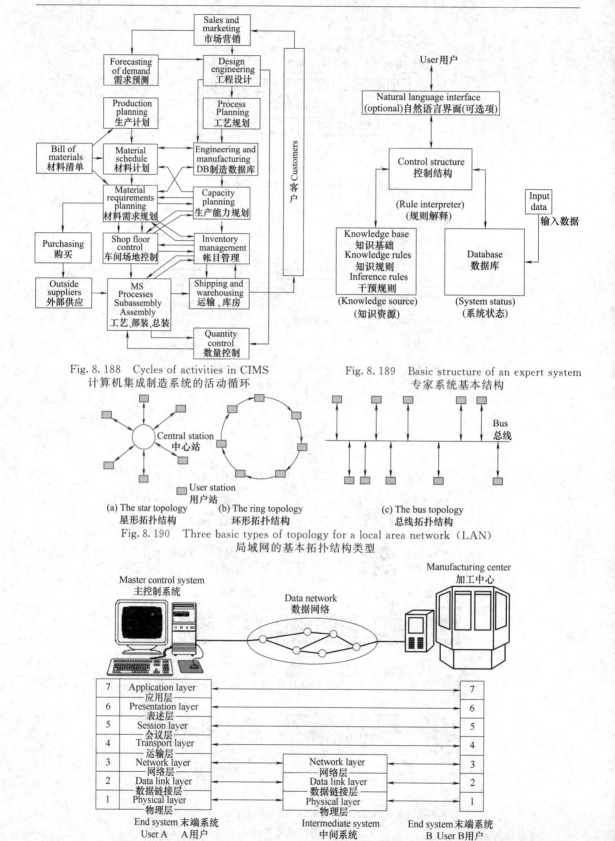

Fig. 8.188　Cycles of activities in CIMS　计算机集成制造系统的活动循环

Fig. 8.189　Basic structure of an expert system　专家系统基本结构

Fig. 8.190　Three basic types of topology for a local area network (LAN)　局域网的基本拓扑结构类型

Fig. 8.191　The ISO/OSI reference model for open communication　开放式通信 ISO/OSI 参考模型

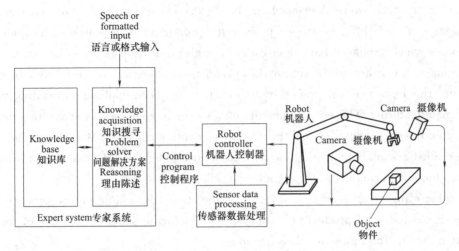

Fig. 8.192 Expert system, as applied to an industrial robot guided by machine vision
专家系统用于视觉引导的工业机器人

Fig. 8.193 A general view of a flexible manufacturing system 柔性制造系统外观图

8.6 Short passage for reading 阅读短文

Evolution of Automation

Some metalworking processes were developed as early as 4000 B.C.. However, it was not until the beginning of the Industrial Revolution in the 1750s (also referred to as the First Industrial Revolution) that automation began to be introduced in the production of goods. Machine tools (such as turret lathes, automatic screw machines, and automatic bottle-making equipment) began to be developed in the late 1890s. Mass-production techniques and transfer machines were developed in the 1920s. These machines had fixed automatic mechanisms and were designed to produce specific products best represented by the automobile industry which produced passenger cars at a high production rate and low cost.

The major breakthrough in automation began with numerical control (NC) of machine tools. Since this historic development, rapid progress has been made in automating most aspects of manufacturing. These developments involve the introduction of computers into automation, computerized numerical control (CNC), adaptive control (AC), industrial robots, computer-aided design, engineering, and manufacturing (CAD/CAE/CAM), and computer-integrated manufacturing (CIM) systems.

Manufacturing involves various levels of automation, depending on the processes used, the product desired, and production volumes. Manufacturing systems in order of increasing automation include the following classifications:

Job shops: These facilities use general-purpose machines and machining centers with high levels of human labor involvement.

Stand-alone NC production: This uses numerically controlled machines but with significant operator/machine interaction.

Manufacturing cells: These use a designed cluster of machines with integrated computer control and flexible material handling—often with industrial robots

Flexible manufacturing systems: These use computer control of all aspects of manufacturing, the simultaneous incorporation of a number of manufacturing cells, and automated material-handling systems.

Flexible manufacturing lines: Organize computer-controlled machinery in production lines instead of cells. Part transfer is through hard automation, product flow is more limited than in flexible manufacturing systems, but the through put is larger for higher production quantities.

Flowlines and transfer lines: Consist of organized groupings of machinery with automated material handling between machines. The manufacturing line is designed with limited or no flexibility, since the goal is to produce a single part.

自动化发展沿革

早在公元4000年前有些金属加工工艺就已出现，然而，直到18世纪50年代的工业革命开始（又称为第一次工业革命），自动化才开始进入产品的生产。机床（如转塔车床、自动螺纹加工机、自动制瓶设备）始于19世纪90年代后期。批量生产工艺和传输线始于20世纪20年代。这些机器配备固定的自动机构，设计用于生产特色产品，最具代表的就是高效低成本生产乘用车的汽车工业。

自动化的主要突破始于机床数控技术，从此，制造领域的各个方面取得了巨大进步。这些进步包括计算机进入自动化领域、计算机数字控制、适应控制、工业机器人、计算机辅助设计、计算机辅助工程、计算机辅助制造、计算机集成制造系统。

制造业涉及不同程度的自动化水平，主要取决于所采用的工艺方法、需求产品、产品规模。按照自动化程度增加的序列，制造系统有如下类别。

修理车间：设备主要为通用机床和涉及高水平人力的加工中心。

单机数控机床：采用数控机床，显然需配备操作人员干预机床。

制造单元：采用一系列的专门设计机床，配备计算机集成控制和通常为工业机器人的柔性材料处理装置。

柔性制造系统：制造的各个环节采用计算机控制，涉及诸多同步制造单元和材料自动处理系统。

柔性制造生产线：计算机控制生产线代替制造单元，通过刚性自动化传输工件。与柔性制造系统相比，产品品种和传输方式受到限制，但是其传输量大，用于大量生产。

流水线和传输线：包括成组的机器设备和机器之间的自动材料处理装置。生产性柔性受限或没有柔性，因为其目标在于单一工件。

Unit 9　Engineering Materials and Mould
工程材料和模具

9.1　Engineering materials　工程材料

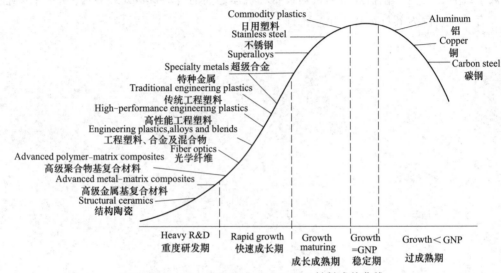

Fig. 9.1　Materials maturity curve　材料成熟曲线

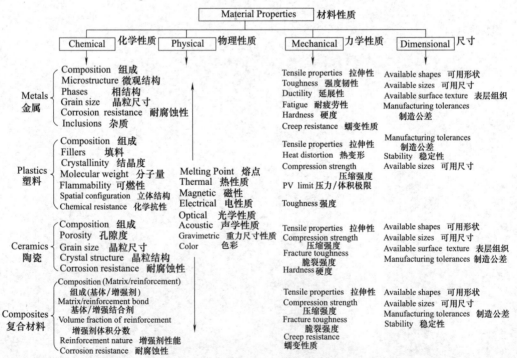

Fig. 9.2　Spectrum of material properties　材料性质图谱

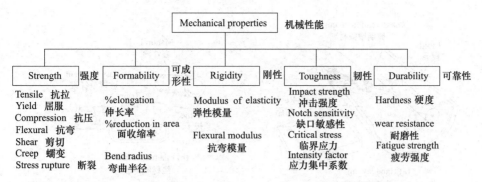

Fig. 9.3　Spectrum of mechanical properties　机械性能图谱

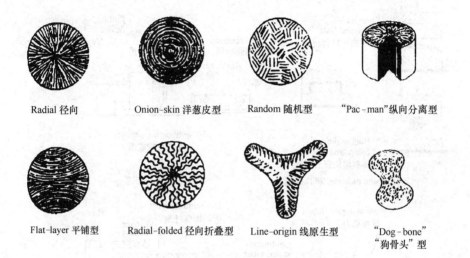

Fig. 9.4　Summary of possible carbon fiber morphologies
可能的碳纤维形状汇总

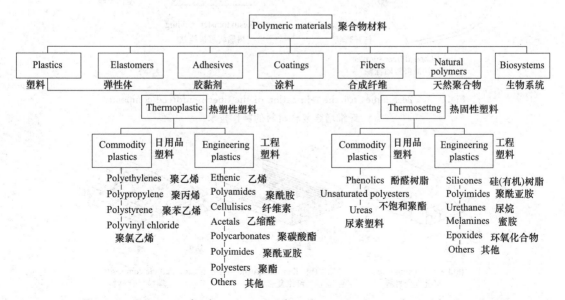

Fig. 9.5　Spectrum of polymeric materials and some important thermoplastic and thermosetting plastic families　聚合物材料及重要的热塑性、热固性塑料族谱

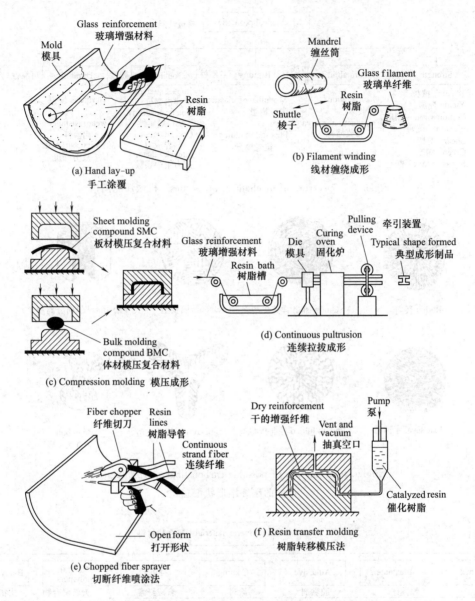

Fig. 9.6　Techniques for the fabrication of the fiber-reinforced composites
纤维增强复合材料的制作技术

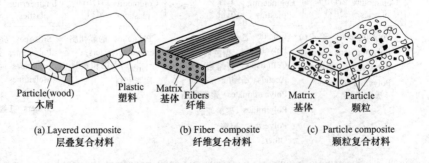

Fig. 9.7　Typical composites　典型复合材料

Unit 9 Engineering Materials and Mould 工程材料和模具

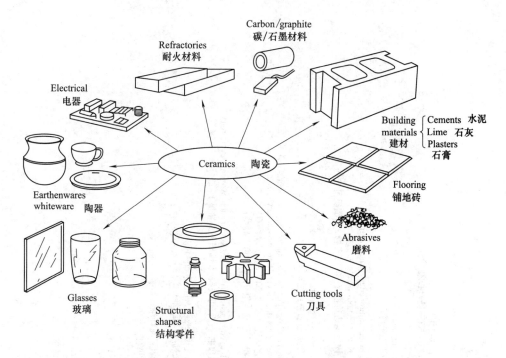

Fig. 9.8　Spectrum of ceramic uses　陶瓷材料应用谱图

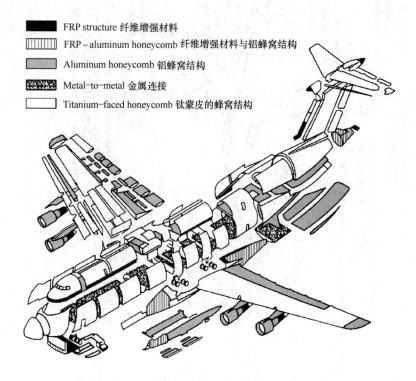

Fig. 9.9　Advanced materials used on transport aircraft
运输机上采用的先进材料

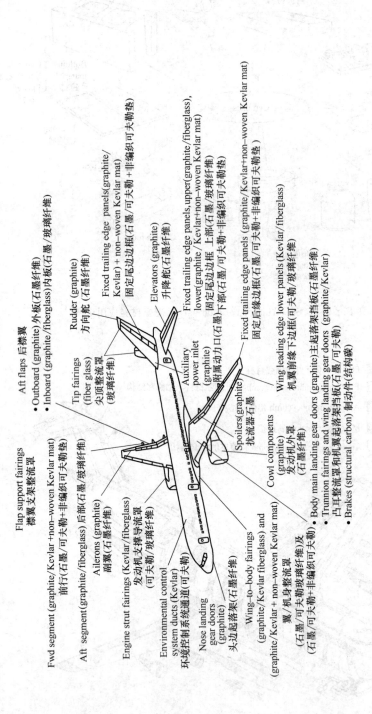

Fig. 9.10 Application of advanced composite materials in commercial aircraft
商用飞机上应用的先进复合材料

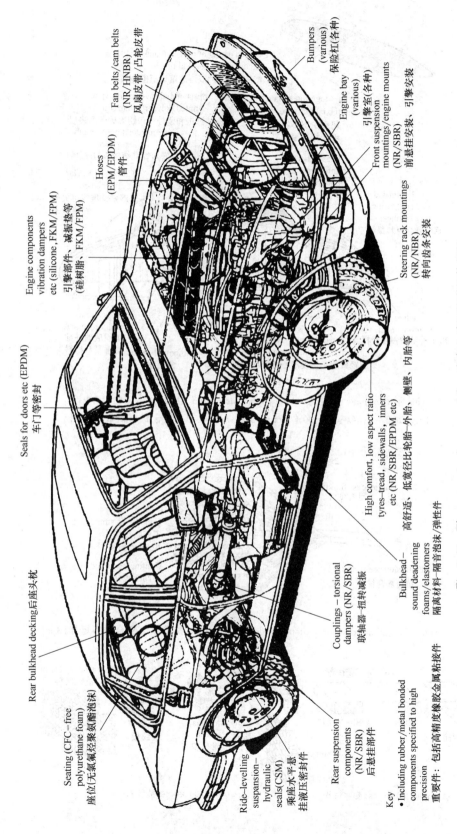

Fig. 9.11　Elastomers in the automobile　汽车上采用的弹性体材料

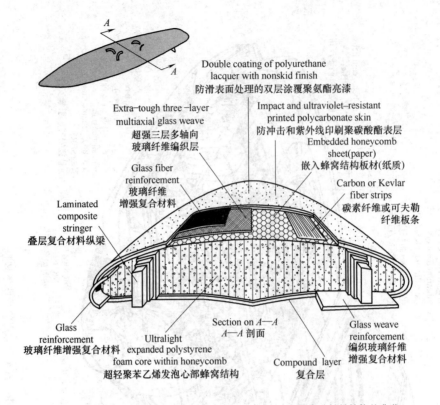

This is an example of advanced materials construction. 这是先进材料结构的典范
Fig. 9.12 Cross-section of a composite sailboard 复合材料帆板断面图

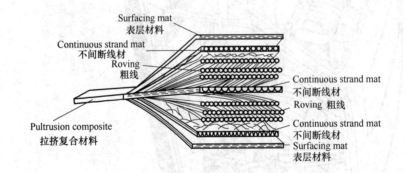

Fig. 9.13 Exploded view of pultruded composite 拉挤成形复合材料爆炸图

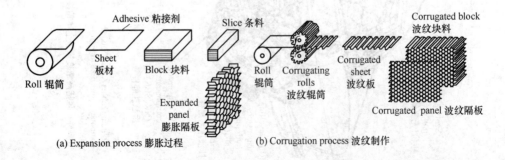

(a) Expansion process 膨胀过程　　(b) Corrugation process 波纹制作

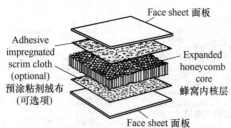

(c) Assembling a honeycomb structure into a laminate 安装蜂窝结构在夹层板里

Fig. 9.14 Methods of manufacturing honeycomb structures 蜂窝夹层结构制造方法

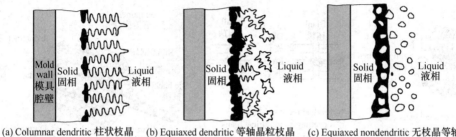

(a) Columnar dendritic 柱状枝晶　(b) Equiaxed dendritic 等轴晶粒枝晶　(c) Equiaxed nondendritic 无枝晶等轴晶粒

Fig. 9.15 Three basic types of cast structures 三种基本晶粒铸件结构

9.2 Mould and die for metals 金属模具

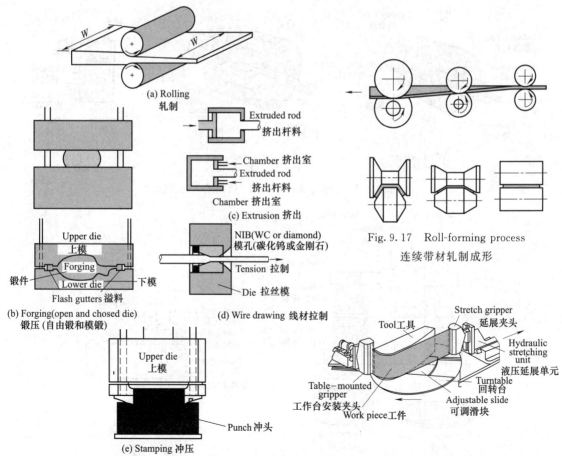

Fig. 9.16 Metal forming processes that make use of cold working as well as hot working 金属的冷态及热态成形工艺

Fig. 9.17 Roll-forming process 连续带材轧制成形

Fig. 9.18 Stretch Bending 延展折弯

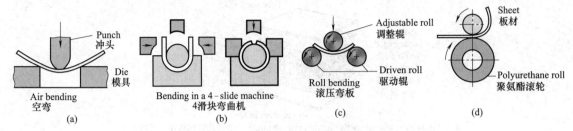

Fig. 9.19　Examples of various bending operations　几种弯曲工艺示例

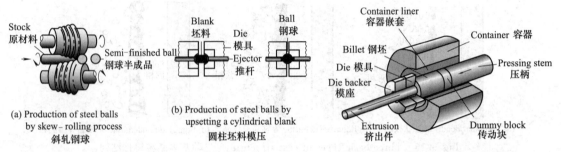

Fig. 9.20　Steel ball machined by dies　模具加工钢球

Fig. 9.21　Illustration of the direct-extrusion process　直接挤出工艺

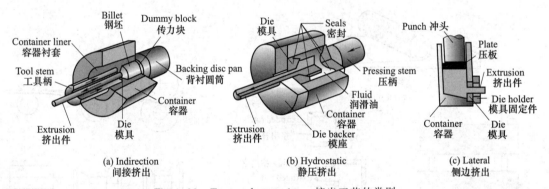

Fig. 9.22　Types of extrusion　挤出工艺的类别

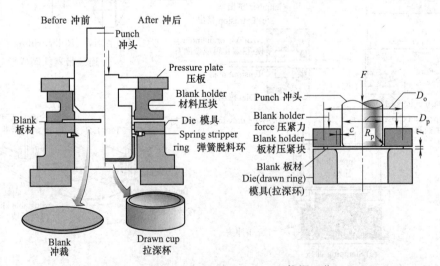

Fig. 9.23　Deep-drawing process　拉深工艺

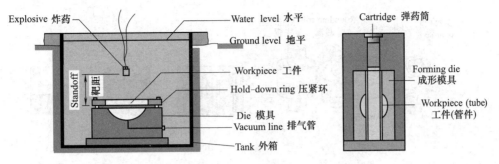

Fig. 9.24　Explosive forming process　爆炸成形工艺

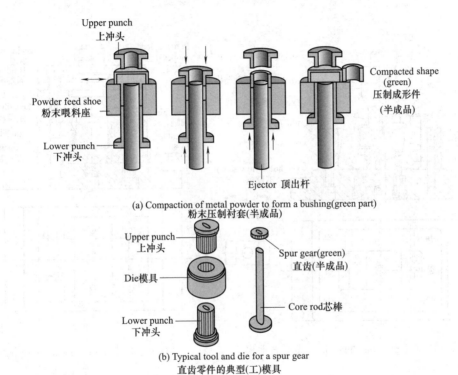

Fig. 9.25　Powder metallurgy process　粉末冶金成形工艺

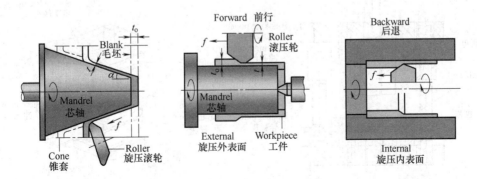

Fig. 9.26　Shear-spinning process　剪旋工艺

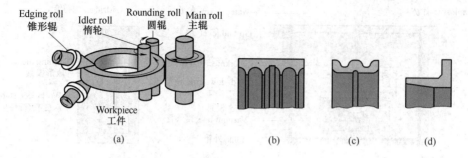

Fig. 9.27 Ring rolling operations 环件的滚压加工

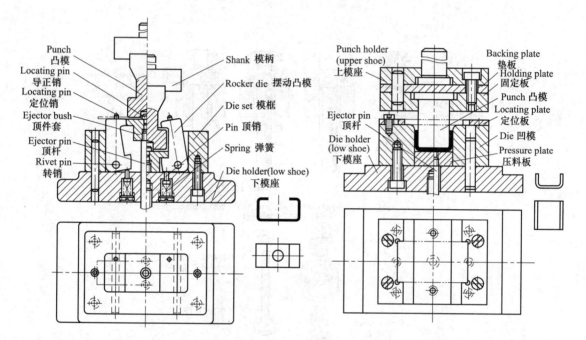

Fig. 9.28 Complex bending dies 复合弯曲模

Fig. 9.29 Bending die for U-type job U形件弯曲模

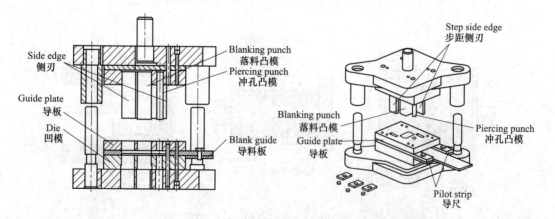

Fig. 9.30 Progressive die and its model 连续冲裁模（又称级进模）及模型

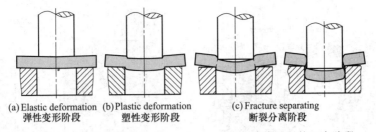

Fig. 9.31 Deformation process of stamping 冲裁过程的三个阶段

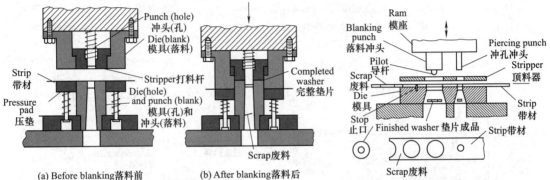

Fig. 9.32 Before and after blanking a common washer in a compound die 复合模具对普通垫片落料前、后图

Fig. 9.33 Schematic illustration of making a washer in a progressive die 级进模加工垫片图解

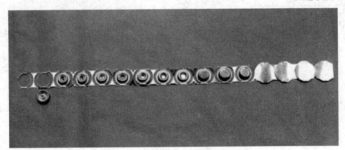

Fig. 9.34 Forming of the top piece of an aerosol spray can in a progressive die 级进模上喷雾罐顶片的成形

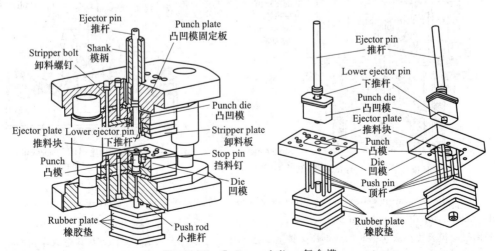

Fig. 9.35 Compound die 复合模

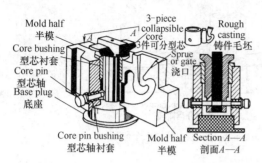

Fig. 9.36　A typical permanent mold arrangement for nonferrous casting　典型有色金属永久型铸造

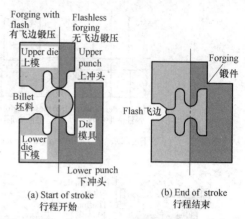

Fig. 9.37　Comparison of closed-die forging to precision or flashless forging of a cylindrical billet　圆柱坯料闭合模具精锻与无飞边锻压的比较

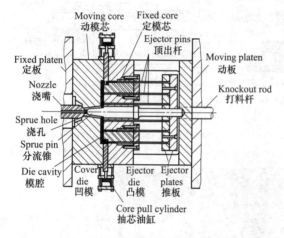

Fig. 9.38　Sectional drawing of a typical die cast　典型压铸模具剖面图

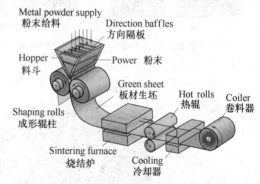

Fig. 9.39　An illustration of powder rolling　粉末滚压成形

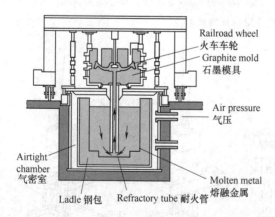

Fig. 9.40　The bottom-pressure casting process utilizes graphite molds for the production of steel railroad wheels　采用石墨模具生产火车钢轮的底部压力铸造工艺

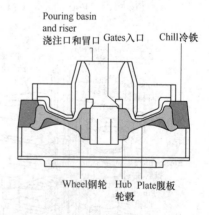

Fig. 9.41　Gravity-pouring method of casting a railroad wheel　重力浇注方法铸造火车钢轮

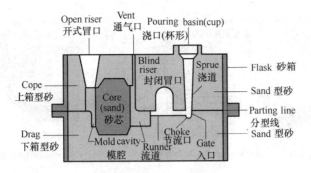

Fig. 9.42　Schematic illustration of a sand mold, showing various features
砂型模具结构特征

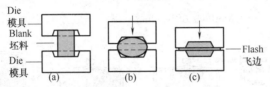

Fig. 9.43　Stages in impressin-die forging of a solid round billet
实心圆形棒料的型腔模锻的不同阶段

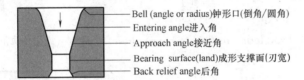

Fig. 9.44　Terminology of a typical die used for drawing round rod or wire
圆形棒料或线材拉制典型模具术语

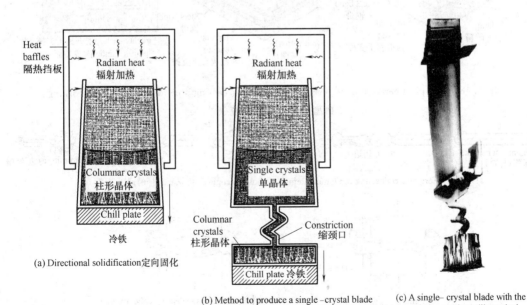

Fig. 9.45　Methods of casting turbine blades　涡轮叶片铸造方法

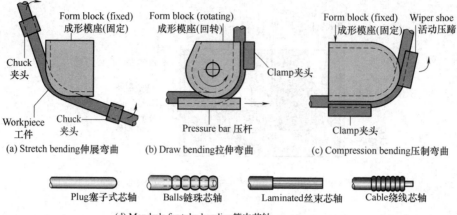

Fig. 9.46 Methods of bending tubes 弯管方法

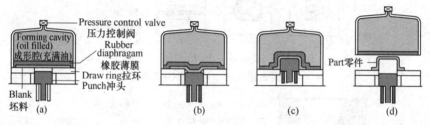

Fig. 9.47 The hydroform (or fluid forming) process 液压（流体）成形工艺

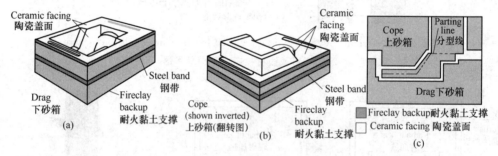

Fig. 9.48 A typical ceramic mold (shaw process) for casting steel dies used in hot forging 典型的热锻铸钢陶瓷模

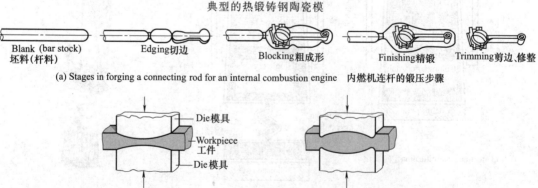

Fig. 9.49 Forging a connecting rod 连杆的锻压

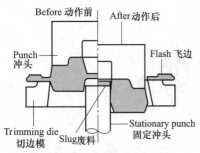

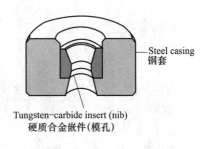

Fig. 9.50　Trimming flash from a forged part　锻件飞边去除

The thin material at the center is removed by punching
中心薄片材料靠冲头去除

Fig. 9.51　Tungsten-carbide die insert in a steel casing　钢套里嵌入硬质合金模具

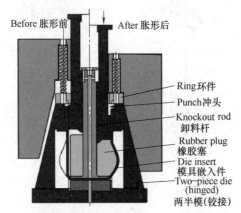

(a) The bulging of a tubular part with a flexible plug
管件柔性塞子胀形

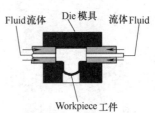

(b) Expanding tubular blanks under internal pressure
管件(流体)内压膨胀

Fig. 9.52　Bulging　胀芯成形

Fig. 9.53　Comparison of sheared edges produced by conventional (left) and by fine-blanking (right) techniques　传统方法落料（左图）和精密落料（右图）的剪切边口比较

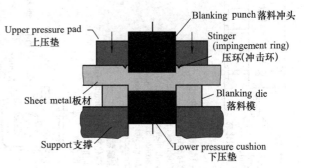

Fig. 9.54　Schematic illustration of one setup for fine blanking　精密落料装置图

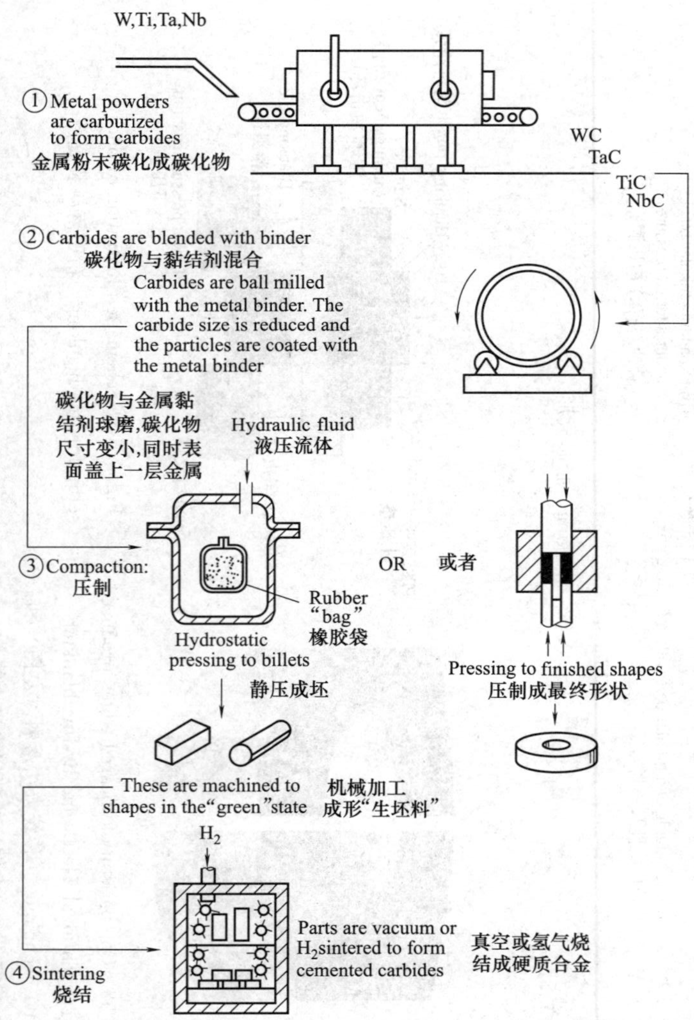

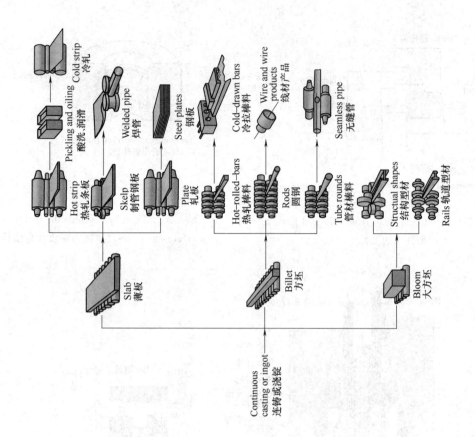

Fig. 9.56 Schematic outline of various flat-rolling and shaped-rolling 板材和型材轧制工艺示意图

Fig. 9.55 Making of cemented carbide steps 硬质合金的制备过程

9.3 Die and mould for plastics 塑料模具

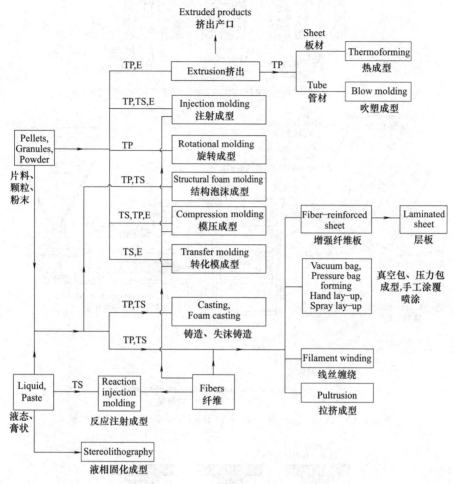

Fig. 9.57 Outline of forming and shaping processes for plastics, elastomers, and composite materials
塑性、弹塑性、复合材料的成型工艺概览

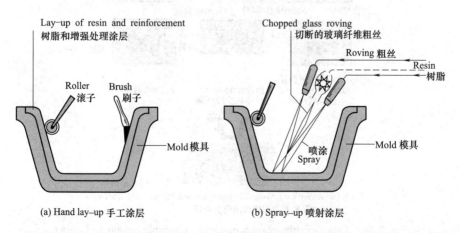

Fig. 9.58 Manual methods of processing reinforced plastics 手工制造增强塑料的方法

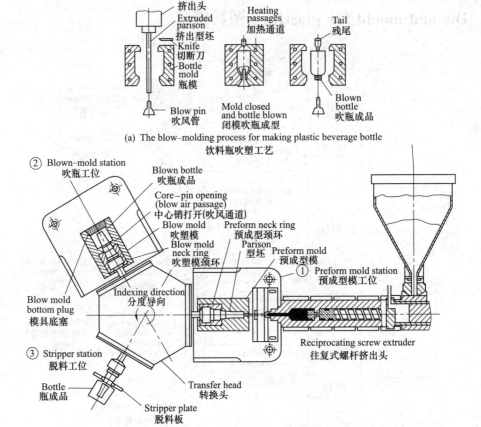

Fig. 9.59 Schematic illustration of the blow-molding 吹塑图解

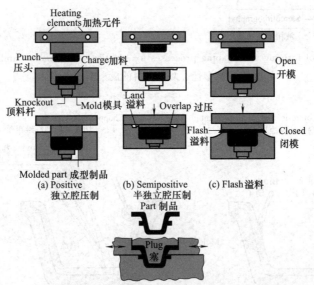

Fig. 9.60 Types of compression molding, a process similar to forging
模具压制成形的类别，方法类似于锻压

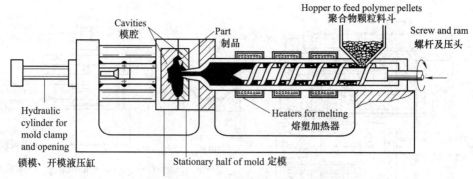

Fig. 9.61　Injection molding　注射成型

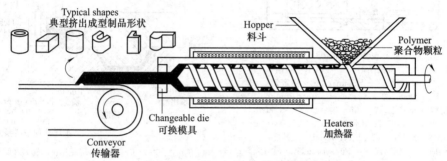

Fig. 9.62　Extrusion　挤出成型

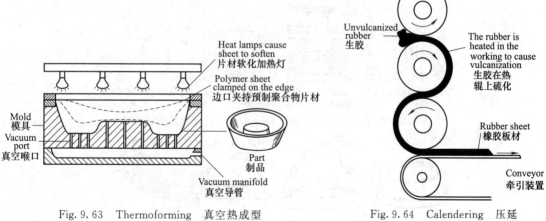

Fig. 9.63　Thermoforming　真空热成型　　　　Fig. 9.64　Calendering　压延

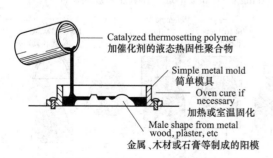

Fig. 9.65　Casting　浇铸成型

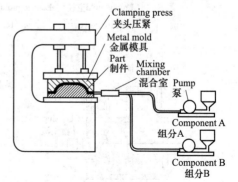

Fig. 9.66　Reaction injection molding
反应注射模具

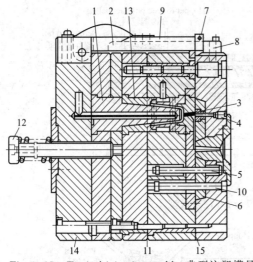

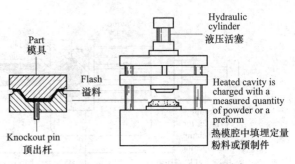

Fig. 9.68　Compression molding　压制成型

Fig. 9.67　Typical injection mold　典型注塑模具
1—Mold core 模具型芯；2—Latch 插销；
3—Sprue 直浇道；4—Retainer pin 固定销；
5,10—Bolt head 插销头；6—Sprue-stripping plate 注料口分模板；7—Pin 销；8—Guide strip 导轨；9—Waterway 冷却水道；11—Main parting line 主要分型线；12—Ejector rod 顶料杆；
13—Stripper sleeve 分型套；14—Plate assembly 模板装置；
15—Sprue separating area 浇道分型面

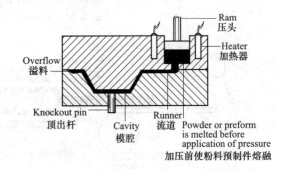

Fig. 9.69　Transfer molding　转移模压法

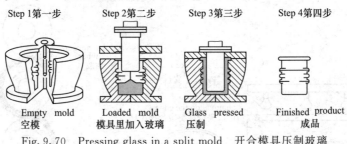

Fig. 9.70　Pressing glass in a split mold　开合模具压制玻璃

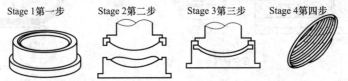

Fig. 9.71　Manufacturing a glass item by pressing glass in a mold　模具压制玻璃器件

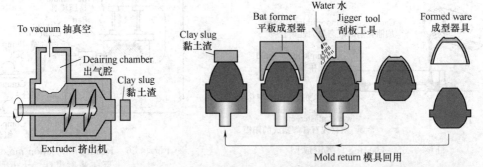

Fig. 9.72　Extruding　挤出工艺　　Fig. 9.73　Jiggering operations　刮板模具工艺

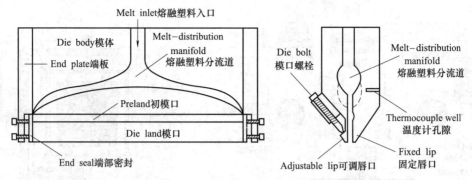

Fig. 9.74　Die geometry for extruding sheet　板材挤出模具几何形状

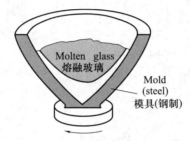

Fig. 9.75　Centrifugal casting of glass　玻璃的离心铸造

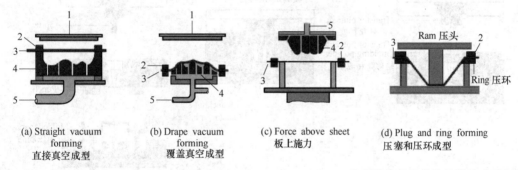

Fig. 9.76　Various thermoforming processes for thermoplastic sheet　热塑性板材的几种热塑性成型方法
1—Heater 加热器；2—Clamp 夹头；3—Plastic sheet 塑料板；4—Mold 模具；5—Vacuum line 真空管

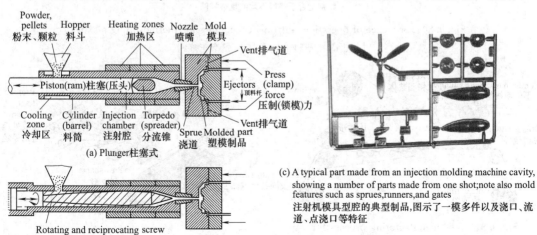

Fig. 9.77　Injection molding　注射模

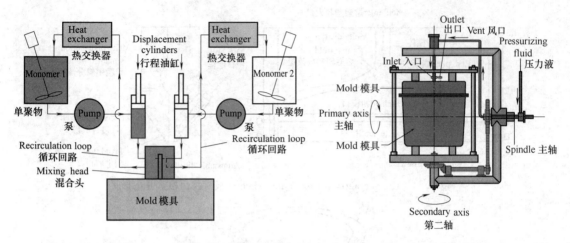

Fig. 9.78　Reaction-injection molding process
反应注射模具成型工艺

Fig. 9.79　The rotational molding (rotomolding or rotocasting) process　回转模具成型工艺

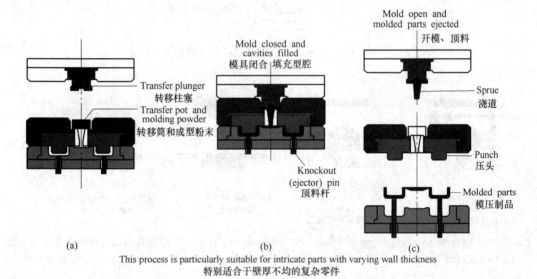

This process is particularly suitable for intricate parts with varying wall thickness
特别适合于壁厚不均的复杂零件

Fig. 9.80　Sequence of operations in transfer molding for thermosetting plastics
热固性塑料的转移模具成型工序

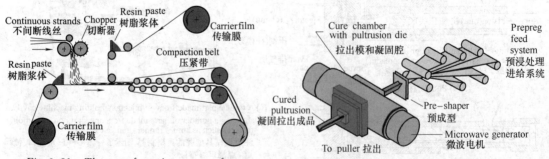

Fig. 9.81　The manufacturing process for producing reinforced plastic sheets
增强塑料板材生产过程

Fig. 9.82　Pultrusion process　拉出工艺

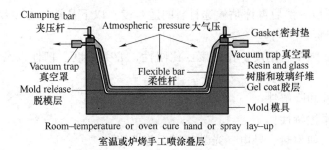

Fig. 9.83　Vacuum-bag forming　真空包成型

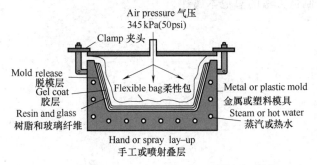

Fig. 9.84　Pressure-bag forming　压力包成型

9.4　Short passage for reading　阅读短文

Selection of Plastics

Material selection is not as difficult as it might appear but it does require an awareness of the general behaviour of plastics as a group, as well as a familiarity with the special characteristics of individual plastics. The first and most important steps in the design process are to define clearly the purpose and function of the proposed product and to identify the service environment. Then one has to assess the suitability of a range of candidate materials. The following are generally regarded as the most important characteristics requiring consideration for most engineering components:

① mechanical properties - strength, stiffness, specific strength and stiffness, fatigue and toughness, and the influence of high or low temperatures on these properties;

② corrosion susceptibility and degradation;

③ wear resistance and frictional properties;

④ special properties, for example, thermal, electrical, optical and magnetic;

⑤ moulding and/or other methods of fabrication;

⑥ total costs attributable to the selected material and manufacturing route.

塑料材料的选择

材料的选择并非它所呈现的那么困难，但是也需要了解某类塑料或某一族塑料的通用特征及个别塑料的特性。设计过程的第一步也是最为重要的一步，就是要明确产品的目标和功能，了解其工作环境。然后再评估候选材料的适合度。以下是被认为多数工程零件需要考虑的最重要的性能指标。

① 力学性能：强度、刚度、比强度、比刚性、疲劳强度、韧性以及温度的高低对这些性能的影响情况。

② 腐蚀敏感性和降解性。

③ 抗磨性和摩擦特性。

④ 特殊性能，如耐热、导电、光学、磁学等性能。

⑤ 模具和/或其他的生产方法。

⑥ 所选材料及制造方法的总成本属性。

Vocabulary with Figure Index
词汇及图形索引（英中对照）

4-way valve 四通阀 104

A

abrasive 磨具 138
abrasive disc grinder 圆盘打磨机 112
abrasive disc precision polisher 圆盘精密抛光机 112
abrasive disc 磨盘，砂轮 150
abrasive slurry 研磨膏 192
abrasive tank 磨料箱 113
abrasives process 磨削加工 291
absorption 吸振 4
absorption filter 吸收过滤器 34
accumulator 蓄能器 120
acme thread 梯形螺纹 49
acoustic horn 变幅杆 227
actuator 启动器 7
adapter 适配连接器 76
addative 添加剂 141
adhesive bonding 粘接 185
adjustable slide 可调滑块 337
adjuster cable 调节绳 76
adjusting snob 调节旋钮 111
adjustment nut 调节螺母 84
air cushion 气垫 97
air lock 气动锁 6
air supply gas mask 供气面罩 5
air vent 通气孔 67
air-gage system 气动测量仪 30
air-operated clutch 气动离合器 75

AJ 磨料射流加工 236
aligner 定位器 231
allen key 内六角扳手 150
alternator housing 发电机箱 195
amplifier 放大器 33,36
anchor plate 固定板 76
angle iron(plate) 角铁 146
angle milling cutter 角度铣刀 125,286
angle plate 角铁 284
angularity 倾斜度 15
annular worm 环面蜗杆传动 62
annulus wheel 内齿轮 146
anvil 铁砧,砧座 150,154
arbor 刀杆,刀柄 93,150
arch 顶梁 103
arc welding 电弧焊 206
armature 衔铁 73,74,147
arrowhead 箭头 16
atomized spray 雾化喷射束 213
automatic powder feed 自动进粉器 199
AWJ 磨料水射流加工 236
axial piston pump 轴向柱塞泵 164
axial rake 轴向前角 126
axial relief 轴向铲背角 126
axial relief angle 轴向后角 126
axial thrust stop 轴向推力挡块 93

B

back rake angle 前角 122
bag filter 袋式过滤器 5

baghouse 布袋式除尘室 4
balancing arbor 平衡杆 92

ball 滚动体 70
ball bearing 球轴承,滚珠轴承 19,65,146,149
ball check 球体浮标 86
ball end mill 球形端铣刀 127
ball nut 滚珠套 54
ball screw 滚珠丝杠 54
ball screw assembly 滚珠丝杠组件 54
band 环带 70
bandsaw 带锯 150
bar stock 棒料,杆件 125,280
barometer 气压表 266
barrel 滑套 96
barrel lock 滑套锁柄 96
barrier guard 障碍防护罩 3
base circle 基圆 61
beam compass 长臂划规 150
beam deflector 离子束反射器 231
beam monitor 离子束监控器 231
bearing ball 滚珠 54
bearing cap 轴承盖 69
bearing cover 轴承盖 69
bearing plate 支承板 19
bearing surface 支撑面 141
bed 床身 93
bellows coupling 波纹管联轴器 71
bell-type outer race 钟罩形外滚道 70
belt drive 带传动 58
belt pulling wheel 砂带收卷轮 296
bending 弯曲 183
bent roughing tools 弯头粗加工刨刀 136
bevel gear 锥齿轮 146
bevel pinion 锥齿轮 280
bevel teeth on scroll plate 转盘锥齿 280
bifurcated rivot 开口铆钉 146
billet 钢坯 338
bladder-type accumulator 气囊式蓄能器 174
blanker 支座 231
blanking 落料 183
blasting gun 喷枪 120,237
blender 混合搅拌机构 41
blind hole 盲孔 290

blind hole with flat bottom 平底盲孔 290
blind riser 闭式冒口 197
blow molding 吹塑成型 184
board 转换板 122
body 泵体,刀体 20,130
body diameter clearance 钻孔间隙 130
bolt 螺栓 20
bolt coupling in reamed hole 铰制孔螺栓连接 49
bolted connection 螺栓连接 186
bond 粘接剂 139
boot 护套 76
boot seal 套形密封件 70
boring bar 镗杆 100,101
boring machine 镗床 100
boring process 镗削加工 290
boring tool 镗刀 128,284
box spanner 套筒扳手 150
brace 弓形钻 150
brake cylinder 制动油缸 195
brake drum 制动鼓 195
brake fluid 制动液 76
braking disk 制动盘 76
brazing 铜焊 186
breast drill 胸压手摇钻 150
broaching 拉削 91,185
breathing air line 呼吸管 5
broaching fixture 拉削夹具 105
broaching taper 拉削丝锥 134
brush cap 刷帽 19
brush with spring 弹性电刷 19
buffer plunger 缓冲柱塞 168
buffing wheel 抛光轮 150
bulging 胀芯成形 345
bull gear 大齿轮 104
burnishing operation 挤齿加工 301
bush 套筒,轴套 20,57
bush chain 套筒链 57
bush-roller chain 套筒滚子链 57
buttress thread 锯齿螺纹 49

C or horseshoe washer C形/马蹄形垫片 55

cable clamping jaws 电缆夹爪 159

caliper 卡钳 76
cam shaft 凸轮轴 42
cam blank 凸轮毛坯 287
cap nut 外套螺母 147
capstan wheel 绞轮 96
carbide bur 硬质合金毛刺刀 129
carbide insert 刀片 130
carbon dioxide extinguisher 二氧化碳灭火器 6
carbon electrode 碳电极 218
carriage 拖板 93
carriage handwheel 刀架手轮 96
carrier film 传输膜 352
carry handle 提把 6
case 腔体 87
casing 外壳 75
casing ring 腔体环 87
cast ingot 铸锭 205
casting 铸件 116
castle nut 开槽螺母 49,50
caulking gun 填缝枪 150
cavity 模腔,型腔 117,118
cavity milling 铣型腔 127
center drill(drilling) 中心钻 129,290
centered grinding 中心磨削 192
centerless grinding 无心磨削 185,192
centesimal dial indicator 百分表 27
central screw 中心螺杆 93
centralising spring 对中弹簧 36
centre 顶尖 96
centre punch 中心冲 150
centre-pod silencer 中心柱形消声器 3
centrifugal casting 离心铸造 182
ceramic-mold casting 陶瓷模具铸造 182
chain 链条 57
chain drive 链条传动 57
chain wheel 链轮 147
chainless transportation device with one degree of freedom 单自由度无链传输装置 308
chainless transportation device with two degrees of freedom 两自由度无链传输装置 308
chamfering form tool 倒角成形车刀 124
chaser 螺纹梳刀 150
check valve 单向阀 22
cheese-head screw 圆柱头螺钉 147

chemical machining 化学加工 185
chemical vapor deposition process(CVD) 化学气相沉积工艺 230
chip auger 排屑螺旋 266
chip breaker 断屑器 190
chip excavator 排屑器 114
chisel 凿子 150
chisel edge 横刃 130
chisel edge angle 横刃斜角 130
CHM 化学加工 118
choke 节流口 197
chopper 切断器 352
chuck 夹头,卡盘 19,93,150
chuck key 夹头松紧匙 19
chuck spacer 夹头隔套 19
circular blade saws 圆盘锯 157
circular die 圆板牙 135
circular 圆弧插补 interpolation 249
circular runout 圆跳动 15
circular saw blade 圆盘锯 138
circularity 圆度 15
clamp 夹头,压板 70,104,123
clamp base 夹座 111
clamp handle 夹紧手柄 157
clamp screw 压紧螺钉 122,123
clamping bar 夹压杆 353
clamping base 夹紧盘 157
clamping dog 夹头 316
clamping flange 夹紧法兰 82
clapper box 夹持架 104
clean-gas outlet 净气出口 4
clearance diameter 钻孔直径 130
clearance surface 铲背面,容屑表面 126
clevis pin 叉杆销 48
closed-loop control system 闭环控制系统 249
closed die 模锻 205
closed die forging 模锻 183
closed loop system 闭环系统 264
closed ring 闭形 46
closed-track cam 闭合滚道凸轮 43
closing cylinder 闭合油缸 118,203
clutch plate 离合器片 75
CNC drilling machine 数控钻床 252
CNC milling machine 数控铣床 253

CNC turning and lathe 数控车床 254
coach bolt 半圆头方颈螺栓 146
coated abrasive 涂覆磨具 141
coated abrasive process 涂覆磨具磨削加工 296
coil 线圈 34
coil spring 平面涡卷弹簧,螺旋弹簧 46,146,151
cold extrusion 冷挤出 183
cold welding 冷焊 186
collar 螺纹套筒 93
collar bolt 环螺栓 146
collet 弹性套,弹性夹套 92,280
collet chuck 弹性夹套 280
collecting tube 集收管 6
column 立柱 93
common bolt coupling 普通螺栓连接 49
compaction belt 压紧带 352
compass 圆规 11
compressed air hose 压缩空气管 155
compression molding 压缩模 184
compression packing 压缩密封 83
compression spring 压缩弹簧 46
compression stroke 压缩冲程 147
computer integrated manufacturing system(CIMS) 计算机集成制造系统 325
concavity 中凹面 126
concentricity 同轴度 15
cone 锥盘 88
cone-ended screw 开槽锥端紧定螺钉 49
cone-shaped spring 圆锥形压缩弹簧 46
conical brake 锥形制动器 309
conical or belleville washer 锥形或钟罩形垫片 54
conical point screw 锥端螺钉 52
conical reamer 锥形铰刀 151
connecting rod 连杆 279
contact plate 接触板 208
contact point 触针 35
contact roller 接触辊 111
contact wheel 接触轮 111
container liner 容器衬套 338
container support 容器支撑 7
continuous air tube 连续供气管 75
continuous transportation device 连续传输装置 307
contour milling 轮廓铣削 127
control panel 控制箱,控制面板 35,36
conventional grinding 常规磨削 295
coolant tube 冷却液管 108
cooler 冷却器 86
cooler of snake-shaped tube 蛇形管冷却器 173
cooling fan 冷却风扇 4
coordinate-measuring machine 坐标测量机 30
cope 上箱型砂 197
copper electrode 紫铜电极 191
core 型芯 117
core drilling 扩孔 290
corrosion defect 腐蚀缺陷 33
corrugated block 波纹块料 336
corrugated panel 波纹隔板 336
corrugated sheet 波纹板 336
corrugating roll 波纹辊筒 336
cotter pin 开口销,销钉,圆锥销 48,147
counterboring 沉孔加工 290
counter bore 沉孔 290
counter sink 沉坑 290
countersink bit 锪钻,沉头钻 151
countersinking 锪锥面 290
countersunk 反锥垫片 washer 55
counter-boring tool with pilot 沉孔导向镗刀 128
coupling 联轴器 22,69
coupling bolt 连接螺栓 146
cover die 凹压(定)模 197
cover disc 定模板 118,203
cradle 托架 92
crane 鹤式起重机构 41
crank 曲柄压力机 121
crank pin 曲柄销 297
crank shaft 曲轴 69
crank-rocker 曲柄摇杆机构 41
creep feed grinding 大切深缓进给磨削 295
creep resistance 抗蠕变能力 33
cross rail 横梁 103
cross-feed handwheel 横进手轮 96
cross-slide 中拖板 95,282
cross-slide handwheel 横向滑板手轮 96
cup point 杯端螺钉 52

cup shell 杯罩 175
cup washer 杯形垫片 55
cutting station 切割站 237
cutter radius compensation 刀具半径补偿 269
cutting edge 主切削刃 122
cutting teeth 切削齿 136
cutting tool 镗刀,刀片 100,135
cutting zone 切削部分 122
cylinder 液压缸 22

cylinder tube 柱塞筒 174
cylinder-head gasket 气缸密封垫 146
cylindrical cam 圆柱形凸轮 43
cylindrical joint 柱面铰链 42
cylindrical mandrel 圆柱芯轴 316
cylindrical worm 圆柱蜗杆 62
cylindrically curved washer 圆柱拱曲垫片 54
cylindricity 圆柱度 15

datum code 基准代号 16
DC generator 直流发动机 89
DC motor 直流电动机 89
dead center 死顶尖 284
deep drawing 拉深 184
deep-drawing process 拉深工艺 338
delivery line 输送管 86
depth gauge 深度尺 151
detector 探测器 33
dial indicator 刻度表 29
diamond grinding wheel 金刚石砂轮 142
diaphragm spring clutch 膜片弹簧离合器 74
diaphragm 隔板 202
diaphragm unit 膜盒系统 7
die 模具,锻模 117,122
die casting 压铸 182,195
die cavity 模腔 197
diestock 板牙扳手 151
differential gear 差动齿轮 146
differential housing 差速器箱 195
digital vernier height gauge 数字高度尺 26
dimension figure 尺寸数字 16
dimension line 尺寸线 16
direct arc 直接电弧 218
direct extrusion 定向挤出 183
direct manual switch interlock 手动互锁开关 3
disc 基盘 138
disc cam 盘形凸轮 43
discharge horn 喇叭排放头 6
discharge nozzle 排泄喷嘴 6
discharge pipe 排水管 6
discharge tube 排放管 6
disk brake 盘式制动器 76

divider 分规 11
dog clutch 齿式离合器 146
dog point screw 柱端螺钉 52
dosing cylinder 剂量缸 310
dotted erosion on face 齿面点蚀 61
double-crank 双曲柄机构 41
double-ended cutter or boring tool 双端镗刀 128
double-rocker 双摇杆机构 41
double pawl ratchet 双爪式棘轮机构 44
double slider coupling 十字双滑块联轴器 70
dove-tail cutter 燕尾槽铣刀 128
dovetail milling 铣燕尾槽 127
dovetail slide cutting tool 燕尾槽斜面刨刀 136
dowel 销轴,固定销,榫钉 57,146
dowel pin 圆柱销 48
down milling 顺铣 285
drag 下箱型砂 197
drain 接水槽 120
drain hole 排泄孔 166
drain plug 排泄塞 166
drawing 棒料拉制 183
drawing board 绘图板 11
drawn ring 拉深环 338
drill 钻头 151
drill bush(bushing) 钻套 131,318
drill chuck 钻夹头 102
drill plate 钻模板 318
drilling 钻削 91,185,290
drilling machine 钻床 102
drive head 驱动箱 35
driven chain wheel 从动链轮 57
driven disc 从动盘 72

driven element 从动件 73
driven gear 从动齿轮 72
driven member 从动件 72
drive-pin type of blind rivet 销驱动类盲孔铆钉 78
driving belt 传动带 59
driving chain wheel 主动链轮 57
driving element 驱动件 73
driving sleeve 驱动套 72
drum brake 鼓式(形)制动器 76,147
dry powder extinguisher 干粉灭火器 6
dual oil ring 双层油封环 166
dummy block 传力块 338
dust discharge 排尘口 4
dynamic seal 动密封 83

EBM 电子束加工 118
eccentric wheel 偏心轮(盘) 147
ECM 电化学加工 118
eddy currents 电涡流 32
EDM 电火花加工 118
ejector 推料杆 117
ejector box 动模箱,推出箱 118,203
ejector die 凸压(动)模 197
ejector pin 推料杆 200
ejector platen 动模板 118
electric drill (手)电钻 152
electric furnace 电炉 230
electrical brush 电刷 191
electrical contact 触点 147
electrochemical polishing 电化学磨抛 185
electrode 电极 191
electrode carrier 电极支架 223
electrode holder 电极夹头 209
electrode wheel 电极轮 208
electrodynamic contourogragh 电动轮廓仪 35
electrolysis 电解 151
electrolytic fluid 电解流 191
electromagnetic tooth clutch 电磁齿盘离合器 75
electron beam welding 电子束焊接 206
electro-magnetic coil 电感线圈 35
electro-slag welding 电渣焊 206
emergency escape bottle 紧急逃生瓶 5
enclosure 密闭装置 120
encoder 编码器 250
encoder feedback 反馈编码器 264
end clearance 端部铲背角 126
end cutting edge angle 主切刃角,刀尖刃倾角 122,126
end gash 端部齿隙 126
end mill 端铣刀 128
end relief 刀尖后角 126
end relief angle 主后角 122
end support 尾端支撑 100
end surface grinding 端面磨削 294
end-drive adapter 末端驱动适配器 92
epicyclic gear 行星轮系 146
equalizing piston 等压活塞 202
excessive undercut 过切 209
exhaust muffler 排出隔音板 4
exhaust scrubber 排气净化器 230
exhaust stroke 排气冲程 147
exhaust valve 排气门 147
existing hole 预孔 100
expanded metal 网眼钢板 147
expanded panel 膨胀隔板 336
expanding drill 扩孔钻 131
expanding ring 膨胀环 72
expansion bolt 膨胀螺栓 52
explosion welding 爆炸焊接 186
explosive blind rivet 爆炸盲孔铆钉 78
explosive forming process 爆炸成形工艺 339
extension line 尺寸界线 16
extension spring 拉伸弹簧 46
external involute spline 外渐开线花键 46
external-tooth locking washer 外齿锁紧垫片 55
extract slot 抽吸槽 5
extrusion 挤出成型,挤出(件) 184,205,338
eye bolt 眼孔螺栓,带孔螺栓 52,146
eye hook 眼孔吊钩 80
eye-splice 眼孔接头 80

F

face 前刀面 122
face cam 端面凸轮 43
face cutter 端面铣刀 125
face milling 端面铣削,端铣平面 125,127
face milling cutter 端铣刀 99
face plate 花盘 92,147
face wear 齿面磨损 61
fasten nut 紧固螺母 20
fatigue life 疲劳寿命 33
feed change gear box 进给交换齿轮箱 95
feed hand wheel 进给手轮 102
feed reel 进给丝筒 213
feed rod 进给光杆 95
feed shaft 进给轴 96
feedback signal 反馈信号 249
feedback transducer 反馈传感器,反馈装置 25,250
fillet 过渡圆弧 126
fillister screw 开槽盘头螺钉 49
filter 过滤器 22
filtering core 滤芯 175
filtering cup 滤杯 175
filtering grid 过滤网格 202
filtering station 过滤站 237
finger clamp 指状压板 286
finish groove 精车沟槽 284
finishing teeth 精齿 136
fire extinguisher 灭火设备 6
firmer chisel 榫孔凿 151
fixed shaft 固定芯轴 69
fixture 夹具 104
flange 法兰 81
flange coupling 凸缘联轴器,法兰联轴器 70,146
flanged pulley 法兰盘带轮 60
flap wheel 页轮 112
flash welding 闪光焊 206
flask 砂箱 116,197,200
flat belt 平带 58
flat rolling 平板轧制 183
flat spring 板弹簧 46
flatness 平面度 15

flatter 平锤 155
flat-jawed tong 平口夹钳 157
flexible axle of steel cord 钢丝软轴 69
flexible bar 柔性杆 353
flexible connector 柔性接头 7
flexible high-pressure hose 高压软管 6
flexible line 柔性管 86
flexible manufacturing cell(FMC) 柔性制造单元 321
float 浮子 86
floating lever 浮动杆 36
flood coolant reservoir 冷却液箱 266
floor line 地脚 121
flow plate 导流板 175
flow stabilizer 流体稳定器 241
fluid coupling 液力离合器 75
fluid forming process 流体成形工艺 344
fluid nozzle 冷却液喷嘴 191
fluidized abrasivetank 流化磨料箱 113
flute 刀齿槽,韧带 126,130
flux 焊药 214
flux-cored arc welding 药芯焊丝电弧焊 186
flywheel 飞轮 59,69
focusing nozzle 聚焦喷嘴 240
focusing tube 混合集束管 237
forged boring tools 锻制镗刀 128
forging 锻压 205
forging stock 锻坯 122
form loop chain 成形环扣链 57
form milling 成形铣削 127
form relieved circular cutter 铲背圆弧成形铣刀 125,286
four flute end mill 四槽端铣刀 127
four-jaw chuck 四爪卡盘 280
four-stroke engine 四冲程发动机 147
fracture toughness 断裂强度 33
free floating piston 浮动柱塞 174
fret saw 钢丝锯,加工锯 152
friction clutch 摩擦离合器 72
friction disk 摩擦片 74
friction plate 摩擦盘 72
friction stir welding 摩擦焊接 185

friction welding 摩擦焊 206
front bearing 前支承 69
front pilot 前导部 136
fuel pump 机油泵 146
fuller 套柄铁锤 154

furnace 熔炉 197
fused deposition modeling 熔融沉积成型 184
fused-deposition-modeling process(FDM) 熔丝堆积成形工艺 235
fusion welding 熔焊 206

G-clamp 弓形钩,夹钳 151
galvanometer 电流计 235
garter spring 箍簧,环形弹簧 82
gas chamber 气腔 174
gas valve 气门 42
gas welding 气焊 206
gasket 垫片,密封垫 20,81,353
gasket cup 密封垫盖罩 83
gas-metal arc welding 气体保护金属弧焊 186
gas-tungsten arc welding 气体保护钨极弧焊 186
gauge 量仪、量具 151
gear 齿轮 20
gear box 齿轮箱 147
gear coupling 齿式联轴器 70
gear cutting 齿轮加工 299
gear cutting machine 齿轮加工机床 113
gear cutting tool 齿轮刀具 144
gear gauge 齿轮规 28
gear hobbing 滚齿 91
gear hobbing machine 滚齿机 113
gear hob 齿轮滚刀 145
gear housing 齿轮盒 19
gear lapping 研磨齿轮 301
gear lever 变速杆 147

gear pump 齿轮泵 165
gear rack 齿条 92
gear shaving 剃齿 301
gear train 齿轮系 149
gearcutter 齿轮铣刀 150
gel coat 胶层 353
geneva mechanism 槽轮机构 44
goose nose 鹅颈刨刀 136
gooseneck clamp 鹅颈形压板 286
goose-neck tong 鹅颈夹钳 157
gouge 弧口凿,半圆凿 150
grain 磨粒 139
graphite mould 石墨模具 201
grinding abrasive wheel 砂轮 141
grinding disc 磨盘,砂盘 142
grinding machine 磨床,砂轮机,磨床 106,151
grinding wheel 磨轮,砂轮 106,108,150
groove 沟槽 170
grooving tool 开槽刨刀 136
grub screw 平头螺钉 148
gudgeon pin 活塞销 149
guide 导向块 42
gun drill 枪钻 131,290
gylindrical grinding 外圆磨削 91

hairspring 游丝 147
hand reamer 手动铰刀 133
hand ring 手调环 92
handle 手把 19
handwheel 手轮 96
hard hat 硬头盔 5
head cap assembly 头盖组件 6
heading 锻头 183
headstock 主轴箱,床头箱 93,95,152

heat exchanger 热交换器 120
heat treatment 热处理 33
heater 加热器 86
heavy boring tool 重载镗刀 128
heel 刀棱 126
helic angle 螺旋角 130
helical gear 斜齿齿轮 301
helical joint 螺旋铰链 42
helical peripheral cutter 螺旋圆周铣刀 125

English	中文	页码
helical slot milling	铣螺旋槽	127
hemming	卷边	183
herringbone gear	人字齿	147
hex bolt	六角头螺栓	49
hex nut	六角螺母	49
hexagon socket head screw	内六角螺钉	51
hexagon(main)turret	六角(主)刀架	96
high frequency coil	高频线圈	208
high pari	高副	42
high pressure pump	高压泵	119, 237
high speed steel bur	高速钢毛刺刀	129
hinge	铰链	88
hokke's joint	十字架式万向节	149
holding fixture	夹具	198
hole bolt	开孔螺栓	50
hole type nozzle	孔式喷油器	147
hole-making tool	钻扩铰孔加工刀具	129
hollow spindle	空心轴	69
honing	珩磨	91
honing head	珩磨头	297
honing operation	珩磨加工	297
hook bolt	钩头螺栓	146
hooks coupling	十字轴万向联轴器	70
hot working equipment	热加工设备	114
hydraulic	液压机	121
hydraulic clutch	油压离合器	72
hydraulic coupling	液压联轴器	71
hydraulic cylinder	液压缸	167
hydraulic jack	液压千斤顶	151, 155
hydraulic motor	液压马达	22, 167
hydraulic oil	液压油	104
hydraulic piston	油压活塞	72
hydraulic press	水压机	151
hydraulic pump unit	液压泵单元	36
hydraulic ram	液压头,液压夯锤	36, 151
hydraulic shot cylinder	液压注射缸	197
hydraulic unit	液压单元	120
hydrodynamic thrust bearing	动压推力轴承	68
hydroform process	液压成形工艺	344
hydroforming	液力挤压	183

English	中文	页码
IBM	离子束加工	230
idle wheel	惰轮	111
idler gear	惰轮	147
idler pulley	张紧带轮,惰轮	147
illustration of powder rolling	粉末滚压成形	342
impeller	叶轮	34, 75, 165
indexing table	分度台	309
indicating line	指引线	16
indicator	指示表	35
indirect arc	间接电弧	218
induction	感应炉	218
induction coil	感应线圈	216
induction motor	感应电机	89
induction stroke	进气冲程	147
industrial hand-held sound level meter	工业手持声压计	2
ingate	浇口	197
injection molding	注射成型	184
inlet valve	进气门	147
inner bearing	内轴承	76
inner flange	内端法兰盘	141
inner hex fillister screw	内六角圆柱头螺钉	49
inner plate	内链板	57
inner race	内滚道	70
inner surface abrasive	内圆磨具	107
inner-hexagon nut	内六角螺母	20
inspection coil	检测线圈	32
instrument screwdriver	手捻,仪表起子	151
insufficient throat	缩喉	209
insulating board	绝热板	216
insulating layer	绝缘层	223
insulation	绝热层	201
intake muffler	吸入隔音板	4
intensifier	增压器	120, 237
intermediate gear	中间齿轮	19
internal spline	内渐开线花键	46
internal grinding	内圆磨削	106
internal centerless grinding	内圆无心磨削	295
investment casting	熔模(失蜡)铸造	182
ion implantation process	离子注入工艺	230
ion-plating process	离子镀过程	230
iron core	铁芯	35

J

jack 千斤顶 151
jaw 卡爪 280
jaw screw 卡爪螺杆 280
jet 射流 120
jet cutting 射流加工 118

jet tube 射流管 221
jig bushing 夹具衬套(钻套) 317
journal bearing 滑动轴承 68
jubilee clip 箍圈 148

K

key 键 20
key way 键槽 69
key way milling 铣键槽 127
keyhole saw 鸡尾锯，狭手锯 151
knee 升降台 93

knife-edge rule 刀口尺 29
knob 手把 111
knuckle joint 肘节压力机 121
knurling 滚花 151

L

ladle 铸勺 117
laminated-object manufacturing 叠(分)层实体制造 184
laminated-object-manufacturing process(IOM) 薄片分层叠层制造 235
land 刀刃厚度，刃带 126,130
landing-gear fork 拨齿叉 279
lapping 研磨 185
laser machining 激光加工 185
laset welding 激光焊接 206
lathe 车床 95
LBM 激光束加工 118
lead screw 丝杠 93
leading screw 丝杆 118
leadscrew 丝杆，滚珠丝杠 95,249
left cap 左端盖 20
left hand turning tool 左车刀 124
lens 透镜 148
level indicator 液面指针 86
lever 操纵杆 279
light boring tool with bend shank 弯头轻载镗刀 128
limit switch 极限开关 37
limit valve 极限阀 179
line with fixed restriction 固定节流线路 22

linear 直线插补 interpolation 249
line-of-action 啮合线 61
lining 衬片 75
link coupling 连杆联轴器 71
lip 刀刃 126,130
lip angle 刀尖角 126
lip-relief angle 刃倾角 130
lip seal 唇形密封 82
liquid vacuum pump 液体真空泵 166
live center 活顶尖 283,284
locating datum 定位基准 303
locating datum surface 定位基面 303
lock bolt coupling 紧定螺钉连接 49
lock screw 锁紧螺钉 69
lock washer 锁紧垫圈 49
locking needle roller 锁紧滚针 75
locking nut 锁紧螺母 93
locking roller 锁紧滚子 75
lockplate washer 锁紧垫片 55
logo plate 铭牌 19
longitudinal feed lever 纵向进给柄 96
loop spring 环形弹簧 46
loose-proof by wire connect 串联钢丝防松 50
loose-proof with self-lock nut 自锁螺母防松 50
loose-proof with spring washer 弹簧垫圈防松

50
loose-proof with stop washer 止动垫片防松 50
loose-proof with two nuts 双螺母防松 50
loose-proof with undismantle methods 不可拆卸防松 50
lost foam casting 失沫铸造 182
lower lap 下研磨板 192
lub point 润滑点 86

mach. frame 机架 67
machine column 机床立柱 251
machine reamer 机动铰刀 133
machine tool 机床 89
machining center 加工中心 257
magazine 料斗 179
magnetic drain plug 磁力排泄塞 166
magnetic field 磁场 32
magnetic-pulse forming 磁脉冲挤压 184
magnetizing coil 磁化线圈 32
major flank 主后刀面 122
mandrel 芯轴 92
manhole 人孔 148
manifold 管道 7
manipulator 机械手 258
manual adjustable reamer 可调式手用铰刀 133
manual metal-arc welding 手工金属弧焊 206
manual reamer 手用铰刀 133
manual taper reamer 手用锥孔铰刀 133
margin 刃边,韧带 130
margin flute 排屑槽 131
measure box 检测箱 257
measuring datum 测量基准 303
mechanical seal 机械密封 82
mechanical strength 机械强度 33
mechatronics 机电一体化 245
melt-spinning process 熔旋快速固化 182

metal active-gas(MAG)welding MAG熔焊 206
metal arc welding 金属弧焊 206
metal inert-gas(MIG)welding MIG熔焊 206
metal sleeve 金属套筒 118,203
metric thread 普通螺纹 49
micrometer for external diameter 外径千分尺 26
middle bearing 中间支承 69
milling 铣削,铣削加工 91,185,285
milling machine 铣床 98
milling tool 铣刀 125
minor cutting edge 副切削刃 122
modular jig 组合夹具 318
mold 模具 353
mold cavity 模腔 197
mold oscillation 模具振动器 199
mold release 脱模层 353
morse taper 莫氏锥度 16
motor coupling 电机联轴器 92
movable clamp 活动钳口 157
movable sleeve 活动套 74
muff coupling 套筒联轴器 70
multi flute end mill 多槽端铣刀 125,127
multiple-cutter boring tool 多刃镗刀 128
multi-edges belt 多楔带 58
multi-pipe cooler 多管式冷却器 172
multi-plate clutch 多片离合器 72

nail puller 起钉器 152
NC grinding machine 数控磨床 257
NC high speed gear cutting machine 数控高速滚齿机 114
neck 颈部 130
needle bearing 滚针轴承 19
needle valve 针阀 147

negative load bearing 受压轴承 93
non-groove taper 无槽丝锥 134
non-traditional machining equipment 特种加工机床 118
nose radius 刀尖圆角半径 122
nozzle holder 喷嘴座 241
nut 螺母 20

O

O-ring　O 形密封圈　82
objective lens　物镜　231
offset　偏置量　126
offset path of cutter　刀具补偿轨迹　269
offset translating roller follower　偏心滑移滚子从动件　43
off-set roller　偏置滚子　93
oil cup　油杯　83
oil distributing plate　配油盘　167
oil frog absorber　抽油烟机　114
oil inlet cavity　回油腔　167
oil reservoir　油箱,储油器　89,266
oil retainer　油保持器　67
oldham coupling　十字联轴器　146
one-way clutch　单向离合器　75
one-way valve　单向阀　310
open die forging　自由锻　183
open loop system　开环系统　264
open-loop control system　开环控制系统　249
open ring　开环　46
open riser　开式冒口　197
open sleeve bearing　开式套式轴承　93
operating lever　操纵杆　6
operating sleeve　工作套　72
operation datum　工序基准　303
optical projector　光学投影仪　27
orifice　小孔　116
oscillating mechanism　振动机构　229
oscillator　振荡器　33
outer bearing　外轴承　76
outer flange　外端法兰盘　141
outer plate　外链板　57
overarm　悬梁　98
overlap　搭接　209
overload relief valve　卸荷阀　104
overrunning clutch　超越离合器　75
overrunning ratchet mechanism　（自行车后轴）超越棘轮机构　44

P

packed gland　填塞密封　84
packing cup　密封盖罩　83
pallet storage　托盘库　258
panel operator　操作面板　264
panel stiffener　隔板支架　4
parallel　平行仪　11
parallel baffle muffler　平行吸振隔音板　4
parallelism　平行度　15
parting tool　切断刀　124
partingline　分型线　197
PBM　等离子束加工　118
PECVD process　等离子体增强化学气相沉积工艺　230
pendulum　摆锤　31
perforated tray　打孔槽　86
peripheral cutting edge　周边铣削刀刃　126
peripheral grinding　周边磨削　294
peripheral milling　周铣平面　127
permanent magnet　永磁铁　34,242
permanent-mold casting　永久性铸型　182
perpendicularity　垂直度　15
personal dust sampling pump　个人操作的粉尘采样泵　2
phillips screwdriver　十字旋具　153
phillips screw　十字槽（沉头）螺钉　49,148
pierce　冲孔　184
piercing　锻孔　183
pilot operated relief valve　先导型溢流阀　168
pilot valve　导向阀　104
pin　圆柱销　20
pinion　小齿轮　104
pinion cutter　插齿刀　113
pipe thread　管螺纹　49
pipe vice　管子台虎钳　150
piston air compressor　活塞式空压机　179
piston ring　活塞环　147
piston seal　活塞密封　84
piston-type accumulator　活塞式蓄能器　174
pitch　齿距　136
pitch point　节点　61

pivot 枢轴 86
plain washer 普通平垫片 54
plain slotted clamp 普通开槽压板 286
planar joint 平面铰链 42
planar four-bar linkage 平面四杆机构 42
planar six-bar linkage 平面六杆机构 42
planetary wheel 行星齿轮 146
planing 龙门刨削 91
plasma arc turning(PAT) 等离子弧车削 232
plasma arc welding 等离子体弧焊 206
plastic deformation of face 齿面塑性变形 61
plate clutch 盘式离合器 146
plate die 搓丝板 135
plate cam 盘形凸轮 43
platform 支承平台 235
plinth 底座 92
plug gage 塞规 29
plunge grinding 切入式磨削 107,295
plunger 活塞 117,118
plunger ratchet pawl 柱塞式棘爪 44
plunger rod 活塞杆 118,197
pneumatic drill 风钻 152
pneumatic propel wheel 气动叶轮 111
pneumatic system 风动系统 154
pneumatically actuated brake 气动制动器 76
pneumatically driven indexing table 气动分度台 310
point angle 顶尖角 130
polishing cloth wheel 抛光布轮 142
polishing machine 抛光机 153
poppet valve 气门,提升阀,顶杆阀 148,174
porosity 孔隙 139
portable belt grinder 手提式砂带机 112
portable oxygen analyser 便携式氧气分析仪 2
portable welding seam polisher 手提式焊缝打磨机 112
position 位置度 15
position sensor 位置传感器 249
pot 熔锅 197
pouring basin(cup) 浇口,浇注口 116,197
pouring hole 浇孔 118
powder metallurgy process 粉末冶金成形工艺 339
power hammer 气锤 153

power stroke 工作冲程 147
power switch 电源开关 266
presence-sensing device 存在(有无)感应装置 3
pressing stem 压柄 338
pressure angle 压力角 61
pressure cartridge 压力筒 6
pressure differential indicator 压差指针 87
pressure gage 压力表 22
pressure plate 压力板,施压盘 72,74
pressure ring 压力环 75
pressure spring 压力弹簧 72
pressure switch 压力开关 7
pressure toggle 压力肘节 72
pressure wheel 施压滚轮 201
pressure-fed bearing 静压轴承 68
pressure-reducing valve 减压阀 169
pressurized oil cavity 压油腔 167
primary 初级线圈 209
primary shoe 领蹄 76
prismatic joint 棱柱型铰链 42
process chamber 加工室 235
profile grinding 轮廓磨削 107
profile line 轮廓线 15
profile surface 轮廓面 15
projection welding 凸出焊接 206
projector 喷水头 7
propeller 螺旋桨 148
propeller shaft 传动轴 147
proportional divider 比例规 11
protective boot 防护鞋 5
protective glove 防护手套 5
protective suit 防护服 5
protractor 量角器,半圆规 11,92
pull broach 拉刀 136
pull end 拉头 136
pulley 带轮 102
pull-through-type riveting 贯通型铆钉 78
pulltrusion 拉出成型 184
pulse power 脉冲电源 118
pulse train 脉冲系列 249
pump casing 泵体 82
pump housing 泵体 82
pump impeller 泵叶轮 82

pump motor starter 泵电机启动器 36
punching 冲裁 184

pushrod 推杆 149

quick exhaust valve 快速排气阀 175

quill 主轴 99

radial arm 摇臂 94
radial bearing 径向轴承 67
radial clearance angle 径向铲背角 126
radial cutting edge 径向切削刃 126
radial drilling machine 摇臂钻床 94
radial land 径向刃宽 126
radial piston pump 径向柱塞泵 164
radial rake angle 径向前角 126
radial relief angle 径向后角 126
radial slot 径向槽 170
radial translating roller follower 径向滑移滚子从动件 43
radius turning form tool 圆弧成形车刀 124
rag bolt coupling 地脚螺栓连接 49
rail head 横梁刀架 103
ram 顶杆,滑枕,锤头,电极坐板 94,96,104,203
ratchet 棘轮机构 44,147
ratchet brake 棘轮制动器 44
ratchet rack 棘爪棘条机构 44
ratchet screwdriver 棘轮式旋具 153
rawhide hammer 皮锤 153
rawl bolt 膨胀螺栓 52
reactor 反应器 209
reactor coil 反应器线圈 209
reamer 铰刀 153
reaming 铰削 290
rean hole 铰孔 284
rear bearing 后支承 69
rear pilot 后导部 136
reciprocating machine 往复运动机床 103
reciprocating machining processes 往复式加工 291
reciprocating process tool 往复运动加工刀具 135
reciprocating vibration flat grinder 往复振动平面磨光机 112
recorder 记录器 35
rectangular section spring 矩形截面圆柱形压缩弹簧 46
rectifier 整流器 220
regulating wheel 调节轮 170
release handle 释放把手 6
relief valve 泄压阀,卸荷阀 87,89,169
reservoir 储液箱 120,221
resistance butt welding 电阻对焊 206
resistance welding 电阻焊 186,206
retaining cage 保持架 70
retaining ring 扣环,保持环 19,70
retaining spring 保持弹簧 73
return line 回流管线 86
return tube 回珠管,溢流管 54
reversible ratchet 可变向棘轮机构 44
revolute joint 回转铰链 42
revolution frame 转架 111
revolving head 旋转头 283
right cap 右端盖 20
right hand turning tool 右车刀 124
right-angled screwdriver 直角旋具 152
ring gage 环规 29
ring rolling 环件轧制 183
ring rolling operation 环件滚压加工 340
ring spanner 梅花扳手,闭口扳手,眼孔扳手 152
rivet 铆钉 148
rocker arm 摇杆臂 104
rocker cam 摇臂凸轮 97
rod seal 活塞杆密封 84
roll forging 辊锻 183
roll forming 滚压 184
roller 滚子 57
roller bearings 滚子轴承 19,65

Vocabulary with Figure Index 词汇及图形索引（英中对照）

roller follower 滚子从动件 42
roller mechanism 滚筒 235
roller-chain coupling 滚子链联轴器 71
rolling 轧制 205
rolling bearing 滚动轴承 65
root diameter 基圆 136
rotary arbor 转动芯轴 69
rotary base 转盘座 157
rotary file 回转锉 129
rotary shaft 转轴 69
rotary table 回转工作台 99
rotating pair 转动副 42
rotating shaft 回转轴 82
rotating-link coupling 回转连杆联轴器 71

rough bore hole 粗镗孔 284
rough groove 粗切槽 284
rough turn 粗车 284
roughening teeth 粗齿 136
roughing filter 粗过滤 6
roughness 粗糙度 233
round nose 圆头刨刀 136
round belt 圆带 58
RP 快速成形 234
rubber case 橡胶腔体 82
rudder follow-up linkage 舵随动连接 36
rudder 船舵 36
runner 流道 67,75,197
runner bar 流道 197

S

saddle 主轴箱,床鞍 94,96,100
saddle bearing insert 鞍形轴承内件 93
saddle support 床鞍支撑 100
safety cover 安全护罩 102
safety guard 安全罩 92
safety pin 安全销 6
safety tag 安全栓 6
sand casting 砂型铸造 182
sand lining 砂衬 116
sander 打磨机,磨光机 152
sapphire nozzle 宝石喷嘴 120
sarvo amplifier 伺服放大器 264
sauce spring 碟形弹簧 46
saw blade 锯片 138
saw hand 锯条 106
scoring of face 齿面胶合 61
screw 螺钉,丝杠,螺旋压力机 19,96,121
screw coupling 螺钉连接 49
screw drive 螺纹传动 53
screw lead 丝杠 157
scribing block 划线盘 153
scroll plate 转盘 280
seal casing 密封腔 82
seal face 密封面 82
sealing ring 密封圈 20
seam welding 缝焊 206
secondary 次级线圈 209
secondary shoe 从蹄 76

segment 锯片 138
segmental carbon ring 扇形碳环 82
selector fork 换挡拨叉 147
self aligning equalizing base 自找平平衡座 67
self closing door 自动门 6
self-plugging blind rivet 自插式盲孔铆钉 78
self-tapping screw 自攻螺钉 51,148
semifinishing 半精齿 136
semi-finish bore hole 半精镗孔 284
sensor 传感器 35
sequence valve 顺序阀 169
servo driver 伺服驱动器 262
servo motor 伺服电机 262
set screw 锁定螺钉,紧固螺钉 52,148
set square 三角板 11
shaft 轴 20
shank 刀杆 123
shank diameter 刀柄间隙 130
shape of tolerance zone 公差带形状 16
shape rolling 型材轧制 183
shaped coil 成形线圈 219
shaper 牛头刨床 94
shaping 牛头刨削 91
shaping cutter 插齿刀 145
shaping machine 牛头刨床 153
shaping tool 刨刀 135
shear-spinning process 剪旋工艺 339
shell 外壳 87

shell end mill 中空端面铣刀，空心端铣刀 125,286
shell-mold casting 壳型造型 182
shielded metal arc welding 自动保护金属极电弧焊 185
shielding setup 隔离屏蔽装置 3
shock absorber 减振器，缓冲器 149
shoe 蹄块 67
shoe retaining nail 蹄块保持钉 76
shot cylinder 注射缸 118
shot sleeve 推料筒 118
shoulder face milling 铣削台阶面 127
shroud 盖罩 92
side cutting edge angle 副切刃角 122
side face milling 铣削侧面 127
side head 侧刀台 103
side rake angle 副前角 122
side relief angle 副后角 122
silencer 消声器 3
silent chain 齿形链 57
silent ratchet mechanism 摩擦式棘轮机构 44
silent-chain coupling 无声链联轴器 71
sine bar 正弦尺 28
single-crystal casting 单晶铸造 182
single-plate clutch 单片离合器 72
slab milling cutter 平面铣刀 286
slave bearing 从动轴承 93
sleeve bearing carriage 套式轴承座 93
sleeve bearing housing 套式轴承盖 93
sleeve bearing insert 套式轴承内轴 93
slide valve 滑阀 176
sliding pair 移动副 42
slitting (铣)切断,剪板机,切开 127,156,183
slitting saw 切断铣刀 286
slitting saw cutter 锯切铣刀 125
slot drill 铣槽钻头 128
slot milling 铣沟槽 127
slotted 开槽螺钉,开槽垫片 52,54
slotted head machine screw 端头开槽机制螺钉 52
slotted spring pin 开槽弹性销 48
slotted-head cap screw 一字开槽螺钉 52
slotting 插削,铣沟槽 91,127
slotting tool 开槽刨刀 136

slurry 磨浆 227
smoke tube 风烟试验管 2
snap gage 卡规 29
snip 白铁剪 151
socket spanner 套筒扳手 153
soldering 低温焊接 214
solenoid member 电磁铁组件 73
solenoid valve 电磁阀 36
solid abrasive 固结磨具 138
space sleeve 隔套 69,168
spade drill 铲形钻 130
spanner 扳手 153
sparking plug 火花塞 147
spatial RCCR four-bar linkage 空间 RCCR 四杆机构 42
spherical four-bar linkage 球面四杆机构 42
spherical joint 球形铰链 42
spindle 主轴 69
spindle box 主轴箱 102
spindle carrier 主轴箱 99,258
spindle nut 主轴螺母 141
spindle speed selector 主轴转速选调器 96
spindle with gear 齿轮轴 19
spinning 旋压 184
spiral fluted tap 螺旋槽丝锥 134
spiral(helical)gear 螺旋齿轮 149
spirit level 水平仪 153
spline 花键 46
splined shaft 花键轴 149
split pin 开口销 50,149
split valve 多路阀 241
splitter silencer 分隔片式消声器 3
spot facing 锪孔 290
spot welding 点焊 153,206
sprag clutch 斜撑离合器 75
spring washer 弹簧垫片 54
spring loaded type relief valve 弹簧直动型溢流阀 170
spring stripper ring 弹簧脱料环 338
spring-locking washer 弹簧锁紧垫片 54
spring-type interlock 弹簧式互锁开关 3
sprue 浇道 197
spur gear 直齿轮,正齿轮 149,301
square spline 矩形花键 46

square head flat point screw 方头平顶螺钉 52
square nose planer 方头刨刀 136
square or rectangular key with gib head 钩头方形/矩形键 47
square thread 方螺纹 148
square turret 方刀台 96
square-head bolt 方头螺栓 146
squeeze head 压头 202
squeeze casting 压实铸造 182
squeeze roll 压辊 208
staggered tooth cutter 错齿铣刀 125,286
stamping set 冲压设备 121
stand-off distance(SOD) 靶距 236
static screw driving 静压螺旋传动 54
stationary plate 定模板 118
stationary sealing head 静止密封头 82
stator 定子 92
steel rule 钢尺 11
steering engine 转向引擎 36
steering knuckle 转向接头 76
step drilling 阶梯钻孔 290
stepping motor 步进电机 118,167,249
stereolithography 立体光固化成型 184
stiffener 加强筋 86
still clamp 固定钳口 157
stopcock valve 旋塞阀 149,153
stop rod 停车杆 96
storage hopper 料斗 202
stored pressure type of water extinguisher 储存压力水灭火器 6
straight shaping tool 尖直刨刀 136
straight line ratchet 直线棘轮 44

straight roughing tool 直柄粗加工刨刀 136
straight shank 直柄 130
straightness 直线度 15
straight-flute drill 直槽钻 130
stretch forming 延展 183
stretch gripper 延展夹头 337
stud 双头螺柱 49,148
stud coupling 双头螺柱连接 49
stylus 触针 38
submerged-arc welding 埋弧焊 206
sub-base 下底板 92
suction splitter 吸入口分流锥 166
sump 油槽,油底壳 82,86
sun wheel 恒星齿轮 146
superfinishing 超精加工 91,296
supply roll 放卷轮 235
support blade 托板 192
supporting rod 支承杆 111
surface flaw 表面裂纹 33
surface grinding 平面磨削 91,185
surface hardness 表面硬度 33
surface roughness 表面粗糙度 33
surface stress 表面应力 33
surface treatment 表面处理 33
swage 旋锻工具 154
swage block 陷型砧座 154
swinging roller follower 摆动滚子从动件 43
swivel hook 旋转吊钩 80
symbol of tolerance 公差符号 16
symmetry 对称度 15
synchronous belt 同步带 58

T

table 工作台 93
tailstock 尾座 93,257,270
tang 扁尾 130
tang drive 扁尾驱动 130
tank 油箱 22,104
tap wrench 丝锥扳手 150
tape reader 读带机 265
taper shank 锥柄 130
taper worm 锥蜗杆传动 62
tapped cover 锥形盖 141

tapper bushing 锥套 111
tappet 挺杆 149
telescoping cover 伸缩盖 223
template 样板 11
tenon saw 开榫锯 152
tension adjusting bar 张紧调节杆 111
tension roller 张紧辊 111
tension wheel 张紧轮 111
terminal block 接线端 265
terminal clamp screw 端头夹持螺钉 158

test and measuring gauge 测试仪器 2
thermal spray operation 热喷涂工艺 232
thermal wire spray 热丝喷涂 232
thermo-forming 热成型 184
thermostat 恒温器 120
thread cutting tool 螺纹车刀 124
thread-cutting screw 牙形切断螺钉 52
three-dimension printing 立体打印 184
three-jaw chuck 三爪卡盘 280
three-jaw micrometer for internal(inner/inside) diameter 三爪内径千分尺 27
throttle valve 油门,节流阀 149,221
through hole 通孔 290
through-feed grinding 贯通磨削 295
thrust ball bearing 轴向/推力球轴承 66
thrust bearing 推力轴承,止推轴承 34,149,167
thrust block 推力块 67
thumb screw 拇指形螺钉 51
tie rod 固定杆 83
tiebar 系杆 92
tiebar arm 系杆臂 92
time-saving continuous transportation device 节时连续传输装置 308
timing chain 正时链 149
toggle joint 肘节 149
toggle link 肘节连杆 74
tolerance 公差数值 16
tommy bar 套筒扳手旋转手把 150
tool base 刀座 122
tool changer 刀库 258
tool face 刀面 122
tool interchange arm 换刀臂 258
tool length compensation 刀具长度补偿 269
tool point 刀尖 122
tool post 刀台 93
tool post slide 刀架溜板 113
tool stem 工具柄 338
toolbox 工具箱 150
toolholder 刀体(夹持部分) 122
tool-post 刀台架 95

tooth 刀齿 126
tooth breakage 轮齿折断 61
tooth face (刀)齿面 126
torch 焊距 214
torque wrench 扭力扳手 150
torsion spring 扭转弹簧 46
total runout 全跳动 15
transducer 换能器 216
transfer launder 流槽 201
transfer molding 转移成型(传递模) 184
translating cam 移动凸轮 43
transmission gear 传动齿轮 20
transmission lever 调整杆 92
trasmission housing 变速箱 195
transmission shaft 传动轴 69
travelling column 移动立柱 258
traverse grinding 进给磨削 107
trepanning tool 套料刀,套料钻 135
triangular spline 三角形花键 46
trip dog 行程挡块 104
try square 直角尺,矩尺 151
tube drawing 管材拉制 183
tubeplate 管板 87
tungsten insert-gas(TIG)welding TIG焊接 206
turning 车削 91,185
turning tool 车刀 122,124
turnstile 转杆 96
turret (转塔)刀架 252,270
turret chuck 转塔夹头 252
turret stop 转塔挡块 96
twist drill 麻花钻 130,256
two flute end mill 双槽端铣刀 127
two-stoke engine 二冲程发动机 149
T-head bolt T形槽用螺栓 146
T-slot T形槽 92
T-slot cutter T形槽铣刀 128
T-slot cutting tool T形槽刨刀 136
T-slot milling 铣T形槽 127
T-slot for clamping 夹紧T形槽 99

U-bolt U形螺栓 148
U-clamp U形压板 286
ultrasonic vibration 超声振动 226

unflanged pulley 无法兰盘带轮 60
universal coupling 十字轴万向联轴器 70
universal joint 万向节 149

universal joint(drive)shaft 万向节(驱动)轴 92	upper lap 上研磨板 192
up milling 逆铣 285	USM 超声加工 118

V-belt V带 88	vane pump 叶片泵 164
V-block V形块 35,93	vee V形槽 208
V-positioning(locating)block V形块 316	vee type V带 59
V-roller carriage V形滚子架 93	vehicle axis 车轴 279
V-slot milling 铣V形槽 127	vent 通气口 197
V-thread 三角螺纹,V形螺纹 148	vent connection 通风接头 83
V-positioning(locating)block V形块 316	vent cup 通风杯 83
vacuum pump 真空泵 150	ventilator 通气口 86
vacuum sucker 真空吸盘 175	Venturi tube 文丘里管,缩喉管 148
vacuum trap 真空罩 353	vernier caliper 游标卡尺 26
vacuum-bag forming 真空包成型 184	vernier depth gauge 游标深(高)度尺 26
valve master 阀控制器 7	vertical column 立柱,主柱 101,102
valve mechanism 配气机构 42	vertical feed rod 垂直进给丝杠 101
valve protector 阀罩 174	vertical way 垂直导轨 101
valve slave 阀受控器 7	vibrofeeder 振动进给装置 307
vane 叶片 165	vice 钳工台虎钳 151,157
vane anemometer 叶片式风速计 2	vise 虎钳 104

washer 垫片,垫圈 19,49	wing screw 蝶形螺钉 51
water exhaust valve 排水阀 175	wing shaped plate heat exchanger 板翅式换热器 172
water extinguisher 水灭火器 6	wire clamp screw 夹线螺钉 158
water fender 挡水板 175	wire clamping jaw 线丝夹爪 158
water tank 水箱 120	wire EDM 电火花线切割 185
water-jet machining 水射流加工 185	wire gauze 线网 87
wave soldering 波焊 186	wire spool 储丝筒 118
wax pattern 蜡模 200	WJ 水射流加工 236
wear pad 耐磨垫 131	wood screw 木螺钉 51
web 钻心 130	woodruff key 半圆键 47
weld 焊点 208	woodruff key cutter 半圆键铣刀 286
weld nugget 焊核 208	woodruff key milling 铣半圆键 127
welding with pressure 压力焊 206	wood-grip washer 抓木垫片 55
wheel head 砂轮头架 108	work pan 工件槽 120
wheel head column 砂轮头架立柱 108	worm 蜗杆 149
wheel spindle 砂轮主轴 141,257	worm gear 蜗轮(蜗杆)副 149
wheel stud 车轮螺栓 76	worm wheel 蜗轮 149
wide belt 宽砂带 111	

Vocabulary with Figure Index
词汇及图形索引（中英对照）

A

安全护罩　safety cover　102
安全栓　safety tag　6
安全销　safety pin　6

安全罩　safety guard　92
鞍形轴承内件　saddle bearing insert　93
凹压(定)模　cover die　197

B

靶距　stand-off distance(SOD)　236
白铁剪　snip　151
百分表　centesimal dial indicator　27
摆锤　pendulum　31
摆动滚子从动件　swinging roller follower　43
扳手　spanner　153
板翅式换热器　wing shaped plate heat exchanger　172
板弹簧　flat spring　46
板牙扳手　diestock　151
半精齿　semifinishing　136
半精镗孔　semi-finish bore hole　284
半圆键　woodruff key　47
半圆键铣刀　woodruff key cutter　286
半圆头方颈螺栓　coach bolt　146
半圆凿　gouge　150
棒料　bar stock　125
棒料拉制　drawing　183
宝石喷嘴　sapphire nozzle　120
保持环　retaining ring　70
保持架　retaining cage　70
保持弹簧　retaining spring　73
爆炸成形工艺　explosive forming process　339
爆炸焊接　explosion welding　186
爆炸盲孔铆钉　explosive blind rivet　78
杯端螺钉　cup point　52
杯形垫片　cup washer　55
杯罩　cup shell　175
泵电机启动器　pump motor starter　36

泵体　body, pump housing, pump casing　20, 82, 130
泵叶轮　pump impeller　82
比例规　proportional divider　11
闭合滚道凸轮　closed-track cam　43
闭合油缸　closing cylinder　118, 203
闭环控制系统　closed-loop control system　249
闭环系统　closed loop system　264
闭式冒口　blind riser　197
闭形　closed ring　46
编码器　encoder　250
扁尾　tang　130
扁尾驱动　tang drive　130
变幅杆　acoustic horn　227
变速杆　gear lever　147
变速箱　trasmission housing　195
便携式氧气分析仪　portable oxygen analyser　2
表面处理　surface treatment　33
表面粗糙度　surface roughness　33
表面裂纹　surface flaw　33
表面应力　surface stress　33
表面硬度　surface hardness　33
拨齿叉　landing-gear fork　279
波焊　wave soldering　186
波纹板　corrugated sheet　336
波纹隔板　corrugated panel　336
波纹管联轴器　bellows coupling　71
波纹辊筒　corrugating roll　336

波纹块料　corrugated block　336
薄片分层叠层制造　laminated-object-manufacturing process(LOM)　235
不可拆卸防松　loose-proof with undismantle methods　50
布袋式除尘室　baghouse　4
步进电机　stepping motor　118,167,249

C

操纵杆　operating lever, lever　6,279
操作面板　panel operator　264
槽轮机构　geneva mechanism　44
侧刀台　side head　103
测量基准　measuring datum　303
测试仪器　test and measuring gauge　2
叉杆销　clevis pin　48
插齿刀　pinion cutter, shaping cutter　113,145
插削　slotting　91
差动齿轮　differential gear　146
差速器箱　differential housing　195
铲背面　clearance surface　126
铲背圆弧成形铣刀　form relieved circular cutter　125,286
铲形钻　spade drill　130
长臂划规　beam compass　150
常规磨削　conventional grinding　295
超精加工　superfinishing　91,296
超声加工　USM　118
超声振动　ultrasonic vibration　226
超越离合器　overrunning clutch　75
车床　lathe　95
车刀　turning tool　122,124
车轮螺栓　wheel stud　76
车削　turning　91,285
车轴　vehicle axis　279
沉坑　counter sink　290
沉孔　counter bore　290
沉孔导向镗刀　counter-boring tool with pilot　128
沉孔加工　counterboring　290
沉头钻　countersink bit　151
衬片　lining　75
成形环扣链　form loop chain　57
成形铣削　form milling　127
成形线圈　shaped coil　219
尺寸界线　extension line　16
尺寸数字　dimension figure　16
尺寸线　dimension line　16
齿距　pitch　136
齿轮　gear　20
齿轮泵　gear pump　165
齿轮刀具　gear cutting tool　144
齿轮规　gear gauge　28
齿轮滚刀　gear hob　145
齿轮盒　gear housing　19
齿轮加工　gear cutting　299
齿轮加工机床　gear cutting machine　113
齿轮铣刀　gearcutter　150
齿轮系　gear train　149
齿轮箱　gear box　147
齿轮轴　spindle with gear　19
齿面　Tooth face　126
齿面点蚀　dotted erosion on face　61
齿面胶合　scoring of face　61
齿面磨损　face wear　61
齿面塑性变形　plastic deformation of face　61
齿式离合器　dog clutch　146
齿式联轴器　gear coupling　70
齿条　gear rack　92
齿形链　silent chain　57
冲裁　punching　184
冲孔　pierce　184
冲压设备　stamping set　121
抽吸槽　extract slot　5
抽油烟机　oil frog absorber　114
初级线圈　primary　209
储存压力水灭火器　stored pressure type of water extinguisher　6
储丝筒　wire spool　118
储液箱　reservoir　120,221
触点　electrical contact　147
触针　contact point, stylus　35,38
传动齿轮　transmission gear　20
传动带　driving belt　59
传动轴　transmission shaft, propeller shaft

69,147
传感器　sensor　35
传力块　dummy block　338
传输膜　carrier film　352
船舵　rudder　36
床鞍支撑　saddle support　100
床身　bed　93
吹塑成型　blow molding　184
锤头　ram　122
垂直导轨　vertical way　101
垂直度　perpendicularity　15
垂直进给丝杠　vertical feed rod　101
唇形密封　lip seal　82
磁场　magnetic field　32
磁化线圈　magnetizing coil　32
磁力排泄塞　magnetic drain plug　166
磁脉冲挤压　magnetic-pulse forming　184

次级线圈　secondary　209
从动齿轮　driven gear　72
从动件　driven member, driven element　72,73
从动链轮　driven chain wheel　57
从动盘　driven disc　72
从动轴承　slave bearing　93
从蹄　secondary shoe　76
粗糙度　roughness　233
粗车　rough turn　284
粗齿　roughening teeth　136
粗过滤　roughing filter　6
粗切槽　rough groove　284
粗镗孔　rough bore hole　284
存在（有无）感应装置　presence-sensing device　3
搓丝板　plate die　135
错齿铣刀　staggered tooth cutter　125,286

搭接　overlap　209
打孔槽　perforated tray　86
打磨机,磨光机　sander　152
大齿轮　bull gear　104
大切深缓进给磨削　creep feed grinding　295
带传动　belt drive　58
带锯　bandsaw　150
带轮　pulley　102
袋式过滤器　bag filter　5
单晶铸造　single-crystal casting　182
单片离合器　single-plate clutch　72
单向阀　check valve, one-way valve　22,310
单向离合器　one-way clutch　75
单自由度无链传输装置　chainless transportation device with one degree of freedom　308
挡水板　water fender　175
刀柄　arbor　150
刀柄间隙　shank diameter　130
刀齿　tooth　126
刀齿槽　flute　126
刀齿面　tooth face　126
刀杆　arbor, shank　93,123
刀架溜板　tool post slide　113
刀架手轮　carriage handwheel　96
刀尖　tool point　122

刀尖后角　end relief　126
刀尖角　lip angle　126
刀尖圆角半径　nose radius　122
刀具半径补偿　cutter radius compensation　269
刀具补偿轨迹　offset path of cutter　269
刀具长度补偿　tool length compensation　269
刀口尺　knife-edge rule　29
刀库　tool changer　258
刀棱　heel　126
刀面　tool face　122
刀片　carbide insert　130
刀刃　lip　126,130
刀刃厚度　land　126,130
刀台　tool post　93
刀台架　tool-post　95
刀体　body　20,130
刀体（夹持部分）　toolholder　122
刀座　tool base　122
导流板　flow plate　175
导向阀　pilot valve　104
导向块　guide　42
倒角成形车刀　chamfering form tool　124
等离子弧车削　plasma arc turning(PAT)　232
等离子束加工　PBM　118
等离子体弧焊　plasma arc welding　206

等离子体增强化学气相沉积工艺　PECVD process　230
等压活塞　equalizing piston　202
低温焊接　soldering　214
底座　plinth　92
地脚　floor line　121
地脚螺栓连接　rag bolt coupling　49
点焊　spot welding　153,206
电磁齿盘离合器　electromagnetic tooth clutch　75
电磁阀　solenoid valve　36
电磁铁组件　solenoid member　73
电动轮廓仪　electrodynamic contourogragh　35
电感线圈　electro-magnetic coil　35
电弧焊　arc welding　206
电化学加工　ECM　118
电化学磨抛　electrochemical polishing　185
电火花加工　EDM　118
电火花线切割　wire EDM　185
电机联轴器　motor coupling　92
电极　electrode　191
电极夹头　electrode holder　209
电极轮　electrode wheel　208
电极支架　electrode carrier　223
电极坐板　ram　223
电解　electrolysis　151
电解流　electrolytic fluid　191
电缆夹爪　cable clamping jaws　159
电流计　galvanometer　235
电炉　electric furnace　230
电刷　electrical brush　191
电涡流　eddy currents　32
电源开关　power switch　266
电渣焊　electro-slag welding　206
电子束焊接　electron beam welding　206
电子束加工　EBM　118
电阻对焊　resistance butt welding　206
电阻焊　resistance welding　186,206
垫片　washer,gasket　19,20
垫圈　washer　49
叠(分)层实体制造　laminated-object manufacturing　184
碟形弹簧　sauce spring　46
蝶形螺钉　wing screw　51
顶杆　ram　96

顶杆阀　poppet valve　174
顶尖　centre　96
顶尖角　point angle　130
顶梁　arch　103
定模板　stationary plate,cover disc　118,203
定位基面　locating datum surface　303
定位基准　locating datum　303
定位器　aligner　231
定向挤出　direct extrusion　183
定子　stator　92
动密封　dynamic seal　83
动模板　ejector platen　118
动模箱　ejector box　118,203
动压推力轴承　hydrodynamic thrust bearing　68
读带机　tape reader　265
端部铲背角　end clearance　126
端部齿隙　end gash　126
端面磨削　end surface grinding　294
端面凸轮　face cam　43
端面铣刀　face cutter　125
端面铣削　face milling　125
端头夹持螺钉　terminal clamp screw　158
端头开槽机制螺钉　slotted head machine screw　52
端铣刀　face milling cutter,end mill　99,128
端铣平面　face milling　127
断裂强度　fracture toughness　33
断屑器　chip breaker　190
锻孔　piercing　183
锻模　die　122
锻坯　forging stock　122
锻头　heading　183
锻压　forging　205
锻制镗刀　forged boring tools　128
对称度　symmetry　15
对中弹簧　centralising spring　36
多槽端铣刀　multi flute end mill　125,127
多管式冷却器　multi-pipe cooler　172
多路阀　split valve　241
多片离合器　multi-plate clutch　72
多刃镗刀　multiple-cutter boring tool　128
多楔带　multi-edges belt　58
舵随动连接　rudder follow-up linkage　36
惰轮　idle wheel,idler gear　111,147

E

鹅颈夹钳	goose-neck tong	157
鹅颈刨刀	goose nose	136
鹅颈形压板	gooseneck clamp	286

| 二冲程发动机 | two-stoke engine | 149 |
| 二氧化碳灭火器 | carbon dioxide extinguisher | 6 |

F

发电机箱　alternator housing　195
阀控制器　valve master　7
阀受控器　valve slave　7
阀罩　valve protector　174
法兰　flange　81
法兰联轴器　flange coupling　146
法兰盘带轮　flanged pulley　60
反馈编码器　encoder feedback　264
反馈传感器　feedback transducer　25
反馈信号　feedback signal　249
反馈装置　feedback transducer　250
反应器　reactor　209
反应器线圈　reactor coil　209
反锥垫片　countersunk washer　55
方刀台　square turret　96
方螺纹　square thread　148
方头螺栓　square-head bolt　146
方头刨刀　square nose planer　136
方头平顶螺钉　square head flat point screw　52
防护服　protective suit　5
防护手套　protective glove　5
防护鞋　protective boot　5

放大器　amplifier　33,36
放卷轮　supply roll　235
飞轮　flywheel　59,69
分度台　indexing table　309
分隔片式消声器　splitter silencer　3
分规　divider　11
分型线　partingline　197
粉末滚压成形　illustration of powder rolling　342
粉末冶金成形工艺　powder metallurgy process　339
风动系统　pneumatic system　154
风烟试验管　smoke tube　2
风钻　pneumatic drill　152
缝焊　seam welding　206
浮动杆　floating lever　36
浮动柱塞　free floating piston　174
浮子　float　86
腐蚀缺陷　corrosion defect　33
副后角　side relief angle　122
副前角　side rake angle　122
副切刃角　side cutting edge angle　122
副切削刃　minor cutting edge　122

G

盖罩　shroud　92
干粉灭火器　dry powder extinguisher　6
杆件　bar stock　280
感应电机　induction motor　89
感应炉　induction　218
感应线圈　induction coil　216
钢尺　steel rule　11
钢坯　billet　338
钢丝锯　fret saw　152
钢丝软轴　flexible axle of steel cord　69
高副　high pari　42

高频线圈　high frequency coil　208
高速钢毛刺刀　high speed steel bur　129
高压泵　high pressure pump　119,237
高压软管　flexible high-pressure hose　6
隔板　diaphragm　202
隔板支架　panel stiffener　4
隔离屏蔽装置　shielding setup　3
隔套　space sleeve　69,168
个人操作的粉尘采样泵　personal dust sampling pump　2
工件槽　work pan　120

词汇及图形索引(中英对照)

工具柄　tool stem　338
工具箱　toolbox　150
工序基准　operation datum　303
工业手持声压计　industrial hand-held sound level meter　2
工作冲程　power stroke　147
工作台　table　93
工作套　operating sleeve　72
弓形钩　G-clamp　151
弓形钻　brace　150
公差带形状　shape of tolerance zone　16
公差符号　symbol of tolerance　16
公差数值　tolerance　16
供气面罩　air supply gas mask　5
沟槽　groove　170
钩头方形/矩形键　square or rectangular key with gib head　47
钩头螺栓　hook bolt　146
箍簧　garter spring　82
箍圈　jubilee clip　148
鼓式(形)制动器　drum brake　76,147
固定板　anchor plate　76
固定杆　tie rod　83
固定节流线路　line with fixed restriction　22
固定钳口　still clamp　157
固定芯轴　fixed shaft　69
固结磨具　solid abrasive　138
管板　tubeplate　87
管材拉制　tube drawing　183

管道　manifold　7
管螺纹　pipe thread　49
管子台虎钳　pipe vice　150
贯通磨削　through-feed grinding　295
贯通型铆钉　pull-through-type riveting　78
光学投影仪　optical projector　27
辊锻　roll forging　183
滚齿　gear hobbing　91
滚齿机　gear hobbing machine　113
滚动体　ball　70
滚动轴承　rolling bearing　65
滚花　knurling　151
滚筒　roller mechanism　235
滚压　roll forming　184
滚针轴承　needle bearing　19
滚珠　bearing ball　54
滚珠丝杠　ball screw,leadscrew　54,249
滚珠丝杠组件　ball screw assembly　54
滚珠套　ball nut　54
滚珠轴承　ball bearing　146
滚子　roller　57
滚子从动件　roller follower　42
滚子链联轴器　roller-chain coupling　71
滚子轴承　roller bearings　19,65
过渡圆弧　fillet　126
过滤器　filter　22
过滤网格　filtering grid　202
过滤站　filtering station　237
过切　excessive undercut　209

焊点　weld　208
焊核　weld nugget　208
焊接(TIG)　tungsten insert-gas(TIG)welding　206
焊距　torch　214
焊药　flux　214
鹤式起重机构　crane　41
恒温器　thermostat　120
恒星齿轮　sun wheel　146
珩磨　honing　91
珩磨加工　honing operation　297
珩磨头　honing head　297
横进手轮　cross-feed handwheel　96

横梁　cross rail　103
横梁刀架　rail head　103
横刃　chisel edge　130
横刃斜角　chisel edge angle　130
横向滑板手轮　cross-slide handwheel　96
后导部　rear pilot　136
后支承　rear bearing　69
呼吸管　breathing air line　5
弧口凿　gouge　150
虎钳　vise　104
护套　boot　76
花键　spline　46
花键轴　splined shaft　149

花盘 face plate 92,147
滑动轴承 journal bearing 68
滑阀 slide valve 176
滑套 barrel 96
滑套锁柄 barrel lock 96
化学加工 CHM,chemical machining 118,185
化学气相沉积工艺 chemical vapor deposition process(CVD) 230
划线盘 scribing block 153
环带 band 70
环规 ring gage 29
环件滚压加工 ring rolling operation 340
环件轧制 ring rolling 183
环螺栓 collar bolt 146
环面蜗杆传动 annular worm 62
环形弹簧 loop spring,loose-proof by wire connect,garter spring 46,50,82
缓冲器 shock absorber 149
缓冲柱塞 buffer plunger 168
换挡拨叉 selector fork 147
换刀臂 tool interchange arm 258
换能器 transducer 216
回流管线 return line 86
回油腔 oil inlet cavity 167
回珠管 return tube 54

回转锉 rotary file 129
回转工作台 rotary table 99
回转铰链 revolute joint 42
回转连杆联轴器 rotating-link coupling 71
回转轴 rotating shaft 82
绘图板 drawing board 11
混合集束管 focusing tube 237
混合搅拌机构 blender 41
锪孔 spot facing 290
锪锥面 countersinking 290
锪钻 countersink bit 151
滑枕 ram 94,104
活顶尖 live center 283,284
活动钳口 movable clamp 157
活动套 movable sleeve 74
活塞 plunger 117,118
活塞杆 plunger rod 118,197
活塞杆密封 rod seal 84
活塞环 piston ring 147
活塞密封 piston seal 84
活塞式空压机 piston air compressor 179
活塞式蓄能器 piston-type accumulator 174
活塞销 gudgeon pin 149
火花塞 sparking plug 147

机床 machine tool 89
机床立柱 machine column 251
机电一体化 mechatronics 245
机动铰刀 machine reamer 133
机架 mach. frame 67
机壳 mach. housing 19
机械密封 mechanical seal 82
机械强度 mechanical strength 33
机械手 manipulator 258
机油泵 fuel pump 146
鸡尾锯 keyhole saw 151
基盘 disc 138
基圆 base circle,root diameter 61,136
基准代号 datum code 16
激光焊接 laset welding 206
激光加工 laser machining 185
激光束加工 LBM 118

极限阀 limit valve 179
极限开关 limit switch 37
棘轮机构 ratchet 44,147
棘轮式旋具 ratchet screwdriver 153
棘轮制动器 ratchet brake 44
棘爪棘条机构 ratchet rack 44
集收管 collecting tube 6
挤齿加工 burnishing operation 301
挤出成型 extrusion 184
挤出(件) extrusion 205,338
计算机集成制造系统 computer integrated manufacturing system(CIMS) 325
记录器 recorder 35
剂量缸 dosing cylinder 310
加工锯 fret saw 152
加工室 process chamber 235
加工中心 machining center 257

加强筋	stiffener	86
加热器	heater	86
夹持架	clapper box	104
夹紧法兰	clamping flange	82
夹紧盘	clamping base	157
夹紧手柄	clamp handle	157
夹紧T形槽	T-slot for clamping	99
夹具	fixture, holding fixture	104,198
夹具衬套(钻套)	jig bushing	317
夹钳	G-clamp	151
夹头	chuck, clamp, clamping dog	19,70,104,316
夹头隔套	chuck spacer	19
夹头松紧匙	chuck key	19
夹线螺钉	wire clamp screw	158
夹压杆	clamping bar	353
夹座	clamp base	111
尖直刨刀	straight shaping tool	136
间接电弧	indirect arc	218
检测线圈	inspection coil	32
检测箱	measure box	257
剪旋工艺	shear-spinning process	339
减压阀	pressure-reducing valve	169
减振器	shock absorber	149
键	key	20
键槽	key way	69
箭头	arrowhead	16
浇道	sprue	197
浇孔	pouring hole	118
浇口	ingate	197
浇注口	pouring basin(cup)	116,197
胶层	gel coat	353
角度铣刀	angle milling cutter	125,286
角铁	angle iron(plate)	146,284
绞轮	capstan wheel	96
铰刀	reamer	153
铰孔	rean hole	284
铰链	hinge	88
铰削	reaming	290
铰制孔螺栓连接	bolt coupling in reamed hole	49
阶梯钻孔	step drilling	290
接触板	contact plate	208
接触辊	contact roller	111
接触轮	contact wheel	111
接水槽	drain	120
接线端	terminal block	265
节点	pitch point	61
节流阀	throttle valve	221
节流口	choke	197
节时连续传输装置	time-saving continuous transportation device	308
金刚石砂轮	diamond grinding wheel	142
金属弧焊	metal arc welding	206
金属套筒	metal sleeve	118,203
紧定螺钉连接	lock bolt coupling	49
紧固螺母	fasten nut	20
紧急逃生瓶	emergency escape bottle	5
进给光杆	feed rod	95
进给交换齿轮箱	feed change gear box	95
进给磨削	traverse grinding	107
进给手轮	feed hand wheel	102
进给丝筒	feed reel	213
进给轴	feed shaft	96
进气冲程	induction stroke	147
进气门	inlet valve	147
精车沟槽	finish groove	284
精齿	finishing teeth	136
颈部	neck	130
径向槽	radial slot	170
径向铲背角	radial clearance angle	126
径向后角	radial relief angle	126
径向滑移滚子从动件	radial translating roller follower	43
径向前角	radial rake angle	126
径向切削刃	radial cutting edge	126
径向刃宽	radial land	126
径向轴承	radial bearing	67
径向柱塞泵	radial piston pump	164
净气出口	clean-gas outlet	4
静压螺旋传动	static screw driving	54
静压轴承	pressure-fed bearing	68
静止密封头	stationary sealing head	82
矩形花键	square spine	46
矩形截面圆柱形压缩弹簧	rectangular section spring	46
矩形螺纹	square thread	49
锯齿螺纹	buttress thread	49

锯片	saw blade,segment 138		卷边	hemming 183
锯切铣刀	slitting saw cutter 125		绝热板	insulating board 216
锯条	saw hand 106		绝热层	insulation 201
聚焦喷嘴	focusing nozzle 240		绝缘层	insulating layer 223

卡规	snap gage 29		抗蠕变能力	creep resistance 33
卡盘	chuck 93,150		壳型造型	shell-mold casting 182
卡钳	caliper 76		可变向棘轮机构	reversible ratchet 44
卡爪	jaw 280		可调滑块	adjustable slide 337
卡爪螺杆	jaw screw 280		可调式手用铰刀	manual adjustable reamer 133
开槽螺钉	slotted 52,54		刻度表	dial indicator 29
开槽螺母	castle nut 49,50		空间 RCCR 四杆机构	spatial RCCR four-bar linkage 42
开槽盘头螺钉	fillister screw 49		空心轴	hollow spindle 69
开槽刨刀	grooving tool,slotting tool 136		孔式喷油器	hole type nozzle 147
开槽弹性销	slotted spring pin 48		孔隙	porosity 139
开槽锥端紧定螺钉	cone-ended screw 49		控制面板	control panel 35,36
开环	open ring 46		扣环	retaining ring 19
开环控制系统	open-loop control system 249		快速成形	RP 234
开环系统	open loop system 264		快速排气阀	quick exhaust valve 175
开孔螺栓	hole bolt 50		宽砂带	wide belt 111
开口铆钉	bifurcated rivet 146		扩孔	core drilling 290
开口销	cotter pin,split pin 48,50,147,149		扩孔钻	expanding drill 131
开式冒口	open riser 197			
开式套式轴承	open sleeve bearing 93			
开榫锯	tenon saw 152			

拉出成型	pulltrusion 184		冷却风扇	cooling fan 4
拉刀	pull broach 136		冷却器	cooler 86
拉伸弹簧	extension spring 46		冷却液管	coolant tube 108
拉深	deep drawing 184		冷却液喷嘴	fluid nozzle 191
拉深工艺	deep-drawing process 338		冷却液箱	flood coolant reservoir 266
拉深环	drawn ring 338		离合器片	clutch plate 75
拉头	pull end 136		离心铸造	centrifugal casting 182
拉削	broaching 91,185		离子镀过程	ion-plating process 230
拉削丝锥	broaching taper 134		离子束反射器	beam deflector 231
拉削夹具	broaching fixture 105		离子束加工	IBM 230
喇叭排放头	discharge horn 6		离子束监控器	beam monitor 231
蜡模	wax pattern 200		离子注入工艺	ion implantation process 230
棱柱型铰链	prismatic joint 42		立体打印	three-dimension printing 184
冷焊	cold welding 186		立体光固化成型	stereolithography 184
冷挤出	cold extrusion 183		立柱	column,vertical column 93,101

连杆　connecting rod　279
连杆联轴器　link coupling　71
连接螺栓　coupling bolt　146
连续传输装置　continuous transportation device　307
连续供气管　continuous air tube　75
联轴器　coupling　22,69
链轮　chain wheel　147
链条　chain　57
链条传动　chain drive　57
两自由度无链传输装置　chainless transportation device with two degrees of freedom　308
量角器(半圆规)　protractor　11,92
量仪(量具)　gauge　151
料斗　magazine, storage hopper　179,202
领蹄　primary shoe　76
流槽　transfer launder　201
流道　runner, runner bar　67,75,197
流化磨料箱　fluidized abrasive tank　113
流体成形工艺　fluid forming process　344
流体稳定器　flow stabilizer　241
六角螺母　hex nut　49
六角头螺栓　hex bolt　49
六角(主)刀架　hexagon(main) turret　96
龙门刨削　planing　91

滤杯　filtering cup　175
滤芯　filtering core　175
轮齿折断　tooth breakage　61
轮廓面　profile surface　15
轮廓磨削　profile grinding　107
轮廓铣削　contour milling　127
轮廓线　profile line　15
螺钉连接　screw coupling　49
螺钉　screw　19
螺母　nut　20
螺栓　bolt　20
螺栓连接　bolted connection　186
螺纹车刀　thread cutting tool　124
螺纹传动　screw drive　53
螺纹梳刀　chaser　150
螺纹套筒　collar　93
螺旋槽丝锥　spiral fluted tap　134
螺旋齿轮　spiral(helical) gear　149
螺旋桨　propeller　148
螺旋角　helic angle　130
螺旋铰链　helical joint　42
螺旋弹簧　coil spring　146,151
螺旋压力机　screw　121
螺旋圆周铣刀　helical peripheral cutter　125
落料　blanking　183

M

麻花钻　twist drill　130,256
埋弧焊　submerged-arc welding　206
脉冲电源　pulse power　118
脉冲系列　pulse train　249
盲孔　blind hole　290
铆钉　rivet　148
梅花扳手　ring spanner　152
密闭装置　enclosure　120
密封垫　gasket　81,353
密封垫盖罩　gasket cup　83
密封盖罩　packing cup　83
密封面　seal face　82
密封腔　seal casing　82
密封圈　sealing ring　20
灭火设备　fire extinguisher　6
铭牌　logo plate　19
模锻　closed die forging, closed die　183,205

模具　die, mold　117,353
模具振动器　mold oscillation　199
模腔　cavity, die cavity, mold cavity　117,197
膜盒系统　diaphragm unit　7
膜片弹簧离合器　diaphragm spring clutch　74
摩擦焊　friction welding　206
摩擦焊接　friction stir welding　185
摩擦离合器　friction clutch　72
摩擦盘　friction plate　72
摩擦片　friction disk　74
摩擦式棘轮机构　silent ratchet mechanism　44
磨床　grinding machine　106
磨浆　slurry　227
磨具　abrasive　138
磨粒　grain　139
磨料射流加工　AJ　236
磨料水射流加工　AWJ　236

磨料箱　abrasive tank　113
磨轮　grinding wheel　106,108,150
磨盘　grinding disc,abrasive disc　142,150
磨削加工　abrasives process　291

末端驱动适配器　end-drive adapter　92
莫氏锥度　morse taper　16
拇指形螺钉　thumb screw　51
木螺钉　wood screw　51

N

耐磨垫　wear pad　131
内齿轮　annulus wheel　146
内端法兰盘　inner flange　141
内滚道　inner race　70
内渐开线花键　internal spline　46
内链板　inner plate　57
内六角扳手　allen key　150
内六角螺钉　hexagon socket head screw　51
内六角螺母　inner-hexagon nut　20
内六角圆柱头螺钉　inner hex fillister screw　49

内圆磨具　inner surface abrasive　107
内圆磨削　internal grinding　106
内圆无心磨削　internal centerless grinding　295
内轴承　inner bearing　76
逆铣　up milling　285
啮合线　line-of-action　61
牛头刨床　shaper,shaping machine　94,153
牛头刨削　shaping　91
扭力扳手　torque wrench　150
扭转弹簧　torsion spring　46

P

排尘口　dust discharge　4
排出隔音板　exhaust muffler　4
排放管　discharge tube　6
排气冲程　exhaust stroke　147
排气净化器　exhaust scrubber　230
排气门　exhaust valve　147
排水阀　water exhaust valve　175
排水管　discharge pipe　6
排泄孔　drain hole　166
排泄喷嘴　discharge nozzle　6
排泄塞　drain plug　166
排屑槽　margin flute　131
排屑螺旋　chip auger　266
排屑器　chip excavator　114
盘式离合器　plate clutch　146
盘式制动器　disk brake　76
盘形凸轮　disc cam,plate cam　43
抛光布轮　polishing cloth wheel　142
抛光机　polishing machine　153
抛光轮　buffing wheel　150
刨刀　shaping tool　135
配气机构　valve mechanism　42
配油盘　oil distributing plate　167
喷枪　blasting gun　120,237
喷水头　projector　7

喷嘴座　nozzle holder　241
膨胀隔板　expanded panel　336
膨胀环　expanding ring　72
膨胀螺栓　expansion bolt　52
皮锤　rawhide hammer　153
疲劳寿命　fatigue life　33
偏心滑移滚子从动件　offset translating roller follower　43
偏心轮(盘)　eccentric wheel　147
偏置滚子　off-set roller　93
偏置量　offset　126
平板轧制　flat rolling　183
平锤　flatter　155
平带　flat belt　58
平底盲孔　blind hole with flat bottom　290
平垫片　plain washer　54
平衡杆　balancing arbor　92
平口夹钳　flat-jawed tong　157
平面度　flatness　15
平面铰链　planar joint　42
平面六杆机构　planar six-bar linkage　42
平面磨削　surface grinding　91,185
平面四杆机构　planar four-bar linkage　42
平面涡卷弹簧　coil spring　46
平面铣刀　slab milling cutter　286

平头螺钉　grub screw　148
平行度　parallelism　15
平行吸振隔音板　parallel baffle muffler　4
平行仪　parallel　11

普通开槽压板　plain slotted clamp　286
普通螺栓连接　common bolt coupling　49
普通螺纹　metric thread　49

Q

气锤　power hammer　153
气垫　air cushion　97
气动测量仪　air-gage system　30
气动分度台　pneumatically driven indexing table　310
气动离合器　air-operated clutch　75
气动锁　air lock　6
气动叶轮　pneumatic propel wheel　111
气动制动器　pneumatically actuated brake　76
气缸密封垫　cylinder-head gasket　146
气焊　gas welding　206
气门　gas valve　42
气囊式蓄能器　bladder-type accumulator　174
气腔　gas chamber　174
气体保护金属弧焊　gas-metal arc welding　186
气体保护钨极弧焊　gas-tungsten arc welding　186
气压表　barometer　266
启动器　actuator　7
起钉器　nail puller　152
千斤顶　jack　151
前刀面　face　122
前导部　front pilot　136
前角　back rake angle　122
前支承　front bearing　69

钳工台虎钳　vice　151,157
枪钻　gun drill　131,290
腔体　case　87
腔体环　casing ring　87
切断刀　parting tool　124
切断器　chopper　352
切断铣刀　slitting saw　286
切割站　cutting station　237
切入式磨削　plunge grinding　107,295
切削部分　cutting zone　122
切削齿　cutting teeth　136
倾斜度　angularity　15
球面四杆机构　spherical four-bar linkage　42
球体浮标　ball check　86
球形端铣刀　ball end mill　127
球形铰链　spherical joint　42
球轴承　ball bearing　19,65,149
曲柄销　crank pin　297
曲柄压力机　crank　121
曲柄摇杆机构　crank-rocker　41
曲轴　crank shaft　69
驱动件　driving element　73
驱动套　driving sleeve　72
驱动箱　drive head　35
全跳动　total runout　15

R

热成型　thermo-forming　184
热处理　heat treatment　33
热加工设备　hot working equipment　114
热交换器　heat exchanger　120
热喷涂工艺　thermal spray operation　232
热丝喷涂　thermal wire spray　232
人孔　manhole　148
人字齿　herringbone gear　147
刃边　margin　130
韧带　flute,margin　130

刃倾角　lip-relief angle　130
容器衬套　container liner　338
容器支撑　container support　7
熔锅　pot　197
熔焊　fusion welding　206
MIG熔焊　metal inert-gas(MIG)welding　206
MAG熔焊　metal active-gas(MAG)welding　206
熔炉　furnace　197
熔模(失蜡)铸造　investment casting　182
熔融沉积成型　fused deposition modeling　184

熔丝堆积成形工艺　fused-deposition-modeling process(FDM)　235
容屑表面　clearance surface　126
熔旋快速固化　melt-spinning process　182
柔性杆　flexible bar　353
柔性管　flexible line　86
柔性接头　flexible connector　7
柔性制造单元　flexible manufacturing cell(FMC)　321
润滑点　lub point　86

S

塞规　plug gage　29
三角板　set square　11
三角螺纹(V形螺纹)　V-thread　148
三角形花键　triangular spline　46
三爪卡盘　three-jaw chuck　280
三爪内径千分尺　three-jaw micrometer for internal(inner/inside) diameter　27
砂衬　sand lining　116
砂带收卷轮　belt pulling wheel　296
砂轮　grinding abrasive wheel　141,150
砂轮机　grinding machine　151
砂轮头架　wheel head　108
砂轮头架立柱　wheel head column　108
砂轮主轴　wheel spindle　141,257
砂箱　flask　116,197,200
砂型铸造　sand casting　182
闪光焊　flash welding　206
扇形碳环　segmental carbon ring　82
上箱型砂　cope　197
上研磨板　upper lap　192
蛇形管冷却器　cooler of snake-shaped tube　173
射流　jet　120
射流管　jet tube　221
射流加工　jet cutting　118
伸缩盖　telescoping cover　223
深度尺　depth gauge　151
升降台　knee　93
失蜡铸造　lost foam casting　182
施压滚轮　pressure wheel　201
十字槽(沉头)螺钉　phillips screw　49,148
十字架式万向节　hokke's joint　149
十字联轴器　oldham coupling　146
十字双滑块联轴器　double slider coupling　70
十字旋具　phillips screwdriver　153
十字轴万向联轴器　hooks coupling, universal coupling　70
石墨模具　graphite mould　201

适配连接器　adapter　76
释放把手　release handle　6
手把　handle, knob　19,111
(手)电钻　electric drill　152
手调环　hand ring　92
手动互锁开关　direct manual switch interlock　3
手动铰刀　hand reamer　133
手工金属弧焊　manual metal-arc welding　206
手轮　handwheel　96
手捻　instrument screwdriver　151
手提式焊缝打磨机　portable welding seam polisher　112
手提式砂带机　portable belt grinder　112
手用铰刀　manual reamer　133
手用锥孔铰刀　manual taper reamer　133
受压轴承　negative load bearing　93
枢轴　pivot　86
输送管　delivery line　86
数控车床　CNC turning and lathe　254
数控高速滚齿机　CNC high speed gear cutting machine　114
数控磨床　CNC grinding machine　257
数控铣床　CNC milling machine　253
数控钻床　CNC drilling machine　252
数字高度尺　digital vernier height gauge　26
刷帽　brush cap　19
双槽端铣刀　two flute end mill　127
双层油封环　dual oil ring　166
双端镗刀　double-ended cutter or boring tool　128
双螺母防松　loose-proof with two nuts　50
双曲柄机构　double-crank　41
双头螺柱　stud　49,148
双头螺柱连接　stud coupling　49
双摇杆机构　double-rocker　41
双爪式棘轮机构　double pawl ratchet　44
水灭火器　water extinguisher　6

词汇及图形索引(中英对照)

水平仪　spirit level　153
水射流加工　WJ(water-jet machining)　185,236
水箱　water tank　120
水压机　hydraulic press　151
顺铣　down milling　285
顺序阀　sequence valve　169
丝杆　leadscrew, leading screw　95,118
丝杠　screw, lead screw　93,96,157
丝锥扳手　tap wrench　150
死顶尖　dead center　284
四槽端铣刀　four flute end mill　127
四冲程发动机　four-stroke engine　147
四通阀　4-way valve　104
四爪卡盘　four-jaw chuck　280

伺服电机　servo motor　262
伺服放大器　sarvo amplifier　264
伺服驱动器　servo driver　262
榫孔凿　firmer chisel　151
缩喉　insufficient throat　209
锁定螺钉(紧固螺钉)　set screw　52,148
锁紧垫片　lockplate washer　55
锁紧垫圈　lock washer　49
锁紧滚针　locking needle roller　75
锁紧滚子　locking roller　75
锁紧螺钉　lock screw　69
锁紧螺母　locking nut　93
榫钉　dowel　146

T

弹簧垫片　spring washer　54
弹簧垫圈防松　loose-proof with spring washer　50
弹簧式互锁开关　spring-type interlock　3
弹簧锁紧垫片　spring-locking washer　54
弹簧脱料环　spring stripper ring　338
弹簧直动型溢流阀　spring loaded type relief valve　170
弹性电刷　brush with spring　19
弹性夹套　collet chuck　280
弹性(夹)套　collet　92,280
探测器　detector　33
碳电极　carbon electrode　218
镗床　boring machine　100
镗刀　cutting tool, boring tool　100,128,135,284
镗杆　boring bar　100,101
镗削加工　boring process　290
陶瓷模具铸造　ceramic-mold casting　182
套柄铁锤　fuller　154
套料刀(套料钻)　trepanning tool　135
套式轴承盖　sleeve bearing housing　93
套式轴承内轴　sleeve bearing insert　93
套式轴承座　sleeve bearing carriage　93
套筒(轴套)　bush　20,57
套筒扳手　box spanner, socket spanner　150,153
套筒扳手旋转手把　tommy bar　150
套筒滚子链　bush-roller chain　57
套筒联轴器　muff coupling　70

套筒链　bush chain　57
套形密封件　boot seal　70
特种加工机床　non-traditional machining equipment　118
梯形螺纹　acme thread　49
提把　carry handle　6
提升阀　poppet valve　148
蹄块　shoe　67
蹄块保持钉　shoe retaining nail　76
剃齿　gear shaving　301
添加剂　addative　141
填缝枪　caulking gun　150
填塞密封　packed gland　84
调节轮　regulating wheel　170
调节螺母　adjustment nut　84
调节绳　adjuster cable　76
调节旋钮　adjusting snob　111
调整杆　transmission lever　92
铁芯　iron core　35
铁砧(砧座)　anvil　150,154
停车杆　stop rod　96
挺杆　tappet　149
通风杯　vent cup　83
通风接头　vent connection　83
通孔　through hole　290
通气孔　air vent　67
通气口　ventilator, vent　86,197
同步带　synchronous belt　58

同轴度　concentricity　15
铜焊　brazing　186
头盖组件　head cap assembly　6
透镜　lens　148
凸出焊接　projection welding　206
凸轮毛坯　cam blank　287
凸轮轴　cam shaft　42
凸压（动）模　ejector die　197
凸缘联轴器　flange coupling　70
涂覆磨具　coated abrasive　141
涂覆磨具磨削加工　coated abrasive process　296

推杆　pushrod　149
推力块　thrust block　67
推力轴承　thrust bearing　34,167
推料杆　ejector pin　200
推料筒　shot sleeve　118
托板　support blade　192
托架　cradle　92
托盘库　pallet storage　258
拖板　carriage　93
脱模层　mold release　353

外齿锁紧垫片　external-tooth locking washer　55
外端法兰盘　outer flange　141
外渐开线花键　external involute spline　46
外径千分尺　micrometer for external diameter　26
外壳　casing,shell　75,87
外链板　outer plate　57
外套螺母　cap nut　147
外圆磨削　gylindrical grinding　91
外轴承　outer bearing　76
弯曲　bending　183
弯头粗加工刨刀　bent roughing tools　136
弯头轻载镗刀　light boring tool with bend shank　128
万向节　universal joint　149
万向节（驱动）轴　universal joint(drive)shaft　92
网眼钢板　expanded metal　147
往复式加工　reciprocating machining processes　291

往复运动机床　reciprocating machine　103
往复运动加工刀具　reciprocating process tool　135
往复振动平面磨光机　reciprocating vibration flat grinder　112
位置传感器　position sensor　249
位置度　position　15
尾端支撑　end support　100
尾座　tailstock　93,257,270
文丘里管　Venturi tube　148
蜗杆　worm　149
蜗轮　worm wheel　149
蜗轮（蜗杆）副　worm gear　149
无槽丝锥　non-groove taper　134
无法兰盘带轮　unflanged pulley　60
无声链联轴器　silent-chain coupling　71
无心磨削　centerless grinding　185,192
物镜　objective lens　231
雾化喷射束　atomized spray　213

吸入隔音板　intake muffler　4
吸入口分流锥　suction splitter　166
吸收过滤器　absorption filter　34
吸振　absorption　4
铣半圆键　woodruff key milling　127
铣槽钻头　slot drill　128
铣床　milling machine　98
铣刀　milling tool　125
铣沟槽　slot milling,slotting　127

铣键槽　key way milling　127
铣螺旋槽　helical slot milling　127
（铣）切断　slitting　127,156,183
铣削侧面　side face milling　127
铣削台阶面　shoulder face milling　127
铣削　milling　91,185,285
铣V形槽　V-slot milling　127
铣T形槽　T-slot milling　127
铣型腔　cavity milling　127

铣燕尾槽 dovetail milling 127
系杆 tiebar 92
系杆臂 tiebar arm 92
狭手锯 keyhole saw 151
下底板 sub-base 92
下箱型砂 drag 197
下研磨板 lower lap 192
先导型溢流阀 pilot operated relief valve 168
衔铁 armature 73,74,147
线圈 coil 34
线丝夹爪 wire clamping jaw 158
线网 wire gauze 87
陷型砧座 swage block 154
橡胶腔体 rubber case 82
销钉 cotter pin 147
消声器 silencer 3
销驱动类盲孔铆钉 drive-pin type of blind rivet 78
销轴 dowel 57
小齿轮 pinion 104

小孔 orifice 116
斜撑离合器 sprag clutch 75
斜齿齿轮 helical gear 301
泄压阀 relief valve 87,89,169
卸荷阀 overload relief valve 104
芯轴 mandrel 92
行程挡块 trip dog 104
行星齿轮 planetary wheel 146
行星轮系 epicyclic gear 146
型材轧制 shape rolling 183
型腔 cavity 118
型芯 core 117
胸压手摇钻 breast drill 150
蓄能器 accumulator 120
悬梁 overarm 98
旋锻工具 swage 154
旋塞阀 stopcock valve 149,153
旋压 spinning 184
旋转吊钩 swivel hook 80
旋转头 revolving head 283

压板 clamp 123
压柄 pressing stem 338
压差指针 pressure differential indicator 87
压辊 squeeze roll 208
压紧带 compaction belt 352
压紧螺钉 clamp screw 122,123
压力板(施压盘) pressure plate 72,74
压力表 pressure gage 22
压力弹簧 pressure spring 72
压力焊 welding with pressure 206
压力环 pressure ring 75
压力角 pressure angle 61
压力开关 pressure switch 7
压力筒 pressure cartridge 6
压力肘节 pressure toggle 72
压实铸造 squeeze casting 182
压缩冲程 compression stroke 147
压缩弹簧 compression spring 46
压缩空气管 compressed air hose 155
压缩密封 compression packing 83
压缩模 compression molding 184
压头 squeeze head 202

压油腔 pressurized oil cavity 167
压铸 die casting 182,195
牙形切断螺钉 thread-cutting screw 52
延展 stretch forming 183
延展夹头 stretch gripper 337
研磨 lapping 185
研磨齿轮 gear lapping 301
研磨膏 abrasive slurry 192
眼孔吊钩 eye hook 80
眼孔接头 eye-splice 80
眼孔螺栓(带孔螺栓) eye bolt 52,146
燕尾槽铣刀 dove-tail cutter 128
燕尾槽斜面刨刀 dovetail slide cutting tool 136
样板 template 11
摇臂 radial arm 94
摇臂凸轮 rocker cam 97
摇臂钻床 radial drilling machine 94
摇杆臂 rocker arm 104
药芯焊丝电弧焊 flux-cored arc welding 186
叶轮 impeller 34,75,165
叶片 vane 165
叶片泵 vane pump 164

叶片式风速计　vane anemometer　2
页轮　flap wheel　112
液力挤压　hydroforming　183
液力离合器　fluid coupling　75
液面指针　level indicator　86
液体真空泵　liquid vacuum pump　166
液压泵单元　hydraulic pump unit　36
液压成形工艺　hydroform process　344
液压单元　hydraulic unit　120
液压缸　cylinder,hydraulic cylinder　22,167
液压机　hydraulic　121
液压联轴器　hydraulic coupling　71
液压马达　hydraulic motor　22,167
液压千斤顶　hydraulic jack　151,155
液压头（液压夯锤）　hydraulic ram　36,151
液压油　hydraulic oil　104
液压注射缸　hydraulic shot cylinder　197
一字开槽螺钉　slotted-head cap screw　52
移动副　sliding pair　42
移动立柱　travelling column　258
移动凸轮　translating cam　43
溢流管　return tube　54
硬头盔　hard hat　5
硬质合金毛刺刀　carbide bur　129
永磁铁　permanent magnet　34,242
永久性铸型　permanent-mold casting　182
油保持器　oil retainer　67
油杯　oil cup　83
油槽（油底壳）　sump　82,86
油门　throttle valve　149
油箱　tank　22,104

油箱　oil reservoir　89,266
油压活塞　hydraulic piston　72
油压离合器　hydraulic clutch　72
游标卡尺　vernier caliper　26
游标深（高）度尺　vernier depth gauge　26
游丝　hairspring　147
右车刀　right hand turning tool　124
右端盖　right cap　20
预孔　existing hole　100
圆板牙　circular die　135
圆带　round belt　58
圆度　circularity　15
圆规　compass　11
圆弧插补　circular interpolation　249
圆弧成形车刀　radius turning form tool　124
圆盘打磨机　abrasive disc grinder　112
圆盘精密抛光机　abrasive disc precision polisher　112
圆盘锯　circular saw blade,circular blade saw　138,157
圆跳动　circular runout　15
圆头刨刀　round nose　136
圆柱度　cylindricity　15
圆柱拱曲垫片　cylindrically curved washer　54
圆柱头螺钉　cheese-head screw　147
圆柱蜗杆　cylindrical worm　62
圆柱销　pin,dowel pin　20,48
圆柱芯轴　cylindrical mandrel　316
圆柱形凸轮　cylindrical cam　43
圆锥销　cotter pin　48
圆锥形压缩弹簧　cone-shaped spring　46

Z

凿子　chisel　150
增压器　intensifier　120,237
轧制　rolling　205
粘接　adhesive bonding　185
粘接剂　bond　139
张紧带轮　idler pulley　147
张紧调节杆　tension adjusting bar　111
张紧辊　tension roller　111
张紧轮　tension wheel　111
胀芯成形　bulging　345
障碍防护罩　barrier guard　3

针阀　needle valve　147
真空包成型　vacuum-bag forming　184
真空泵　vacuum pump　150
真空吸盘　vacuum sucker　175
真空罩　vacuum trap　353
振荡器　oscillator　33
振动机构　oscillating mechanism　229
振动进给装置　vibrofeeder　307
整流器　rectifier　220
正时链　timing chain　149
正弦尺　sine bar　28

支撑面 bearing surface 141	轴向铲背角 axial relief 126
支承板 bearing plate 19	轴向后角 axial relief angle 126
支承杆 supporting rod 111	轴向前角 axial rake 126
支承平台 platform 235	轴向推力挡块 axial thrust stop 93
支座 blanker 231	轴向/推力球轴承 thrust ball bearing 66
直柄 straight shank 130	轴向柱塞泵 axial piston pump 164
直柄粗加工刨刀 straight roughing tool 136	肘节 toggle joint 149
直槽钻 straight-flute drill 130	肘节连杆 toggle link 74
直齿轮(正齿轮) spur gear 149,301	肘节压力机 knuckle joint 121
直角尺(矩尺) try square 151	主动链轮 driving chain wheel 57
直角旋具 right-angled screwdriver 152	主后刀面 major flank 122
直接电弧 direct arc 218	主后角 end relief angle 122
直流电动机 DC motor 89	主切刃角(刀尖刃倾角) end cutting edge angle 122,126
直流发动机 DC generator 89	主切削刃 cutting edge 122
直线插补 linear interpolation 249	主轴 spindle,quill 69,99
直线度 straightness 15	主轴螺母 spindle nut 141
直线棘轮 straight line ratchet 44	主轴箱 saddle spindle carrier(box) 94,99,102,258
止动垫片防松 loose-proof with stop washer 50	主轴转速选调器 spindle speed selector 96
止推轴承 thrust bearing 149	主柱 vertical column 102
指示表 indicator 35	注射成型 injection molding 184
指引线 indicating line 16	注射缸 shot cylinder 118
指状压板 finger clamp 286	柱端螺钉 dog point screw 52
制动鼓 brake drum 195	柱面铰链 cylindrical joint 42
制动盘 braking disk 76	柱塞式棘爪 plunger ratchet pawl 44
制动液 brake fluid 76	柱塞筒 cylinder tube 174
制动油缸 brake cylinder 195	铸锭 cast ingot 205
中凹面 concavity 126	铸件 casting 116
中间齿轮 intermediate gear 19	铸勺 ladle 117
中间支承 middle bearing 69	抓木垫片 wood-grip washer 55
中空端面铣刀(空心端铣刀) shell end mill 125,286	转动副 rotating pair 42
中拖板 cross-slide 95,282	转动芯轴 rotary arbor 69
中心冲 centre punch 150	转杆 turnstile 96
中心螺杆 central screw 93	转换板 board 122
中心磨削 centered grinding 192	转架 revolution frame 111
中心柱形消声器 centre-pod silencer 3	转盘 scroll plate 280
中心钻 center drill(drilling) 129,290	转盘锥齿 bevel teeth on scroll plate 280
钟罩形外滚道 bell-type outer race 70	转盘座 rotary base 157
重载镗刀 heavy boring tool 128	转塔挡块 turret stop 96
周边磨削 peripheral grinding 294	(转塔)刀架 turret 252,270
周边铣削刀刃 peripheral cutting edge 126	转塔夹头 turret chuck 252
周铣平面 peripheral milling 127	转向接头 steering knuckle 76
轴 shaft 20	转向引擎 steering engine 36
轴承盖 bearing cap(cover) 69	

转移成型（传递模） transfer molding 184
转轴 rotary shaft 69
锥柄 taper shank 130
锥齿轮 bevel gear(pinion) 146,280
锥端螺钉 conical point screw 52
锥盘 cone 88
锥套 tapper bushing 111
锥蜗杆传动 taper worm 62
锥形盖 tapped cover 141
锥形或钟罩形垫片 conical or belleville washer 54
锥形铰刀 conical reamer 151
锥形制动器 conical brake 309
紫铜电级 copper electrode 191
自插式盲孔铆钉 self-plugging blind rivet 78
自动保护金属极电弧焊 shielded metal arc welding 185
自动进粉器 automatic powder feed 199
自动门 self closing door 6
自攻螺钉 self-tapping screw 51,148
自锁螺母防松 loose-proof with self-lock nut 50
（自行车后轴）超越棘轮机构 overrunning ratchet mechanism 44
自由锻 open die forging 183
自找平平衡座 self aligning equalizing base 67
纵向进给柄 longitudinal feed lever 96
组合夹具 modular jig 318
钻床 drilling machine 102
钻夹头 drill chuck 102
钻孔间隙 body diameter clearance 130
钻孔直径 clearance diameter 130
钻扩铰孔加工刀具 hole-making tool 129
钻模板 drill plate 318
钻套 drill bush(bushing) 131,318
钻头 drill 151
钻削 drilling 91,185,290
钻心 web 130
左车刀 left hand turning tool 124
左端盖 left cap 20
坐标测量机 coordinate-measuring machine 30

Dactylology: One-hand Alphabet
附录 单手势字母表

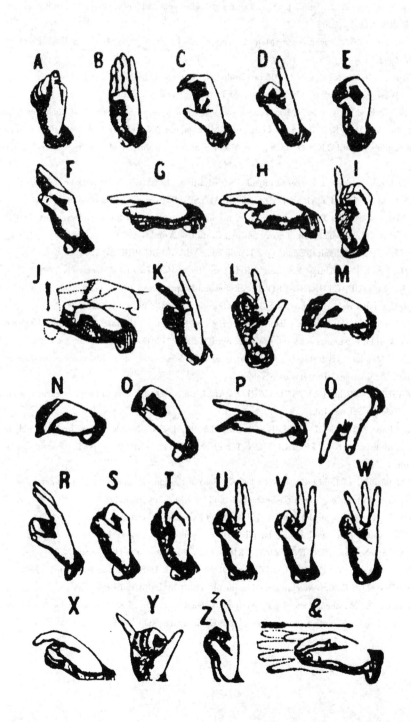

参 考 文 献

[1] 黄云，朱派龙编著. 砂带磨削原理及其应用. 重庆：重庆大学出版社，1993.
[2] 朱派龙，孙永红主编. 机械制造工艺装备. 西安：西安电子科技大学出版社，2006.
[3] 朱派龙主编. 机械专业英语图解教程. 北京：北京大学出版社，2008.
[4] 朱派龙主编. 图解机械制造专业英语. 北京：化学工业出版社，2009.
[5] Serope Kapakjian, Stever R. Schmid. Manufacturing Engineering and Technology. Fifth Edition. 制造工程与技术. 北京：清华大学出版社，2006.
[6] Rao P N. Manufacturing Technology—Metal Cutting & machine tool. 制造技术－金属切削与机床. 北京：机械工业出版社，2003.
[7] Carvill, James. Mechanical Engineer's Data Handbook. Butterworth-Heinemann, 2003.
[8] Ronald A. WasherHandbook of Machining and Metalworking and calculations. McGraw-Hill, 2001.
[9] Heinz P. Bloch, Fred K. Geitner. Major process equipment maintenance and repair. Gulf Publishing Company, 1997.
[10] Heinz P. Bloch, Fred K. Machinery Component Maintenance and Repair, Gulf Publishing Company, 1999.
[11] Ben-Zion Sandier. ROBOTICS Designing the Mechanism for Automated Machinery. Second Edition. ACADEMIC PRESS, 1999.
[12] John S. Oakland. Statistical Process Control. Fifth Edition. Butterworth-Heinemann, 2003.
[13] R. Keith Mobley. ROOT CAUSE FAILURE ANALYSIS. Butterworth-Heinemann, 1999.
[14] Ioan D. Marinescu et al. Tribology of abrasive machining processes. William Andrew, Inc. 2004.
[15] Thomas Childs. Metal Machining Theory and Applications. Arnold, 2000.
[16] Dan B. Marghitu. Mechanical Engineer's Handbook. ACADEMIC PRESS, 2001.
[17] Edward H. Smith. Mechanical Engineer's Reference Book. Butterworth-Heinemann, 2000.
[18] Singh U K. MANUFACTURING PROCESSES Second Edition New Age International (P) Itd, 2009.
[19] Bob Mercer. (Industrial Control Wiring Guide) (Second Edition). Newnes, 2001.
[20] Eric H. Glendinning. Oxford. English for Electrical and Mechanical Engineering. Oxford University Press, 1995.
[21] John Ridley, John Channing. Safety at Work. Sixth Edition. Butterworth-Heinemann, 2003.
[22] Andreas W. Momber. Hydrablasting and Coating of Steel Structures. 2003 Elsevier Science Ltd.
[23] John Campbell. Castings. Butterworth-Heinemann, 2003.
[24] Ei-ichi YASUDA. Michio INAGAKI. CARBON ALLOYS Novel Concepts to Develop Carbon Science and Technology. 2003 Elsevier Science Itd.
[25] J. Edward Pope. RULES OF THUMB FOR MECHANICAL ENGINEERS. 1997 by Gulf Publishing Company.
[26] R. Keith Mobley. AN INTRODUCTION TO PREDICTIVE MAINTENANCE. Second Edition. Butterworth-Heinemann, 2002.
[27] NEALE M J. THE TRIBOLOGY HANDBOOK. Second Edition. Butterworth-Heinemann, 2001.
[28] Soares, Claire. Process engineering equipment handbook, McGraw-Hill, 2002.
[29] Frank Kreith. The Mechanical Engineering Handbook Series. CRC Press, 2005.
[30] Mobley, R. Keith. Plant engineering-Handbooks, manuals. Butterworth-Heinemann, 2001.
[31] Gwidon W. Stachowiak. ENGINEERING TRIBOLOGY. Butterworth-Heinemann, 2000.
[32] Joseph E. Shigley. STANDARD HANDBOOK OF MACHINE DESIGN. McGraw-Hill, 1996.
[33] ERIK OBERG. 27th Edition Machinery's Handbook. 2004 by Industrial Press Inc.
[34] Youssef, Helmi A. Machining technology: machine tools and operations. CRC Press. Taylor & Francis Group, 2008.
[35] Prof. J. S. Colton. Manufacturing Processes and Engineering. GIT 2009.